88 The Giants of Jazz Piano

by Robert L. Doerschuk

Backbeat
Books

San Francisco

Published by Backbeat Books
600 Harrison Street, San Francisco, CA 94107
An imprint of the Music Player Network
United Entertainment Media, Inc.

The Earl Hines, Keith Jarrett, and Cecil Taylor chapters are
based on interviews previously published in *Keyboard* magazine.

Distributed to the book trade in the U.S and Canada by
Publishers Group West, 1700 Fourth Street, Berkeley, CA 94710

Distributed to the music trade in the U.S. and Canada by
Hal Leonard Publishing, P.O. Box 13819, Milwaukee, WI 53213

Cover Design by Doug Gordon
Text Design and Composition by Leigh McLellan
Front Cover Photo of Thelonious Monk by Lee Tanner

Library of Congress Cataloging-in-Publication Data
Doerschuk, Robert L.
    88 : the giants of jazz piano / by Robert L. Doerschuk.
        p. cm.
    Includes bibliographical references (p.) and index.
    ISBN 0-87930-656-4

    1 . Pianists–Biography. 2. Jazz musicians–Biography. 3.
Piano music (Jazz)–History and criticism. I. Title: Eighty-eight.
II. Title
ML397 .D64 2001
786.2'65'0922–dc21
[B]   200043708

Printed in the United States of America

01 02 03 04 05   5 4 3 2 1

Contents

Foreword *by Keith Jarrett*   v

Introduction   vii

The Man Who Invented Jazz

   1. Jelly Roll Morton   2

Masters of Stride

   2. James P. Johnson   13
   3. Willie "the Lion" Smith   16
   4. Fats Waller   19

Singing & Swinging

   5. Duke Ellington   23
   6. Earl Hines   27
   7. Count Basie   39
   8. Mary Lou Williams   42
   9. Teddy Wilson   48
   10. Nat "King" Cole   52
   11. Dorothy Donegan   54

"God Is in the House"

   12. Art Tatum   58

Deep in the Mainstream

   13. Erroll Garner   69
   14. Ahmad Jamal   71
   15. Oscar Peterson   75
   16. Phineas Newborn   78

In Walked Bud

   17. Bud Powell   82

It Started at Minton's

   18. Tadd Dameron   91
   19. Hank Jones   93
   20. Jaki Byard   97
   21. Red Garland   100
   22. Tommy Flanagan   102
   23. Barry Harris   106
   24. Sir Roland Hanna   108

Brilliant Corners

   25. Thelonious Monk   112

Hard Bop to Funk

   26. Horace Silver   121
   27. Wynton Kelly   125
   28. Ray Bryant   127
   29. Ramsey Lewis   129
   30. Les McCann   131
   31. Bobby Timmons   134
   32. Herbie Hancock   137

Everybody Digs Bill Evans

   33. Bill Evans   144

The Sophisticates

   34. George Shearing   157
   35. Marian McPartland   161

36. John Lewis   164
37. Dave Brubeck   168
38. Roger Kellaway   172

The Neo-Traditionalists

39. Jimmy Rowles   175
40. Dick Hyman   177
41. Dick Wellstood   180
42. Dave McKenna   182
43. Gene Harris   184

The Endurance of Postbop

44. Billy Taylor   187
45. Toshiko Akiyoshi   190
46. Cedar Walton   193
47. Steve Kuhn   196
48. Chick Corea   198
49. JoAnne Brackeen   201
50. Kenny Barron   203
51. Richie Beirach   206

Old World/New Flavors

52. Joe Zawinul   209
53. Adam Makowicz   212
54. Michel Petrucciani   214

Outside Looking In

55. Sun Ra   219
56. Lennie Tristano   223
57. Paul Bley   227
58. Ran Blake   229

Order Within Chaos

59. Cecil Taylor   234

Back to the Fountain

60. Randy Weston   245
61. Mal Waldron   248

62. Muhal Richard Abrams   251
63. Abdullah Ibrahim   253
64. McCoy Tyner   255
65. Don Pullen   258

Improvisation as Revelation

66. Keith Jarrett   262

The Latin Connection

67. Chucho Valdés   273
68. Monty Alexander   275
69. Michel Camilo   279
70. Eliane Elias   281
71. Gonzalo Rubalcaba   282

The Future Is Now

72. Henry Butler   285
73. Mulgrew Miller   287
74. Kenny Kirkland   290
75. Fred Hersch   293
76. Billy Childs   295
77. Geri Allen   297
78. Renee Rosnes   299
79. Cyrus Chestnut   300
80. Benny Green   303
81. Marcus Roberts   305
82. Jacky Terrasson   308
83. Bill Charlap   310
84. Harry Connick, Jr.   312
85. Stephen Scott   314
86. Eric Reed   316
87. Brad Mehldau   318
88. Geoff Keezer   321

Photo Credits   325

Index   326

Foreword

BY KEITH JARRETT

T he piano is not a jazz instrument. The voice, the drum, and the horn strike me as the real jazz instruments. But if we take the feeling we've got and apply it to the piano, it *can* be jazz. But *will* it be
jazz? In this, the musicians themselves are the only experts, and even they can be wrong. Nobody
seems to be able to define what line separates jazz from non-jazz. But we can hear it.

Some continuing characteristics of jazz piano are: forward motion, emphasis on pulse, emphasis of line, simulation of voice or horn phrasing, left hand as accompanist, subject matter in treble
voice, angularity (sometimes from lack of touch), seeming desire to free the mechanism (transcend
the instrument), linearity rather than verticality. I could go on, but I won't because none of these words
get us any closer to why it is jazz. In the end the pianists speak for themselves.

There is one overriding characteristic shared by *all* the great jazz pianists: individuality. They had
their sound, no one else's. Jazz is one of the few places where opinion, if strong enough, prevails over
pseudo-objectivity. Monk's opinion, for example, was strong enough to change many people's concept
of what jazz should be, even though there were players who wouldn't have wanted to play with him, especially in the early days. Cecil Taylor had to practically create players who could play with him, but
again, his opinion didn't change to suit everyone else, and he, too, changed the face of jazz.

The result of strong opinion does not have to be "radical" music, however. Bill Evans added beauty
to the world of jazz with his commitment to touch, and jazz piano wasn't the same anymore.

But, in general, the quality of commitment to what a particular player heard is what determined
that pianist's value to the world of jazz. I would even venture to say that it wasn't as important how a
player could play as how well a player could hear what he or she *wanted* to play. And maybe this desire holds the key to what jazz is: a certain kind of commitment to the rough edge of desire in order
to participate in the process of becoming. Players are willing to trade the veneer for the action. This
may be why when we hear old jazz piano recordings, the "funky" piano (out of tune, etc.) makes a
certain sense, not because jazz and depression (financial or otherwise) have such a close relationship, but because the rough edge of desire comes through better on a rough instrument.

Pianists are used to battling for their rights to play a decent instrument, and I think things are
better than they used to be, but the struggle to "get it out" of a good piano just becomes a different

formula. Because the piano is not a jazz instrument, it is possible to lose the music *to* the instrument. (I've often said that Hamburg Steinways can't play the blues.)

People have remarked that I seem to be having a love affair with the piano when I play. The truth is that it is a wrestling match. The piano is so stiff and unbending in essence that it takes all my effort to get it to sing. When we hear Bud Powell or Erroll Garner or countless other pianists grunt, squeal or moan, this is mostly the result of the effort to "move" the instrument—to get it to translate a feeling not essentially "pianistic" and phrasing not intrinsically piano-like. The thing just wasn't built by singers, and jazz is full of singers.

The history of jazz piano is rich with characters. Jazz asks for *your* statement about who you are. The process of improvising is one of self-revelation (or disgust), *not* one of playing for the public alone. The piano, with its 88 keys, has no right to be called a jazz instrument, but what would jazz have done without it?

Introduction

A confession: As a pianist myself, I admit to a certain bias. For me, this has always been the greatest of instruments, with a unique position in the greatest of all styles of music. It's the only instrument in the standard jazz rhythm section that can trade fours or entire choruses with the horn soloists. It can also stand out, with no support from bass, drums, or anyone else, and captivate listeners all on its own. Its range is bigger by far than that of any horn or woodwind, bigger than the human voice itself. It can play an endless melody, unbroken by pauses for breath. You can use it to spell the most complex harmonies, or ripple a silken ostinato, or pound an irresistible dance beat. It can be as quiet as thought, or loud enough to summon the cops to a Harlem rent party.

Perhaps the most important quality of the piano is its endurance. The pianos played by Jelly Roll Morton a century ago are essentially identical to those played by Jason Moran today. This means that the changes we hear in jazz piano are due not to the tinkerings of manufacturers but to an evolution in expression by the pianists themselves.

For jazz musicians, this means that an awareness of the history of their music, specifically as reflected on their instrument, is essential. Wynton Marsalis and Wallace Roney and Nicholas Payton didn't just pick up their horns and start playing from scratch; they had to understand how Joe Oliver and Louis Armstrong led to Bix Beiderbecke and Hot Lips Page, and on to Roy Eldridge and through Dizzy Gillespie and Miles Davis. They had to climb the whole tree before finding their own branch.

And so it is with the piano—only more so, because of its self-sufficiency. Unlike trumpeters, piano players have to understand how ragtime, a solo form built on a rhythmic pattern generated by the pianist with no help from percussion or any other instrument, transformed into the New Orleans style, with its more diverse references. In this style there lay the seeds of the New York stride school, a more technically demanding variation on the original ragtime rhythm. Today's pianists need to know how Art Tatum provided the bridge from stride to the ensemble school of jazz piano, which dated back to Earl Hines and moved up through Teddy Wilson and the big band players. Then came the bebop players, who de-emphasized the stride elements of Tatum and focused instead on his fleet right-hand lines. Their streamlined style, with its daring rhythms and advanced harmonic implications, blossomed in a dozen directions: the hard bop of Horace Silver and his descendants, the harmonic genius of Bill Evans, and then another bridge in the form of Herbie Hancock, linking these schools. And on, and on again.

Every step forward in jazz piano has been taken within a context of what came before, by an artist who is seeking or has found a new direction. That direction could lead back to something from the past, but because it would begin in the present it would still uncover something new. Even archival players such as Dick Hyman belong to the present; his motivation is to preserve aspects of stride piano, while James P. Johnson and Willie "the Lion" Smith saw stride as a dynamic new form. This inevitably puts a different spin on the music played by Hyman, Dick Wellstood, and Ralph Sutton, and therefore will have a different effect on those who are inspired by their work.

Clearly, then, jazz piano is nothing other than the story of the people who played it, how they learned from their teachers and how their peers and subsequent generations learned from them. Other than their decision to devote their lives to sitting on a bench or a stool and pressing on a row of keys, the only thing these artists have in common is their individualism. There is no single stereotypical jazz pianist; instead, we have a parade of colorful scoundrels and soft-spoken wallflowers, hilarious extroverts and narrow-tied introverts, an elegant Englishwoman and more than one sad, drugged-out case, big, robust men and a tiny, fragile Frenchman, unable to walk until late in his life.

We also have, it must be said, far more worthy souls in this congregation than the 88 profiled in this book. Sadly, there isn't enough room to give proper recognition to all of the pianists who have left their mark on jazz. Each of these will have his or her champions who will be outraged at this omission—and rightly so. From Charles "Luckey" Roberts through Jay McShann, Peck Kelly, and Jess Stacy, up from Jimmy Jones and Junior Mance to Dodo Marmarosa, Joe Albany, Mose Allison, Ellis Larkins, Hampton Hawes, Joe Sample, and Andrew Hill, all the way to Hilton Ruiz and Tania Maria, the list is long, and each name on it too distinctive, for one book to encompass.

Who, then, are our 88 notables? First of all, they are not necessarily the greatest of the great players—at least that wasn't my intention in choosing them to write about. There's no way to prove that one musician, or one artist of any kind, is greater than another—this is, in fact, the allure of the arts, in which the absence of absolute truths mirror the vagaries of human nature. Rather, this is a representative selection. Each of these pianists testifies to the impact one person can make. Taken together, their stories form a narrative that flows across the generations, from areas as diverse as suburban Wisconsin and apartheid-era South Africa, and into one stream of creative accomplishment.

Individualism and harmony—the attributes of the piano mirror those of all human endeavor. There is no more compelling metaphor, and no richer story, than that of the pianists who play jazz.

Special thanks to Peter Dale and Encore Recordings of Ann Arbor, Michigan, for their help on this project.

Robert L. Doerschuk

For Beth and Vanya, with love

The Man Who Invented Jazz

JELLY ROLL MORTON

Born: October 20, 1890, New Orleans, Louisiana
Died: July 10, 1941, Los Angeles, California

There is no more contradictory figure in jazz piano history than Jelly Roll Morton. No one swaggered through the spotlight with more bravado; his talent for self-promotion was epic, on the scale of Muhammad Ali. If it was his purpose to establish a legacy not just as the original jazz pianist but possibly as the inventor of jazz itself, then he must be judged at least a partial success.

Yet his notoriety came at a price. Even during the years of his greatest fame, when he would drape his fabulous coat across the piano, with the expensive lining turned carefully toward the audience, and smile so that the lights would catch the diamond inset into his front tooth, he was one of the least-liked individuals in his business. His tireless sermons on his own importance drove other musicians to distraction. He ridiculed New York jazz even while trying to keep his career afloat in New York; he preached again and again on the superiority of New Orleans, though he was a rare visitor to his hometown.

Today, the picture seems clear: a view of life muddied from the start by the racial hierarchies peculiar to New Orleans. A turbulent childhood that ended too soon. Years spent hustling pool, pimping, and playing piano throughout much of the country. A preoccupation with sexual conquest and a fear of being judged as effeminate. A tendency to hold grudges, to see betrayal and treachery in all the corners of his life. And ultimately, a terror of being mocked or, worse, forgotten.

It's an almost irresistible subject for modern myth-makers. The picture of Morton as a washed-up bartender, sure that he was being wasted slowly away by a voodoo spell, has stimulated at least one colorful novel as well as a dubious Broadway musical. Along with the dissipated Bix Beiderbecke, Morton casts a tragic shadow, one that time seems bound to distort and darken.

In fact, the decline in his musical reputation toward the end of his life was hastened by the annoyance he provoked from younger artists. Louis Armstrong lived long enough to argue about music with bebop incendiaries in the forties, though without losing their affection or respect. Morton, on the other hand, was baited by players who laughed at his impotent rages against modern jazz. Billy Taylor admitted to this author that he trekked to the Jungle Inn, the Washington dive managed by Morton in the late thirties, specifically to make fun of the pianist. Like his friends, Taylor dismissed him as a throwback and, by modern standards, a crude technician at best—until Morton shut him up by sitting at the old upright and tearing through a selection of his classic tunes. Taylor left that bar a bit wiser than he had been when he walked in.

Others held to their prejudices. Duke Ellington never found a kind word for Morton. Though courteous and complimentary to just about everyone else, Ellington sniffed that Morton "played piano like one of those high school teachers in Washington. As a matter of fact," he added, twisting the knife, "high school teachers played better jazz."

It is no disrespect to Ellington to remember that there had been bad blood between him and Morton as far back as the late twenties, when the two were nearly embroiled in a lawsuit. According to Morton, the young Duke had plagiarized several ideas from him. They never went to trial over the issue, though there may have been reason for resentment. In his book *Duke Ellington*, James Lincoln Collier cites the quote from Chopin's *Funeral March* at the end of Ellington's *Black and Tan Fantasy*, recorded in April 1927, as a device arguably lifted from Morton's use of the New Orleans funeral dirge "Flee as a Bird" in "Dead Man Blues."

The point is that even if Ellington's opinions were untainted by personal animosity, Morton certainly did about as little to endear himself to the Duke as he did to his other colleagues.

With firsthand memories of Morton faded, it's easier now to appreciate not only his role in launching jazz, but the skill he brought to the task as a player. His full voicings and surging two-handed rhythms weren't overly admired during the swing era, when a spare left hand and quick single lines in the right hand defined jazz piano. There is another irony here, in that Morton's playing was just as tied to writing as was the Duke's—and in some respects, it was better. Perhaps Ellington himself knew this, if clarinetist Albert Nicholas's story is true that he once declined an invitation to follow Morton at the piano during a jam session in New York.

Ellington was a master of harmony. To many of his works, idiomatic and adventurous voicings are intrinsic. One cannot simplify the chords to "Sophisticated Lady," "Prelude to a Kiss," or "In a Sentimental Mood" without compromising the structure of the tune. In contrast, Morton's attempts at advanced harmonies seem superfluous. His knotty theme on "Freakish" has a self-conscious quality. Rather than outline the direction of the tune, it gives way to the more traditional—and more graceful—chords of the second half of the verse. The title, as much as the music, betrays Morton's attitude toward "modern" harmonies; like freaks, these chords are unnatural, if not unnecessary.

Yet in terms of rhythm, and specifically in using rhythm to build tension and momentum, Morton exceeded anything that many more accomplished pianists would ever play. The unaccompanied piano verse on Morton's Red Hot Peppers recording of "Black Bottom Stomp" from September 15, 1926, practically explodes off the disc, especially when he shifts from a simple right-hand theme to shorter octave figurations that ignite against a ferocious left-hand stride. Nearly two years later, with a different group of Peppers in New York, he played a more fluid but equally compelling solo on "Georgia Swing." Here, the impact comes from a sixteenth-note rising line, played in octaves and mirrored by a descending line in the left hand. By kicking all this off in the middle of the fourth bar rather than at the end, he extends rather than obliterates the ideas explored in the first part of the solo. It is fireworks, but this is a musical rather than a gimmicky display.

These solos, played with verve and precision, reflect a compositional mentality. Ironically, by the advent of the swing era, only Ellington, among pianists, would hold onto and advance this approach—at least up until the arrival of Thelonious Monk.

For Morton, the roots of his piano playing grew from the unique diversity available to him as a child in New Orleans. As with all self-styled and actual figures of legend, details about his past were, and to a degree remain, mysterious. He was said to have been born in Gulfport or Freeport, Louisiana, though he was actually a native of New Orleans, born in a house at the corner of Frenchmen and Robertson Streets, in the heart of the neighborhood known locally as Creoleville, not far from the boyhood homes of jazzmen Manuel Perez, Freddie Keppard, and Sidney Bechet. Reports of his birth date were confused—intentionally, it turns out—for years. Though born on October 20, 1890, Morton insisted on 1885 as the correct year, in order to make his claims to inventing jazz in 1902 more believable.

In his song "Winin' Boy Blues," Morton crooned the line, "Don't deny my name." Yet no one did so more than Morton himself, who variously claimed LaMothe and Le Menthe as his handle. In fact, his name was Ferdinand Joseph Lamott; though his family went by LaMothe, this was misspelled on the baby's baptismal certificate. Eventually he changed his name to Morton, after his stepfather, because, as he told folklorist Alan Lomax, "I didn't want to be called Frenchy." The fact that his stepfather actually spelled his name Mouton seems almost anticlimactic.

More important is Morton's lineage as a mixed-blood Creole, with West Indian and other elements in his background. His parents were middle-class, strict Catholics, with a preference for European rather than neo-African cultural references. French was spoken more often than English in Creole homes, and opera and the classics, rather than the blues of the lower black classes, was their music. Creoles, who called themselves *les gens de couleur libres*, tended to see themselves as distinct from and socially superior to black society. Whites were indifferent to this stratification; in fact, a state law passed in the 1880s labeled all groups with "colored blood" as "negroes." This collision of class consciousness and legislated racism did little to soothe sensitive Creole psyches as Jelly Roll Morton entered the world.

Life was turbulent at the LeMothe household. The father, a carpenter who played trombone on the side, abandoned the family not long after Ferdinand's birth. Louise Monette, his mother, did her best to provide stability at home, but she could do nothing to thwart her son's disinterest in schooling and fascination with music and its temptations. His classroom was in the streets, where he took note of the "spasm bands"—street musicians who "did a lot of ad-libbing in ragtime style" on traditional and homemade instruments. At an early age he was banging on pots and pans. He took some guitar lessons at age six from "a Spanish gentleman in the neighborhood," and apparently played trombone and drums as well.

He was seven years old when he began to play in public. "I played in the string bands that were common at the time," he would recall for Alan Lomax. "These little three-piece combinations, consisting of bass, mandolin, and guitar, used to play serenades at late hours, from twelve to two, in the houses of friends. Naturally, the folks would welcome us when they heard those old tunes like 'Hot Time in the Old Town Tonight,' 'Wearing My Heart for You,' 'Old Oaken Bucket,' 'Bird in a Gilded Cage,' 'Mr. Johnson, Turn Me Loose,' as well as different little blues and ragtime numbers we knew. There was plenty of liquor in those old-time New Orleans homes, and they were liberal about entertaining us musicians"—even, apparently, if they were as young as seven.

Around the age of ten, he began playing piano. "I was inspired to play piano by going to a recital at the French opera house," he remembered in his conversations with Lomax. "There was a gentleman who rendered a selection at the piano, very marvelous music that made me want to play the piano very, very much." Though he studied for a while with several teachers, including a music professor from St. Joseph's Seminary College, he never developed into a proficient reader or built what might be called a strong "legitimate" technique. Instead, he learned by listening to the pianists who were established in the elegant salons and less reputable establishments throughout the 38-block red-light district known as Storyville, including Morton's main mentor, Tony Jackson, composer of "Pretty Baby" and "The Naked Dance." It soon became clear that the piano was his ticket to adventure and success. While his mother most likely wasn't thrilled about all this, she didn't order him to give it up either.

Everything changed with her death in 1904. Jelly and his two sisters were taken in by their great-grandmother Mimi Pechet and their uncle. By this time he was already earning money and a reputation through his own whorehouse gigs. Inevitably this created a conflict, and Pechet, concerned about his influence on his sister, called him a "bum and a scalawag" and kicked him out of the house. Jelly, all of 16 years old, set off for Biloxi, Mississippi, to live with his godmother, Eulalie Echo.

He never made it. Instead, in Biloxi, he picked up a gig at a brothel; it was here that he got his first pistol and had his first taste of whiskey. After a short stay in Meridian, and a quick return trip to New Orleans for some work at Hilma Burt's whorehouse, he spent the rest of his formative years wandering from town to town, playing one-night stands or short engagements, hustling the local pool or card sharks, and living on his wits. At first he covered Louisiana and Mississippi, then he expanded to Missouri, Illinois, California, New York, and other far-flung territories.

The following years sound like something out of folklore. Jelly toured with a vaudeville company called McCabe's Troubadours, and put together a music and comedy duo with a partner named Rose. During 1907 he performed in Chicago, Texas, California, Oklahoma, and New Orleans—with, he would later insist, a different girlfriend and plenty of money earned through gambling at each stop. He met W. C. Handy, the "Father of the Blues," during a visit to Memphis in 1908. He spent parts of 1909 and '10 touring the South with Billy Kersand's minstrel show, and performed on the vaudeville circuit with Will Benbow in 1910 and '11. He was arrested on false charges of train robbery in Mississippi and sentenced to one hundred days on a chain gang—from which he quickly managed to escape. He joined up with another New Orleans pianist, Jack the Bear, to swing through the Deep South and sell Coca-Cola laced with salt as a cure for tuberculosis. His travels took him to Chicago late in 1914, where he played at the Deluxe and Elite No. 2 clubs. The following year he performed at the Exposition in San Francisco, after which he wound up in Detroit, playing solo piano at the Fairfax Hotel; during 1915 he also found time to publish one of the first jazz tunes ever released on sheet music, his own "Jelly Roll Blues."

Somewhere along the line he picked up the name with which he would earn his renown. The story was that he found himself on a vaudeville bill one night, following a comedian who presented himself to the audience as "Sweet Papa Cream Puff, right out of the bakery shop." This sounded like a challenge to the young pianist, who improvised his own introduction as "Papa Jelly Roll, with stove pipes in my hips and all the women in town dyin' to turn my damper down." Other reports suggest that he lifted the name directly from another pianist he encountered on his travels. No matter—the name became his.

Throughout these adventures, and those that would follow before he settled for a while in Chicago, Morton saw himself as something of a gunfighter. But though he always packed a pistol, music, gambling, fast talk, and style were his real weapons. Nothing pleased him more than to ease into some new saloon and run a routine that would impress everyone in the room and leave him with money in his pocket. He outlined his strategy to Alan Lomax:

"I would . . . get a room, slick up, and walk down the street in my conservative stripe. The gals would all notice a new sport was in town, but I wouldn't so much as nod at anybody. Two hours later I'd stroll back to my place, change into a nice tweed, and stroll down the same way. The gals would begin to say, 'My, my, who's this new flash-sport drop in town? He's mighty cute.' About four in the afternoon I'd come by the same way in an altogether different outfit, and some babe would say, 'Lawd, mister, how many suits you got anyway?' I'd tell her, 'Several, darling, several.' 'Well, do you change like that every day?' 'Listen, baby, I can change like this every day for a month and never get my regular wardrobe half used up. I'm the suit man from suit land.' The next thing I know, I'd be eating supper in that gal's house and have a swell spot for meeting the sports, making my come-on with the piano, and taking their money in the pool hall."

This sort of behavior didn't draw only admiring glances. More than once Morton was threatened by gamblers who resented his suspicious winnings. Though he managed to avoid serious beatings or engaging in an actual gunfight, it can't be said that he left a trail of fond memories as he wheeled and dealed from town to town.

In 1917 he finally put down roots for a while, in Los Angeles. Here he settled with Anita Gonzales, an old girlfriend from New Orleans whose three brothers were musicians. They bought a small rooming house, which generated a trickle of income as Morton pursued gigs at places like the Cadillac Café, Baron Long's, the U.S. Grand Hotel, and the Jump Steady Club. He picked up some extra scratch with out-of-town work at the Regency Hotel in Vancouver, in Caspar, Wyoming, and, for a short while, with a band led by George Morrison in Denver.

Morrison's recollections of Morton in Whitney Balliett's book *Jelly Roll, Jabbo, & Fats* explain both the appeal and travail of working with the hotshot pianist in those days. "He couldn't stay in one band too long, because he was too eccentric and too temperamental, and he was a one-man band himself," he remembered. "Oh, but he could stomp the blues out. When he got to pattin' his foot, playing the piano, and a cigar in his mouth, man, he was *gone!*"

These performances, plus a few sideline activities that included promoting boxing matches, kept Jelly and Anita solvent enough to enjoy a few indulgences, such as the matching diamonds they set into their teeth. But as the jazz age dawned after World War I, Morton began to feel the pull of Chicago, the city that was drawing the best players from New Orleans. Perhaps he was itching for another challenge, or for a chance to play with some of his old colleagues. In any event, when a business proposition beckoned from the Windy City, he didn't hesitate.

In 1923, hoping to capitalize on the jazz craze and on the success they'd already enjoyed with the music of New Orleans cornetist King Joe Oliver, the Melrose Brothers Music Company offered Morton a contract to write piano music, which they would sell through their store in Chicago. Further, Melrose had a deal with the Gennett label that allowed artists to record their own music. This was enough to reel Morton in from way out West.

He arrived in spectacular cowboy-like attire, ready to take over the town. That July, a month after making his debut recordings in Chicago for another label, he was sent to Gennett's studios, in a former Ku Klux Klan meeting hall in Richmond, Indiana; only by claiming to be of Spanish descent was he able to secure a hotel room. Though he wasn't the leader on that date, he did make history by re-

Jelly Roll in 1939: Morton casts a tragic shadow, one that time seems bound to distort and darken.

placing pianist Kyle Pierce on three songs with the New Orleans Rhythm Kings, a major white band, thus playing on what would for several years be the only interracial jazz studio session.

In the months that followed, Morton cut many of his best piano solo recordings, and in 1926 he recorded some wonderful dates as leader of the Red Hot Peppers, a band he put together to fulfill a contractual obligation with the Victor label. The New Orleans all-stars recruited for these sessions lock into the groove as if it were the most natural thing they could do. On "Black Bottom Stomp," recorded on September 15, 1926, John Lindsey's thumping double-time bass electrifies Johnny St. Cyr's banjo solo, and on the final chorus trombonist Kid Ory plays one of the most thrilling two-bar breaks ever recorded. And no better example of momentum at relaxed tempos exists in traditional jazz than the version of "Grandpa's Spells," recorded three months later, with Andrew Hilaire contributing some inspired drum fills.

Great as these performances are, the success of these records stems more from Morton's writing. New Orleans bands were fundamentally improvisational; the essence of their art involved simultaneous collective extemporization. Arranged sections were rare and, almost always, simple enough to be mastered by ear. Not so on the Red Hot Peppers discs, where Morton wrote complex parts that owed more to notated music, such as ragtime, marches, and the music favored by Creoles, than to the bluesy looseness of Joe Oliver, Louis Armstrong, and their ensembles. Each section of these arrangements would receive its own treatment, with constant variation in the rhythm instrumentation. And by giving each player plenty of room to solo, Morton nudged jazz closer to the practices of swing and even bebop.

For our purposes, the many solo piano performances that Morton recorded during this same period have an even greater significance. There's no shortage of exciting material here. In one day alone, on June 9, 1924, Morton cut 11 unaccompanied pieces for Gennett, including the memorable "Shreveport Stomp," "Perfect Rag," and "Jelly Roll Blues." These recordings, along with his solo versions of works like "Kansas City Stomp," "Smokehouse Blues," and "The Pearls" (which he modestly described as one of the two most difficult piano pieces ever written, the other being another of his compositions, "Finger Breaker"), mark the spot where ragtime piano gives way to the more flexible structures and melodic freedoms of jazz performance. As Morton scholar and pianist James Dapogny told author Rick Kennedy in *Jelly Roll, Bix, and Hoagy*, "No other records before Morton's Gennett sides give us such a glimpse into the future possibilities for jazz piano."

Chicago was Morton's home base for five years. Though he didn't play that often locally, he recorded copiously, not just for Gennett but for Paramount, most notably Victor, and other labels. Most of his gigs took him on brief tours, including a short stint as second pianist with Fate Marable in 1924 and longer treks as front man for bands led by pianists Gene Anderson and Henry Crowder. Morton also performed a bit with W. C. Handy. Unlike his earlier routine in L.A., he devoted himself almost entirely to music—perhaps, it has been suggested, because gangsters already had gambling, prostitution, and other former Morton indulgences locked up. In fact, rumors suggest that Morton's departure for New York in 1928 owes as much to unspecified frictions with Al Capone as to the possibilities for greater success in the even bigger city.

Arriving in February 1928, Morton dove into the turbulent musical scene with his familiar cocky confidence. There was music everywhere, but it didn't take him long to decide that none of it met his standards. He found a room at a boardinghouse run by Lottie Joplin (Scott Joplin's widow), and almost immediately began making enemies by getting into arguments with other residents about the sorry state of musicianship in New York.

None of this really mattered to Morton, who saw this city as his last, greatest conquest. He found work quickly, with a two-month gig at the Rose Danceland in Harlem, and inked a publishing partnership with Harrison Smith, who had previously arranged a Victor contract for King Oliver. In June Morton also began recording more discs, solo and with a local incarnation of the Red Hot Peppers, for Victor at the label's studios in Camden, New Jersey. This version of the band featured Omer Simeon, who was playing clarinet with Morton at Rose Danceland, and other New Orleans expatriates who were playing at the Strand Ballroom in Brooklyn.

There's more diversity on these discs than in the Chicago recordings. As on his "Georgia Swing" solo noted earlier, Morton brings depth to his work with the full band by positioning his effects carefully: A sparkling right-hand trill pops up in the middle, not the beginning, of one of his choruses on "Shoe Shiner's Drag," thus enhancing rather than interrupting his momentum. In a trio rendition of "Shreveport Stomp," with Simeon and drummer Tommy Benford, Morton proves himself an inventive accompanist as well; behind the clarinet solo, he avoids repetitive comps and instead keeps feeding Simeon with surging dynamics and counter-figures. Their interaction helps explain jazz producer Nesuhi Ertegun's description of this track as "the greatest jazz record of all time."

The solo piano tracks cut in Camden offer insight into the importance of compositional structure in Morton's playing. Like the New York artists who were busy carving out the stride piano style, he anchors his performances on a boom-chuck left-hand pattern; his touch, however, seems a little heavier than theirs, and his conceptions highlight the structure of each piece, an emphasis that places him closer to ragtime tradition than to the specifically pianistic aesthetic of stride. There's an implication of how a song might be orchestrated in Morton's work; with James P. Johnson or Fats Waller, all of the ideas and execution refer solely and exclusively to the piano.

In other words, relative to the emerging stride school, Morton was beginning to sound a little old-fashioned. His frequent insistence that good piano performance involved "giving an imitation of a band" didn't agree with either the stride approach or the more revolutionary single-line orientation of Earl Hines. Further, Morton's occasionally heavy pedal work contrasted disturbingly with the crisp articulations of the younger pianists. Almost without noticing it, he had begun to slip from the pedestal he had built for himself. More modern trends were passing him by—a process only aggravated by an arrogance that was turning from colorful to just plain nasty.

Harlem-based musicians in the late twenties spent much of their time hanging out at a place called the Rhythm Club, at 2235 Seventh Avenue. New Orleans veterans like Louis Armstrong and Sidney Bechet mingled there with stride pianists like Waller and Johnson, as well as with Duke Ellington, Coleman Hawkins, and other more visionary musicians. Morton was a regular there too, but where he perhaps expected adulation he found himself being ridiculed by his rivals.

In his book *A Life in Jazz*, Danny Barker paints a depressing picture: "Jelly would drive up in front of the Rhythm Club some days, and when the musicians saw him they would start to laugh, for they knew they could anticipate a show and many laughs. As Jelly would stop his large, high-powered Lincoln car and step out to the sidewalk, one of the group was sure to gleefully ask him, 'Jelly, what's that you said about New York musicians yesterday?' Jelly would prop up his lips and exclaim crisply, 'What I said yesterday and today and on Judgment Day and also my dying day is that it takes one hundred live New York musicians to equal one dead police dog.' The group would laugh hysterically as Jelly went into his daily tirades."

Perry Bradford outlines similar memories in *Born with the Blues*, where he writes, "Long about sun-up found some of us making a bee-line for the Rhythm Club. . . . Everybody was crowded around Jelly Roll Morton as we entered, and Jelly was dishing out the usual morning lectures: 'You New York musicians don't know anything about jazz—can't play it because you don't know how.'"

If there was an element of bear-baiting in these encounters, Morton asked for it. As onlookers snickered, he would tell the great drummer Chick Webb that he couldn't play and that his band stank. He would insist that he was the first jazz musician to record with a string bass instead of a tuba. He'd complain that he was playing "St. Louis Blues" years before W. C. Handy claimed to have written it. He'd credit himself as the inventor of wire brushes for drummers, or scat singing, or jazz itself.

Work began to dry up. On the eve of the Great Depression Morton organized an all-girl musical revue, but the act dissolved after a few months. He recorded a few more times for Victor before the label dropped him in 1930. Investments he had made in a cosmetics company disappeared as tough times grew tougher. Eventually he had to sell even the diamond from his front tooth.

To make things worse, it started getting harder to find sidemen for occasional live dates who would put up with his authoritarian ways. As reedman Joe Darensbourg remembers in his autobiography *Jazz Odyssey*, "He never believed in paying guys too much money to start with. I think I got $30 for two weeks [with Morton]. A lot of musicians wouldn't even play with him because they were afraid they wouldn't get their money."

After scuffling around New York for several more years, Morton abandoned the big city and retreated to Washington, D.C. There, late in 1936, he opened his own bar, a second-floor walkup that he called the Jungle Club. He might have faded completely from sight there, were it not for a radio show that caught his attention one night. The popular program *Ripley's Believe It or Not* innocently introduced W. C. Handy one night in 1938 as "the originator of jazz and the blues." In a last burst of pride, Morton decided to set the record straight.

His letter to the jazz magazine *Down Beat* might have amused the young pups back at the Rhythm Club, but like so many of his extravagant gestures in years past, it did push him back into the spotlight one last time. After disparaging Handy as, essentially, a phony, Morton informed readers that "New Orleans is the cradle of jazz, and I, myself, happened to be the creator in 1902." That would have made him 12 years old at the time of this epochal event—but considering that he was in fact already playing gigs in Storyville at that age, it is difficult to write off this boast as completely without merit.

Yet, characteristically, he couldn't leave it at that. "I may be the only perfect specimen today in jazz that's living," he declared. "Speaking of jazz music, anytime it is mentioned, musicians usually hate to give credit, but they will say, 'I heard Jelly Roll play it first.'"

Certainly this broadside got the attention of Alan Lomax, a folk music archivist at the Library of Congress. He met with Morton and persuaded the pianist to sit with him in the Coolidge Auditorium at the Library and record music and reminiscences of his life onto Lomax's disc recorder for preservation in the Library archive. Though he planned only a single short conversation, the result was more than eight hours' worth of material, including thoughtful renditions of more than 100 compositions, all of which would later be pressed onto 52 discs. These recordings, as well as Lomax's transcriptions and reflections on them in his book *Mister Jelly Roll*, are among the most precious artifacts in American culture. For all the hyperbole thrown about by Morton throughout his youth, here we have a more insightful picture of the artist and his world.

Time was already running out as Morton recounted his life for Lomax. They began their sessions in May 1938. That fall, the pianist was wounded in the head and chest by an assailant with a knife—predictably, during an argument at the Jungle Club about music. Doctors warned him not to play the piano during his recovery, so in his final meeting with Lomax on December 14, Morton reached far back into his past to accompany his recollections on guitar. He even recorded an a cappella vocal, a prostitute's lament titled "Trix Ain't Walkin' No More," that is as moving in its own way as his best keyboard performances.

A few more opportunities presented themselves in the wake of the *Down Beat* diatribe and the Lomax recordings. Toward the end of 1938 Morton moved back to New York, where he founded another publishing company. In September 1939 he returned to the Victor studios for a final series of all-star sessions, organized by record store owner Stephen Smith. With many of his old friends in attendance—

Sidney Bechet, Albert Nicholas, and Zutty Singleton among them—he waxed, as a last testament, rousing versions of his tribute to the original jazz trumpet icon "I Thought I Heard Buddy Bolden Say" and the "Winin' Boy Blues," in a considerably cleaner version than he revealed to Lomax at the Library sessions. For a while Morton pondered an offer to put a band together and tour the Soviet Union.

But storm clouds were gathering. Beset by heart problems, asthma, and after-effects of the knife wounds, Morton began insisting that some mysterious enemy had bedeviled him with a voodoo spell. As if to confirm his suspicions, he learned in the fall of 1940 that Eulalie Echo—the godmother he had gone to live with when his wanderings began back at age 16—had passed away in California. For some reason he became convinced that there was a small fortune in jewelry stashed away at her house; recovering them became a mission of desperate necessity.

With that, Morton hooked his Cadillac to his Lincoln and began one last picaresque journey, this time from East Coast to West. In letters to his wife Mabel, he told harrowing tales of being stuck in snowstorms in ten states, skidding off the road in Wyoming, and being trapped on an Oregon mountain until being rescued by police. Somehow he made it to California, where, of course, no cache of diamonds awaited him. There is a symmetry to this story of finally making it to his godmother's place, many long years after he had set off to live with her, but whether Morton noticed it is a mystery.

With his last energies Morton tried to revive his career in Los Angeles. Once again he formed a publishing company and organized a band. Once more he ran into trouble, this time with the local musicians' union, to whom he paid a $45 fine for an unspecified offense. A few months later, he became seriously ill. In June 1941 he checked into a sanatorium to attempt a recovery. It was too little too late, and after one last collapse that took him to Los Angeles County General Hospital, Morton died. He had lived several lifetimes, antagonized countless real and imagined rivals, made a few friends, and changed the course of music history.

All in the space of 50 years.

Masters of Stride

2. JAMES P. JOHNSON

Born February 1, 1894, New Brunswick, New Jersey
Died November 17, 1955, New York, New York

The most important transitional figure in early jazz piano is James P. Johnson. His playing, though rooted in East Coast ragtime, pointed the way toward a different kind of sound and spirit.

In his youth he performed for liquor-slicked dancers in disreputable dives. He was only eight when a woman hired him to play at her place for several hours at a time, as long as he kept his eyes fixed on the piano throughout the gig. Years would pass before Johnson realized that he was providing mood music for the neighborhood madame—by that time he was composing orchestral works, which never quite earned him the respectability he deserved.

Even within the legacy of stride piano, which owed everything to Johnson's trailblazing blend of African-American expression and European techniques, he was overshadowed by his pupil, sometime rival, and great friend Fats Waller, whose flamboyant personality drew attention from the more reflective and dignified Johnson. For all the fame that Waller enjoyed, Johnson was the greater visionary, and possibly the better musician.

Johnson never understood why he couldn't enjoy the ring shouts that he heard at his mother's lively parties as much as the classical music he was exposed to through his lessons with a local teacher named Bruto Giannini. In his hierarchy of influences, Eubie Blake, Luckey Roberts, and Abba Labba, all of whom he heard in New York as a teenager, were no more or less valuable than the classical virtuosi Josef Hoffman and Sergei Rachmaninoff, or the New York Philharmonic, which he first heard at the age of 11.

His mission, as a young pianist, was to build a foundation strong enough to support a union of these disparate styles. He practiced to exhaustion, sometimes draping a sheet over the keyboard and working in the dark in order to make his bond with the instrument more intuitive. He began playing

in a black area of New York called the Jungles, where a tough clientele of transplanted South Car-
olinians demanded ragtime accompaniment for the frenzied dance that Johnson would immortalize
in his most famous composition, "Charleston." Yet he would scatter quotes from Liszt or Grieg over
the beat, and keep pushing against the limits of the style by exploring fuller chords, a more insistent
rhythm, and greater improvisational liberties.

Johnson's great contribution was to invent stride piano from these elements. It was, from the
start, a style based in New York, where audiences who could visit Harlem one night and Carnegie Hall
the next tended to develop high expectations. Stride piano met and exceeded these standards, and
in such compositions as "Carolina Shout," "Jingles," and "You've Got to Be Modernistic," he made
it clear that a solid command of the instrument was essential in this idiom.

In fact, heavyweight technique was the calling card of every pianist who tried to build a name for
himself in stride circles in the wake of World War I. Many of these young players had trained for this
assignment by studying Johnson's piano rolls; both Fats Waller and Duke Ellington learned to play
"Carolina Shout" by slowing down the player piano mechanism and memorizing Johnson's performance as it danced across the keys.

The earliest of these rolls capture Johnson as a pure ragtime player in the East Coast style of Eubie
Blake. His "Steeplechase Rag" and "Twilight Rag"—both recorded in 1917, the latter as a duo with
E. E. Wilson—adhere to ragtime form, with essentially no improvisation. But on rolls that he cut just
a few years later, he displayed a looser approach, with three-against-two counter-rhythms and a bigger selection of figurations in the left hand, and more blues inflections in the melody. Ragtime still dictated his compositional approach on tunes like "Harlem Strut," "Carolina Shout," and the waltz novelty
"Eccentricity," and old-timey tremolos kept cropping up in midsections of his tunes, but throughout

James P. Johnson with guitarist Danny Barker, trumpeter Marty Marsala, and clarinetist Albert
Nicholas on a Hudson River jazz excursion, 1946: For all the fame Fats Waller enjoyed, Johnson
was the greater visionary, and possibly the better musician.

the twenties a swing feel and a more sophisticated harmonic sensibility in his playing reflected Johnson's interest in more contemporary expressions.

By the end of the decade Johnson was working elaborate variations, beyond the limits of ragtime, into his improvisations. His recordings of "What Is This Thing Called Love" and "Crying for the Carolines," both cut on January 21, 1930, show a dedication to creating a completely integrated performance more than to dazzling listeners. His right hand, in particular, had advanced dramatically, with looser, more natural phrasing and a preference for solid voice-leading over single lines. It is as much a solo piano style as ragtime, but more responsive to modern tastes and temperaments.

Still, the self-sufficiency of stride began to sound dated as the swing craze erupted in the thirties. Though he did perform with groups, including gigs with Mezz Mezzrow, Johnson's style didn't fit as neatly into the rhythm section as the more spare playing epitomized by Count Basie. At the historic *Spirituals to Swing* concert organized by John Hammond at Carnegie Hall in 1939, Johnson plays gracefully while sitting in with the Basie band behind singer Helen Humes, but he seems to be playing more than he needs to—not in the sense of setting off fireworks, but rather in not embracing a more economic role offered by the band dynamics.

As opportunities for stride pianists diminished, Johnson began to concentrate more on serious composition. He was writing ambitious works as far back as the late twenties, some of which won brief attention: His piano rhapsody *Yamekraw*, based on impressions of black life in Savannah, Georgia, was premiered by Fats Waller during his debut at Carnegie Hall in 1928. The same venue would feature a program in 1945 that consisted entirely of Johnson's works.

More typically, the classical establishment persisted in its indifference toward Johnson. Comments from observers suggest that prejudice had at least as much to do with this neglect as any questions about quality. In his book *The Story of Jazz*, after proclaiming Johnson's piano concertos "quite as complex and, in a sense, twice as difficult to play as Mozart's," Marshall Stearns muses, "Perhaps his Afro-American folk origins betrayed him, for the average classical musician is utterly incapable of the rhythmic sensitivity that is necessary to play Johnson's pieces."

Things were made worse by health problems, beginning with a mild stroke in 1940. Johnson continued to record, with elegance and restraint, in the forties, though a growing unsteadiness in his tempo forced him to bring in a drummer on a number of dates. Another stroke in 1950 left him bedridden until his death five years later.

Johnson's decline, along with faster changes in jazz style during the forties, left him largely forgotten: *Down Beat* embarrassed itself, and did little to cheer him up, by publishing an obituary months before his actual demise. Yet his memory would be kept alive by disciples of Harlem stride, including Dick Wellstood, who wrote in the August 1960 issue of *Jazz Review*, "James P. is the focal point. The rags, cotillions, mazurkas, and all those other unknown phenomena all came together in James P., who made jazz out of them. And then the harmonics of James P. went into Duke, the showiness into Tatum, the good-timiness into Fats, and the rhythmic possibilities into Monk."

Indeed, it was the modernist Thelonious Monk who had the final word, after listening one day to his own recording of an original tune, "Functional." Turning to producer Orrin Keepnews, he commented, "I sound just like James P. Johnson."

WILLIE "THE LION" SMITH

Born: November 25, 1897, Goshen, New York
Died: April 18, 1973, New York, New York

He wasn't the greatest of the stride pianists, but Willie "the Lion" Smith personified the style as vividly as his friend and younger rival Fats Waller. Each was an unforgettable personality, though Smith was closer in spirit to the flashy, combative Jelly Roll Morton than to the lovable persona that Waller inhabited. His calling cards were a derby hat and a long cigar; together, they created an unmistakable silhouette as he sidled into countless rent parties and all-night jams and hovered menacingly over whoever was playing piano at the moment.

Duke Ellington witnessed many of these intimidating encounters. "The Lion was standing over him, cigar blazing," he recalled in *Hear Me Talkin' to Ya*. "Like, if the cat was weak with the left hand, the Lion would say, 'What's the matter? Are you a cripple?' Or, 'Where did you break your left arm?' Or, 'Get up. I will show you how it's supposed to go.'" To the young Duke, Smith was "a gladiator at heart." He would dedicate one of his own compositions, *Portrait of the Lion*, to Smith.

Another rival and colleague, James P. Johnson, saw music in Smith's behavior: "When Willie Smith walked into a place, his every move was a picture . . . studied, practiced, and developed just like it was a complicated piano piece."

There is insight in these words, for Smith was in fact a composer by nature, as much as he was a fighter by temperament. His works, especially the solo piano pieces, are intricate little masterpieces. More than Waller's songs, and like Johnson's earlier output, many of them reflected a ragtime influence, but with intriguing twists. Swing clarinetist Artie Shaw, who used to sit in frequently with Smith, wrote about these complementary influences: " . . . scattered throughout the ragtime were occasional incongruously modern modulatory passages. I have never heard anyone else play anything like them." Billy Strayhorn would more poetically remember Smith's "strange mixture of counterpoint, chromatic harmony, and arabesque-like figures."

Some degree of mystery surrounds the Lion's nickname. In *Hear Me Talkin' to Ya* Smith himself insists that "James [P. Johnson] gave me the title because of my spunk and enterprise." But he was also fond of claiming that he earned the handle through displaying bravery on the battlefield with an artillery unit in World War I. What's beyond dispute is that the name served him well: "When the Lion roared, you knew what was coming," said blues singer Joe Turner, in words that countless musicians and admirers would echo throughout his long career.

Smith's birth name was equally vivid, though far less concise. William Henry Joseph Bonaparte Bertholoff Smith was how he came into the world—as Smith would later explain it, Joseph derived from the Bible, Bonaparte reflected a French sensibility, Bertholoff was his real father's name, Smith came from his stepfather, and the William and Henry were tossed in essentially to round things off. (By comparison, he had a brother, whose name was, in its entirety, Ralph.) As an infant he moved with his family from upstate New York to an unsavory neighborhood in Newark, New Jersey. His father, a gambler, died when Willie was five years old.

With his father's absence, Smith's mother made a strong positive impact on her son. She was a musician who played organ and piano in church; from her he learned his keyboard rudiments, and from a local teacher, Hans Steinke, he acquired a knowledge of classical repertoire that would feed both his writing and his performing throughout his life. From his grandmother, who performed in a minstrel show, he also learned to play the banjo. When not practicing at home, young Willie would earn spare change for his family by tap dancing in saloons or on busy street corners.

During this time he crossed paths with Jelly Roll Morton. He first heard the legendary New Orleans pianist in 1911, when Smith was just 14 years old. The experience made a strong impression on Smith, in terms both of pianistic performance and showmanship. Looking back in the pages of his autobiography, *The Lion Roars*, he would remember Morton as "a man with strong spiritual and magnetic forces. When he sat down to play, he could hold the audience by the strength of his strong personality. . . . He was intelligent, had something to offer, and as far as I could tell, he was always able to back up what he said." No truer summary of the Lion's own emerging self-image could be written.

By his late teens Smith was well on his way, with gigs in and beyond the New York area. He met and befriended James P. Johnson in 1914, and replaced Eubie Blake for a summer job in Atlantic City the following year. In 1917 Smith joined the Fifteenth Infantry Regiment, a black company, and served for two years in Europe during World War I. Though he did see combat, he spent much of his time in France as a drum major with a black military band as well. With his discharge he returned to New York and promptly made himself indispensable as a focal point of the emerging stride piano style.

He, Waller, and Johnson became the Trinity in that scene, with Charles "Luckey" Roberts, Lippy Boyette, and a few others close in their footsteps. Over the years, after Waller's death and Johnson's incapacity, Smith would roll on as a jazz institution, holding court at assorted New York clubs, working with Dixieland bands led by Max Kaminsky, Jimmy McPartland, and other revivalists, and enlightening talented acolytes such as Joe Bushkin and Mike Lipskin on the persistent art of stride piano.

Smith's style was light and buoyant, with fewer frills than Waller's but more emphatic cross-rhythm interludes. His solo on "What Can I Do with a Foolish Little Girl Like You," recorded in 1935 with his Cubs, begins with a full verse of rumbling sixteenth-notes in which the right hand initially plays a three-against-one "broken" pattern against the left-hand pulse. In the second half of this verse, Smith divides the episode into irregular sub-rhythms, a favorite stride technique, executed here with a blithe insouciance. The second verse reintroduces the familiar boom-chuck figure to the left hand as Smith dances through a sprightly, if unadventurous, extemporization in the upper midrange. Through the rest of the song, as the band barrels toward last two choruses, Smith holds onto a straightforward stride, bearing down with a heavier touch that transforms the piano into a no-nonsense rhythm dynamo.

From the same session, on "Harlem Joys," Smith deviates from his stride with some remarkable left-hand variations. After the opening chorus, he plays his one-chorus solo with a standard theme-and-development improvisation in his right hand. His left hand, meanwhile, lightens up a bit to allow more exposure to the right-hand figures, then moves into a series of ascending passages in bars three and four; these set the stage for another departure from the stride pattern in bars seven and eight—in this case, a deftly executed truncation that momentarily turns the left-hand pulse around in its relation to

Willie "the Lion" Smith at New York's Park Lane Hotel in 1939: He was a composer by nature, as much as he was a fighter by temperament.

the beat, thus creating an illusion of deviation from the four-bar structure of the solo. It all blows by in seconds before Smith straightens it out, with a recurrence of the left-hand ascending line placed symmetrically in the first two bars of the second chorus and leading this time to four final bars played in stop-time against Willie Williams's ongoing washboard rhythm.

Perhaps because his technique wasn't as overwhelming as that of some of his peers in the stride school, Smith pursued more ingenious variations on stride in his solos. Where Waller or Johnson might dazzle with sheer virtuosity, Smith constantly tweaked the formula. On "The Swampland Is Calling Me," recorded with the six-piece Cubs in 1937, he takes the somewhat flowery quality of his own intro as a cue to approach his solo with a fastidious air; his articulation is a pristine staccato, decorated with a few well-placed trills, and the rhythm turns into a rolling arpeggiation, all of which creates a bubbly, fountain-like impression. Smith was capable of moving in the other direction as well, as on "Muskrat Ramble," recorded with another version of his Cubs in 1944; to balance the hot blowing by Max Kaminsky and the rest of the sextet, he plays a scrupulously minimalist solo, which consists essentially of a single simple figure repeated with only minor variation from beginning to end. One can imagine Smith, eyebrows nonchalantly raised, as if to suggest there's no need to prove himself the master on *every* performance.

This thoughtful quality in Smith's ensemble work manifested itself in the intricacy and originality of his solo piano compositions. Since these were generally written out more fully than tunes tailored for improvisational interpretations, Smith's renditions of original material had more in common with a classical pianist interpreting Chopin than Fats Waller jamming on "Honeysuckle Rose." You couldn't reduce the Lion's songs to simple chord charts or lead sheets; their intricate form, and delicate construction of both thematic and accompanimental passages, often left little room for winging it. There were of course exceptions—and when they occur in the meticulously notated contexts that he created, the effect could be thrilling.

Listen, for example, to "Rippling Waters," recorded in 1939: There's almost a ragtime feel as Smith plays through the syncopated chords and trilling theme on the introduction and first verses, but going into the chorus section he suddenly breaks into a bawdy stride, complete with staggered left-hand variations below barrelhouse figurations. Then he slips back to a reprise of the written verse. The B section that follows is classic blowing, as Smith lays down a swinging rhythm bed and tears through three roaring choruses marked by some terrific momentum generated through manipulations of a motivic figure—and interrupted momentarily by an elegant, suspended-breath single note, an ironic diminished fifth, midway through the second verse. Again, there is Lionesque humor in this pause, which functions as a rhetorical question: "So . . . how'm I doing?"

He was doing great, all the way up to his last gig, a duo concert with another gifted young student, Brooks Kerr, in January 1973. Three months later, his boundless energies finally exhausted, the Lion died peacefully in a New York hospital.

4. FATS WALLER

Born May 21, 1904, New York, New York
Died December 15, 1943, Kansas City, Missouri

Like his contemporary Babe Ruth, Fats Waller was a media phenomenon at the dawn of the information age. There were similarities between the two: Each cast a big shadow, with Waller packing nearly three hundred pounds on a five-foot-ten frame. Their personalities filled the venues of their choice, whether Carnegie Hall or Yankee Stadium.

But within their respective disciplines, they represented opposite approaches. Ruth was a romantic: His booming home runs shattered the pristine aesthetics of hit-and-run baseball. In other words, he played the way he looked. Not so with Waller. For all his ribald humor and the excesses of his life, he had a classic temperament, one that prized finesse over power. Ruth's swing at the plate was explosive; Waller's delivery at the piano was economical, with minimal movement punctuated only rarely by thumping, percussive effects.

Stride piano reached its apotheosis in the playing of Fats Waller. He was a more subtle and technically polished player than his teacher and friend, James P. Johnson, and less bound by the structural limitations of ragtime. He worked more successfully with pop song form, and streamlined his improvisations into single lines that had little to do with Scott Joplin or Eubie Blake and everything to do with a more modern swing feel that would always hover beyond Johnson's reach.

This style rose on a foundation of African-American church music, tempered by classical refinement. Born in Harlem, Tom Waller was one of five children. He began learning the basics of piano and organ from his mother at age six and gave his first public performances on harmonium to accompany his father's street sermons. As an overweight kid, Waller compensated by turning himself into a class clown; at home, he sought solace in music, through diligent practice at the keyboard.

He was ten years old when he got his hands for the first time on the thundering pipe organ at the Abyssinian Baptist Church, on Seventh Avenue near 125th Street, where his father served as a lay preacher.

Throughout his life Waller would be captivated equally by the organ, which he fondly called the "God box," and the piano. He sang hymns, both at home and in the church choir; "Abide with Me" would always remain one of his favorite tunes. Yet he was also drawn to secular music, some of it bawdy enough to cause alarm in the Waller household.

As a remedy to this distressing fixation, Fats was taken by his father to hear a recital being given by Ignace Paderewski. While the experience wasn't enough to make him swear off "the Devil's music," Waller did emerge from Carnegie Hall with a respect for what a virtuoso could do with the piano. (On that same night, ragtime giant Scott Joplin, whose music already represented a bygone era, was in the audience, forgotten and syphilitic, with only months more to live.) It must have consoled the older Waller to witness the growth of his son's commitment to explore and master the classical repertoire.

But there weren't that many opportunities in classical music for young black artists—and in any event, Waller's new enthusiasm for European repertoire did nothing to dampen his ardor for funkier material and living large. He was 15 when he quit De Witt Clinton High School to work full-time as a silent movie organist at the Lincoln Theater; there he would entertain friends with hilariously inappropriate improvisations during love scenes, or welcome admirers, from a young Count Basie to Waller's future lyricist Andy Razaf, into the orchestra pit.

In 1920, distraught over his mother's death, Waller moved in with a pianist named Russell Brooks, married too quickly to a woman who would hector him for years after their divorce over his erratic support for their son, and plunged into the rent party circuit that was already a hothouse for the stride style. Word of his talents spread quickly: He visited Chicago, where he performed on organ at the Regal Theater and received a $100 tip from Al Capone. And in 1922, when Willie "the Lion" Smith left his regular gig at Leroy's in Harlem, Waller was hired to replace him, on recommendation from James P. Johnson.

Johnson played a critical role in Waller's life. He was generous with his advice, and in private lessons he worked to strengthen the younger pianist's already powerful left hand. Johnson also introduced Waller to the QRS piano roll company, for whom he cut 22 rolls from 1923 through '27. They wrote some material together for the revue *Keep Shufflin'* in 1927. And when he made his Carnegie Hall debut in 1928, in a program organized by W. C. Handy, Waller stole the show with a performance of Johnson's *Yamekraw*.

He soon surpassed his teacher, as a pianist and more so as an entertainer. Had he never played a note of music, Waller would likely have become just as famous as a comic actor. Audiences learned to expect outlandish entrances at his shows: Sometimes he would perform a lascivious hip swivel as the band simulated hula music. He could deflate the most formal concerts with *sotto voce* comments: At one piano recital, after the opening applause had died away, he settled onto the stool, cast a glance toward his bulky backside, and murmured, loud enough to be heard throughout the house, "Is you all there, Fatsy-Watsy?"

As the radio era dawned, Waller's star rose higher still. He was a natural for the idiom—too natural, by some accounts, as some of his double-entendres stretched the patience of network executives and program sponsors. Still, nobody was foolish enough to consider taking him off the air, and as

Fats Waller at New York's Onyx Club, 1936: For all his excesses, Waller had a classic temperament, one that prized finesse over power.

he launched his own show in 1929, his hilarious ad-libs, campy but artful singing, and impeccable piano became part of the soundtrack for the era.

Much of what Waller played was his own material. He wrote prolifically, beginning with "Squeeze Me" and eventually completing more than five hundred tunes, including such classics as "Black and Blue," "The Jitterbug Waltz," "Keepin' Out of Mischief Now," and "Blue Turning Grey Over You." In 1929 he opened a revue in the Hudson Theater at 48th Street and Broadway: Titled *Connie's Hot Chocolates*, it included such classic originals as "Honeysuckle Rose," with words written by Razaf after Waller had whistled the melody to him over the phone, and "Ain't Misbehavin'," performed in the show by Waller, Edith Wilson, and his close friend Louis Armstrong, billed as "Three Thousand Pounds of Rhythm."

For all the hits credited to Waller, many ended up being owned by someone else. With high living and alimony payments keeping him in debt, he often sold his songs at unbelievably low prices. More than once, he unloaded rights to his songs in order to buy hamburgers. "Black and Blue" and "Ain't Misbehavin'" were peddled as part of a nine-song package for $500. Another time, in a moment of real desperation, Waller offered fellow musician Don Redman ownership of his entire catalog for no more than $10; Redman had the decency to turn him down. Some songs that endure to this day, including "I Can't Give You Anything But Love" and "On the Sunny Side of the Street," are rumored to have begun life as Waller compositions before being surrendered.

Still, there was never enough to keep up. In 1928 he spent six months in the New York County Jail for failure to provide support for his first wife and their four-year-old son. His impulsive habits didn't make budgeting any easier: Throughout his adult life Waller consumed enormous amounts of food and drink. He was known to eat as many as four steaks at a single dinner, and his dressing room table groaned under piles of burgers and beer at gigs. When Waller was threatened again with prison after returning from a European tour in 1932, his agent threw in the towel and quit. For the next decade his successor, Ed Kirkeby, would find it more than a full-time job to keep his client's riotous affairs in order.

Nothing, however, stopped the music. Waller, like James P. Johnson, dreamed of writing concert works. Inspired by Kirkeby's descriptions of historic sites in England, he composed six programmatic piano sketches, collectively titled *London Suite*. He delighted in bringing classical and jazz elements together, and would sometimes perform "Honeysuckle Rose" in the styles of Bach, Beethoven, and Brahms. But buffoonery was his bread and butter, and after a Victor executive heard him play at a party given by George Gershwin and signed him in 1934, Waller sank into a long denouement of recording corny songs that came cheap to the label.

On occasion Waller raged over the tripe he was forced to record, yet in the end he proved himself capable of overcoming the most mediocre material. No one else could take a song like "The Curse of an Aching Heart" and ridicule it through melodramatic vocals even while leading his band through a ferociously swinging interpretation. Working most often with a six-piece lineup known as Fats Waller and his Rhythm, on tunes that ranged from classic to inane, he improvised brilliantly constructed solos and, more important, created a scaled-down concept of accompaniment that adapted perfectly to the jazz framework.

Among scores of examples, his recording of "Stop Pretending," cut on July 16, 1940, with his sextet, features Waller in a masterful opening chorus, with quarter-note chords creating a stately foundation under the right hand. The stride pulse doesn't kick in until the bridge, but even here the piano explores a variety of rhythms, all of which lock onto the bass and drum groove. Then, during Bugs Hamilton's muted trumpet lead, Waller cuts further back, with octave counter-themes that nudge the solo toward blues phrasing and a final twinkling trill that leads to a delicate but infectious piano break on the bridge.

Waller's last years were a tumble of fame, financial crisis, and accelerating health problems. Hollywood beckoned, and his appearance in *Stormy Weather* arguably stole the show from co-stars Lena Horne, Cab Calloway, and Bill "Bojangles" Robinson. But there were erratic moments as well, including a notorious recital at Carnegie Hall on July 10, 1942; there, in front of an audience that included James P. Johnson and the gifted young pianist Dick Hyman, Waller followed a lackluster first set with an embarrassing finale in a state of obvious intoxication.

In December 1943, after wrapping up a six-week engagement at the Florentine Gardens in Los Angeles, Waller boarded a luxury train bound for New York, where he planned a long overdue vacation, followed by discussions for a movie project with Abbott and Costello. He was exhausted and ill, in part from having to play in cold air conditioning at the Florentine. The temperature in his compartment dropped through the night as the train rolled through the Midwest. Somewhere near Kansas City, the pianist died in his sleep.

Ironically, a train bearing his close friend Louis Armstrong, heading west, passed through Kansas City even as a local doctor was making Waller's death official. When told the news, Armstrong reportedly spent the entire night in tears.

Singing & Swinging

5. DUKE ELLINGTON

Born: April 29, 1899, Washington, D.C.
Died: May 24, 1974, New York, New York

A perception has long existed—more of a preconception, perhaps—that pianists who lead big bands tend not to play with the authority of those who present themselves mainly as soloists or in smaller groups. Earl Hines, who had established himself initially as an outstanding and innovative performer before putting his ensemble together, is seen often as the exception to this perceived rule. But Duke Ellington, uniquely distinguished and revered, is usually the focus of those on both sides of this debate.

It is obvious that Ellington had as distinctive a sound as a pianist. But the piano also played a subsidiary role in his greater mission of highlighting his band, with its brilliant soloists and impeccable execution of his written ideas. You would often hear Ellington at the keys, playing an introductory verse or two in order to set the tempo and the feel for his ensemble. He took solos too, often with a buoyant rhythm, or a reflective, poetic sensibility on ballads. In these exposed moments Ellington was impossible to mistake for any other player, yet everything he played was conceived to serve the arrangement, rather than to draw too much attention to himself. As Paul Bley put it to the author, "Duke was the composer's pianist personified . . . always thinking in terms of an orchestral sense, and in a sense writing for the orchestra in real time."

His longtime friend and collaborator Billy Strayhorn was more succinct, saying, "Ellington plays the piano, but his real instrument is the orchestra." No one knew Ellington the pianist better than Strayhorn, who in 1950 recorded a series of duets with him at one keyboard. Available on the album *Great Times!,* they radiate an exuberant energy and more than a little playfulness, but much of what Ellington offers on tracks like "Cottontail" echoes devices—especially a pearly descending run—that occur repeatedly in his catalog. As a player, it seemed more important for him to apply familiar harmonies, licks, and fills, which had long been evident as a part of his compositional sound, rather than test less familiar waters in the fashion of a virtuoso performer.

The piano was indispensable to Ellington. He used it while composing, and insisted on having one in his hotel room while on the road. It was, however, not the culmination of his work but a first solid step. That he could maintain as fresh an identity on it as the greatest masters of the instrument testifies to the depth of his encompassing artistry.

He was an only child for 16 years, the son of a butler who kept his family in reasonable comfort. He was Edward Kennedy Ellington in those days, by his own admission an indifferent kid whose main interest involved playing in the streets with his friends. He took piano lessons from a neighborhood teacher, the improbably named Marietta Clinkscales, and he learned well enough to earn her praise after playing some simple pieces at a church concert. But it took an encounter with another pianist, Harvey Brooks, during a vacation in Philadelphia to persuade Ellington to start practicing in earnest and to think about music as a career. He was fifteen years old at the time.

As a student at Armstrong High School, Ellington juggled his interests in music and in art—he won a poster contest sponsored by the NAACP and was offered a scholarship to attend the Pratt Institute of Applied Arts in Brooklyn. But he also studied with the school music teacher, Ernest Amos, and took private advanced lessons in composition from Henry Grant. A fascination with ragtime, beginning in 1916, drew him out of school and into Washington's club scene. He started playing at the Poodle Dog Café while picking up tips from more established ragtime players, such as Sticky Mick, Louis Brown, Doc Perry, and someone known only as the Man with a Million Fingers. By 1921 Ellington was probably the top player in town, good enough to impress visiting stride giants such as James P. Johnson, whose "Carolina Shout" he had learned by following keyboard patterns from a piano roll. He worked ensemble jobs as well, including a stretch as one of *five* pianists who shared the stage with orchestra leader Russell Wooding.

In 1923, the young king of New York stride, Fats Waller, was a dinner guest at the Ellington home in Washington. His tales of musical opportunity convinced his host to make the move up to Harlem. After a short period of getting situated and working under banjoist Elmer Snowden's leadership, Ellington put together the nucleus of his band, including his longtime drum wizard Sonny Greer, and began chasing his destiny as a composer and leader. But he kept up with the piano players as well, especially Willie "the Lion" Smith, whose elegant and musically informed way with stride appealed to Ellington's nature more than the flash and fireworks of Waller or even Art Tatum. At his peak he could hold his own with many of the leaders of that school, as proven by his thrilling unaccompanied intro to "Lots o' Fingers," recorded with his band in 1932 and available on *Solos, Duets and Trios.* The opening emphasizes the dexterity of his right hand, with very clean streams of sixteenth-notes blowing past simple quarter-note chords from his left. After two verses, a transitional section follows, in which the right hand crosses the left to jab out a dotted-eighth descending figure in the bass range under chords articulated now in eighth-notes. By engaging the left hand more actively against the right, this section builds the intensity of the rhythm, which grows stronger still in the following verse as a true left-hand stride supports fleet ascending runs toward the top of the keyboard. Now, after a key change, Elling-

Duke Ellington with Bud Freeman in New York, 1939: His piano sound stood out for its seductive combination of sophistication and tactility.

ton turns up the heat even more with a tempo acceleration; his almost frantic counter-rhythms and supercharged stride make it clear that, at least in his early days, he had more than enough chops to compete in the arena of performance.

The endurance of stride as his foundation is clear decades later, in his performance of "The Second Portrait of the Lion," another tribute to Willie "the Lion" Smith. Recorded in 1965 at the Pittsburgh Jazz Festival, it is a classic stride romp, played at a medium tempo and according to the old rules: An opening figure leads to two choruses over a left hand that alternates stride and a bouncy line or two, followed by a B-section in which the articulated rhythm gives way to a brief suspension of the beat and some bluesy figurations. The more familiar Ellington touch comes in when he suspends the rhythm, plays a series of thick chords that lead to a free-tempo section, with Impressionistic whole-tone harmonies and splashy right-hand ornaments. Even here, however, he builds rather than blows . . . before seeming to shrug it all off and jump back into a reprise of the stride-driven earlier material. Listening to this typical example of Ellington is more like eavesdropping on a writer than witnessing a performance.

Throughout most of his career, though, he played quietly and with understatement—not as Basie did, with spare notes popped into the pocket, but with a salon-like intimacy, tinted by Romantic and Impressionistic elements and a polished replication of the blues. From the twenties through the seventies, the Ellington piano sound stood out for its seductive combination of sophistication and tactility.

He expressed these qualities most often in brief chords that he would drop—and often repeat—in the holes he had written into his arrangements. These staccato intrusions were enough to inject a unique flavor into the music, as distinctive as Basie's simpler licks. All it takes is one Ellington chord—aromatic, mysterious, sometimes vaguely Arabian—to color an entire ensemble performance. This magic can be heard clearly in the CD bonus track "Solitude," from *Duke Ellington Meets Coleman Hawkins.* Recorded in August 1962, this track features Ray Nance on the first verse, with Ellington masterfully shifting chords behind the violin's long notes; his lush bitonal voicings, especially on the bridge, and the expressive power of the individual notes he drops so delicately in the following verse build the perfect frame to complement Nance's plaintive caress of the melody—which, in turn, sets up a key change and opens the door to Hawkins's entrance. This performance perfectly illustrates why Ellington's playing, moving as it could be, was so often under-appreciated, being hidden in the shadows beyond the aura of his soloists.

Ellington's version of "Frankie and Johnny," recorded in 1945, emphasizes the rigor of his compositional perspective. The performance opens with a romping piano introduction, unaccompanied for four bars until Sonny Greer slips in on drums; they drive together to the end of the verse, where they break for a fill by bassist Junior Raglin. The verse that follows has a more improvised feel, but even here Ellington turns a cascading arpeggio into a thematic element before hitting an out-of-tempo transitional passage to another key. At a moderate walking tempo now, he spends a verse stating the theme in octaves around more arpeggios and some Deco chord movement in the left hand. Another key change leads into a faster section, in which Ellington now applies some stride piano figures to the right hand for one verse, then switches to a riffing redux of figure introduced at the beginning of the track. Everything in Ellington's performance reflects polish and intelligence, but there's very little true blowing going on.

Even when playing the blues, Ellington treated each performance as primarily an arrangement. In his "B Sharp Blues," recorded in April 1953 with bassist Wendell Marshall and drummer Butch Ballard and available on *Piano Reflections,* Ellington's improvisation is built within severely restricted lines: Each chorus begins with a simple figure, which is faithfully repeated, with minimal or no variation, as a riff. The playing here, in other words, reflects precisely the conventions of writing for a horn section rather than any inclination to seriously extemporize. But within these restrictions, Ellington offers bits of insight into his sense for orchestration: On the bridges to "Prelude to a Kiss," also from *Piano Reflections,* he drops the last two notes of each of the main two-bar phrases down an octave, to create the kind of displacing impression one might derive from by shifting it from brass to saxophones; the fact that he does so without variation four times further establishes his preference for writing over soloing.

Generous in small settings, Ellington ceded the spotlight almost entirely to Jimmy Blanton in their series of duo recordings from October 1, 1940. Of course, his personality projects as clearly as that of his bassist, with highly recognizable pearly descending arpeggios and, on "Mr. J. B. Blues," some quirky minor seconds and other harmonic stretches. That these occur on both the first and second takes of the tune emphasizes again Ellington's preference for staying with established notions of arrangement, rather than play more adventurously; though he certainly fills well behind Blanton, most often with big band-like, two-handed riffs, one wonders what they could have developed together if there was a little more risk-taking from the piano.

How much of a literalist was Ellington? Compare his two versions of "Solitude," both recorded solo on May 14, 1941. He opens the first with a lovely ostinato, almost Satie-like in its hypnotic oscillation between the fifth and diminished fifth alternating with a simple major third in a dreamlike, slow-motion stride. He uses the same figure to launch his second version as well, but the feel is a little brighter; he cuts the pattern two bars shorter than on the first version, stretching out a transitional passage rooted on the fifth to balance things out. His opening verse is animated by little smears from the right hand, a series of quarter-note chords that briefly interrupt the left-hand pulse, and a few quick arpeggios and trills in the opening verse; the tempo doesn't quite breathe as freely as on the other performance. In both renditions he executes a key change, using slightly different chord movements each time. Other than that, the differences are minimal; Ellington treats his gem gently, taking few risks, bringing out its inner qualities as he best knew how.

Even so, during a remarkable session that paired him with one of the great modernists of the early sixties, Ellington proved himself able to adapt to a more loosely improvisational setting. *Duke Ellington & John Coltrane*, recorded on September 16, 1962, paired the two giants with their rhythm sections in various combinations. The saxophonist's free, streaming style was ill-suited to Ellington's form-oriented approach, so the older musician made the adjustment. True, his arrangement mentality drives his three-chorus solo on "Stevie," though the regularity of its components also reflect his elevated conception on the harmonic possibilities inherent in the blues. But in his chord-dominated solo on the Coltrane composition "Big Nick," his rhythmic placement is varied rather than repetitive, and his meticulous pace suggests a linear contour rather than a riff-like repetition.

In the end, the argument over Ellington the pianist can be settled best by acknowledging that in this area, as in all areas of music, he is best appreciated as a singular figure. On relatively narrow foundations of ragtime and stride, he built an edifice of accomplishment unlike any other in American culture. If the best that can be said about his piano playing is that it reflected the vast dimensions of his art, then that alone is saying plenty.

6. EARL HINES

Born: December 28, 1903, Duquesne, Pennsylvania
Died: April 22, 1983, Oakland, California

Early in 1982, in a high-rise apartment overlooking a scenic slice of Oakland on the east side of San Francisco Bay, I had the opportunity to spend some time with one of the few artists who could be said to have single-handedly affected the evolution of jazz piano. At the time of our meeting Earl Hines was, as he put it, "semi-retired." His world, which once spread as far as the sound of jazz itself, had narrowed down to the few rooms in his flat. Once proud of his athleticism and prowess at sports, he now moved stiffly, taking long seconds to cross his living room in short, slow steps. He wasn't inclined to dwell on the past, partly because of his remarkable self-effacement; when he asked why in the world I wanted to interview him, his incredulity seemed genuine.

He was still doing occasional performances; at the time of our meeting he was preparing for a month-long tour through South America. Yet the past surrounded him. Rows of plaques covered his walls. Photos of old friends, some long departed, smiled down at him. For all of his modesty, he wasn't unaware of his legacy. And it was with pride that he invited his visitor to sit behind his most cherished memento, his Steinway grand piano, and try it out.

An intriguing plaque was mounted in the fallboard of this handsome instrument: "Presented by jazz lovers from all over the world. This piano is the only one of its kind in the world and expresses the great genius of a man who has never played a melancholy note in his lifetime on a planet that has often succumbed to despair."

"Scott Newhall, a very close friend who was the executive editor of the *San Francisco Chronicle,* gave this piano to me," Hines remembered as he lit one of his omnipresent cigars. "I was giving a concert down at the Sheraton Palace Hotel in San Francisco, and he unveiled it for me, right there at the concert. I didn't know anything like that was going to happen until he unveiled it. And, you know, I was rehearsing down there in the afternoon too, so he must have had a heck of a time keeping me from seeing it all day."

The piano, purchased originally in 1904 by Leander Sherman of the sheet music chain Sherman Clay, had been spotted by Newhall, a pianist himself, in the window of an antique shop. Despite its age, it was in terrific condition. "Everybody knows I prefer a Steinway," Hines smiled. "A Steinway always has a medium action. Now, a Baldwin is too stiff for me, but Steinway is just about right. And this Steinway is my favorite. I recorded with it once. Did you see the album *Earl Hines at Home*? That was recorded in my house before I moved here. Everything was just right on that record. Everything!"

Did recording at home, surrounded by souvenirs and memories, make it easier for Hines to play as well as he did on that album? He shook his head. "No, no, no, no. It's a funny thing. I never play better in one place than I do somewhere else. I don't care where I'm at; I just play the way I feel. Now, when I record in Japan, I think they like to hear more bass on the piano than they do over here, so there might be some difference, but that's the way *they* feel. Whether it was my best playing, that's up to the public to decide."

There is no shortage of material to choose from in the Hines catalog. His first recordings date back to October 3, 1923, when at the age of 17 he entered Gennett Studios in Richmond, Indiana, to record two songs with singer Lois Deppe and his 11-piece band; on November 6 he cut four more backing Deppe by himself. After this debut, Hines would perform with Louis Armstrong's Hot Five on some of the most important recordings in the jazz catalog, as well as on dozens of sides as leader of his own band, in reunion gigs with Armstrong in the late forties and fifties, and on countless other sessions recorded over a span of more than half a century.

Despite the many sides he cut with small groups and on his own, Hines never really thought of himself as a solo pianist. Some observers disagreed, like the English critics Brian Case and Stan Britt, who asserted that "Hines is invariably at his magical best when performing alone." Nonetheless, Hines confided, "I never did like any solo album that I recorded. I always thought I could do better than I did. Even now, when I record something, I say to myself when I listen to it, 'Now, what the heck did I do that for?'"

Several points are beyond argument, the first being that Hines introduced a style that permanently affected the way jazz pianists approached their art. Equally important is the fact that this style stemmed from his view of himself as a band pianist. Even as a teenager, Hines understood that playing jazz with a group demanded a different set of concepts and techniques than working solo, like the great stride players of New York. Further, he could recognize that the kind of playing represented by Jelly Roll Morton with the Red Hot Peppers set severe limits on how far a piano player could go within the context of a jazz band. Where Morton used the instrument to reflect his compositional aesthetic, Hines empathized more with the horn players: He wanted to *blow*.

It was no easy thing, though, for a pianist to take his or her place in the spotlight as a soloist. Amplification for pianos was largely hypothetical in the twenties, a fact that tended to bury the instrument deep within the rhythm section, where basses thumped and banjos strummed in anonymous supportive roles. If he was going to be heard as clearly as a blaring trumpet or a piercing clarinet, Hines knew he would have to deviate from common practice by streamlining, simplifying, and projecting more effectively onstage.

This realization came early to Hines—as early as 1918, when the precocious young pianist began playing with Deppe at a place in Pittsburgh called the Liederhouse. He was tall for his age, which made it easier for the bandleader to bring him into the gig. His hands were large as well, capable even in those days of spanning an octave on the keyboard comfortably enough for him to hit both notes hard with his thumb and fifth finger. By doubling the same note, he increased his volume and hardened his tone to the point that the piano could finally be heard above the din of the rhythm section. As obvious as this device seems today, it was novel in those earlier days of jazz, especially when adapted by Hines to the business of playing trumpet-like lines in his solos.

"I got the trumpet style on the piano from playing with bands," he explained from within a blue haze of cigar smoke. "See, I used to use regular fingering when I was playing at home, but then when I started working with big bands and they gave me a solo, nobody could hear me. Now, my father played the trumpet, so I started using his particular style, going back to the melody, and it cut through that way. Soon all the pianists began to use it."

And yet, Hines cautioned, he never studied the playing patterns of horn patterns as a young man. "I never did copy nobody or use anybody's ideas," he insisted. "Never! I always had my own way of doing it. I never did sit down and rehearse. I might sit down and rehearse the first thing that I'd feel might be advantageous to the program I was going to use, but that's all."

Whether or not he consciously copied anyone in developing his style, Hines was able to absorb plenty of musical influences during his formative years. He was born in Duquesne, Pennsylvania, into one of only 12 black families in the steel mill country outside of Pittsburgh. His father worked days on the coal docks, and by night performed locally with the Eureka Brass Band; an uncle, Bill Phillips, played brass instruments as well. Earl, one of three siblings, loved hearing the trumpet and in fact tried—unsuccessfully—to master it before laying his hands on a keyboard.

After a while, the piano began to catch his attention. One of his aunts was friendly with two outstanding pianists of the day, ragtime giant Eubie Blake and stride icon Luckey Roberts. His mother, taking notice, traded in the organ she played at home and brought in a piano, on which Earl began taking lessons at age nine. Under his first teacher, Emma D. Young, and in more advanced instruction from a strict German named Von Holz, he drilled on classical repertoire and laid the foundation for what would become his strong technique—in part to escape the sharp raps on his knuckles that Von Holz would deliver with his ruler as punishment for sloppy execution.

Though he loved the European repertoire, Hines never dreamed of a career as a classical player. If anything, his thoughts centered more on playing sports with his pals; when asked what he intended to do for a living, he assumed in those days that he would wind up being a barber. "I didn't know what I was going to be, to tell you the truth," he said. "I loved classical music because it was given to me by my mother and my dad. I was just surrounded by music. That's the reason I stuck with it, even though I didn't know what I was going to do."

Popular music eventually drew his thoughts away from clippers and shears and more toward music as a profession. His first attempts at playing non-classical pieces involved ragtime, and he listened carefully to piano rolls cut by James P. Johnson and Zez Confrey. "You know, when the music had syncopation, I sort of liked that," he said. "I heard that foot patting, I liked it, and I kept on going from there.

"But after you play the classics for a certain length of time," he continued, "a lot of it sticks with you. There are some things you can't get from them—like, you'll very seldom find a classical musician who can memorize. Your symphonic musicians can't remember anything. I don't care how many times they've played their overtures; they still can't memorize them. That happens with a lot of classical pianists. Classical music is good for things like learning to read. I was always a fast reader, and I would always read four or five measures ahead, so I could see the chord structures before I got to them. I was always exploring, trying to find something new. A lot of times I played things I didn't even know I could do myself, until I heard the record."

Hines was quiet for a minute. "But now," he finally added, "I'm much older. I don't think as fast as I used to, and even my fingers don't work the way they did then. Let's face it."

Earl's hands were delicate that day in Oakland, and animated by a slight tremor, as if endlessly running over the long tremolo at the end of his "Boogie Woogie on 'The St. Louis Blues.'" He laid them on the table. "I used to do stretching. You see that?" His fingers were now spread wide open. "That's a tenth. I don't need no more than that. Now, I can't hardly do a tenth on a D chord or a B-flat chord. On a D-flat, A-flat, and F, I can touch it. I'm getting stronger with them too, but in the old days I wasn't doing much playing in those keys. When I first started playing tenths, I had to roll my wrist. I was only fifteen when I started, you know! So I'd simplify a lot of the time. In other words . . . I cheated!"

In those days pianists weren't even thinking about arranging their hands into chords based around intervals of a tenth. While others were bothering only to bounce the occasional tenth in the midst of an octave stride, a 15-year-old kid was already mulling over voicings that are at the root of today's jazz harmonies. Part of that kid came to the surface as Hines looked back on some of the pianists whose reach he envied long ago.

Earl Hines in the late forties: At age fifteen he was already mulling over voicings that are at the root of modern jazz harmony.

"I had two different pianists I was listening to then," he said. "I wasn't making but $15 a week, but I would have paid $15 a day just to see those guys. One had a heck of a right hand, and one had a heck of a left hand. Jim Fellman was the left hand, and Johnny Watters was the right hand. He was a guy with a hell of a style. His left hand didn't do much, but his right hand used to play tenths *and* the melody at the same time. Man, I couldn't do that! He could stretch a B chord: B, F-sharp, and D-sharp.

"But, you know, I didn't use their style," he pointed out. "What I did was put their styles together, then put my ideas with that. It's not good when you copy a person. If you copy somebody, you're only going to make that person popular. Now, I used a lot of ideas from other pianists, but they didn't know it because I put those ideas in other tunes. Now and then I'd be playing something, then all of a sudden one of those things I heard from somebody would just strike me, and I'd think, 'Oh, God, I've got to put that thing in here!'"

For more abstract lessons, like learning to improvise, Hines advised players to follow their own instincts rather than to seek answers through a teacher, especially if that teacher is oriented toward the classics. He chuckled while remembering one fast and desperate bit of improvising he had to do early in life. "My music teacher had a contest at the end of the season, and I had to do a piece with about 45 pages to it. I was into it when my mind went blank. I just blacked out, and I didn't know what the hell to do, so I started faking it. The teacher was trying to find out where I was! I could see her sitting right there by the piano with the music, looking all through it. However, it finally came back to me, so I got back to the right changes."

There was a punch line: "At the end she said to me, 'You did a hell of a job getting back there.' I said, 'I know I did.' And she said, 'Yeah, but nobody knew—only me! I didn't know where you was!' And I said, 'Neither did I!'"

With his command of the keyboard fully established and his head filled with fresh ideas, Hines took some advice from Eubie Blake and left Pittsburgh in order to find work in Chicago. Already the biggest stars in jazz were performing in the city's clubs, and Jelly Roll Morton had just arrived to stake his claim as the king of the keyboard. None of this intimidated Hines, who quickly settled into a gig on a portable piano with a small group at the Club Elite No. 2, which was owned by an acquaintance in Pittsburgh. In 1925 he moved up to a slightly larger venue, the Entertainer's Café, where he met and eventually joined bandleader Carroll Dickerson for a long road trip to California and back.

While still working with Dickerson's band, Hines found his ticket into jazz history in 1926, when he met Louis Armstrong one afternoon at the black musicians' union headquarters. They jammed together that day, on a tune titled "The One I Love Belongs to Somebody Else." That same year, Dickerson landed a gig at the Sunset Café, on the corner of Calumet Avenue and 35th Street, and persuaded Armstrong to join Hines in the band's lineup. This was a prestige job, with a mixed-race clientele drawn by an elaborate floor show and potent bootleg liquor. Despite the band's success, the Sunset's talent coordinator, Joe Glaser, was forced to fire Dickerson in February 1927 when the bandleader began developing a drinking problem. Armstrong got the nod to take Dickerson's place, while Hines was appointed musical director and the group was rechristened Louis Armstrong and His Stompers.

Despite their obvious musical chemistry, Armstrong and Hines began developing personal problems. Ever the professional, Hines resented the trumpeter's indifference toward leading the band in fact as well as in name. As he told writer Dempsey J. Travis in *The Los Angeles Odyssey,* Armstrong "was a guy who always said he didn't want any responsibility at all. He wanted the agency to take care of his everyday life and handle the band. So Glaser took all that responsibility away from Louis and just let him blow his horn."

Even so, when the Sunset was shut down at dawn on Sunday, November 5, 1927, for selling illegal booze and tolerating "lewd" dancing, the three cornerstones of the band—Armstrong, Hines, and drummer Zutty Singleton—resolved to start their own place together. Further, they agreed to accept only those gigs that would hire all three of them. The idea was to sell the package rather than the individuals within it—and, given each man's distinctive personality and talent, there's no way that this was going to work.

First, their pact was strained by the failure of their new club. After only two days of searching, they signed a lease on Warwick Hall, a space on the second floor at 593 E. 47th Street, for $375 a month. Supremely confident, they paid for the entire year in advance and put a band together, which they called the Hot Six. Unfortunately, on Thanksgiving, their opening night, the far more glitzy Savoy Ballroom also opened, just two blocks away. Crowds flocked to the glare of the Savoy's neon sign, and after a short and ignoble run Hines and his partners ate their loss and closed the Warwick. They found another gig at a smaller spot on the West Side, but trouble followed here as well: On opening night a drunken customer waved a gun toward the musicians and sent Hines diving under the old upright piano for protection.

Relations between the musicians were strained by these events, and made even worse when Armstrong and Singleton took a gig with Dickerson at the Savoy despite Dickerson's insistence on keeping Gene Anderson at the piano. For weeks Hines was furious over what he saw as their betrayal. He scuffled around for a while before finding work with a quartet led by clarinetist Jimmie Noone at the Apex Club, another second-floor venue, on East 35th Street between Calumet and Prairie Avenues. It was a grinding schedule, running from midnight until six in the morning seven days a week, yet when Armstrong and Singleton sheepishly appeared at the Apex at the end of a gig in February 1928 to apologize and convey an offer from Dickerson to join his group, Hines brusquely blew them off.

Even so, the musical ties between these three proved too strong to deny, and only a few months after their confrontation Hines accepted an invitation from Armstrong to replace Lil Hardin as a member of the Hot Five. This band, which included trombonist Fred Robinson, clarinetist Jimmy Strong, banjo player Mancy Carr, and Singleton, played a variation on New Orleans jazz, with slightly less emphasis on collective improvisation because of Armstrong's unprecedented and unmatchable power as a soloist.

Unmatchable, that is, until Hines's arrival. Though Hardin would spend a number of years married to Armstrong, she was a more limited and traditional player. The idea of stepping forward as a soloist wasn't foreign to her disposition, but she lacked the chops and imagination to make an impact that way. Richard Hadlock, in his excellent book *Jazz Masters of the Twenties,* recalls a night when she was performing with seminal New Orleans trumpeter Joe Oliver; after she threw a few too many intricate runs into the mix, Oliver told her to cut it out because "we already have a clarinet player in the band."

Of course, Hines was driven by his ambition to solo as freely as any clarinetist or other band member, and unlike Hardin he had the artillery to make it happen. More than that, his playing proved as volatile as Armstrong's within the Hot Five. On a series of recordings made by the band in June, July, and December 1928 at Okeh Studios, energy crackles repeatedly between the two and drives each toward higher levels of performance. Their arrangement of "Fireworks" is in fact built around Hines's ability to match, by himself, the entire band's drive and inventiveness. After the first verse, the pianist delivers an unaccompanied verse whose staggered rhythms and unexpected harmonies provide an explosive introduction for Jimmy Strong's clarinet solo. Using the same device, Hines lights a similar match in launching the trombone and trumpet solos that follow. Though Armstrong is the leader here, this arrangement is built around the novel power of the piano in Hines's hands.

Even more important, to the jazz piano lineage as well as to music in general, is the Hot Five recording of Joe Oliver's "West End Blues." Here, Armstrong and Hines find a brilliant balance: The trumpet playing, from the opening cadenza to the thrilling sustained note toward the end, represents the peak of Armstrong's playing in its blend of primal energy and exuberant virtuosity. Rather than compete at this level, Hines complements Armstrong with an eloquent solo chorus, in which he conjures a delicate melody and frames it with elaborate filigree. But even in this performance, with all its restraint, Hines can't resist breaking into double-time figurations, as if to proclaim that he takes second place to no one, not even Armstrong, as a dynamo of rhythmic improvisation.

Even while recording with Armstrong, Hines stuck with Noone for much of the year, recorded some piano rolls for QRS, and most important, played his first jobs as head of his own band. And these weren't just any jobs; the debut of his orchestra, which took place on his birthday, December 28, 1928, marked the beginning of Hines's emergence as a major artist, entirely on his own terms.

It was one of the best deals ever signed by a bandleader. Ed Fox owned the Grand Terrace, a lavish club with mirrored walls and starry lights, at the corner of Oakwood and South Parkway. A shrewd businessman with gangland connections, Fox saw the handsome, charismatic pianist as his key to making the Grand Terrace a landmark in Chicago, equivalent to New York's famous Cotton Club. So strong was his commitment to Hines that he offered him a 20-year contract to assemble and run the house band. Not being a fool, Hines signed up and went to work making history.

The Hines ensemble worked hard, playing six nights a week from ten in the evening until four in the morning; on the seventh night, Saturday, they played an hour longer and quit at five. Like the Duke Ellington and Cab Calloway bands at the Cotton Club, they were fundamentally about entertainment. They accompanied gaudy floor shows, which featured rows of chorus girls or taller "parade girls" as well as guest stars like Ethel Waters, the Step Brothers, Buck and Bubbles, and Bill "Bojangles" Robinson. Dancers, black and white, twirled and spun on an elevated floor. And bootleg hooch flowed endlessly. Al Capone himself was a regular customer—and a good tipper, with a hundred-dollar bill always ready to hand over to Hines for a job well done.

With dancers, gangsters, customers, and even a few armed waiters swirling before him, Hines beamed from the piano bench, a musical monarch enthroned before his people. Ross Russell paints a memorable picture of the scene in *Bird Lives:* "Hines sat at the piano as befitted a member of jazz royalty, tall, of broad shoulder, immaculately dressed in formal black, unshakable in his self-confidence, cigar tucked in one corner of his mouth, cueing his all-star bands with pianistic signals, tossing off sparkling runs and tremolos that rippled through the texture of the bands."

His realm expanded further in 1934, when a radio hookup began broadcasting his Grand Terrace shows throughout North America. On one broadcast the announcer unintentionally bestowed Hines with the regal nickname that stayed with him for the rest of his days. With the band's theme song, the medium-tempo "Deep Forest," playing, he intoned, "Here comes Fatha Hines through the forest with his children!" From that point, each show would open with band members chanting "Fa-tha Hines! Fa-tha Hines!" as the pianist played a solo chorus.

Not surprisingly, much of the band's repertoire was built around the personality and performance of its leader. Though Hines kept its musical range fairly broad by working with a variety of talented arrangers, the essence of its sound was riff-oriented swing, which anticipated Count Basie. On song after song the highlight would be the piano solo, which might stretch out on any given night as members of the band playfully called on their boss to take another chorus.

Quite often, the longer the solo, the more Hines would fall back on tricks and effects that were guaranteed to please the crowd. On "Blue Drag," recorded in New York on July 14, 1932, he unleashes an anarchic improvisation that's riddled with spasms of double-time stride, cascading runs, and quick tremolos; the intention is clearly to play off the "jungle" feel of the beat with primitive effects. Even more revealing are the band's two takes of "I Love You Because I Love You," from the same session: On the first, Hines unaccountably obliterates his line with some frantic scampers up the keyboard. The relative restraint of his solo on the second take suggests that he wanted to create something with a little more substance the second time around.

His showpiece numbers could be even more disheartening. He has plenty of room on "Piano Man," as one might expect, but the band's July 12, 1939, recording captures him in an uncertain dance between straightforward stride and a more modern and spare approach. After a few choruses his playing develops an awkward, jerky quality, from which he escapes at the end by lapsing back into a stride groove. Another flag-waver, his "Boogie Woogie on 'The St. Louis Blues'," is really nothing but entertainment, with band member George Dixon hollering cornball encouragement as Hines trudges through a solo that's undistinguished except for one long, carefully controlled octave tremolo.

As if to confirm his reluctance to be critiqued as a solo pianist, Hines plays best when his solos are short or he's working within an arrangement. He is stronger still when being pushed by a solid beat. On "Sensational," with the tempo racing almost at a bebop clip, he responds to the challenge and delivers a strong solo spiced by impeccable octaves and tremolos. At slower but still swinging tempos, when the emphasis of the chart is pure rhythm, Hines is even stronger: "G. T. Stomp" and "Grand Terrace Shuffle," both recorded in 1939, open with an emphatic solo piano intro, and during solos Hines keeps the heat up with off-beat stabs and left-hand fragments that enhance the voicings of the chord changes. Even his gimmicky smears and spurts work brilliantly when confined within an arrangement, as on "Riff Medley," also from '39.

Throughout the life of his band, Hines played joyfully, and always with a restlessness that drove him to explore new possibilities in rhythmic phrasing. His showmanship, and indeed his obligations at the Grand Terrace, tended to discourage deeper explorations; aside from the occasional dissonant left-hand jab (which, in fact, may have been intended as a "jungle" effect), Hines didn't stray too far from basic harmonies in his solo lines. In fact, his tendency to trot out smears, quick arpeggios, and other fireworks generally impeded whatever inclination he might have had to create longer, more coherent improvisations.

After six years of celebrity on the air, Hines bought his way out of the Grand Terrace and began taking his band on tour. Throughout the early forties they played in the major swing venues before enthusiastic fans and on military bases for young servicemen. During these years Hines began recruiting a new generation of players. Silky-voiced Billy Eckstine, the "sepia Sinatra," was discovered by the pianist at Chicago's Club De Lisa in late 1939. Dizzy Gillespie joined the band in Baltimore late in January 1943, and brought several exciting original tunes, including "A Night in Tunisia," into the band's book. Charlie Parker was picked up as a tenor saxophonist to replace Budd Johnson after Hines heard him jamming after hours at Monroe's Uptown House in Chicago. And Sarah Vaughn—she wasn't yet spelling her name "Vaughan"—joined Hines as a second pianist and singer during an appearance at the Apollo Theater in April 1943.

This was certainly the most intriguing of all the Hines bands, as the creative energies of more conservative players and the fresher talent sought accord. Although they never recorded, due to a strike imposed by the American Federation of Musicians against the record industry, reports of their performances tease our imaginations to this day. Parker, Gillespie, and other seminal boppers in the band were already testing the limits of tradition during their stints with Hines. Under their influence, the band developed a progressive reputation, though the leader himself apparently harbored reservations. But, as he put it to a BBC interviewer in 1980, he put up with their experiments because that's what younger fans wanted—again, reflecting his concern with entertaining, more than educating, the fans.

In the late forties, though, the band broke up, following the defection of several key members: Eckstine, distressed at having to go through yet another barnstorming tour of the Jim Crow South, bailed to take a gig on 52nd Street in New York, as did Sarah Vaughan. Ever the showman, Hines responded by organizing a twelve-member all-female group, which lasted just two months and was dismissed by *Variety* as a "$20,000 flop." This was followed by a more ambitious venture, with a 24-piece orchestra that included strings, a French horn, and an oboe. This, too, went nowhere.

Faced with financial difficulties for the first time in years, Hines swallowed a bit of pride and accepted an invitation to replace pianist Dick Cary in Louis Armstrong's All-Stars in 1948. With its emphasis on traditional jazz, the All-Stars represented an artistic step backward for the pianist; on the other hand, Armstrong's popularity guaranteed some degree of security—and the presence of trombonist Jack Teagarden, clarinetist Barney Bigard, bassist Arvell Shaw, and drummer Sid Catlett ensured that the music, though retro, would at least be played with style.

Hines debuted with the band at the Nice Festival in France. Once again, he proved a brilliant counterpart for Armstrong; the crisply executed piano solo on "Indiana," from *Louis Armstrong: The California Concerts,* creates a twinkling contrast to Armstrong's razzle-dazzle brassiness. But old unsettled scores between the two created an uneasy atmosphere off the stage. As Bigard recalls in his autobiography *With Louis and the Duke,* "Earl sounded great with the band and was a fantastic showman in himself. . . . [But] they never really hit it off too well, Earl and Louis. . . . Sometimes Louis would get after Earl because he put too much show into it all and wasn't giving the soloists the support he should have."

Armstrong himself put it more succinctly, after Hines gave his notice in 1951: "Hines and his ego, ego, ego. If he wants to go, the hell with him. He's good, sure, but we don't need him."

With that, Hines packed his cigars, grabbed his hat, and headed out to San Francisco. The Bay Area was at that time at the center of the so-called trad jazz revival, with scores of young musicians reviving the sound of New Orleans jazz. As always, Hines knew what the people wanted to hear, and so in 1955 he began a stint with an old-fashioned sextet at Doc Dougherty's Hangover Club; originally signed for eight weeks, they ended up there for more than five years. With old-timers like bassist Pops Foster, cornetist Muggsy Spanier, and an old friend from the Grand Terrace, clarinetist Darnell Howard, in the lineup, Hines dusted off—or, in many cases, learned for the first time—"Jazz Me Blues" and other ancient tunes that the tourists lined up to hear.

It was steady work, but it also had the effect of pulling Hines away from the vital center of jazz, to the point that hipsters of the late fifties and early sixties had all but forgotten him. His star seemed to be setting even among locals: In 1963 Hines was offered a "lifetime" contract to perform at the Cannery on San Francisco Bay, yet after playing to a packed house on opening night he was never invited back. That same year he ended up playing in a lounge at the Claremont Hotel in Oakland, in an odd group composed of a tenor saxophonist, an organist, a drummer, Hines at the piano, and a Japanese singer.

All that changed in 1964, when Hines accepted perhaps the unlikeliest opportunity of his career: a trio gig at the Little Theater in New York. He met his sidemen, bassist Ahmed Abdul Malik and drummer Oliver Jackson, only about an hour before going onstage on opening night. Yet he had no trouble bowling over the critics and earning himself a follow-up engagement at Birdland and a few solo piano sessions in local studios.

The Little Theater performances, documented by the Delmark label on *The Legendary Little Theater Concert,* put Hines on course for nearly another 20 years as, once again, one of the great attractions in jazz. A stream of albums throughout the seventies and into the eighties yielded more than a few disappointments, such as a bizarre mutation of Joe Zawinul's "Birdland," with Red Callender oomphing the bass line on a tuba. Yet to many new listeners, Hines possessed an invigorating vitality, and in his far-flung tours, including a sojourn to the Soviet Union as the Vietnam War was heating up in 1966, he delighted a new crop of listeners who had never heard, much less heard of, the Grand Terrace broadcasts.

As we spoke in Oakland, Hines reflected that his connection to great artists and ideas from years long past gave him a responsibility to educate as well as to entertain these younger fans. "Years ago the composers wrote about everyday life," he mused. "That's why songs like 'Tea for Two' and 'Body and Soul' still live; they're about true life! Of course, one or two tunes might come nowadays that do the same thing, but just go back about ten years, after Dick Clark started rock, and find out how many tunes have come along that are still alive. There's no comparison with what the guys did years ago. They don't write those kinds of tunes anymore."

Hines closed his eyes and hummed a few bars from "These Foolish Things." "Beautiful tunes. I listen to a lot of what the kids are writing now, and they get to a place where they just run out of ideas and fade out the record at the end. That's what discourages me so much. They write whatever comes into their heads, and a lot of it *doesn't make sense.* Everything has changed. You've got a new type of person nowadays. You don't have the romantic type of feeling that people had years ago, when everybody danced together. I remember when they had those big ballrooms; they'd turn the lights down, put a screen down the middle of the floor, and put the lyrics of the tune you were dancing to on the screen. Some people met their girlfriends by a tune, some people were married by a tune, some people were even divorced by a tune! You don't have that no more."

An example came to mind. "I'll never forget this guy, George E. Lee, a blues singer out of Kansas City. One of his favorite songs was 'You Go to My Head.' Man, he sang the hell out of it, and every time I hear that tune I think of him, because he romanced the vocalist I had in my band to that tune. Those are the things that stick with you."

Never mind rock; jazz itself had changed to the extent that much of what was going on within that label left Hines, in his last years, unmoved. "See, jazz is from the heart," he said, "but a lot of kids are going by what they see on the paper. As I said before, I used to look four or five measures ahead in my chord structures. Well, a lot of guys don't do that now. They use a lot of chord structures, and they read well, but sometimes the modern things have too many changes, so they can't do much with it. When I'm playing these things, I can't think through all those things at the same time. Not now. I was doing it when I was playing, but I didn't realize it."

With fewer gigs on his calendar, did Hines take more time to play for his own pleasure at home? He looked aghast at the suggestion. "Oh, no, no, no! Man, I've been playing for 57 years." Then, with a hint of resignation, he added, "I don't play much because I don't think as fast as I used to. That gets disturbing to me. If I don't feel like I played the thing right, I just don't want to play at all."

Given all of the artists he had played with, was there anyone he missed along the way, anyone he never got the chance to jam with? Hines mentally ran through the lengthy list, then answered, "Well, I don't think so. There were so many of them over the years, and everybody at that time used to help each other. When I was working in a club, they'd all come in after a show to jam, and the proprietor would charge to see it! When Ben Webster would show up, they'd put his name up there on the marquee! There'd be maybe $3000 or $4000 worth of talent jamming inside, and nobody was making any money off of it but the man! But even though that wasn't so good for the musicians, I'm glad I got to play with so many of those wonderful guys."

Another memory came alive. "Like my good friend Bill Evans," he smiled. "Man, what a beautiful pianist he was, but his style was different. You had to understand what he was playing. Then there's George Shearing. Shearing is a guy who thinks he's doing jazz, because he wants to show his versatility. You know, when he first came over here from England he was trying to play like me, then he finally got to a more commercial style. He'd say, 'I won't swing anything too hard.' I'd laugh like hell and say, 'Go ahead, man, the people will go for it anyway.'"

On the question of whether he still had any musical goals, Hines drew long on his cigar and said, "Oh, I've pretty much done everything I've wanted to. But there is one thing I'd like to do before I give up the business, and that would be to have one more nice band with a string section. We'd get use of a nice ballroom right here in Oakland. Through the week we'd play waltzes and nice things like that. Then on Friday and Saturday we'd do Latin music and all the modern things, with the strings as background for me and the vocalists. Then I'd like to do a little classical music on Sunday. I'd like to do all that and charge the kids only a dollar to get in. I don't know if we'd be able to draw as large an audience as Lawrence Welk, because he's on TV all the time, but I'd like to try that."

I ventured that the kids—and the grown-ups—would love to see him do something like that. One could imagine older folks, drawn by the same memories that Hines had from his youth, and their kids, hearing perhaps for the first time the melodies and lyrics that played across the screens of the ballrooms where lovers met and danced long ago. For a moment, shrouded in smoke, Hines seemed to envision that scene, but then he shook his head, breaking free of a dream.

"No," he concluded. "I want to relax now. Let's face it. I've played everywhere a person can play. I've been everywhere a person can be. I've seen everything a person can see. So I want to relax now. If I get something I can handle, all right. If it's too much hassle, I won't bother with it. I don't need that now."

Less than a year later, slowed by arthritis and crippled by heart problems, Hines passed away in an Oakland hospital.

7. COUNT BASIE

Born: August 21, 1904, Red Bank, New Jersey
Died: April 26, 1984, Hollywood, California

The Basie style is one of the marvels of jazz piano. It is, for one thing, absolutely distinctive, and proof positive that less actually is more. There is no more recognizable style in all of jazz—not just piano. The Basie coda—those three little plinks—is enshrined in American culture, as evocative a riff as "We have nothing to fear but fear itself" or "You ain't seen nothin' yet!"

This came to pass in spite of the fact that Basie was, by temperament, hardly a driven soloist. Quite the contrary: Most of the time he worked as one cog in the mighty machinery that was his band. Indeed, his playing pointed to other musicians more than to himself; we noticed Freddie Green's guitar because of the way Basie danced against that unstoppable pulse.

Basie was, then, a magician of sorts. A note here, a seventh-chord there, and all the big-band fire and fury that follows somehow seems galvanized, as if driven to come back home, to that essential piano lick, completing the circle of the most powerful swing ensemble in the history of jazz.

The power of Basie stems from the piano. His mother gave him his first lessons; his father was a horn player who gigged around the area. Young William Basie initially wanted to be a drummer, but gave up and decided to concentrate on the keys when another local kid, future Duke Ellington stalwart Sonny Greer, proved himself better on sticks and skins.

In his teens Basie crossed the river into New York to seek his fortune. It was a perfect time and place for a young keyboardist to learn. Both James P. Johnson and Fats Waller gave him informal instruction; their stride orientation became the basis of Basie's style, though he would pare it down in order to fit into band settings, in which the bass, drums, and horn section would take over the rhythm responsibilities of the stride player's left hand. Still in his teens, the young pianist polished his chops on the job, in Harlem speakeasies and rent parties that would run past dawn, and then on the road with the blues shouters, "eccentric" dancers, and other entertainers who toured the black vaudeville circuit.

It was fate that led Basie to Kansas City in 1927. After working a while as the house organist at a silent movie theater, he accepted an offer to join bassist Walter Page's Blue Devils, one of the top bands in what was becoming a turbulent local jazz scene. Working with Page planted an appreciation for the city's "jump" rhythm style, which complemented the New York stride on which he had trained; it also forged a friendship and artistic bond between Basie and the band's singer, Jimmy Rushing.

He left the band after six months to work some solo jobs in some of the more torrid dives of Kansas City, then joined the very successful Bennie Moten band in 1929. Known throughout the Midwest for its riff-driven, rocking sound, the Moten band was a perfect workshop for Basie as he continued to distill his playing to its skeletal elements; it also allowed Moten, a pianist as well, to spend most of the night leading the group from the front of the stage as his new hire took his place on the bench.

By the time of Moten's death after a botched tonsillectomy in 1935, Basie was established as the definitive rhythm section pianist in Kansas City. It was inevitable that, after working briefly with his own trio, he would put together a bigger group, Count Basie and His Barons of Rhythm. While broadcasting from the Reno Club over radio station WHB in Kansas City, the group was heard by John Hammond; the famous record producer and jazz entrepreneur was in Chicago with another of his discoveries, the Benny Goodman band, during their engagement at the Congress Hotel. Hammond persuaded Basie to take his band to New York in 1936, where they laid down the first of the many tracks for Decca that would establish themselves as the hardest-swinging band in the land.

Few other bands provoked the kind of excitement onstage that came naturally to Basie and his group. Their earliest work was driven by bare-bones riffs, over which soloists like Herschel Evans, Buck Clayton, and Lester Young would blow urgent, bluesy choruses. Dancers filled the aisles when the band played its first gig on Broadway in December 1936. Customers clamored for copies of their hits—"One O'Clock Jump," "Jumpin' at the Woodside," and on the later Columbia releases, "Lester Leaps In," "Taxi War Dance," and much more. More than 3,000,000 Basie discs were sold in one year alone, 1944.

In live settings the energy that Basie could generate from these spare gestures was sometimes especially easy to feel. At the historic 1938 concert memorialized on *Benny Goodman Live at Carnegie Hall,* he takes his turn on "Honeysuckle Rose" after a couple of choruses from saxophonist Lester Young. He begins with a quick figure that leads to some syncopated articulations of the tonic. Elegant triplet trills fill the bridge, and the following verse reprises the written motif in the melody. Everything after that is about fitting the piano into the pumping beat. Most aspects of the solo get recycled at least once—the syncopated tonic notes, a flat-five riff built on the seventh of the IV chord—but, to risk the double negative, nothing doesn't help push the rhythm. It is, typical of Basie, a totally generous performance, devoted entirely to celebrating the ensemble more than the soloist.

For those who can't get enough of these *nouvelle cuisine* portions of tasty jazz piano, *Count Basie and the Kansas City 7,* from the early 1960s, is essential. It's a delight to hear the Count, with fewer horns crowding against him, stretch out a bit more—precisely because "stretching out" is a relative concept. There are no Tatum-like blizzards, no Tyneresque landslides. Instead, there's Basie finding limitless variations on his style. He opens "Count's Place" with a spectacularly understated intro on the V chord, then when the beat kicks in the fun begins: On the first verse he states a theme that echoes "Lady, Be Good," lets a measure go by, then alludes to the riff with a grand total of one note, followed by some more silence and a couple of chords that accompany our lingering memory of that opening figure. The second verse dishes up another little riff, which Basie this time repeats intact against the blues changes. Third verse? A shorter motif, and this one boils quickly down to one off-beat minor ninth interval. The fourth verse is also more silence than substance, after which a dotted-eighth repetition of the dominant note leads to the horn riff.

In these smaller settings we can also hear more clearly how Basie the pianist patterned himself on swing arrangements. Throughout "Tally Ho, Mr. Basie!" his accompaniment is precisely based on principles of horn section riffs; as Thad Jones or one of the other horn players solos, Basie repeats a snippet of a riff, occupying but not filling up the spaces. On the bridge to the first horn section verse he drops a few "outside" augmented chords, which one notices only in contrast to his more often simpler style; at the end, he pounds a descending octave figure in the lower range, obviously aware of the humorous effect induced by this unexpected bravado. Nothing, however, is awkward; every single note

Count Basie was a magician: A note here, a seventh-chord there, and all the big-band fury that follows somehow seems galvanized.

(even their length, slightly held out during the first four bars of the Thad Jones solo) is in place and in full service to the groove.

Could it be that the economy of Basie's style owes to some technical limitation on the keys? This may in fact have something to do with it: When you listen to him at a very up-tempo, there are occasional smudges and hesitations. Consider, for example, "Baby Lawrence," from the trio album *For the First Time,* recorded with bassist Ray Brown and drummer Louis Bellson in 1974. Playing at a clip more typical of bop carving sessions than dance gigs, Basie seems to have a bit of trouble now and then executing even his more familiar licks, and at the one point where he does try to stretch—with a blues figure, during just the first two bars of one verse in the middle of the performance—it immediately bumps to an awkward halt, as if he was unable to execute the complete idea. Certainly he doesn't attempt any stride action at this tempo. And some of his devices, especially a simple run from the I to the V in the right hand, and an eighth-note ascension from the V to I in the left hand, definitely get a little repetitive.

Of course, repetition is an important part of the Basie style—but when it's grounded in a trio jam, rather than at a more moderate tempo as an element within an arrangement, it can start to cloy after just a minute or two. But then, on even the slowest blues, such as "Blues in the Alley," from *For the First Time,* he maintains his skeletal approach; the piano part is more space than substance, with no fast passagework aside from the infrequent four-note smear. His harmonic language also remains very traditional, with only one jagged lick in the entire tune making what might be considered a vague reference to that other master of minimal piano, Monk. Though born from necessity, Basie's style was almost never altered, even under circumstances in which a less gifted player would have no trouble shooting off fireworks.

The "almost" qualification best applies to a pair of two-piano albums recorded by Basie and Oscar Peterson, who represent in some ways a complete antithesis, not just as keyboardists but as soloists on any instrument. Backed by Brown, Bellson, and guitarist Freddie Green, each soloist seems to edge toward a middle ground in which they might find their connection. For Peterson this means toning down the excess, while still recalling it in his brief but ornate ornaments. Basie, on the other hand, lengthens his lines and avoids the riffs that had become his trademark. The opening chorus on "Buns Blues," from *Satch and Josh* in 1974, tosses snippets of the theme back and forth every bar over a moderate swinging beat. From the start Peterson's parts have a freer feeling, while Basie restricts himself to answering—and generally simplifying—his partner's ideas. Basie solos from the first chorus, and already by the third bar or so he drops in a Peterson-like filigree. Of course Basie does keep it simple, and even reverts now and then to his modular approach, with a different figure guiding him in different sections of the tune. Nonetheless, to however slight a degree, he does loosen up a bit as Peterson makes his presence known.

It works both ways, of course. When Basie makes the unusual move of playing a bridge during "These Foolish Things" in a lower register, with some atypical departures from and variations beyond the written line, Peterson responds with a more characteristic burst of rapid runs in the following verse—inspired, perhaps, to assert himself a bit more by Basie's low-key but effective display.

From 1950, when he split up his history-making band and (two years later) began assembling larger, more musically ambitious ensembles, Basie kept recording and performing, even after a 1976 heart attack; his last appearances with his orchestra often found him playing the piano from a wheelchair. Today, nearly 20 years after the Count's death from cancer, his band continues to play, while his solos endure, more beautiful and enigmatic than ever in an era of excess.

8. MARY LOU WILLIAMS

Born May 10, 1910, Atlanta, Georgia
Died May 28, 1981, Durham, North Carolina

Forget the piano: Mary Lou Williams was a player virtually without parallel on any instrument in jazz. Only Coleman Hawkins could match her accomplishment, with a career that began as a teenage sideman for blues diva Mamie Smith, stretched through the bebop era, and ended up entwined with postmodern and even bossa nova. Like Hawkins, Williams became a master of her instrument because she never stopped learning, even from those who were far younger than her. Musicians can be threatened by the innovations of their students; Williams and Hawkins remained intrigued with new ideas throughout their long careers.

More important, they both embraced the visionaries who would emerge with each new generation. It is true that, in her last years, Williams was less than charitable with players who she felt had lost touch with their roots; in the seventies she made it a point to let the world know that her new mission as a performer was to "save jazz." On the other hand, when assessing the fusion school, for which volume knobs arguably had replaced nuanced technique, she may have had a point. In any event, if anyone had a right to critique any rogue strain of jazz, Williams had earned that right.

By riding the currents of change for more than six decades, Williams actually cheated herself in some ways. Many observers were distracted by her adaptability from being able to appreciate the qualities that defined her own style. Whitney Balliett wrestled with this paradox when he wrote, in *The New Yorker,* "The triumph of Mary Lou Williams's style is that she has no style. . . . She is a gifted and delicate appreciator who distills what affects her in the work of other pianists into cool, highly individual synopses. The grapes are others', the wine is her own."

It took a close friend, sometime rival, and canny observer to identify and pay respect to the essence of Williams as a pianist. In a 1957 issue of *Down Beat* Marian McPartland admitted that the Williams sound "is not so stylized as to be recognized by the average man in the street . . . yet it is all her own—not flowery, but not too spare. . . . Hers is the exact opposite of a 'busy style,' yet she eschews the Spartan approach which characterizes so many of the up-and-coming pianists. She exhibits a fine disdain for those who favor the more technical aspects of the keyboard." In a later *Down Beat* piece McPartland elaborated: "Mary Lou's playing is real. Earthy. Running through all the emotions, it speaks volumes, for there is much in its creator that comes out in the music . . . so that at times one has the feeling almost of intruding on her thoughts."

This fearless candor in Williams's performance is made even more remarkable by her decision, at a peak period of her career, to separate herself from jazz and surrender to her swelling devotion to Roman Catholicism. Though she was away from the piano for only three years, this sabbatical brought a new kind of strength to this already formidable artist—one that confirmed her instinct that music is sustained by spirit.

How does a performer develop this kind of courage? Maybe being a woman in a man's game had something to do with it as well. Most likely, it's nothing more than the collision of exceptional talent and a unique personality, in which integrity, intelligence, hard work, and old-fashioned stubbornness played their parts.

She was born Mary Elfreida Scruggs in Atlanta, then raised in Pittsburgh. For whatever reason, her mother arranged for all her daughters—except Mary—to take piano lessons. Undaunted, Mary listened as her sisters went through their lessons and drills, and at age four began to play back what she had heard. Her progress at teaching herself was prodigious; neighboring families would invite her in to practice on their own pianos. She would remember a boogie-woogie player named Jack Howard as her first influence, but before long Mary was studying recordings by Jelly Roll Morton, Earl Hines, and Fats Waller, and discovering her own voice between the lines that they played.

At age ten she began playing with local musicians at picnics and other affairs. In her early teens she performed with the Hottentots, a vaudeville group whose pianist had taken leave to wrestle with a drug problem, and began sitting in with McKinney's Cotton Pickers and other established bands as they passed through Pittsburgh. Work piled up, and after completing her freshman year in high school Mary dropped out to go on the road with another vaudeville act, Seymour and Jeannette.

When Jeannette died unexpectedly, the young pianist resolved to pursue her fate alone and set off for New York. She plunged into its bustling music world, meeting and befriending artists as diverse as Jelly Roll Morton and Andrés Segovia. Duke Ellington let her sit in with his band at the Lincoln Theater. She played for Fats Waller too, who was so delighted by her precocious gifts that he picked her up and tossed her in the air. At the age of 15 she began working with bandleader John Williams, who married her just one year later. In 1927 she made her recording debut with his band, the Synco Jazzers.

When her husband quit the Synco Jazzers, Mary took over as leader. But when John was hired by Andy Kirk's Clouds of Joy in 1929, Mary followed him from New York out to Kansas City, where Kirk was building his reputation as the top bandleader in what was then a hot music town. Marion Jackson was already playing piano with Kirk, so Mary got her own gigs in local blues and boogie-woogie clubs. Significantly, when the band made its first recordings that year, producer Jack Kapp insisted that Mary be used for the piano parts.

With Clark's departure in 1931, the piano bench was turned over to Mary full-time, along with the job as Kirk's chief arranger. In the years that followed, her charts and compositions powered the Clouds of Joy to swing stardom. In the mid-thirties, when the band relocated to New York, Williams also began writing freelance arrangements: In addition to writing "Roll 'Em" and "Camel Hop" for Benny Goodman and "What's Your Story, Morning Glory" for Jimmie Lunceford, she contributed to the band books of Tommy Dorsey, Louis Armstrong, Earl Hines, and other luminaries.

She kept her piano chops up as well: Many of her works with Kirk, and as leader of Mary Lou Williams and Her Kansas City Seven, featured her hard-rocking solos and fills. During an extended engagement with Kirk in Cleveland, Williams also spent a lot of time at Val's in the Alley, where she and Art Tatum would play together and for each other through the night and up to eleven in the morning.

Her gig with Kirk and her marriage ended in 1942. Williams and her new husband, Harold "Shorty" Baker, led their own group for a while before Ellington hired them both, Baker to play trumpet and Mary to do some arranging. For two years in the mid-forties she fronted an all-female band, whose talented lineup included guitarist Mary Osborne. At the same time Williams was pushing herself to write more ambitious, long-form pieces, including *Zodiac Suite,* a musical meditation on astrological signs, which the New York Philharmonic presented at Carnegie Hall in 1946.

She was also opening her ears to the sounds of bebop. Where most swing musicians backed away from the challenging new style, Williams invited Dizzy Gillespie, Charlie Parker, Thelonious Monk, Bud Powell, Tadd Dameron, and the other pioneers to come by and work out their ideas in her apartment. Their influence began to creep into her work as pianist at Café Society Downtown and on records that she made with a diverse range of artists, from Coleman Hawkins to folk blues artist Josh White.

But changes in her life were already beginning to affect her work. A growing involvement with charitable causes lowered her profile in the city's musical circles. Discontented with New York, Williams moved to Europe in 1952, where she recorded in England and France, performed in continental clubs, and stepped up her search for something that might settle her restless soul. Two years of irresolution came to an end in 1954, at the Boeuf Sur Toit, a nightclub in Paris. She recalled the epiphany that changed her life that night in a *Down Beat* interview: "I was sick and tired of all the selfishnness. . . . When playing all those years, I never felt a conscious desire to get close to God. But it seemed that night at the Boeuf Sur Toit that it all came to a head. I couldn't take it any more. So I just left."

Typical for Williams, once she knew what had to be done, she didn't hesitate. In the middle of the gig at that Paris club, she stopped playing, stood up, turned her back on the piano, walked out the door, and returned to America. For the next two years she refused to touch the keyboard and instead immersed herself in study with a Jesuit priest, Father Anthony Woods. Hours of listening to records gave way to hours of meditation. For three years her commitment to the church and attendant charitable work was complete.

Yet inevitably Williams did return to music. After gentle prodding from Dizzy Gillespie and from Father John Crowley, a Catholic priest and erstwhile jazz saxophonist, she returned to performance with a surprise appearance at the Newport Jazz Festival in 1957, where she played her *Zodiac Suite* with Gillespie and his band. Once again her calendar filled with activity: recording again, playing concerts and club dates, and taking on additional responsibilities as a teacher. With art and faith reconciled, she accepted a commission from the Vatican to compose *Mary Lou's Mass,* with choreography by Alvin Ailey. As founder of the Bel Canto Foundation, Williams worked to help musicians who were down on their luck or struggling with addiction. From Duke University to ad-hoc classrooms for street kids in New York, Williams initiated a new generation of players into the mysteries of jazz, always emphasizing the feeling of the blues over any niceties of technique.

And more than ever, she challenged herself as well. In 1969, during a visit to England, she went to hear Cecil Taylor perform at Ronnie Scott's in London. They struck up an acquaintance that led eventually to their decision to present a joint concert in New York during 1977. It was a breathtaking concept, this attempt to build a bridge between Williams, whose roots stemmed from actual encounters with Jelly Roll Morton and the founding fathers of this music, and Taylor, who embodied the most extreme language of the avant-garde. Though a complete meshing of minds failed to transpire, there was something inspirational even in the attempt by these two giants to seek a connection.

In addition to their fearlessness, Taylor and Williams shared a fascination with improvisation. That other acquaintance of Williams, Art Tatum, excelled at creating performances of such architectural design that they seemed composed. Williams couldn't match these standards of perfection; she would occasionally muff one of the faster descending runs that often decorated her solos—which apparently didn't bother her, or her audience, in the least. Instead, her style embraced the unexpected. She never hesitated to switch ideas; even in the middle of a phrase, she might veer from a low-down boogie-woogie into a jump blues, as on "Overland (New Froggy Bottom)," a trio piece recorded in the late thirties. In the fashion of most great improvisers, Williams was capable of surprising her listeners, and even her fellow musicians, without warning.

Her adventurous approach is especially evident on familiar repertoire: "The Pearls," performed by its composer Jelly Roll Morton over a tuba-driven two-beat rhythm, becomes an intimate salon piece in the Williams trio version. The brush snare beat provides a steady, simmering swing, which allows the pianist complete freedom to slip between stride, chorded passages, off-beat spikes in her melody or accompaniment, and one quick, dramatic gliss halfway through the performance. (This sweeping little zip up the keys to one sustained note was one of the pianist's trademark figures, all the way up to her last years.) Only Earl Hines, in those days, showed as much willingness to ignore stylistic limits, but Williams did so with more subtlety and less preoccupation with showy effects.

When he heard her in her early teens, Fats Waller was so delighted by Mary Lou Williams's precocious gifts that he picked her up and tossed her in the air.

Leaping ahead to 1971, Williams reaches even further back on *Nite Life*, with a series of stunning performances of Scott Joplin rags. These performances expose aspects of this repertoire that persistently elude more archival players. On "Elite Syncopations" Williams presents the written material faithfully, then builds on it with repeated triplet figures that extend the melody, her familiar quick glissando, and other examinations of the theme that leave the audience gasping and laughing in delighted surprise—a response that Williams, with an audacious imagination and vast creative range, could elicit at will.

Williams owned a complete command of the stride style, marked by a vigorous rhythm and a hint of barrelhouse. On her original composition "Night Life," recorded in 1930 and available on the French EPM album *Mary Lou Williams Story: 1930-1941,* she displays a technique that's more emphatic than nimble, with snappy chord repetitions and deft broken figurations in the opening verse. Williams packs a punchy stride throughout the piece with a lot of muscle.

Practically nobody played the blues with the emotional conviction and inventive spirit that Williams routinely displayed. On "Twinklin'," recorded in 1936 with Andy Kirk and His 12 Clouds of Joy, she digs into several opening choruses over a spare rhythm accompaniment; beginning with an ascending figure in the left hand, to which she returns after the first bridge, her solo is a marvel of melodic variety, with a bracing balance of motivic riffs and loose extemporizing. A modernist mentality yet to blossom in jazz piano is hinted at in bar ten, where the melody snares on a minor sixth that anticipates Monk's whole-tone explorations and jagged attack. It blows by pretty quickly but leaves a flavor of where jazz piano would be moving in another decade or so.

There is no parallel in jazz that compares to changes in style that Williams underwent from the thirties to the seventies. In her youth she was already an anomaly, capable of displaying equal authenticity in every extant school of jazz piano. But one can listen to her rendition of "I Can't Get Started," on the duo album with bassist Brian Torff that she recorded in 1975 for *Live at the Cookery,* and be justified in disbelieving that she wasn't any older than Bill Evans. Her harmonization of this tune is completely attuned to the most advanced practice of the time; her left hand adheres to a postbop, free-comping style, with no reference to more historic styles. Later in the same set, Williams offers a sprightly interpretation of "The Man I Love," with knotty harmonies built on extensions of the prominent minor seventh in the melody; aside from a certain Oriental reference in some of the fourths-based chords, nothing here brands Williams as anything less than a thoroughly modern stylist.

Her treatment of "Over the Rainbow," from *Montreux Jazz Festival 1978,* is an even more disorienting performance. The free-tempo introduction, based on the bridge, layers a mirror variation on the harmony over a foundation of complex harmonic extension. The verses in this performance are relatively straightforward, with each bridge serving as a laboratory for ever more ambitious reharmonizations. Williams's increasingly clustered chords push nearly into abstract territory toward the end of the performance—as it to anchor her experiments, she shifts into an old-fashioned slow stride with her left hand even while twisting the changes into enigmatic patterns with her right. In its downplayed way, this is bipolar virtuosity, an example of looking forward by reaching backward.

This same range was a cinch for Williams at faster tempos as well. Her trio rendition of Duke Ellington's "The Jeep is Jumping," from the 1979 live album *At Rick's Café Americain,* makes an undeniable case for Williams as the greatest swing pianist of her time; from emphatic low-register accents to her driving right-hand lines, she pushes the beat with an almost ferocious and impatient aggression. At the same time, her powerful attack and blunt tone, and the gradually intensifying dissonances of her chorded passages, draw much more from Monk than from Teddy Wilson. In these sorts of performances we are reminded again of the difference between archival performers, who would meticulously reconstruct the aesthetic of past styles, and Williams, who never lost touch with the thrill of the new.

It is no surprise that, a year before succumbing to cancer, Williams established a foundation dedicated to financing lessons for promising young musicians with established jazz artists. On practical matters, as in the realm of faith, she was an artist in the service of a greater good than her own.

9

TEDDY WILSON

Born: November 24, 1912, Austin, Texas
Died: July 31, 1986, New Britain, Connecticut

I t's not as easy to appreciate Teddy Wilson's contributions as it was back in the thirties, when his ability to improvise long, silky lines suggested a more subtle complexity than that offered by stride piano. Wilson radiated class: He was a trim young man with movie-star looks and a style that suggested swank salons rather than funky uptown rent parties. Precision was as important in his playing as, say, a muscular projection was to the sound of Earl Hines.

It's an important distinction, since the two pianists were often considered kindred spirits. Certainly there were similarities: Both favored single lines in the right hand, which suggested a temperament more characteristic of horn players than keyboardists. Each was comfortable within a rhythm section, unlike some stride players who never learned to make room for the bass and drums.

In retrospect, though, Wilson represents a deviation from the path first opened by Hines. The older pianist's strategy was to attack his lines; rather than slip them into a neat fit with the band, he battled his own musicians to be heard. Wilson, who was more reserved than Hines, benefited from advances in amplification that were unavailable when his predecessor was loading his pianistic weapons. Without needing to pound over the din, he could develop a more intimate approach, with minimal physical effort and an aesthetic that was more bouncy than bluesy.

This sleek, smooth sound made it easier for Wilson to play an important role in the social history of jazz. Though black and white musicians had jammed together for years, it wasn't until clarinetist Benny Goodman invited the pianist to join his trio that an integrated band achieved prominence. In manner and music, Wilson possessed a quiet dignity that did little to encourage controversy. Like Jackie Robinson in baseball, he avoided confrontation yet changed his world through the force of his principles.

Wilson was bred to play this role. He moved with his family at age six from Austin, Texas, to Alabama, where his mother was a librarian and his father headed the English department at the Tuskegee Institute. An appreciation for eclectic culture guided his formative years, through exposure in equal parts to opera and blues in his parents' record collection; Wilson's early favorites included Bix Beiderbecke's "Singin' the Blues," King Oliver's "Snag It," and Hines and Louis Armstrong, whose performances he isolated in his listening from the rest of their band, on Hot Five discs.

He saw his first live jazz performances during a summer visit to an aunt's home in Detroit. As a student at Tuskegee, Wilson took lessons on piano and violin, and played E-flat clarinet and oboe in the school band. Though eager to play professionally, he agreed to attend Talladega College as a music theory major, but one fateful day he happened to hear another young pianist swinging through some tunes in a neighbor's house. That was enough to persuade Wilson to drop out and, all of 17 years old, seek his fortunes as a musician in Detroit.

Shortly after arriving, he picked up a gig through his brother Augustus, who was working alongside trombonist Vic Dickenson and trumpeter Roy Eldridge in a band led by drummer Speed Webb. A couple of years later, in mid 1931, he took over the piano chair in saxophonist Milton Senior's band. This might have been the toughest assignment ever tackled by a jazz piano player, since Wilson had to take the place of the already formidable Art Tatum. Inevitably, their paths would cross; in fact, at age 19, Wilson moved into an apartment in the building where Tatum lived in Toledo. The two became friends, and spent many hours tossing ideas back and forth. Their mutual influence proved enduring, with Tatum learning something about left-hand voicings and linear improvisation from Wilson, in exchange for some insights on harmony.

Both pianists advanced quickly into approximations of their more mature styles. Before the end of 1931 Wilson moved to Chicago, where he began playing at the Gold Coast, a lavish private club which was frequented, like a lot of clubs seemed to be in those days, by Al Capone. Over the next several years he worked with Jimmie Noone, Eddie Mallory, Erskine Tate, and Louis Armstrong, with whom he made his recording debut in January 1933. During a performance with Clarence Moore's band, which was subbing for Earl Hines and his orchestra on a national radio broadcast from the Grand Terrace Ballroom, Wilson was noticed by the young jazz enthusiast and producer John Hammond; on the basis of that program, Hammond persuaded Benny Carter, who was looking for a new pianist, to bring Wilson out to New York.

By October 1933, when he cut his first tracks with Carter's Chocolate Dandies, Wilson had pretty much developed his distinctive sound; where he initially tended to restrict himself to the middle range of the piano, he was now spiraling his lines into the high, undampered strings, whose resonance contrasted with the lightly pedaled, dry stride in his left hand. He became a top-call pianist in New York, with Red Norvo, Mezz Mezzrow, Mildred Bailey, and other prominent performers hiring him for sessions.

Two important opportunities opened for Wilson in 1935. With more help from John Hammond, he wound up leading a series of recordings with Billie Holiday, who was just emerging as a significant vocalist. For four years he worked closely with Holiday, for whom he assembled all-star ensembles that featured members of whatever big bands happened to be in New York with some time off from the road.

An even bigger break presented itself that same year at a party given by Mildred Bailey, where Wilson met and jammed with Benny Goodman. Once again Hammond played the key role, persuading Goodman and drum superstar Gene Krupa to join forces with Wilson in a history-making interracial trio. After some initial recordings, they made their debut in public on Easter Sunday in 1936, with a performance at the Congress Hotel in Chicago. Several months later another black artist, the vibraphonist Lionel Hampton, made it a quartet.

It was an electrifying combination, a daring balance of styles and personalities that thrilled fans throughout the world. Krupa and Hampton, the two percussionists, played hot rhythms with clearly sexual insinuations, each spraying sweat and pummeling his instrument in unprecedented proximity for a white and a black man onstage. Wilson, cool and composed, channeled their energy through the filter of his sophisticated piano; with no bass player in the band, he slid his stride and slippery tenths into the stampede of drums and vibes, reined them in, then built momentum by keeping tension high between his restraint and their abandon. Goodman, the authority figure, presided over all this, his clarinet teasing the beat, skimming the surface of the rhythm or digging into it, switching from milky legato to suggestive, syncopated growls.

The lineup would change within a few years. When Dave Tough took Krupa's place, and when John Kirby signed on as bass player late in 1938, the group actually improved; the drumming became less thumpy, the grooves more locked in, and the bass allowed Wilson more freedom. But the significance of the original foursome was unmatchable. In their many reunion appearances over the next few decades, the quartet meant nothing but Goodman, Krupa, Hampton, and Wilson; there was really no alternative.

The quartet also marked the peak of Wilson's career. He was a celebrity when he left in April 1939 to form his own band, and he did put together a solid outfit, with saxophone giant Ben Webster on board as a featured soloist. They recorded some impressive performances, most of them featuring arrangements by Wilson. But these discs didn't sell, and the band's shows had none of the incendiary quality that was essential to Goodman and the other swing headliners. The problem was that Wilson's cool demeanor had no hot foil; his band was tight but lacked fire. For years after the demise of his band in June 1940 he spoke bitterly of its failure, blaming his label for its lack of support, or the industry as a whole for making it tougher to keep large groups together. Only when discussing his band did Wilson betray what was, for him, an uncharacteristic bitterness.

Throughout the forties he pretty much kept to New York. He played with small groups, most often sextets but also in a trio with bassist Al Hall and drummer J.C. Heard. He began a twenty-year association with CBS as a staff musician, assumed a teaching position at Juilliard, took private students, and spent four years playing at the two popular Café Society clubs, one uptown, the other downtown.

In the fifties Wilson began booking himself more often on international tours, which gave him steady work into the seventies. He could count on drawing well in his club and on festival dates in Europe and Japan, where his performances took on a nostalgic quality. Wilson, in fact, did little to discourage his growing perception as a gentlemanly senior statesman of jazz, who always appeared in sober coat and tie, sat with correct posture and virtually no emotional engagement at the keyboard, and played familiar tunes in succinct, four-minute bits that offered no threat of disruption or promise of surprise.

Although the Wilson style changed little through his many active years, a kind of half-heartedness grows more apparent with time. During many of his sessions in the thirties he sounds fresh and fully interactive. On "Where the Lazy River Goes By," for example, recorded on December 16, 1934, he seems almost playful, allowing himself a very brief boogie-woogie paraphrase toward the end of his solo. Very seldom does anything like even this brief deviation intrude on his later recordings, whose consistencies create an impression, in the end, of boredom.

Only rarely did Wilson allow himself to be rushed beyond medium tempos, and on "Jeepers Creepers," which he recorded with Benny Carter in the fifties, it's clear why: With Jo Jones laying down a quick clip, Wilson seems slightly overwhelmed. His lines cling to the structure of each chord, which creates a sense of repetition as he tries to blow through the changes and chops his solos into symmetrical bits that end too often on the tonic note. The discomfort that's apparent on this track says a lot about why, on his own later albums, he never pushed the envelope. On this same album there is equally convincing proof that Wilson had practically no feeling for the blues, as he leads into "Birth of the Blues" with an octave line whose prissy articulation has nothing to do with the messier expressiveness often associated with the style.

Teddy Wilson with Benny Goodman: His movie-star looks and style suggested swank salons rather than funky rent parties.

Within this context, though, he was always capable of delivering an impeccable performance. His solo behind Lester Young on "This Year's Kisses," recorded on January 12, 1956, is built on a familiar but effective foundation of shifting tenths. His right-hand figuration has a spare beauty up until the final section of his solo, where nimble runs skim up and down the keys. The intention is not to build a big finish but to balance the thoughtful architecture of his preceding passages. It's a tasteful exercise, symmetrical and elegant. Only when you pull back and consider his catalog as a whole does this kind of performance stand revealed as, also, redundant.

It may seem strange, given his long denouement into something resembling cocktail music, that Wilson never gave up the idea that jazz was fundamentally more about dancing than listening. In fact, this does explain his preference for medium tempos and his lifelong habit of outlining the beat in his left hand. His skepticism about pianists who lost the pulse in their phrasing, and abstract rhythm sections that played without rhythm, may say more than Wilson intended about his disinterest in exploring beyond certain limits.

But no one could have coasted as long as he did without having generated some significant energy at the beginning of his journey. When asked, toward the end of his life, who was his favorite pianist, Wilson replied, "I am." Like the best of his music, his answer was brief, honest, and eloquent.

10

NAT "KING" COLE

Born March 17, 1919, Montgomery, Alabama
Died February 15, 1965, Los Angeles, California

I f you take away that smoldering, smoke-and-satin croon, and then the handsome features and sly, seductive smile, what remains is Nat "King" Cole, an extraordinary pianist. He played with an appealing blend of sophistication and understatement. His blues had a sleek uptown feel, and at every tempo he swung. His technical resources were among the strongest of his time, yet his temperament drew him toward a minimal approach that was well suited for the trio format. No one surpassed him in his use of syncopation; the spaces between his phrases spoke louder than the notes other pianists would have played.

None of this was a secret in the forties, when musicians such as Art Tatum were borrowing from Cole for their own trio work. Jazz fans noticed too, and voiced their appreciation by naming him best jazz pianist in *Esquire*'s annual tabulation in 1946 and '47, and in *Metronome*'s poll for 1947 through '49. Certainly it was no tragedy that wider fame obscured these accomplishments just a few years later, though some hipper longtime listeners groused, inevitably, as his having "sold out."

From our perspective, Cole's jazz recordings become jewels that had been hidden behind the veils of his own fame, and whose value has grown inestimable.

It was St. Patrick's Day when Edward James Coles, a Baptist minister, and his wife Perlina Adams Coles welcomed their son Nathaniel Adams into the world. Though later he would suggest that he had been born in 1915 or 1916, the correct year is now accepted as 1919. He had three brothers and two sisters, all of whom were musical; each would perform at their father's church services. But from the start Nat showed the most talent; he was four years old when he first played in public, and in kindergarten showed a precocious delight in entertaining his friends. At the age of eleven he began performing at his father's church, doing double duty on the organ and in the choir.

By this time the family had long settled in Chicago, where his father preached at the True Light Baptist Church. Jazz flourished in the city during the twenties, and the music of hometown hero Earl Hines made a particular impression on Nat. He was leading his own band by the age of 16, and in 1936 he left high school and made his recording debut with Eddie Coles' Solid Swingers, a six-piece band led by his brother on bass.

Later that same year, Nat hit the road with a traveling production of the Noble Sissle and Eubie Blake musical *Shuffle Along*. When the company disbanded unexpectedly, he found himself stranded in Los Angeles with his future first wife, a dancer from the show. Necessity led him to a gig at the Swannee Inn, on La Brea Boulevard, late in 1937. This proved to be a pivotal engagement, for it was here that he was persuaded by club owner Bob Lewis to drop the final "s" from his last name. Also, though booked as a quartet, Cole's group turned into a trio, with guitarist Oscar Moore and bassist Wesley Prince, when the drummer, saxophonist Lester Young's brother Lee, missed opening night.

And it was at the Swannee Inn that Cole debuted as a singer, after a drunk customer reportedly bullied him into singing "Sweet Lorraine." It may or may not have happened this way, but Cole did start adding vocals to his performances at this gig, and as a result became a hot local act before hitting his twenty-first birthday.

Without the lush strings that would cushion his vocals on future commercial blockbusters, Cole learned to stretch the resources of his trio through brilliant, precision-executed arrangements. As jazz theorist Gunther Schuller would observe, "one has to wait for the remarkable Lennie Tristano Trio of 1946 and the early Modern Jazz Quartet of a decade later to hear such sensitively integrated playing again."

These standards survived several personnel changes; in many respects, no other jazz piano trio has exceeded them. Sometimes the group went a little overboard; their adaptation of Rachmaninoff's *C# Minor Prelude* is Emerson, Lake & Palmer without the electronics. Mostly, though, their virtuosity was exuberant, and their enthusiasm contagious. They raced through tricky chorded passages without a stumble, or danced through diminished patterns in perfect sync.

They also jammed. When improvising, the threesome approached telepathic levels of communication. But when Cole soloed, the bass and guitar typically fell back into a steady groove, while the pianist could release long, fluid lines whose syncopations bounced against the pulse.

The real tribute to Cole is that he could make his statements with the barest gestures. Where the New York pianists of the Tatum school fired heavy fusillades, Cole underplayed to an extreme. On his trio recording of George Gershwin's "The Man I Love," from *The Best of the Nat King Cole Trio: The Instrumental Classics,* he achieved a certain eloquence in the simplicity and spare adornment of his line. His improvisation follows the melody with great care, departing momentarily for a quote from *Rhapsody in Blue* during the turnaround at the end of the first verse, but otherwise basing every gesture on the written theme.

Cole was capable of moving beyond conventional ideas of melodic variation. His solo on "How High the Moon," from the same album, anticipates the George Shearing "locked hands" approach, in which the line emerges in the upper and lower voices of a thickly chorded passage—but in the second half of the verse, Cole scales down to a single proto-bop line in the right hand. Structurally, it is flawless, and typical of this pianist's conceptions.

In many other performances, Cole showed a sensitivity toward breath as a measure of when the solo line should be broken up. On "It's Only a Paper Moon," a quartet performance with guest trumpeter Harry "Sweets" Edison on *The Complete After Midnight Sessions,* he plays sparely, with practically no left hand and a solo line that's parsed into almost conversational segments. By letting pauses speak within his line, Cole invested them with as much rhythmic emphasis as any articulated notes.

Eventually, though, Cole traded his jazz threads for the mantle of pop stardom. He sold more than $50,000,000 worth of upbeat, easy-listening hits, enough income to merit characterization of the Capitol Records building in Hollywood as "the house that Nat built." Beginning in 1946, he hosted his own radio show every Saturday, and would follow eight years later with his own television show. His hit recording of "Nature Boy" in 1948 accelerated his move from jazz into mainstream pop. He even played himself in an autobiographical film. At the end of the forties his trio was already on its way to becoming a memory.

By the time of his death—from lung cancer, after years of smoking three packs of cigarettes daily—Cole had transformed himself into something dramatically different from what he had been. Yet just as admirers of Louis Armstrong learned to look past "Hello, Dolly!" for the essence of his music, those who love jazz piano know that the art of Cole is more complex, and the search for it more rewarding, than anything suggested by the spectral video sentiment of "Unforgettable."

11. DOROTHY DONEGAN

Born April 6, 1924, Chicago, Illinois
Died May 19, 1998, Los Angeles, California

The story was that when Dorothy Donegan was booked to play at the Embers, at the time New York's most highly regarded piano room, the manager issued specific instructions that she was to play the instrument at arm's length from the keyboard—far enough away to avert any of the damage one might expect from her exuberant performances.

For Donegan, though often lauded by her supporters as a female Art Tatum, resembled him only in the most transparent aspects of technique. Each pianist was a bravura performer—yet they exhibited completely different temperaments. Tatum's intricate counterpoint and meticulous execution revealed a classical outlook of music for its own sake. A correlation existed between the audience's discernment and the magnitude of the impression made by Tatum; the more musically astute his listeners, the more wonders they could appreciate in his work. And it is doubtful that any piano ever suffered beneath his light, skimming touch.

Not so with Donegan. Though capable of blinding velocity on the keys, she never felt inclined to lock her passions into the tight forms that attracted Tatum. Her pedaling was more generous, and her tempos were determined not by any sense of structural balance but by impulse; if she felt like stopping at some point to quote from assorted classical themes, or take off into simultaneous and unconnected two-handed improvisations, or even to veer into a completely unrelated song, why not? This from-the-gut spontaneity turned Donegan's performances into unpredictable caprices, with bits of different songs tossed like a salad and doused by the dressing of her own personality.

Tatum—stoic, proud, self-assured—was the Joe Louis of jazz piano; Donegan—flamboyant in fashion and manner, with one eye always on the crowd—played the role of Muhammad Ali.

For jazz essayist Whitney Balliett, all this smoke obscured the fire of Donegan's music. He describes her, in *Collected Works 1954–2000,* as "a medium-sized Rubens, with a court jester's face, and everything she plays is translated into action. She rocks back and forth and from side to side. She forms her feet into a giant wedge and stomps it. Her head rolls wildly, and her face is possessed by fearful middle-distance stares, a whorl-like mouth, and bowsprit lips. . . . This frenzy . . . obscures her playing, and that's too bad, for Donegan is a first-rate Tatum pianist."

But it is Donegan's playing, more than her act, that obscures whatever she had to say as a jazz artist. Her melodramatic glissandos, muddy low-register rumbles, and tumbling runs distracted more than they enlightened; in her solo performances, she sounded more like an agitated, somewhat disheveled Liberace than another Tatum or Peterson. What was undeniable was that she was a master of the piano, capable of pushing it to brute levels of response like few pianists this side of McCoy Tyner or Cecil Taylor.

All that power and authority traces back to age six, when Dorothy began taking lessons in Chicago. From the start her style was physical—an extension, in a way, of a tomboyish interest in playing baseball with the neighborhood kids. Her public debut came at age ten, when she began playing organ at the local church. Four years after that she had crossed the tracks and was playing both at nightclubs and at rent parties. All the while she kept up her private studies, with advanced instruction at the Chicago Conservatory and the Chicago Music College.

Donegan was only 16 years old when she talked her way into sitting in with the Lionel Hampton band at the Grand Terrace, site of Earl Hines's influential big-band broadcasts. Saxophonist Illinois Jacquet, who was traveling with Hampton at the time, clearly remembers that meeting; in his liner notes to *Live at the 1990 Floating Jazz Festival,* he writes, "I'd never seen her before in my life, but once she started to play, everyone in the room began to look at each other and listen. She hit those first chords, deep chords, strong chords, just like a symphony. She played so much piano that day it was unbelievable. I'd heard Mary Lou Williams . . . but I'd never heard a woman who played like Dorothy."

Throughout the early forties she established herself as the most popular solo pianist in Chicago—so popular that Art Tatum himself came to pay her a visit in 1942. The story is that he walked up six

The flamboyant Dorothy Donegan always kept one eye on the crowd in her musically rich performances.

flights to make her acquaintance and, in the end, treat her to a series of private lessons. Donegan made a bit of history the following year, when she became the first woman as well as the first African-American to perform at Orchestra Hall. In 1945 she was flown to Hollywood to make a flamboyant appearance in the film *Sensations of '45*. From there Donegan flew to New York and began her lengthy career as a recording and, in the richest sense of the word, performing artist.

From that point, throughout the rest of her life, Donegan maintained an exhaustive schedule, appearing in high-class venues throughout Europe and major American cities and on jazz cruises. Where she didn't work that much was on the jazz club circuit, where her self-described "hip-shakin'" and outlandish commentaries only confirmed apprehensions of her artistic irrelevance.

It is difficult to make a case for Donegan as a profound interpreter of standard repertoire. She scattered classical paraphrases throughout her improvisations and crooned along with herself, inevitably illuminating her own affectations rather than the material she purported to interpret. As far as she was concerned, the point wasn't the material as much as it was her stampede through it all.

Yet a rock-hard musical foundation supported these indulgences. She explodes into "My Funny Valentine," from *Live at the 1990 Floating Jazz Festival*, with a two-handed Lisztian spiral down the keys that has little in common with more intimate treatments of the tune; this hair-raising introduction does lead quite logically, however, to some daring reharmonizations on the opening verse. Plenty of bombastic thundering follows, which stops abruptly in mid-phrase as her trio latches, without warning, onto a steady tempo. Donegan lapses quickly into more technical overkill, but only after she has made clear her command of both the instrument and the composition.

Typically, she leads into a medley of "Misty" and "Caravan," from the same album, with a knee-slap quote from "Night and Day" over a Beethovenian ostinato in the left hand. Her twinkling trills serve as little more than sly slapstick in these shows. Indeed, with the sustain pedal jammed to the floor, Donegan's roaring alternating octaves, her dizzy modal runs up and down and up again, recall circus acts or plate spinners on *The Ed Sullivan Show* more than anything that passes for serious jazz.

Donegan could on occasion settle down—relatively. On *The Incredible Dorothy Donegan Trio*, recorded in 1991, she and her sidemen stick closely to the structure of "Sweet Lorraine" as trumpeter Dizzy Gillespie sits in. In the scattered energy of her phrases, and in the moving tenths of her left hand, Donegan strongly recalls Earl Hines here. But even when focused on the tune, she finds it hard to resist her exhibitionistic tendencies: On "Someday My Prince Will Come," from *1990*, every gesture is huge. Why play the melody as written, when you can disguise it in a frenzy of quick lines, eccentric clusters, pearly descending thirds, broken octaves—each effect followed by the other in an ever more bizarre display?

Very clearly, Donegan was a singular phenomenon. There is no way to approach her objectively. When all is said and done, even her critics cannot deny that Donegan's intro to "Tea for Two," a blistering rush of full-fisted, intricately constructed lines and syncopations, is about as stupendous a moment as one will likely encounter in jazz piano—for better or for worse.

"God Is in the House"

12. ART TATUM

Born: October 13, 1909, Toledo, Ohio
Died: November 5, 1956, Los Angeles, California

In nearly all disciplines and arts, the true giants have had to share their thrones with others of equal or nearly equal stature. Only a very few exceptions come to mind: Shakespeare, for example. Julius Caesar, perhaps.

And, definitely, Art Tatum, by consensus the greatest jazz pianist who ever lived.

Granted, jazz and its practitioners haven't had the kind of impact on history as the Einsteins and Napoleons. But if Tatum's world—a world of all-night jams in clubs choked with the funk of cigarettes and booze—lacks grandeur, it may be more because of the prejudices of the time and place than any deficiencies in talent.

There were many brilliant performers on the jazz circuit in the thirties and forties. But in those days, few avenues were open to blacks, especially those who, like Tatum, suffered physical handicaps. Though he played with an assurance and imagination that stunned even the classical masters, he spent most of his career behind inferior pianos in dingy retreats, like Val's in the Alley, a Cleveland club recalled by Duke Ellington in his memoir, *Music is My Mistress*:

"It was really in the alley, off an alley that was off another alley. . . . Val had a piano that was so old and beat-up that Tatum had to learn to play everything up toward the treble end. But it had a most compelling sound, and the action was obviously just right, because Tatum loved that piano even after he went to New York. Famous as he became, and deserved to be, he would always return to Val's in the Alley to play that piano."

From our perspective, this is a quizzical picture. By near universal agreement, Tatum was unprecedented in his time and unequalled in ours. Yet even after doing four or five shows at Cleveland's RKO Palace, he would drop in at Val's and play the battered upright until well past dawn. Of course, he didn't play exclusively on inferior instruments in saloons, but some observers, including his protégé and friend Billy Taylor, feel that he usually played his best in the club setting, rather than in formal recital or on record.

"Anyone who has ever heard Tatum play after hours in a setting of his own choosing will bear out the fact that this is a completely different Art Tatum from the one who plays either in clubs, jazz concerts, or on records," Taylor wrote in *Down Beat* in 1955. "When he plays for a select audience of his own choosing, even his arrangements take on a new dimension. The fabulous technical facility is then used as it should be used, to present and exploit the creative power which sets Tatum apart from other jazz pianists."

On nights like these, the club was packed with musicians, who maintained a proper silence as Tatum wove his musical webs. But non-musicians were often in attendance too, filling the air with the kind of chatter one doesn't hear in a concert setting. Tatum was sensitive to audience noise, and he did demand respect: When someone was making too much noise for his taste, he would simply stop playing in mid-phrase and sit quietly, his arms hanging motionless at his sides, until the offending party got the message. On one particularly raucous night, writer Barry Ulanov saw an irritated Tatum stop a tune and announce, "Do I have to perform a major operation in here to get quiet?"

This is, again, a part of the Art Tatum paradox. He loved his music and apparently enjoyed his life, but he may have been a jazz musician only in part by chance. To a certain extent, he *had* to love jazz, because that was his only outlet. Tatum did have an affinity for the classics, but there was no room in the concert world then for a nearly blind black man. Occasionally he performed classical pieces, though usually in the same style he used for popular tunes, treating the theme as a *cantus firmus* on which he based his improvisations. In Ellington's memoir, we get another glimpse of Tatum's classical side:

"One night in Los Angeles, some friends from San Francisco and I were roaming around, and we wound up in an after-hours joint on Adams Boulevard called Brother's. Who do you think had stopped by after his job and seated himself at the piano? Nobody but my man Tatum. He was in his usual rare form, and doing all of the most impossible high and harmonic changes. . . . After meeting Art and conversing with him, our friend, Mrs. Archibald Holmes, hit on the subject of Bach, because she had been studying his music. Something in Tatum's playing moved her to utter the next thing to a challenge.

"'Well, Mr. Tatum, do you know any Bach?'

"'A little,' Mr. Tatum answered, and then proceeded to execute a parade of Bachisms for the next hour. After getting her breath, the lovely lady said, 'Thanks. I guess I'll keep my big mouth closed now!'"

Pianist, composer, and raconteur Oscar Levant remembered an equally impressive display, before an even more discerning audience, in his book *A Smattering of Ignorance*. His friend George Gershwin was a passionate fan of Tatum's. In fact, Levant writes, "He was so enthused with Tatum's playing that he had an evening for him at his 72nd Street apartment before leaving for Hollywood. Among George's invited guests was Leopold Godowsky, who listened with amazement for twenty minutes to Tatum's remarkable runs, counter-figures, and passage playing. . . . Sometime after he arrived in California, Gershwin discovered that Tatum was playing at a local nightclub, and we went together to hear him. It was a small, dingy, badly lighted room. We joined the group of enthusiasts clustered around the piano where the blind virtuoso was in full swing. To George's great joy, Tatum played virtually the equivalent of Beethoven's 32 variations on his tune 'Liza.' Then George asked for more."

This is a telling passage, for even when playing non-classical repertoire, Tatum worked from what might be called a classical conception. Earlier jazz pianists, even those with formal training, never approached his command of counterpoint, harmony, and texture at the keyboard. His authority reached such a level of sophistication in the historic solo piano sessions with producer Norman Granz that critic Whitney Balliett observed in *Saturday Review*, "Little of the astonishing crystal palace of sound that Tatum has created here is jazz. It is, in fact, difficult to find a single complete chorus of jazz improvisation in the whole series. One hears, rather, a weird cross between a jazz-oriented pianist and one who is, at various times, decked out in Chopin, Debussy, cocktail filigrees, and Frankie Froeba."

Tatum indeed represented no school of jazz piano; he was too good to be confined by any existing categories. He was more the child of the nineteenth-century virtuoso tradition than any other jazz performer of his day. He was a sentimentalist too, and the young bebop generation of the forties and fifties laughed at his "moldy fig" repertoire. But, as Balliett further observed, "People poked fun at his ornate style and his corny interpolations in his solos of *Rhapsody in Blue* and 'Stars and Stripes Forever,' then wept at his next brilliance." Hailed by his peers throughout his career, he nonetheless failed to win a single *Down Beat* jazz piano poll. He counted Horowitz and Gieseking among his admirers, yet lived a jazz life, in Val's and other backstreet bistros, until its early end.

If Tatum was a bitter man, he kept that to himself. Most of his surviving friends remember him as an easygoing companion, always interested in the other player's performance. In the book *Conversations with Jazz Musicians*, Billy Taylor says, "He was extremely sensitive, even though he was blind and could hardly make his way around by himself. What freedom he did have, he guarded jealously. Though he was obviously limited by his handicap, he had a lot of fun. He loved to hang out and party. He was a handicapped person who resented, in many cases, the fact that it limited his mobility. . . . But he didn't mope about. He was a relatively happy guy."

Ultimately, though private by nature, Tatum did seem to be happy, or at least contented. Twice married, he raised two Dobermans at home and enjoyed his family life. He also liked keeping late hours: After finishing a gig at four in the morning, he would seek out another venue, a party or a jam session, and continue playing until noon.

Toward the end of his life, Tatum cut an imposing figure. About five-foot-seven, he was a heavy eater, fond of home cooking and especially of beer. At times he weighed as much as 230 pounds. The younger Tatum, however, is described by Orrin Keepnews in *Jazz Masters of the Thirties* as "not especially noteworthy" in appearance: "His was not a face that one would pick out of a crowd." Others recall that he moved with a slow and deliberate grace, and that he had surprisingly small hands, though his fingers could span a twelfth on the keys.

His friends retain an affectionate memory of him, in the hazy morning light after an all-night jam, looming over the keyboard, yet playing with a light, almost feathery touch, ad-libbing miniature masterpieces from tunes that were already hackneyed in his day by redefining their harmonies and juggling rhythms into complex puzzles that always resolved before the cadence. And on the piano, always, a glass of beer, depleted and refilled many times over as the music went on.

Those who were pianists remember his fingers, always low on the keys, looking, as Keepnews describes them, "almost double-jointed" as they raced through kaleidoscopic patterns. Though partial to Steinways, Tatum spent much of his career on moth-eaten models of dubious vintage. He would warm up with scales—his favorite practice routine—and find the clinkers on each keyboard, then avoid them by playing in whatever keys had the fewest bad notes. Away from the piano, he kept his hands limber by passing a filbert nut between his fingers in quick, intricate patterns, until it had been worn smooth.

Luckily for jazz fans, Tatum was born into a talented family. Both his parents were amateur musicians: His mother played piano, and his father, though he worked as a mechanic, was a guitarist. Art, the oldest of three children, was born with cataracts in both eyes. At first he could see only in black and white. Fairly good vision in color was restored to one eye after thirteen operations, but the doctor's repairs were shattered one day when a robber hit the boy's good eye with a blackjack. From that point on, Tatum had only about 25 percent of his sight in that eye and was completely blind in the other.

At the age of three, he went with his mother to her choir practice. That night, while cooking dinner, she heard him at the piano, picking out the melody of the hymn they had rehearsed. Soon Art was learning his first jazz licks from radio broadcasts and from piano rolls cut by James P. Johnson and Fats Waller. A quick study, he exhibited near-perfect recall; once he heard a song, he never forgot it.

His mother recognized Art's gifts and, after giving him some introductory lessons, she referred him to a local teacher. For four years Tatum built his massive technique, while polishing his Braille music reading at the Jefferson School for the Handicapped; his memory for pieces learned through Braille was soon as faultless as his natural aural retention. The lessons stopped when his teacher made the classic announcement for prodigy pupils: "I've taught you all I can. Now you can teach me."

Following his graduation from the Jefferson School, the 13-year-old Tatum entered the Cousino School for the Blind at Columbia, Ohio. There, he took violin and guitar lessons and, for a while, doubled on accordion, but the piano remained his first love. Soon he was studying with Overton G. Rainey at the Toledo School of Music. Despite Rainey's attempts to steer Tatum toward a classical career, the young pianist was already dedicated to jazz.

He played his first gig with a dance band at 16 and then began working the local circuit—the Rotary Club, the Toledo Club, and so on. Later he subbed for Herman Berry, the ailing pianist in drummer Speed Webb's group; shortly after that, he officially replaced Berry, though only three months later he was in turn succeeded by Fitz Weston. A few years after that Tatum joined another group, this one led by alto saxophonist Milton Senior, with Bill Moore on bass, Fats Mason on drums, Lester Smith on guitar, and Harold Fox on violin; they gigged mainly at the Tabernella and the Chateau de France until mid-1931, with some short tours and more local jobs after that. Except for a few isolated appearances and sessions, that essentially constituted all of Tatum's work in the band format.

Why didn't he follow the path taken by nearly all jazz pianists in those days—the path that led to ensemble jobs? In recalling those early days as a band pianist for *Time* magazine, Tatum revealed that part of the answer may connect to a side of his musical personality that would linger even into his later years. "The other boys used to razz me," he insisted. "They said I had no left hand, so I made up my mind to show them." After he had perfected his stride, even after Horowitz had reportedly declared that he would have given anything for Tatum's left hand, Art was still sensitive to that kind of criticism.

But there were other reasons why Tatum decided to focus on solo performance. As he told *Time*, "A band hampers me. I have to watch out for them." Most critics agree; since Tatum's command of the keys allowed him to express all aspects of rhythm, harmony, and melody effortlessly, this became his natural style. When he shared the stage with horns, rhythm players, or singers, he felt short of space.

Even while working with groups, Tatum was playing solo jobs around Toledo. Around 1928 he became a regular at Chicken Charlie's, with solo spots following in 1930 at the Tabernella, the Chateau de France, a place called Jimmy Jones's near the Majestic Hotel, a nameless little house near Cedar Avenue and 89th Street among the shacks, where the salary was paid in tips and only a dim light illuminated the upright piano, and occasionally in Cleveland clubs.

He was also making a regional impact over the radio. In 1928 or '29, as a result of his performance on an amateur program, WSPD radio in Toledo hired him to play between Ellen Kay's daily shop-
ping hints to housewives. Soon he had a fifteen-minute show of his own, which ran five days a week for
more than two years and was eventually picked up for national broadcast by the old NBC Blue network
(now ABC). Occasionally he played duets on the air with another local pianist soon to make good himself—Teddy Wilson.

Wilson had inherited Tatum's piano gig with Milt Senior's group, and in *The World of Earl Hines*
he told writer Stanley Dance that the radio show "was a much better showcase for him than playing
in a quartet with bass and guitar. He had a great gift for harmonic improvisation, and he would re-
harmonize chorus after chorus on songs like 'Body and Soul,' so the effect of bass and guitar was only
to limit him. Neither he nor I had been to New York at this time, but we would go out together every
night and make the rounds of after-hours places, playing on upright pianos until late morning and
sometimes early afternoon."

Even if his playing hadn't been broadcast over the airwaves, news of Tatum's prowess would have
filtered through the national jazz community via word of mouth from musicians passing through the
area. They carried reports of the nearly sightless young giant back with them to New York, advising
other players to look him up when they were in Ohio. Paul Whiteman, the popular pioneer of sweet
symphonic jazz, did, and was one of the first to proclaim Tatum a genius. The greatest saxophonist
of the day, Coleman Hawkins, heard the pianist and was moved by the experience to completely re-
vise his own improvisatory style. Other jazz tastemakers, such as saxophonists Jimmy Dorsey and Don
Byas, trombonist Jack Teagarden, and bandleaders Glen Gray and Jimmy Lunceford, also crowded
around the old instruments on which Tatum was already restructuring the language of jazz piano.

Musicians would later compete to see who had come across Tatum first. One possible winner
was June Cole, a bassist who insisted that he heard the young pianist, already at his full powers, working in a gambling house around 1925. Another claimant, cornetist Rex Stewart, told *Down Beat* that
he first heard Tatum in 1926 or '27, when he was in town with Fletcher Henderson's band. His description of the scene typifies the reaction that musicians would have to Tatum's playing for years to
come: "To a man, we were astounded, gassed, and just couldn't believe our eyes and ears. . . . As a
matter of fact, the experience was almost traumatic for me, and for a brief spell afterwards, I toyed
with the idea of giving up my horn and returning to school."

Saxophonist Earle Warren of Count Basie's band also recalled the scene in the cramped rooms
where Tatum perfected his playing. "Jam sessions there used to go until seven or eight in the morning," he told Stanley Dance in *The World of Count Basie*. "Art would have beer lined up on top of the
piano. . . . [He] was a good feeder and didn't get in the way. When it was his time to play, he'd really
play, but then he'd come up to the service end of the bar and start arguing about football. Art loved to
discuss the football and basketball players that to his mind were the greatest."

Duke Ellington also heard Tatum for the first time in Toledo. In *Music is My Mistress* he relates
his initial encounter: "Friends had been talking about him, telling me how terrible he was, yet I was
unprepared for what I heard. I immediately began telling him that he should be in New York. Quite
a lot of what he was doing was taken right off the player piano rolls, and I felt that the action and com-

petition would do much good in helping to project that part of himself which was covered up by the carbon-copy things he did so perfectly."

Ellington was not the first to encourage Tatum to move out East—a touring musician named Reuben Harris had that honor—but neither was he the last. Paul Whiteman even took Tatum back to New York with him, but the 19-year-old pianist returned quickly to Toledo. New York was, at that time, the Jazz Mecca, especially for pianists. Tatum had heard of the all-night cutting contests, where the top players in town would try to outdo each other. He knew their names—Willie "the Lion" Smith, Fats Waller, James P. Johnson—and their music, from the piano rolls and radio broadcasts that had introduced him to jazz. The fact is that, despite the famous players who were flocking to his gigs and praising his work, he didn't know if he could cut it in that most competitive of cities.

So it wasn't as a soloist that Tatum went to New York, but in the rather unfamiliar role of vocal accompanist, in a sense testing the waters one foot at a time before jumping in. In 1932 blues singer Adelaide Hall came to Toledo, backed by pianist Francis Carter; Joe Turner, her co-accompanist, had just quit the act, and she was looking for a new pianist to double with Carter behind her. Hall had been told about the incredible local pianist Art Tatum, by Rex Stewart, Fletcher Henderson, her own husband, and Turner, so naturally she looked him up, and they arranged for an audition.

Needless to say, Tatum passed the test. Hall had a feature number, "River Stay Away from My Door," which other pianists had wrestled with for ten days before mastering. It took just three hearings for Tatum to memorize the entire arrangement.

The trio went to New York, and Tatum finally began to be heard by his peers on their own home base. He did a record date with Hall in August 1932, cutting two sides with only her and Carter, and two others in a slightly larger group. There were many live performances too. Hall gave him his first solo spot at a concert in the Palace Theater; from that point on, during the rest of his 18 months with her, Tatum was featured at each concert with one solo number.

Inevitably Tatum received his baptism by fire at the hands of the New York jazz piano elite. His first contact with them was engineered by Fats Waller, who introduced himself backstage at the Lafayette, where Tatum was working with Hall. Waller was not terribly impressed with the newcomer's playing at first, probably because Tatum was restricted that night to stock background chords for the singer. Nonetheless, the two pianists agreed to get together the following night for some serious playing.

After his gig with Hall the next evening, Tatum was met by an imposing welcoming committee: Willie the Lion, James P., and Lippy Boyette, a former pianist turned booking agent. Tatum asked if they could pick up his friend Reuben Harris, at whose house he was staying. They went to Harris's, roused him from his sleep, and went off in search of a piano good enough for the first round of their get-acquainted duel.

Soon they found themselves in Harlem, at a place called Morgan's. Someone played a few numbers to open the proceedings, and then Tatum was talked into taking his seat at the keyboard. The rest of the scene was reconstructed in Maurice Waller's biography of his father, *Fats Waller*:

"Art played the main theme of Vincent Youmans's big hit, 'Tea for Two,' and introduced his inventive harmonies, slightly altering the melodic line. Good, but not very impressive. Then it happened. Tatum's left hand worked a strong, regular beat while his right hand played dazzling arpeggios in chords

Art Tatum at New York's Café Society Downtown, 1940: He counted Horowitz and Gieseking among his admirers, yet lived a jazz life until its early end.

loaded with flatted fifths and ninths. Both his hands then raced toward each other in skips and runs that seemed impossible to master. Then they crossed each other. Tatum played the main theme again and soared to an exciting chorus."

The entourage was stunned; lulled by Waller's preliminary assessment, they hadn't expected anything near Tatum's level of virtuosity. But gamely they tried to meet the challenge. James P. Johnson followed Tatum with "Carolina Shout," playing, Maurice Waller writes, "as if his hands were possessed by a demon. But it wasn't good enough." Waller then presented his showpiece, "A Handful of Keys," but Tatum still had the edge. Then Tatum came up once more and roared through "Tiger Rag." Johnson tried one more time, with his version of Chopin's *Revolutionary Étude*. "Dad told me he never heard Jimmy play so remarkably," Maurice Waller concludes, "but the performance fell short. Tatum was the undisputed king."

Later on, Johnson would admit, "When Tatum played 'Tea for Two' that night, I guess that was the first time I ever heard it really *played*." And in an interview with *The New York Times*, Waller capped his recollection of that night with this: "That Tatum, he was just too good. . . . He had too much technique. When that man turns on the powerhouse, don't no one play him down. He sounds like a brass band."

Perhaps the most appropriate tribute to Tatum lies in the fact that he never saw himself as the "winner" of such contests. Never did he elevate his self-esteem to the point that he could not listen to, enjoy, and learn from other pianists. Ellington confirms this in his memoirs: "After hearing The Lion and being so close to him, I'll always say that you could hear his influence in Art Tatum's playing for the next two years. Tatum was Boss, but he had a deep appreciation of all the other beautiful things in the Top Drawer."

Or, as Tatum himself put it, "You can't create everything. You have to listen to the other fellow."

By late 1932, when he got his first New York solo gig, at the Onyx on 52nd Street, Tatum was revving his career into high gear. In addition to his many club jobs, he spent two weeks subbing for ailing pianist Todd Rhodes with McKinney's Cotton Pickers. And on March 21, 1933, he entered the studio to record his first four piano solos: "Tea for Two," "St. Louis Blues," "Tiger Rag," and "Sophisticated Lady."

These early records hit the music world like a bomb. "Tiger Rag" and "Tea for Two" were exercises in bravura jazz playing—relatively tuneless tunes that were better suited to traditional stride interpretation, with the accent on rhythm, than to more modern melodic invention. Tatum leaned more on this kind of material in his first recordings than in his last, perhaps in part because he was out to prove something, but also because he did feel a stronger empathy with the stride school than with those styles of piano playing that de-emphasized the left hand. Though he was never a "two-fisted" pounder, Tatum always valued his left hand, either as a source of propulsion or as an equal partner to his right hand in harmonic flights of fancy.

The stride school also had an impact on his right hand, but the Earl Hines melodic approach was a more important influence, particularly in the octave tremolos that frequently signaled the end of an improvised Tatum passage. He did extend this concept beyond the reach of any other jazz pianist; the flowing lines that Hines unfurled became spiraling arpeggios from one end of the keyboard to the other, often overlapping, but never interrupting the pulse laid down by the left hand.

There was another ingredient in Tatum's music: a love for the blues. Although his recorded blues output is extremely small—his "Verve Blues" was one of the only twelve-bar tunes he cut during the fifties—and he occasionally indulged in a humorous takeoff on boogie-woogie, Tatum was in fact an accomplished blues player. He had backed up blues shouter Big Joe Turner on several recordings in the early forties, and in New York he often made the rounds with his friend Meade Lux Lewis, the great boogie-woogie pianist. Years after Tatum's death, when a tape turned up of eleven works he had been composing, six of them turned out to be blues tunes.

He favored 32-bar tunes by composers like Gershwin, Cole Porter, Irving Berlin, and Richard Rodgers for his public performances, but when playing for his own pleasure Tatum often played— and sang!—the blues. Another of his friends in the bluesy side of jazz, Jay McShann, testifies to this in *the World of Count Basie*: "Art could really play the blues. To me, he was the world's greatest blues player, and I think few people realized that. As a rule, he'd play all that old technique stuff first, but when he got settled down he played blues."

Occasionally Tatum mixed the "old technique stuff" with the blues, as singer Jimmy Witherspoon relates in the same book: "One day I never forget, we were down at Mike Jackson's, a bar on Central Avenue, and Tatum was drinking a beer. 'Would you like to sing one?' he asked. 'Yeah,' I said. 'What key?' 'Put it in B-flat.' He started in B-flat, but after that he went to every key in the ladder. Jay [McShann] had told me what he would do, so I paid no attention to Art and his chord structures, kept my mind on B-flat, and sang right through. 'Spoon,' he said, hitting me on the shoulder and laughing, 'nobody in the world can do that. I put you through so many keys.' He had a sense of mischief and loved to do things like that."

On the road frequently after 1933, Tatum was in Cleveland in 1934 and '35, working at the Greasy Spoon. From 1935 to '36 he was at the Three Deuces on State Street in Chicago—where, in a sad reminder of music business reality, as Dave Dexter recalls in *Billboard*, "Only musicians applauded and supported his astonishing talent." Then in late 1936 it was on to Hollywood, to perform at the Paramount Theater and the Club Alabam, and to appear on Bing Crosby's radio show. Throughout 1937 Tatum was in Hollywood, in Chicago at the Three Deuces, and then back in New York to work at the Famous Door.

The pianist's first European trip was in March 1938. He drew SRO crowds to Ciro's, the Paradise Club, and other London venues, appeared at the Aston Hippodrome in Birmingham, and played over BBC radio before going on to the Café de Paris and concerts on the Continent. From 1939 to '40 he was back on the West Coast, then he settled mainly in New York before taking another big step.

In 1943, Tatum, the godfather of solo jazz piano, formed a trio, with guitarist Tiny Grimes and bassist Slam Stewart. He had recorded with small groups before: In a 1937 Los Angeles session, he cut several sides with a quintet that included Lloyd Reese on trumpet and Marshall Royal on clarinet, and in 1941 he did some work with a band led by trumpeter Joe Thomas and clarinetist Ed Hall. But the news that he was putting a permanent group together caught many listeners by surprise.

Today, most critics agree that Tatum was not nearly as strong an ensemble player as he was a soloist. Still, many of the sides he cut with Grimes or Everett Barksdale on guitar, and Stewart on bass, show that he did benefit from their interplay. Remember, the most common response induced by his playing was fear; pianists as accomplished as Oscar Peterson talked of being "scared" by him. In this climate, perhaps Tatum found life a little lonely at the top. Which is probably why so much of the music he recorded with his trio sounded like just plain fun.

From 1943 to '53 the Tatum trio played over the radio from Chicago's Blue Note Café. They also played in clubs along New York's 52nd Street and in Harlem hot spots like Lovejoy's. He played with other ensembles during those years as well, most notably as a member of an all-star rhythm section, with guitarist Al Casey, bassist Oscar Pettiford, and drummer Sid Catlett, backing saxophonist Coleman Hawkins, trombonist Jack Teagarden, vibraphonist Red Norvo, and trumpeters Louis Armstrong and Roy Eldridge at the Metropolitan Opera House in January 1944. And he continued his unaccompanied performances and marathon cutting contests with those pianists foolish enough to take him on. One memorable session pitted him against a rival at the Hollywood Bar in Harlem for 24 solid hours, beginning and ending at two in the morning.

From 1945 onward Tatum embarked on national tours, but compared with earlier years, the pickings were leaner. A new generation of musicians was beginning to explore new forms of improvisation. Unfortunately for Tatum, they were moving music in almost the opposite direction from the one he had chosen. For the new breed of pianists, his busy left hand was an artifact; bop style demanded that the left hand only imply the chord occasionally, and nothing more. Right-hand solos were pared down to horn-like single lines. Creative energies were devoted now into extending the melody with exotic dissonances and quirky rhythms, while Tatum preferred to leave melodies relatively untouched, except by his rococo embellishments—which, in later years, he toned down. And the intensity of many young players was foreign to Tatum's more benign temperament.

His contact with boppers was minimal and, with some exceptions, formal. Stories abound of a cutting session that nearly broke out between Tatum and a drunken Bud Powell. The bop pianist supposedly challenged him to a musical shootout, but Tatum dismissed him with an admonition to come back when he had sobered up, and a promise that "anything you play with your right hand I'll play with my left." The next day, Powell actually did spend several hours limbering up in preparation for the encounter, but it never came off.

Apparently record producer Norman Granz also tried to arrange a summit that would bring Tatum together with saxophonist and bebop icon Charlie Parker. Granz almost succeeded in organizing a record date with the two, and actually did set up a Carnegie Hall concert that featured them both, but both plans fell through.

Granz did play a crucial role, though, in setting up the definitive series of Tatum record sessions. The pianist hadn't recorded in the studios since 1947, but when he signed with Granz late in 1953 he returned to the studio with a vengeance, cutting 23 albums, both solo and with various distinguished players, from then until his death three years later. Not quite knowing what to expect, since he didn't know the pianist well when the sessions began in December '53, Granz stocked the studio with ample supplies of beer and held his breath. He was in for two surprises: Despite his preconceptions that Tatum would be aloof and cold, the pianist proved amiable. He declined to listen to playbacks, preferring to move straight on to the next tune, and when the tape ran out in the middle of one number, Tatum simply began on a new tape exactly where he left off, dropping neither a beat, a note, nor an iota of the feeling.

The second surprise? Being a dedicated basketball fan, Tatum brought a radio to the session, which he turned on to the local game after each take.

As to the music itself, these sessions represent the culmination of Tatum's work, and a milestone in jazz history as well. More than 200 songs were laid down, many of them nearly note-identical to versions he had recorded earlier. The dazzling displays that Tatum had loosed on the world more than twenty years before were calmer, his chops always in evidence but now in a mature context. He sounds secure, at home with his place in history. On these albums, in fact, he was sculpting a monument to the older styles he had brought to perfection.

Tatum's last years were content as well as productive. Jazz audiences welcomed him, not as an exponent of a new or old-fashioned school, but as the institution he was. In 1954, '55, and '56 he won the *Down Beat* critics' poll. The gigs were many: In 1955 he drew strong crowds to San Francisco's Black Hawk, and in Toronto. He also made two appearances on television as a guest of host Steve Allen on the *Tonight Show*. For viewers who were unfamiliar with Tatum, these were revelations.

On June 2, with Slam Stewart and Everett Barksdale, he made his first *Tonight* appearance. Allen, overwhelmed with Tatum's facility, asked the pianist to demonstrate some of his three-fingered runs, then commented that watching him in action was like "looking at Da Vinci painting while riding by on a fast bicycle." Then, on July 8, Allen welcomed him back by introducing him as "the number one jazz pianist of all time." Then, after hearing Tatum's rendition of "Someone to Watch over Me," he announced to viewers, "Piano playing might get different, but it's not going to get any better, I can tell you that."

In his last year, Tatum finished his massive Clef/Pablo group sessions and began making plans with Granz for a recital tour that would feature the pianist, billed simply as "Tatum," performing in dignified settings offered by the best classical concert halls. He even bought the white tie and tails he planned to wear onstage. But time was running out. The long hours of drinking and jamming were finally wearing him down. On August 15 Tatum gave his last performance, a triumphant appearance at the Hollywood Bowl before 19,000 fans; he was already seriously ill with uremia. By October he was almost too physically uncomfortable to play at all. He was getting ready to visit his sister in Detroit for an overdue period of rest when, on November 4, he was forced to check into the Queen of Angels Hospital in Los Angeles. The next morning, he was dead.

Tatum was buried at the Rosedale Cemetery in Hollywood. His pallbearers were Benny Carter, Ed Brown, Bill Douglass, Ralph Roberts, Edgar Hayes, and Eddie Beal. Honorary pallbearers and guests included Oscar Peterson, Erroll Garner, Billy Taylor, Cozy Cole, and Dizzy Gillespie. Those jazz giants who weren't in attendance also felt his passing as a personal blow. Commented Count Basie, "It's bad enough when a man and a friend dies. When a man dies with all that talent, it's a disgrace."

After decades of innovation in jazz piano, Art Tatum still stands alone, untouched. Dizzy Gillespie's comment may ring true as long as jazz survives: "First you speak of Art Tatum, then you take a deep breath and you speak of all the other pianists."

Deep in the Mainstream

13. ERROLL GARNER

Born: June 15, 1921, Pittsburgh, Pennsylvania
Died: January 2, 1977, Los Angeles, California

For a while, Erroll Garner was probably the most popular jazz pianist in the world. He was perfect for the fifties: As a longtime presence in the clubs along New York's 52nd Street, he had credibility with his fellow musicians. His playing, a canny blend of romanticism, fidelity to the melody, and blues, went down easy. And, not incidentally, he was physically non-threatening, all of five-foot-two, with an elfin demeanor—no liability for a black artist in those times.

It is difficult to imagine anything like the Garner phenomenon happening today. Credibility is a bigger issue now, and the line between so-called serious musicianship and entertainment cuts deeper than ever. Jazz in particular is supposed to challenge, not soothe; even the accessibility of Wynton Marsalis comes at the price of having to sit through his discourses on tradition. Anyone who decides to simply play with joy and humor for the mainstream public risks being written off as a cultural frivolity.

But that's what Garner did, and it served him well in a less cynical era. Not that he lacked critics: One can sense his defensiveness as he told Nat Hentoff and Nat Shapiro, in *Hear Me Talkin' to Ya*, "I like to play certain tunes because of their melody. Why should I disguise that melody?" The answer, as Garner knew, was that bebop was stretching way beyond melody, partly in order to create an exclusive club that only the hip could dig. Twisting, inverting, and otherwise pulling a tune beyond recognition drew attention away from the composer and created a mystique around the powers of the performer.

Garner could flat a fifth as well as anyone else. For whatever reason, though, he followed his own muse rather than someone else's idea of what was cool. Whether through design or happenstance, his style exemplified the kind of jazz the public wanted to hear. Puzzled or threatened by the inscrutability of bebop's cryptic lines, listeners sought out pianists who emphasized harmony. But where Dave Brubeck could be too cerebral and George Shearing too pretty, Garner found a middle ground that bridged jazz clubs and cocktail lounges. One could listen to him without feeling either stupid or square.

None of this seemed to bother his fellow musicians, who were nearly universal in their affection for him. Mary Lou Williams described Garner as "the Billie Holiday of the piano," and Art Tatum referred to him fondly as "my little boy." If anything, all the attention bothered Garner more than anyone else. When critic Leonard Feather congratulated him on his popularity during the fifties heyday, he somewhat gloomily replied, in part, "I sure wish it could have happened to Art Tatum instead of me."

These sorts of reflections were rare from Garner, who never was comfortable expressing himself through words. But they suggest something, perhaps a feeling of unworthiness, buried beneath his pixie exterior. One of the few things that the public knew about Garner was that he was musically illiterate, though he never took pride in his inability to read notation. This may explain his reluctance to record with orchestras, whose erudition could be intimidating.

Yet left to his own devices, Garner was fantastically prolific. When recording solo he would rush through one song after another, each separated by just a few seconds. Once, during a session for producer George Avakian, he recorded nineteen songs, totaling 97 minutes' worth of music, in just three hours—which included 30 minutes off for lunch. And on one afternoon in July 1954 he laid down 32 songs in three hours, nailing each in just one take.

Despite his commercial appeal, Garner was a real innovator in several respects. His rhythm, though rooted in stride piano, ultimately embraced the four-beat chorded patterns that were more common to guitar players. His willingness to play the extremes of the keyboard, and to break every now and then into rumbling tremolos, fit in with an effective, if somewhat unfashionable, pursuit of dramatic effect through contrasts in volume and timbre.

Both of these traits could get out of control, especially on later recordings. Garner's left-hand beat turns into a ponderous tromp on "For All We Know," recorded in 1965, with bassist Eddie Calhoun and drummer Kelly Martin unable to do more than trudge along in a kind of strip-show groove. And on many Garner performances, the chords he loved to float up in the high range become almost a gimmick, no different in essence from Liberace's arpeggiated frippery. Most unnerving was Garner's tendency to let his hands fall out of sync, so that the melody could drag as far as a full beat behind the left hand before being hurried back into place at the end of a verse. Like the tremolos and tinkles, this practice too often failed to function as more than an affectation.

But when he felt like it, Garner could bring his sound together and play with unmatched verve. His rendition of "The Man I Love," from *Encores in Hi-Fi*, is a bracing workout with bassist Al Hall and drummer Specs Hall, in part because Garner keeps the pulse down in the mix. And on his *Concert by the Sea* live album, he makes greater use of swinging lines in his right hand, which give an extra push to the high-register chords that inevitably follow.

Ironically, Garner and his twin brother were the only kids in his family to receive no formal instruction in music. His father, older brother, and three sisters were all pianists. The problem was that Erroll showed no interest in practicing, though he was picking tunes out on the keys at age two. Even so, he gave his first public performance when he was seven years old, appeared on a local radio show as a member of a group called the Kandy Kids, and even sat in with the legendary riverboat bandleader

Fate Marable, along with the young bassist Jimmy Blanton. He hung out with a musical crowd at Westinghouse High School, where his friends included future bebop pianist Dodo Marmarosa, and was acquainted with another emerging hometown talent, Billy Strayhorn. At one point, he auditioned for and won the piano gig with a local dance band; the guy whose job he inherited, Art Blakey, went on to bigger and better things after switching from piano to drums.

Garner first played in New York at the age of 15 as a vocal accompanist. By the age of 23 he was living in Manhattan, working first as a solo pianist at the Melody Bar on Broadway, then moving uptown to the Rendezvous and Jimmy's Chicken Shack, before settling in at 52nd Street, the heart of the city's jazz club world, at Tondelayo's. Garner was called to substitute for an ailing Art Tatum on a trio gig with guitarist John Collins and bassist Slam Stewart at the Three Deuces in 1944; this became his home base on the Street as he started building his reputation.

Garner's career took a big leap in 1948, with a triumphant set at the International Jazz Festival in Paris. He had an especially big year in 1950, when he signed with manager Martha Glaser, performed a concert at New York's Town Hall, recorded his first Columbia discs with producer Mitch Miller, won the *Grand Prix du Disque* in France for his album *Play, Piano, Play*, and wrote his most famous song, "Misty," during a flight from San Francisco to Denver.

More than many of his peers, Garner had business smarts. His contracts for club and concert dates were unusually comprehensive in guaranteeing him approval over the piano, the lighting, the sound system, the hours of performance, and other details of each appearance. He was assertive in his recording deals as well; when Columbia released *The One and Only Garner* in June 1960 without his approval, he took legal action and became the first recording artist to compel a label to withdraw a release from distribution.

When Garner died at the age of 53, his peak years had long passed, partly because emphysema had forced him to cut down a year or so beforehand, but also because times had changed. His playing, so idiosyncratic yet so commercial, spawned no school of imitators; even more than in the fifties, song players had gone out of fashion. His limitations are perhaps more evident in retrospect than his strengths, with muddy pedaling, occasional clinkers, and those obsessive splashy chords in the upper register marring so much of his work.

It takes a little effort to isolate his strongest moments: his *Concert by the Sea* album, and the often astonishing invention on *Solo Time! The Erroll Garner Collection*. These and a few other recordings remind us of how inventive and ebullient Garner could be—and, equally important, how easy it is to let one's style sink into a kind of self-parody, offering only glimpses of the gifts that it otherwise obscures.

14. AHMAD JAMAL

Born July 2, 1930, Pittsburgh, Pennsylvania

It's often been noted that Ahmad Jamal was Miles Davis's favorite piano player. That would be about as high as praise could get in jazz, given Davis's association with most of the great keyboard artists of the twentieth century's latter half; in fact, the trumpeter at one point instructed his pianist at the time, Red Garland, to try to sound a little more like Jamal. More telling is that fact that Jamal isn't so much an original stylist as an incarnation of all the important elements of style. His sound isn't always instantly identifiable, but that may be because it is the sound of modern jazz piano itself.

When Jamal plays, there's a sense also of what he *could* be playing. His chops are as strong as any among his contemporaries, which means that even in his most elaborate extemporizations there's always something he's editing out. Working like a sculptor, Jamal chisels through whatever gets in the way in his search for the essence of a song. As a song player, in fact, he has no equal; when he does allow himself to ornament a melody with nimble divergent runs or a mercurial arpeggio, the effect is always to animate that tune, not to mask it.

Moving in the opposite direction of most musicians, Jamal began with a fairly economical style, which has bloomed now into a bouquet of brilliant, sometimes clashing colors. His dynamics surge from inaudible to volcanic, often in the space of a second or two. With pedal down, he looses wave after mighty wave of tremolos, then lets them evaporate down to breath-holding hushes and silences. Powerful unison lines blur and build into thundering roars at the bottom of the keyboard. The miracle is that all this never overwhelms the material. Unlike McCoy Tyner, he hasn't invented his own harmonic language, yet his energy in concert frequently pushes past even Tyner's threshold and into Cecil Taylor territory.

An intellectual as well as a musical prodigy, he was born with the name Fritz Jones, which he would discard after his embrace of Islam in the early fifties. Piano lessons began at age three. Jamal progressed quickly, moving to advanced instruction at age seven from the respected black opera singer Mary Caldwell Dawson and, subsequently, with James Miller.

From the beginning Jamal perceived music as a holistic phenomenon, undivided by arbitrary labels. Even disciplines as divergent as jazz improvisation and classical recital impressed him as essentially identical. "Duke Ellington is no different from Bach, as far as I'm concerned," he would tell Neil Tesser of *Down Beat*. "Duke writes what he hears, and Bach wrote what *he* heard. . . . There are many things that Liszt played that aren't written. Many of the things I play *are* written. There's no difference."

Liszt was a beacon for Jamal, so much so that he performed some of his *Études* when he made his public debut in a piano competition at age 11. At the same time he was immersed in the music of Ellington, Teddy Wilson, and Nat "King" Cole. He was near the front lines at the Savoy Ballroom, barely tall enough to peek over the edge of the stage, when Art Tatum, Count Basie, and Dizzy Gillespie came to town. And when hometown hero Erroll Garner played at his school, Jamal was there too, taking it all in.

As a student at Westinghouse High School, already married and a father, Jamal began supporting his family through local gigs. After graduation he went on the road with trumpeter George Hudson's band for a while, then left in 1949 to join a group called the Four Strings. When the leader quit, Jamal took over and fronted the group, now sensibly known as the Three Strings, at the Blue Note in Chicago and the Embers in New York. The band at that point included bassist Ray Crawford and guitarist Eddie Calhoun.

The Three Strings won ample critical attention, especially at the Embers, where producer John Hammond became an early and enthusiastic supporter. As personnel changes eventually led to a settled lineup with Israel Crosby on bass and Vernel Fournier on drums, Jamal found himself with the right partners at last. On January 16, 1958, they recorded *But Not For Me: Live at the Pershing*, which remains a classic in trio performance. Crosby and Fournier's sizzling support allows Jamal to derive maximum effect from the most minimal improvisational gestures. "Surrey with the Fringe on Top" provides the best example here of the pianist's fondness for placing tiny shards of the melody in the highest keys, far above the rhythm bed. This separation of the accompaniment from the solo range allows Jamal to frame each note with brilliant clarity.

Throughout this album, in the snappy call-and-response motifs between Jamal and Fournier, in the bell-like spellings of the thematic chorded riff and understated gospel motifs of "Music, Music, Music," and in the graceful segues between time signatures on "Moonlight in Vermont," Jamal exhibits a strong sense of arrangement, which would support his later development into a more formal and commercial sound.

In the short run, though, *Live at the Pershing* propelled Jamal to the front rank of jazz pianists and marked the beginning of a long and celebrated career. Uncompromising in life as in music, he would for a long time refuse to play in the Jim Crow South. In 1960 he attempted to bring his ascetic

Ahmad Jamal isn't so much an original stylist as an incarnation of all the important elements of style.

values to the club world by opening a dry nightclub, the Alhambra, in Pittsburgh; a year later it was out of business. Disgusted by crass aspects of the industry, Jamal recorded only infrequently for several years in the mid-sixties, then completely retired for a while. Yet when he signed with 20th Century Fox as the label's only jazz artist, he began playing within slicker, more commercial settings, though at no loss to the credibility in which he is still held by his peers.

Whether working with a trio, performing solo, or in one of his easier-listening projects, Jamal never fails to radiate an electric energy, sharp and immediate. From the opening moments of his trio performance of Jobim's "Mahna de Carnaval," recorded during the eighties for the Japanese album *Ahmad Jamal/Gary Burton in Concert*, his take on bossa nova is both original and elemental, with sparkling juxtapositions of fiery lines over an extended trill, adventurous chordal sweeps up from the bass into a brawny midrange climax, booming octaves—and even an extended quote from "My Favorite Things" over ominous stalking harmonies.

This same mix of urgency and fluency distinguishes his solo introduction on "Make Someone Happy," from the 1985 *Live at the Montreal Jazz Festival* album. Here, his phrases push impatiently through quick, splashy arpeggios into steely, dissonant chords. There's always a sense of shoving against the beat, even in Jamal's more spare passages: After a few spacious moments, a lightning run, a string-rattling surge of two-handed chords, an unlikely boogie-woogie crawl, or a statement of the theme exploding unexpectedly in the bass, keep listeners, as well as fellow musicians, in a state of high alert. Even in more intimate circumstances, as in his trio rendition of "All the Things You Are" from the 1992 album *Chicago Revisited*, Jamal constantly kicks at the rhythm section with soft chords dropped just before each beat in the left hand. Alternately, on the same album, he builds a similar tension by comping steadily on all four beats while playing out-of-time or accelerating figures through the changes of "Blue Gardenia."

Jamal's humor and compressed emotional intensity explode on his rendition of "St. Louis Blues," from the 1994 Ray Brown album *Some of My Best Friends are . . . the Piano Players*. Brown plays a free-tempo unaccompanied intro, which leads to a swinging riff as a cue for Jamal's entrance. The pianist comes blasting in with some stinging staccato chords, a quick tremolo, and then a solo that immediately leaps into contrasting keys, thunders through descending chords into the bass, riffs like a big band, and abruptly interrupts itself into a wild series of II–V modulations that climb through parallel lines into more exuberant extemporizations. After a couple of choruses Jamal's exertions begin to sound a little repetitive, and his quote from "Now's the Time" a little predictable; still, when Brown comes back in for a bass chorus, there's a sense that a hurricane has blown through town and suddenly out to sea, leaving a kind of stunned calm in its wake.

At times this headfirst approach tests the limits of good taste. Jamal's performance of "'Round Midnight," on *Montreal Jazz Festival*, is all jerky bursts and melodramatic crescendos, with little attention paid to the virtues of working closer to the written material. Even on an unaccompanied examination of his own "Piano Solo 11," from the 1987 album *Crystal*, Jamal can't resist leaving his otherwise focused performance for an oddly superfluous and repetitive figure in sixths at one of the cadences. It's neither virtuosic nor enlightening; instead, it seems a product of habitual occasional ornamentation.

More often, Jamal's solo performances are models of balance. His 1995 release *I Remember Duke, Hoagy, & Strayhorn* includes some stunning unaccompanied episodes. Consider, for instance, his lead-in to "In a Sentimental Mood." Taken at free tempo, Jamal's improvisation begins on the bridge; by the third bar he is already extending the harmonies through some tricky II–V movement, which become a motif for more abstract impressions of the same section of the tune as well as a setup for the harmonic movement at the beginning of the verse. This section he approaches over a pedal on the dominant, which provides the foundation for some gauzy Impressionistic textures beneath an approximation of the theme. At the end of the verse Jamal surprises with an unadorned triad; its simplicity allows him to move the voicing through a spiral of changes that function as a transition to another examination of the bridge and, eventually, a connect-the-dots pointillistic passage that articulates the last few bars before bassist Ephriam Wolfolk and drummer Arti Dixson make their entrance.

The evidence is there, of Jamal's willingness to stretch out more than he used to, as well as his enduring ability to temper these indulgences with a supreme regard for his material. In this respect he does homage to the spirit of his boyhood hero Liszt, and claims a comparable place for himself as an artist driven by pride and humility, technique and a mastery of technique, a fidelity to tradition and a fascination with learning from what lies beyond its borders.

15. OSCAR PETERSON

Born: August 15, 1925, Montreal, Quebec

No jazz artist has been honored more than Oscar Peterson, a multiple Grammy winner, Companion of the Order of Canada, Officer of French Arts and Letters, chancellor of York University, recipient of Japan's Praemium Imperiale, and a winner of the Glenn Gould Prize and its attendant $50,000.

These tributes mark Peterson's significance as the last link to the golden era of mainstream piano, with Art Tatum as his direct antecedent. His language derives from swing, with a dusting of bebop and blues and an occasional nod toward stride. He is certainly familiar with post-fifties developments, but his interest extends only insofar as they can be folded into his aesthetic. A Peterson performance of "'Round Midnight" is more about dazzling listeners than exploring the composer's intentions.

For Peterson is a throwback: a dynamo whose performance philosophy roots in the old "carving contest" mentality. It is instructive to go back to his Carnegie Hall debut in September 1949, as a surprise guest at one of Norman Granz's Jazz At The Philharmonic extravaganzas. Following the producer's introduction, the young pianist comes out and, with Ray Brown on bass, begins blowing like crazy on "Fine and Dandy." In comparison with most of his later work, he sounds a little nervous . . . after all, as a newcomer from Canada trying to impress a tough New York crowd, he had a lot on the line. But Peterson succeeds, using the formula that would serve him well in the decades to come: blazing chops, driving rhythm.

Almost immediately after that performance, Peterson settled into a long routine of playing on-stage and in the studio with an unshakable sense of assurance. There was nothing tentative about him;

to the contrary, his light-speed lines, rumbling tremolos, and emphatic cadences sounded like challenges, proud and defiant. But who was Peterson's target? At first, it would seem to be his peers, all of whom cleared quickly out of the way and acknowledged him as the new boss on the block. There was nobody, especially from his generation, who could match him in either speed or power.

But another obstacle stood before him. As Peterson began smoking the competition, some of his colleagues wondered out loud where the fire was. Miles Davis mused to one interviewer that Peterson played the blues as if he had studied rather than lived the style. And Thelonious Monk, when treated to a Peterson disc as part of a *Down Beat* Blindfold Test, responded by announcing that he felt a sudden need to use the toilet.

Of course, Davis and Monk weren't known for velocity on their instruments, so perhaps there's a whiff of sour grapes here. On the other hand, for all his command of the keyboard, not to mention the compositional strengths he has exhibited in both small- and large-form works, Peterson cannot be considered a visionary along the lines of Davis, Monk, or another of his occasional critics, Charles Mingus. In the funky figurations he employs repeatedly, in the supersonic stride patterns that he loves to toss into the rhythmic mix, he looks toward the past . . . not as a scholar along the lines of Dick Hyman, or as a student seeking insight into an emerging sensibility, like Marcus Roberts. For Peterson, the past is his home, a fact that reassures listeners of conservative temperament and maybe repels others more drawn to substance than surface attractions.

In life as in music, Peterson is a formidable figure, gracious and elegant, yet stubborn and never inclined to refuse a challenge. His response to those who call him a musical exhibitionist has been to keep playing as he always has. Few artists have recorded as prolifically as Peterson, and those who can rival his output fall short of his consistency. Earl Hines and Erroll Garner could complete an album's worth of solo piano material in a day, though much of what they'd hurl onto tape had an unfortunate slap-dash quality. Not so with Peterson . . . or perhaps not so obviously so: His harmonic eloquence, locomotive momentum, and flash tended to distract from more subtle artistic issues. He could be as repetitive as anyone else, but at a more sophisticated level.

Peterson was the fourth of five children born to immigrants from the British West Indies and the Virgin Islands. He took his first piano lessons from his father, an amateur musician who worked as a porter on the Canadian Pacific Railroad. Oscar was a diligent, even fanatic student; from grade school through high school, he routinely practiced 12 hours a day, and sometimes pushed it up to 18. Even the early onset of arthritis in his hands didn't stop him; in typical fashion, Peterson hunkered down and played through pain that would persist from his teenage years through the rest of his life.

In 1939 the young pianist won an amateur competition sponsored by the Canadian Broadcasting Corporation; the prize included a weekly radio show of his own, *Fifteen Minutes Piano Rambling*, broadcast locally in Montreal over CKAC. Word spread quickly about this new phenomenon, who began playing on national radio shows like *The Happy Gang* and *Light Up and Listen*. After a final year's worth of intensive study with Paul de Marky, a Hungarian whose teacher had learned directly from Liszt, Peterson dropped out of school at age sixteen to pursue music full-time.

His first major gig was as a member of the Johnny Holmes Orchestra in 1944, whose lineup included future trumpet star Maynard Ferguson, with whom he had first played in high school. Inspired by Nat

"King" Cole's trio performances, Peterson put a group together with Ozzie Roberts on bass and Clarence Jones on drums; from 1945 through '49 they recorded for RCA Victor in Canada and toured nationally several times.

The real breakthrough came in 1949. Peterson was then working steadily at the Alberta Lounge. A number of major jazz artists heard him there while passing through Montreal; several, including Count Basie and Jimmie Lunceford, urged him to leave Canada and tackle the big time in New York. Peterson declined repeatedly until one fateful night when he crossed paths with Norman Granz.

Already an established jazz producer, Granz had taken care of his business for the day and was riding to the airport when he happened to hear Peterson on the radio, performing on his regular Alberta Lounge broadcast. Though he had already listened to and written off some of the pianist's boogie-woogie recordings, Granz recognized that there was more than rolling eighth-notes in the young pianist's arsenal. The taxi doubled back toward the venue, and Granz made it in time to meet the artist and book him for the walk-on appearance noted earlier at Carnegie Hall.

Everything fell into place pretty quickly from that point. *Down Beat* gave its pianist of the year award to Peterson in 1950, and repeated the honor annually through 1955. Granz, now signed on as his manager, kept his calendar full. At one engagement in Washington, D.C., Peterson met his hero, Art Tatum, who would soon make it clear that he regarded the Canadian as his heir apparent. Indeed, when the young pianist betrayed a rare set of nerves at having to play before his mentor, Tatum gave him blunt advice: "Get over it. Even if it means having to hate me."

Peterson hit his stride, so to speak, with his new trio, which he put together at Granz's suggestion in 1952. The lineup featured bassist Ray Brown and drummer Charlie Smith, but with Brown and Peterson generating more propulsion on their own than most big bands, it made sense to replace Smith with a second melodic voice, provided initially by Irving Ashby, who had already chalked up trio experience on guitar with Nat "King" Cole. After a short while Barney Kessel took Ashby's place, and a series of highly swinging sides followed on Granz's Verve label. In 1953 Herb Ellis came in as the new guitarist in time for their Japanese tour.

When Ellis left, Peterson shifted back to a bass-and-drums formula, at first with Gene Gammage, who was soon followed by Ed Thigpen in 1959. For the next six years this combination worked exhaustively; in one year alone, 1962, they recorded 11 albums, seven of them in the studio, in addition to backing Ella Fitzgerald and Louis Armstrong on their popular duo release. When Thigpen left in 1966, followed by Brown two years later, the era of classic Peterson trios came to a close.

But there was much more to come, beginning with his first solo album in 1968, extensive work with other trios throughout the seventies, and an association with Granz's new Pablo label that began in 1973 and ended with a live album cut at the Westwood Playhouse in Los Angeles in November 1986. With Pablo, Peterson functioned essentially as house pianist on sessions that reflected Granz's mix-and-match strategies. The catalog included dates with Sarah Vaughan, Joe Pass (with whom he also played several tracks on clavichord), Count Basie, Dizzy Gillespie, and Roy Eldridge.

The Pablo discography offers contradictory insights into Peterson. When working alone or leading his own group, he often played to the crowd, a tendency represented clearly by his solo break on "Caravan," from *Oscar Peterson Plays Duke Ellington*, with a ridiculously and inappropriately fast stride catapulting a fusillade of right-hand notes with much of the facility but none of the finesse that typified Tatum's performances. At a more medium clip, unable to rely on raw speed to impress, he frequently strung blues or funk cliches together in his solos, as in "Lady Be Good," after a Milt Jackson vibraphone break, from *Two of the Few*.

But accompaniment often focused Peterson. When backing Ella Fitzgerald on "Mean to Me," from *Ella and Oscar*, he keeps a swinging pulse alive, provides harmonic support, and scatters counter-figures that never disrupt the vocal line or steal the spotlight. For all the fireworks that illuminate his improvisations, many of Peterson's best moments occur when he defers to other soloists. Arguments rage over his exhibitionistic solos, but there's little dispute over his stature as one of the most sensitive and responsive accompanists in this or any other era of jazz.

Following hip surgery in November 1992, Peterson entered a period of declining health. Onstage at the Blue Note in May 1993, he suffered a stroke that forced him into three months of intensive physical therapy, as well as counseling to deal with depression and anger. Ever the battler, Peterson returned to the stage in July 1994, though with a lingering impairment in his left hand. It is not surprising that he has trimmed back his performing schedule, but it's equally predictable that he would fight to keep himself before the public, as long as he could meet his own standards as a player.

In June 1999 he appeared with his frequent partner, bassist Niels-Henning Ørsted Pedersen, and guitarist Ulf Wakenius, at Carnegie Hall, on the fiftieth anniversary of his debut there. Chances are no one was more sure that he would triumph there once again than Peterson himself.

16. PHINEAS NEWBORN

Born: December 14, 1931, Whiteville, Tennessee
Died: May 26, 1989, Memphis, Tennessee

Intimidation is out of fashion. It's all about musicians helping each other along these days. But not so long ago, the carving contest was the razor hidden in the kid-glove bonhomie of jazz. If you could scare your competition, you were the best on the block—and, bottom line, you kept your gig.

Which explains the impression that Phineas Newborn made as a young pianist. At each of his gigs, he accepted the challenge of being compared with the greatest virtuosos who had preceded him. Neither Tatum nor Peterson seemed to intimidate him, and certainly not any of the players from his own generation. You could hear it in his music, with its extraordinary velocity and rush of inspired ideas.

The critics certainly took note. Writing for *Down Beat* in 1956, Ralph Gleason observed, "He is one of the most impressive pianists to emerge in recent years, a gifted technician, a startling improviser, and a musician with a well-developed harmonic and rhythmic sense." More to the point, Gleason pointed out, "He has a command of the instrument to make other pianists weep, and an ability to say whatever he wishes."

Only five years later, Leonard Feather concluded that, "Bearing in mind that Bernard Peiffer is French and Oscar Peterson Canadian, it would not be extravagant to claim that Phineas has no equal among American jazz pianists, from any standpoint, technical or esthetic."

By all accounts Newborn made his point not in attitude but through performance alone. When there were other pianists in the house, he would often make it a point to begin his set by sliding his right hand into his pocket and playing the first several tunes with just the left. That might be bad form today, but not so long ago this was the stuff that made legends—that and an early decline and demise.

Born about an hour outside of Memphis, Newborn was raised in a musical household; his father was a drummer and a bandleader. With his father's pianist as his first teacher, young Phineas quickly learned his way around the instrument, then expanded his musical education with theory and arranging lessons from Onzie Horne. He was playing R&B gigs with his brother Calvin in his early teens, as well as sessions for B. B. King and other local luminaries. In high school Newborn played a variety of brass instruments and contributed arrangements to the band book.

After graduation, he spent the summer gigging with Lionel Hampton, then left to study music at Tennessee State University. Even as an undergrad he attracted notice: Passing through Memphis, Count Basie heard the young pianist and began a friendship that would soon prove significant. After leaving school in 1952, Newborn worked again with Hampton before getting his draft notice. Two years later, discharge papers in hand, he returned to Memphis to spend more time with his father's band and, subsequently, put his first quartet together.

Newborn's peak years began in 1956, when Basie helped bring him to New York for his first album sessions. He formed a duo in 1958 with bassist Charles Mingus, with whom he collaborated in creating the soundtrack for the John Cassavetes film *Shadows*. A European tour followed later that year, with bassist Oscar Pettiford and drummer Kenny Clarke.

By this time Newborn was fully accredited in the high-velocity school of jazz pianists. Unlike the icons of that school—Art Tatum, Oscar Peterson—who descended more or less directly from stride piano, Newborn was disinclined to treat his left hand as a rhythm generator. But neither could he be connected to a bebop lineage; his fidelity to written themes, and the upbeat feel that permeated almost all of his playing, placed him closer to Ahmad Jamal and other pianists for whom swing and melodic integrity were defining elements.

Newborn's awareness of the relationship between his improvising and the tune is evident even in a bop context, in which other pianists treat the theme purely as a jumping-off point for their own blowing. On "The Blessing," an Ornette Coleman tune recorded in 1964 for *The Newborn Touch*, he uses the quick triplet figure that begins the theme as a recurring motif in his solo: His first notes are a slowed-down reference to this rhythmic element, with frequent reiterations throughout the next several verses. At times Newborn dissects the figure, changing it from a tiny sweep of consecutive notes by tossing one note in the sequence up an octave. (Notice, by the way, the electric communication between Newborn and drummer Frank Butler, as they uncannily extemporized a counter-rhythmic figure in unison at the end of the second verse.)

There is flash in Newborn's performances, but there is also fire. Unlike Tatum and such modern disciples as Adam Makowicz, Newborn worked best within rhythm sections, perhaps because swinging is more fundamental to him than, to be blunt, showing off. Yet in unaccompanied settings, he often succumbed to the temptation to overplay. His performance of "The Man I Love," recorded in 1976 for *Look Out—Phineas is Back!*, is an eruption of heavily pedaled arpeggios, florid runs, and indelicately pounded variations on the melody. Because most of it is played out of tempo, this track is really more about effect than swing—and when Newborn does finally begin a stride beat midway through the piece, it has a heavy, lumbering feel, as well as more than a few glitched notes.

Compare this to "Manteca," recorded with bassist Paul Chambers and drummer Philly Joe Jones in 1961 for *A World of Piano!* Here, Newborn explodes into his solo with hair-raising, rapid-fire unisons in the bass and high midrange—not to dazzle, but to kick off his improvisation with extra bite. Indeed, by the time he hits the bridge, he has broken his solo down to a single octave repeated carefully in the right hand; by holding back here, he widens his options for the verses that follow. In these he mixes and matches, moving from blinding 32nd-note triplets through bumpy dissonances, a Latin allusion or two, and some good old blues licks. All of these episodes are delivered with boundless invention and enthusiasm; as with Tatum, it seems that there is nothing that Newborn cannot play. The difference here is Newborn, in a group setting, also sounds incapable of not swinging.

And Newborn didn't always follow conventional bop practice in pursuing the groove. On "A Walkin' Thing," from *The Newborn Touch*, the pianist embraces the plodding quarter-note beat with jackhammered, heavily pedaled triplet chords at the beginning, after which he states the theme over a quarter-note left-hand chords. The arrangement is faithful to the title of the piece, a potential limitation that Newborn works around by moving his thematic statement up an octave and fashioning a gradual crescendo in the last eight bars of the opening. Then, starting his solo, the pianist begins with a clever sixteenth-note motif divided into irregular groups; he then breaks these down into simpler variations, which in turn reduce to a right-hand trill around the dominant against the steady tread of chords in the left hand. The trill device allows Newborn to bring the verse to a close with some blues inflections; these he contrasts dramatically on the bridge with a loud left-hand repetition of the dominant in the bass. The entire performance is carefully sectioned and then unified by a playfully humorous juxtaposition of contrasts.

Another difference lies in the priorities assigned to harmony and rhythm. Though Newborn possessed the harmonic vocabulary of the best postbop players, he generally gave little attention to chords except as elements for emphasis within a rhythmic statement. Like Tatum, he preferred linear to chordal movement, but where Tatum took this to an extreme of contrapuntal sophistication, Newborn usually restricted himself to unison lines (or, more often than Tatum, to simultaneous and rhythmically independent linear improvisations). The meticulous between-the-beat comps during the first verse of his solo on "Daahoud," from the *World of Piano!* session, reflect an urgency, and a capability of feeding off the bass and drums, that Tatum seldom displayed.

Though he enjoyed a short resurgence in the seventies, Newborn faced physical and emotional problems after moving to Los Angeles in 1961 that would precipitate a long decline in his ability and willingness to perform. Eventually he returned to Memphis to live in relative seclusion during his last ten years, leaving behind a compelling but abbreviated discography and the inevitable speculations of what might have been.

In Walked Bud

17. BUD POWELL

Born: September 27, 1924, New York, New York
Died: July 31, 1966, New York, New York

Genius and anguish were the twin devils that fed on the soul of Bud Powell. Together they accounted for his ferocious piano style, which galvanized the jazz world for about seven years, and together they pushed him into a tragic tailspin through a string of asylums, drove him to seek refuge in Europe, and left him dead at the age of 41.

Even during his lifetime Powell was hounded by devoted fans who seemed eager to lock their hero in a suffocating aura of romantic doom. One is struck by the almost necrophilic flavor running through the articles and liner notes written about him by his contemporaries. The tormented artist was still playing and fighting for emotional equilibrium when one critic wrote, "Bud Powell . . . has influenced whole scores of pianists. He has no influence over himself. Only the final tragedy is missing: He is still alive." No doubt Powell, during his declining years, had many opportunities to read play-by-play accounts of his own disintegration.

Yet in the excruciatingly public life that Powell led, his breakdowns, his spells in mental institutions, and his wildly erratic playing from the mid fifties on were impossible to ignore. The physical deterioration was apparent: His build, lithe and sensually angular during his early years, had ballooned and sagged by the time he returned to the States after his self-imposed French exile in 1966. Journalists and fans who greeted him between sets or on the street were stunned by his obliviousness to the world around him. To people in the know, Bud Powell had no secrets. The love that they felt for him as a musician and as a man perhaps made it impossible for them to sit through his decline as silent witnesses.

Bud's tragedy and his music are fused together in jazz legend. By trying to separate these elements, we can better understand both. The question of whether he would have played with the intensity he exuded in his prime without the stinging impetus of his own neuroses is not relevant. Maybe the same anxieties that distorted his music toward the end of his life pushed it to the levels of frenzy that dazzled listeners when he began making his impact in the mid-forties. No matter. It is his music, not his psyche, that history should consider.

The jazz piano world reeled under the force of Powell's innovations. To this day, he remains the most important pillar in the structure of modern improvisational piano. Those elements that we have come to take for granted—the domination of the right hand over the left, the long single-line solos, the practice of implying harmonies through melodic improvisation rather than stating them directly through chords—were either formulated by Powell, transferred by him from the work of horn players into the language of the piano, or borrowed from earlier piano pioneers and revoiced along the challenging lines of bebop. Powell and Thelonious Monk were the two leading pianists in bop as it emerged in the forties. Eventually, after years of skepticism, the jazz world would accept Monk's economies and integrate the most palatable aspects of his vision into its own mainstream vocabulary. Powell, whose technique was more polished than Monk's and whose passion was more transparent, needed no such grace period. He was the seminal bebop pianist.

It must be added that Powell's left hand was one of his most underrated weapons. Though most of his fireworks exploded in the upper range of the keyboard, Powell's voicings in the low end were far from accidental. Over a tonic chord in his full-speed-ahead chorus on "Get Happy," from *The Genius of Bud Powell*, the bottom note in the left hand rises from the dominant to the major seventh, then sinks back toward the dominant without bothering to resolve; that, set against the repeated dominant at the top of the left-hand chord, creates a tension that's almost subliminal beneath his flashy interpolation of the theme. Abundant recorded evidence of this sort, along with anecdotes about how Powell once duplicated a Tatum right-hand improvisation note-for-note in his left hand, or earned Tatum's congratulations for playing a southpaw rendition of "Sometimes I'm Happy" one night at Birdland, put to rest any rumors that a technical deficiency accounted for his approach.

Powell at his peak was compared frequently to Tatum. Both men boasted formidable chops, and on ballads especially Powell often emulated the older pianist's rococo embellishments. But their musical temperaments differed radically. Tatum was criticized for over-emphasizing technique, for relying on his thorough command of voice-leading, counterpoint, and other formal devices to dazzle his peers and audiences. His improvisations always had a compositional quality, as if more attention had been paid to building a flawless musical structure than to allowing room for inspired disruptions.

Powell took exactly the opposite tack. Though hardly oblivious to structure, he poked and prodded the songs he played with sudden off-beat jabs in the low register, tantalizing interruptions of the rhythmic flow in the improvised line, and dissonant leaps that twisted his melody into a moonscape of peaks and valleys. His love of feverish tempos, even after his technique had worn beyond the point where he could keep up with the rhythm section, inspired countless young players at an emotional depth that Tatum seldom explored. Bassist Ray Brown, who frequently accompanied Powell, was so exhilarated by the fervor of the pianist's performance one night that he put his instrument down in mid-phrase and rushed from the bandstand, hugging himself to keep from shouting out loud.

Echoes of Monk also permeate Powell's work. Time and again we hear the whole-tone runs, emblematic of Monk, though Powell fragments them and mixes them more frequently with other modes or scales. Their piano tones, percussive and bright, are quite similar. And their roots were intertwined in the network of New York clubs from which bebop would emerge. But while Monk came to town from North Carolina at the age of seven, Powell was a native.

Born in New York City and named Earl by his parents, he could claim a musical lineage. His grandfather was a musician, and his father, William Powell, worked professionally as a stride pianist. His brothers were also musical; William, who was older, played trumpet and violin, while younger brother Richie, who picked up the rudiments from Bud, was a promising pianist until his death in the auto accident that also claimed the life of trumpeter Clifford Brown in 1956.

Bud began taking lessons at the age of six. His early grounding was classical; though his preference was Mozart, he studied all the masters from Bach to the twentieth century. Later, he would acknowledge this background in some of his compositions, borrowing from his early technical exercises in "Bud on Bach" and giving a nod to Prokofiev in "Glass Enclosure." In those early days he displayed little interest in jazz; as an altar boy at St. Charles Cathedral, he tried his hand at playing written pieces on the organ, and with his boyhood friend Elmo Hope, later a respected jazz pianist in his own right, he would pass the hours listening to classical records.

The jazz bug bit when Bud reached his mid-teens. His first inspiration was Billy Kyle, who played piano with bassist John Kirby's innovative sextet. When his older brother organized a band in 1938, Bud joined up. Though underage, he played with the group in club dates on Coney Island. The experience whetted his appetite for the jazz life: By age 15 he had dropped out of DeWitt Clinton High School to devote himself full-time to music. Powell was playing solo gigs at the Place in Greenwich Village and the Chicken Coop, run by actor Canada Lee, in Harlem by 1940. Within a short time he was taking jobs throughout Manhattan and the Bronx.

More important, Powell was moving into that community of musicians who were laying the groundwork for the revolution that would shake the foundations of jazz in the next few years. Bebop, or bop, the onomatopoeic name by which this style would soon be named, was concocted at Minton's Playhouse, a jazz club on West 118th Street, where freethinking musicians gathered for after-hours jam sessions. Gradually, in part to keep less skilled musicians from sitting in, the house band there, which featured Thelonious Monk, drummer Kenny Clarke, and other proto-boppers, evolved a style based on a system of syncopations, chord structures, articulations, and melody lines that, despite their internal logic, came across as incomprehensible to the typical swing-type performer, especially when played at the finger-breaking tempos these modernists favored. Bop was too unrepetitive and too fast to dance to, too compelling to ignore. In the wee hours jams at Minton's, jazz began its trek from the dance hall to the concert hall.

Powell was on the periphery of the early Minton's scene. He was first taken to the club by Monk, whom he had met that night in a bar. Grateful for the older pianist's support and impressed by his moody, stark style at a time when few musicians took it seriously, Powell soon formed a rehearsal band that filled its book with Monk charts, which he later supplemented with his own arrangements. When this group split up, Powell went to work with the Sunset Royal Serenaders, which featured trumpeter/singer Valaida Snow. During this same period he was making his homage to Tatum by joining Ram Ramirez, Marlowe Morris, Clyde Hart, Dorothy Donegan, Don Lambert, and other rookie pianists in "carving sessions" at the Hollywood Club before Tatum's arrival, at which time they would clear out of the way and absorb his intricate improvisatory fantasies.

By the age of 18 Powell had already jammed at Minton's with Charlie Parker, guitarist Charlie Christian, and the other bop pioneers. The following year brought him a gig with Cootie Williams, whose solo work on trumpet had been a highlight of the Duke Ellington band. Though Powell was 18 at the time, a rumor was soon circulating that Williams had to have himself appointed the young pianist's guardian to receive permission to take him out on the road.

Powell recorded several sides with the Williams group, starting with eight tunes in a sextet session on January 4, 1944. Later, on August 22, 1944, he cut four songs—"Is You Is or Is You Ain't," "Somebody's Gotta Go," "Royal Garden Blues," and Monk's "'Round Midnight"—with the full band. Most critics agree that while his style was far from mature on these dates, and while the shadow of Art Tatum loomed long over his filigreed ballad treatments, there were clear signs of things to come.

Another rumor was spreading during this time, that Williams, as Powell's guardian, wouldn't let him leave the band to accept Dizzy Gillespie's invitation to play with him at the Onyx, then one of the most happening spots on "the Street," as the exciting club district on 52nd Street was called. Gillespie did want Powell at the piano for this historic gig, the first appearance by a bop outfit at this generally swing-oriented venue, but when Powell couldn't accept the invite, Gillespie opened without a pianist, though he later hired George Wallington for that role.

Still, Powell was soon a familiar figure on the Street. Late in 1943 he had performed at the Stable, another swing bistro that had converted to bop, with Kenny Clarke. By 1945 he had appeared in various establishments there with John Kirby, in whose band his first idol Billy Kyle had played, as well as with Gillespie, saxophonists Don Byas and Allen Eager, drummer Sid Catlett, and others. By 1946 he had established himself as the dominant pianist on the bop scene.

But personal troubles were already clouding his performances. In 1945 he was arrested in Philadelphia's Broad Street Station for drunkenness and disturbing the peace. Reports were soon circulating that the police had beaten him severely on the head, and that his mother had to come down from New York to retrieve him. In any event, he was subsequently sent to Pilgrim State Hospital for ten weeks of treatment—the first of three confinements to mental hospitals that Powell was to experience in the forties alone.

There were other hints of his future erratic behavior. In November of that year he was called to play on Charlie Parker's first record date as a leader, but when the session began Powell was nowhere to be found. In the end Dizzy Gillespie and the Monkish stylist Argonne Thornton, who later took the name Sadik Hakim, covered the piano part in his absence. This no-show habit would become more pronounced as Powell's problems deepened.

During the late forties his musical prowess and mental difficulties grew simultaneously. When he was at his best, he was a chillingly effective player. His work with saxophonist Sonny Stitt on some dates from 1949 and '50, released later on the Prestige album *Sonny Stitt*, are typical. Most of the cuts begin with an unaccompanied eight-bar piano intro, which Powell treats as a highly compressed miniature improvisation, unrelated to the melody of the piece being played. Obviously it was more important to Powell that the piano act as a match for igniting the band's performance than that it state any particular theme, and he excelled at this incendiary task. Once bassist Curly Russell and drummer Max Roach tear into each tune, Powell drops into the rhythm section, not as a steady swing-style comper but as an additional percussionist, dropping accents irregularly where needed. Only occasionally does he mirror Tatum's ensemble technique, by adorning Stitt's solos with fast background runs, as in "Strike Up the Band." Always there is a sense of terrific energy being reined in, especially through Powell's frequent use of the fifth of the tonic chord as a pivot point while the chord changes of the song spin toward resolution.

In his solos, Powell plays with razor-sharp articulation. There are no botched notes; every minor second is apparently an intentional dissonance. He uses practically no sustain pedal, preferring to spell out his precise runs without any blur. His trills are clean and well-placed; in the first take of "Fine and Dandy" they suspend, rather than interrupt, the rhythm to give the line a breathtaking aerial trajectory.

And there is humor in the many quotes he interjects: His snippet from "Turkey in the Straw" from the second take of "Fine and Dandy" inspires Stitt to kick his solo off with a quote of his own.

Throughout the late forties and early fifties Powell generally freelanced, playing sessions with a variety of colleagues. He cut several all-star discs with Stitt, trumpeters Kenny Dorham and Fats Navarro, saxophonist Dexter Gordon, bassist Oscar Pettiford, and drummer Kenny Clarke, among many others. He guested with trombonist J. J. Johnson for a Savoy project, and for Navarro and saxophonist Sonny Rollins on a Blue Note record in 1949.

Yet the problems continued. In November 1947 Powell suffered a nervous breakdown. This time the 23-year-old pianist was packed off to Creedmore Hospital in New York for 18 months, where he was subjected to electro-shock therapy. Within ten weeks of his release in April 1949 he had recorded several fiery trio sides with bassist Ray Brown and drummer Max Roach, including his own compositions "Tempus Fugit," "Celia," and "Strictly Confidential," all of them now on *The Genius of Bud Powell, Vol. 1.*

Bud Powell, 1949: Ray Brown was so exhilarated by a Powell performance that he rushed from the bandstand, hugging himself to keep from shouting out loud.

Then, in the summer of 1951, Powell's fragile recovery was dealt a sharp blow when he was arrested once again, this time for possession of narcotics. Locked up in the grim New York prison known as the Tombs, he went berserk and had to be returned to Pilgrim State Hospital for more electro-shock treatments. After a year he was sent back to Creedmore State Hospital, where he languished until his release in February 1953 to the custody of Oscar Goodstein, the manager of Birdland, who became his temporary legal guardian. It was in '53 that he wrote and recorded the haunting "Glass Enclosure," which was probably inspired by the isolation he experienced during this latest long recovery.

From this point on, the deterioration in Powell's music began to accelerate. Immediately after leaving Creedmore, he played a trio date at Birdland with Oscar Pettiford and drummer Roy Haynes, later released on the Vee Jay album *Bud Powell: 1953*. Though he occasionally breaks into the double-timed rapid runs that marked his earlier work, there is a halting quality on "Lover Come Back to Me" and other tracks, where short bursts replace his formerly coherent long strings of notes. The ideas seem a bit less daring, and a clinker or two crops up where none would have been heard before. Of course there are dazzling moments, such as the tumbling triplet runs in "I Want to Be Happy," but overall Powell's chops seem a little tired, which is certainly understandable; during his confinement he suffered some physical abuse and was allowed to play the piano only once a week. Still, on the historic *Jazz at Massey Hall* album, a live concert taped in Toronto in May 1953 with Parker, Gillespie, Roach, bassist Charles Mingus, and Powell, Bud turns in a solid, if uninspired, performance, whatever the truth of the rumor that he was intoxicated at the time. But the rustiness lingered in his hands. For the rest of his days he was able to shake it only intermittently.

Perhaps to compensate for this, Powell began filtering greater doses of Monk's style into his own work. From the first cut on *The Genius of Bud Powell, Vol. 2*, "Someone to Watch Over Me," recorded with bassist Lloyd Trotman and drummer Art Blakey on January 13, 1955, we hear dramatic adjustments: The touch, the glitched octaves, the whole-tone runs, the rhythmic looseness where tightness had once been the rule, all connect more to Monk than to early Bud. The cynical ragged stride in "Mediocre," the tempo that exceeds his faltering grasp in "I Know That You Know," the apocalyptically simple "It Never Entered My Mind," and the downright frightening sloppiness and disinterest of "I Get a Kick Out of You" paint a darker picture. The latter cut, especially, sounds like the noodlings of an alcoholic, and an ungifted one at that; it makes one want to find a window, open it, and let some fresh air in.

Powell's disintegration was noted by many during the fifties, when he led his own trio on most of his gigs. In *Jazz Masters of the Forties*, Ira Gitler recounts some examples of his increasingly bizarre behavior on the bandstand. "Bud was always on the borderline," is how Dexter Gordon put it to Gitler. And in Whitney Balliett's book *Ecstasy at the Onion*, drummer Elvin Jones went into more detail about Powell during this period.

"Bud was very shaky, very sick," he recalled. "He was almost completely withdrawn. . . . All he needed was a couple of drinks and he'd go berserk. I rationed him to two bottles of beer a day and he was all right. But every once in a while he'd get away from me—like once, when some people poured some wine into him and he was found the next morning in an alley in his underwear with even his shirt and tie stolen. Then one night at Birdland during an intermission he took off, and I didn't see him again for two years."

The death of Charlie "Bird" Parker may have seemed like an omen to Powell. Like the troubled pianist, Parker mixed musical genius with unpredictable self-destructive episodes. Bird recognized the similarities between himself and Powell: On more than one occasion he said, "I taught him everything, including how to be crazy." Powell was at the keyboard for Parker's last gig, at Birdland on March 4, 1955. It was a macabre performance, with the two men verbally abusing each other between songs until Parker suddenly launched into a frenzied tirade. Powell, shaken badly, backed down and pleaded, "Don't hit me, Bird." Parker stopped, then tears welled in his eyes as he quietly answered, "I ain't goin' to hit you, Bud. Never." Eight days later, Parker was dead.

For Powell the crusher came in 1956, with the death of his younger brother Richie. Clearly it was time to get away from an environment that had only been eating away at what was left of his emotional stability. So after a spell in Brooklyn's King's County Hospital, Bud, his wife and guardian Altevia, whom he called Buttercup, and his son Johnny left the States for the more hospitable atmosphere of Paris. As if to celebrate the departure, he recorded a final Blue Note album, *The Scene Changes*, which featured some decidedly upbeat cuts—his first in years.

At least he was able to enjoy a respite. The jazz lovers of Paris gave him an unrestrained welcome, and were hip enough to reports of his habits not to foist drinks and drugs on him. A teeming field of talent awaited him as well, including old friends like Kenny Clarke and Oscar Pettiford, who had become European expatriates. Shortly after setting in Paris, Powell, Clarke, and French bassist Pierre Michelot formed a trio, calling themselves the Three Bosses. With this and other three-piece outfits, Powell became a fixture at the Blue Note club. He lost that gig late in 1961, possibly because of a ruckus that occurred there one night when he drank an entire bottle of cognac. Later the Blue Note would hire him back, but after that incident Bud and Buttercup felt it best for him to withdraw to a hospital in Switzerland, where once again the shock therapy was resumed.

This time, after emerging from treatment, Powell showed strong signs of recovery. He and his family left at once for a tour of Scandinavia, highlighted by a successful four-week stint at a new Stockholm jazz club, backed by a Swedish bassist and drummer, and the filming of a short documentary about the pianist by Jorgen Leth. The Powells spent Easter in a two-room suite at Nyberogatan's Castle Hotel. Following their stay there, they went back to Paris, where Powell played for a short while at the Blue Note before moving on to the Whiskey Jazz Club in Madrid, a series of engagements in Denmark, and three more weeks in Stockholm.

Once again, though, in late 1962, Powell's health took a turn for the worse. He was playing again early in 1963, when he and Buttercup participated in another film project, *The Amazing Bud Powell*, a 30-minute documentary by Jamaican novelist Lebert Bethune. But in mid '63 tuberculosis in both lungs sent him off to Bouffemont Sanatorium outside of Paris; the medical bills were paid through funds raised at benefit concerts in America and Europe.

During his recovery Powell came to rely on a French friend, a commercial artist named Francis Paudras, for support. Paudras, who had kept time with brushes and paper on some recordings Powell made in his apartment, was instrumental in helping Buttercup nurse the ailing pianist back to health. Again, he seemed to be regaining his strength, and within a year he was talking about doing a return visit to the States. Buttercup and Paudras were apprehensive about it, but in the end all the arrangements were made, with the understanding that Paudras would travel with Bud as his guardian. The plan was to open a month-long stint at Birdland on August 25, 1964, followed by further jobs around the U.S. and Japan before heading back to France.

In truth, Powell was in no shape to travel. He still had a severe drinking problem: Often he would walk to and from his Blue Note gigs in order to spend his taxi money on red wine at the Café Echaude. His mental faculties were often fuzzy. And a crowd of old "friends," armed with the drugs they knew he couldn't resist, was waiting for him in New York. As the world would soon realize, Bud's homecoming was a fatal mistake.

His recovery regimen had barely ended when Powell and Paudras took off for America on August 16. The music press greeted him at the airport and reported that he downed his first Stateside meal in six years—a cheeseburger, a vanilla malt, and iced tea—with gusto. Birdland rolled out the red carpet for him, wheeling in a new piano and hiring an ace rhythm section, bassist John Ore and drummer Horacee Arnold, to back him. Finally, on August 25, he played the opening show. Reviews were uneven, but the club extended his contract through December while he made plans to stay in town to record an album for the Roulette label.

Almost immediately, however, Powell began losing his balance. Paudras found himself powerless to shelter his friend from the same temptations that had nearly destroyed him in the past. One night, for example, they returned to their hotel to find an old drug pusher acquaintance of Powell's in their room, carefully spreading his cocaine display across a table. Paudras threw the intruder out, but already the situation was out of control.

On October 10 Bud failed to show up for his scheduled Birdland gig. For two days Paudras searched for him before finding him in Brooklyn, resting at the home of some friends. The club management released him from his contract and encouraged him to return to Paris. On October 18, in the middle of dinner with friends at the home of the Baroness Nica de Koenigswarter in Weehawken, New Jersey, Powell walked off into the night and disappeared again. This time the police were notified, and it was a policeman who happened to be a jazz fan, Thomas McDaniel, who discovered him early in the morning five days later, tattered and bewildered, in a Greenwich Village doorway. Powell was returned to the Baroness, who was known in the jazz world for her willingness to shelter and support talented musicians who have come on hard times. Plans were made for an imminent return to Paris.

But when the plane departed on October 27, it was Paudras who returned, alone. Journalists confronted him as he disembarked and heard the news: Powell had decided to settle in Brooklyn. With that, the denouement began.

In March 1965 Powell played in Carnegie Hall at a tribute concert for Charlie Parker on the tenth anniversary of the saxophonist's death. Reviewers were universally distressed at his shabby performance and appearance. Later that spring Powell did his last gig, sharing a Town Hall bill with some younger musicians; his final selection, "I Remember Clifford," memorialized Clifford Brown, who had died with Powell's brother nearly ten years before. Several months later he nearly died from a liver ailment; after a short recovery, he sank back into a morass of illness and surrender. On July 24, 1966 he was admitted into King's County Hospital one last time. There, drained by pneumonia, liver failure, yellow jaundice, alcohol abuse, tuberculosis, and malnutrition, he died on August 1, a month shy of his 42nd birthday. His last words were, "I'll be all right."

Even in death, tragedy and confusion stalked Bud Powell. Newspaper reports erroneously stated that his body was lying unclaimed in the King's County Morgue. In fact, three claims for it had been submitted—from his new manager, Bernard Stollman, from his daughter Celia, who lived in Brooklyn, and from Buttercup. In the end, custody of the body was granted to Celia until Buttercup's arrival from France, at which time it reverted to the widow.

The funeral was a Roman Catholic service at St. Charles, the same cathedral where young Bud had tried out his early classical pieces on the organ. Five thousand people lined the streets of Harlem to watch as the casket was borne by the pallbearers—Max Roach, clarinetist Tony Scott, trumpeter Kenny Dorham, drummer Willie Jones, bassist Hayes Alvis, and pianists Eddie Bonnemere and Claude Hopkins—to the church. Trombonist Benny Green, saxophonist John Gilmore, trumpeter Lee Morgan, pianist Barry Harris, bassist Don Moore, and drummer Billy Higgins accompanied the procession from atop the Jazzmobile, from which more gala neighborhood concerts were usually performed, doing "Now's the Time," "'Round Midnight," and two Powell compositions, "Bud's Bubble" and "Dance of the Infidels." More members of the jazz aristocracy filled the pews: Monk, Billy Taylor, Yusef Lateef, Randy Weston, and Walter Bishop Jr.

No doubt most of them were remembering the young Bud, the pure Bud, the definitive piano bopper, the proud Bud, whose keyboard acrobatics had inspired them to investigate new sounds and higher possibilities on their own. They laid to rest the restless Bud, the mad and tender Bud, who had softly asked his wife one fine French day, "Buttercup, why are you always trying to save me when you know how bad I want to die?"

It Started at Minton's

18. TADD DAMERON

Born: February 21, 1917, Cleveland, Ohio
Died: March 8, 1965, New York, New York

In his too-brief career, Tadd Dameron was thought of primarily as a writer. Cutting his teeth in the swing era, he wrote charts for a number of established acts before early encounters with Charlie Parker in Kansas City and with Dizzy Gillespie in New York nudged him closer to bop. But unlike many of the practitioners in this style, Dameron approached the music from a compositional standpoint; in a 1961 interview with jazz journalist Ira Gitler, he emphasized that he was "trying to build between popular music and the so-called modern music." Where pioneers of the style cultivated an exclusive attitude based on playing for themselves and their hipper listeners, Dameron sought to open the music to broader audiences without compromising it.

This recognition came at the expense of his reputation as a performer. His playing was easy to write off as "arranger's piano"—light chops, and improvisations guided by visions of band books and horn section parts. Of course, it is just as easy to dismiss Brubeck on these terms—and, for that matter, Basie and Ellington too. But with such distinguished company huddled under this deprecatory umbrella, it becomes obvious that maybe this type of playing is a school in itself, expressive on its own terms, and more elusive to other pianists than it seems.

A piano student since age four, Dameron first heard jazz through the work of his brother Caesar, who played alto sax with local bands in Cleveland. He played his first gigs with trumpeter Freddie Webster, followed by short spells with bands led by Zack Whyte and Cab Calloway's sister Blanche. By the time he arrived in Chicago at age 23, Dameron was already writing; shortly afterward, he worked with Vido Musso in New York and with Harlan Leonard in Kansas City. In the years that followed, while doing home-front defense work, he also stepped up his freelance arranging for Count Basie, Jimmie Lunceford, Sarah Vaughan, Billy Eckstine, and other major-league bandleaders.

From this solid grounding in swing Dameron made the move to bebop after the war. After playing piano for a while with Bab's Three Bips and a Bop, he organized a series of his own combos for jobs at the Royal Roost; his sidemen were drawn from the front ranks of modern jazz, with trumpeters Miles Davis and Fats Navarro, vibraphonist Milt Jackson, and drummer Kenny Clarke sharing the stage with him. On September 26, 1947 Dameron played his first session for Blue Note, using Navarro, alto saxophonist Ernie Henry, and tenor saxophonist Charlie Rouse in the front line, with bassist Nelson Boyd and drummer Shadow Wilson in the rhythm section. He maintained an affiliation with the label through 1949, then left to play at the Paris Jazz Festival with Miles Davis and settle for two years in England, where he wrote extensively for Ted Heath's band.

After returning to the States in 1951, Dameron found work growing scarce as his musical visions grew larger. He found a job touring with R&B saxophone honker Bull Moose Jackson, which he dropped during the summer of 1953 to present an ambitious show in Atlantic City, for which he wrote libretto as well as music and fronted a band that featured the young trumpet star Clifford Brown. As opportunities tightened up, Dameron picked up a heroin habit, which led to his arrest and imprisonment in 1958; while behind bars, he wrote arrangements for a Blue Mitchell album being recorded for Riverside. After being released, he continued to arrange, for Milt Jackson and saxophonist Sonny Stitt, and to record his own album, *The Magic Touch*, in 1962.

Dameron's piano style was as easy to recognize as his crystalline arrangement technique. Like Dave Brubeck, his frequently employed thick two-handed block chords. Often the phrasing on these passages showed a literal rather than an improvisational quality, as on his brief solo during the bridge to "Jahbero," recorded on September 13, 1948, and available on *The Complete Blue Note and Capitol Recordings of Fats Navarro and Tadd Dameron*. Even when playing more linear parts, there was a written, somewhat cerebral aspect to Dameron's phrasing, as on another bridge, on the 1947 recording of "The Chase," from the same album; during this brief passage he thoroughly examines how a single motif might be positioned differently through the changes, to create a symmetrical and satisfying sense of completion in just a few seconds of up-tempo improvising.

Two-handed block chords also dominate his solo on "The Scene is Clean," from his 1956 album *Fontainebleau*. There's an urbane vibe in this performance, though, as Dameron plays with syncopation, half-time passages, and triplet sections—all as Shearingesque harmonies that support an agreeable improvised melody. Played quietly, except for a few teasing and unexpected accents, this solo evaporates down to a whisper on a whimsical final set of verses, bridge, and verse; here, a few Monkish minor seconds add the only moments of contrast with Dameron's hushed and spare conclusion.

On "Dial 'B' for Beauty," recorded in 1953 and available on the OJC album *Clifford Brown Memorial*, Dameron follows a blazing trumpet introduction from Clifford Brown with a piano solo, accompanied only by brush drumming. Playing very quietly, Dameron casts a solemn and dignified spell, briefly building tension with suspended voicings as the drums drop out, then reiterating the theme unaccompanied. Dameron's playing bridges Billy Strayhorn and Bill Evans in its sensitivity to structure and expressive manipulations of tempo.

From the same session, Dameron's solo on "Theme of No Repeat" suggests another bridge. The opening verse of his solo, played over a prowling sequence of notes in the bass range, combines Monk's economy with Ellington's delicacy, while tracing dissonances that reflect the language of both pianists. The closing section of the solo is richly harmonized in a more pure Ellington style, which segues neatly into the full band's entrance.

This same introspective, almost introverted style lent itself well to the blues. On "Bula-Beige," from *Fontainebleau*, Dameron reverses his frequent formula by beginning the piece with a linear statement of the theme on the piano, in order to highlight the minor third and flatted fifth and thus emphasize the intended blue mood. His solo begins with a repetition of the flat-five as well, then moves into a spare opening verse marked by call-and-response fragments separated by leisurely silences. After a quick and somewhat haphazard flurry at the head of the following verse, Dameron lapses back to his minimalist reflections, then begins building his block chords. Occasional notes in the bass range of the keyboard add a gentle push to John Simmons's bass line throughout a performance that, typical for Dameron solos, induce a kind of warm contentment rather than any kind of excitement.

Shortly after cutting *Fontainebleau* Dameron organized a quartet session with Simmons back on bass, Philly Joe Jones on drums, and John Coltrane on tenor sax. Released under the title *Mating Call*, these tracks are animated by the symbiotic encounter of the saxophonist's primal, organic style and the more miniaturist piano. Coltrane is already making his statements through showers of notes that batter against the rhythmic structure; Dameron plays against this phrasing with a conservative approach, based strictly on the beat. Though he syncopates effectively behind the tenor solos, the pianist makes his point by underplaying; on the title track, he begins his solo with a series of two-note motifs separated from each other by neat, two-beat buffers. Dameron plays only a few notes, but the ones he chooses shift the feel back and forth from a silky blues in the Ellington fashion to ear-tickling dissonances jabbed in the manner of Monk, supported by nearly subsonic bass notes on the piano played quietly and entirely in Dameron's own style. At faster tempos, as on "Super Jet," he seems less sure of himself; he fudges more notes, and sometimes slips out of the groove. But his ability to avoid melodic cliché, and his fondness of ending phrases on quirky notes—a major seventh at the very end of his solo—give even this performance an invigorating, pure bop appeal. And on "Romas" Dameron takes the spotlight on several opening choruses, with an extended blues improvisation that never loses focus or feel.

Worn out by his addiction, exhausted by chasing after ever more elusive opportunities to work, Dameron lost a long struggle with cancer at age 48.

19. HANK JONES

Born: July 31, 1918, Vicksburg, Mississippi

Though created largely in response to the exhaustion of older musical forms, bebop would mature along the lines that once outlined its rebellion. There was, in the elbowed edginess of Thelonious Monk and the dizzy trajectory of Bud Powell's solos, a gesture of rejection. But that language that the boppers created to discredit the clichés of swing bore the seeds of a new vocabulary which would chart out a new convention, subject to the same move toward respectability that had discredited earlier innovations.

What would history make of those players who dressed up the insolences of their predecessors and sailed them gently into the mainstream of jazz? Hank Jones is one of those who, depending on how you look at it, either defanged or dignified the aggression implicit in pure bebop. He came to New York after the revolution had begun but before it had ended, and his voice was significant in the music's shift from destabilizing the old order to defining the new order.

Jones understood bebop, in all its extensions of old ideas but also in its potential for establishing a new standard of expression. Where Powell and Monk demanded that audiences make a decision, at the moment of performance, about whether they were part of the solution or part of the problem of stagnation in jazz, Jones opened a path that might satisfy the troops on both sides of the conflict. His ideas grew from Earl Hines and Nat Cole but also conformed to the sound of the new generation. He was alone among pianists who could play one set with Benny Goodman and the next with Charlie Parker, without missing a lick.

In his low-key way, Hank Jones is one of the most significant transitional figures in jazz. His role was to bridge rather than to divide; it is difficult to imagine jazz evolving as it has without his temperance and insight.

Long before Ellis Marsalis turned loose his brilliant brood, Hank Jones stepped forward into his own parade of gifted siblings. He was one of seven children, with two sisters preceding him into the world, and several talented brothers, including trumpeter Thad and drummer Elvin, following. It was a religious household, and during his upbringing in Pontiac, Michigan, Hank absorbed a sense of decency that would dignify his approach to music.

He took classical lessons, not enthusiastically. Chopin and other masters helped him conquer the keyboard, but the music of Fats Waller, broadcast like a siren song from a Canadian station in Windsor, seduced him. After playing outside of Detroit with assorted territory bands, he made the pilgrimage to New York. His first gig was with trumpet legend Hot Lips Page at the Onyx Club, but during intermissions and after hours in the hipper clubs along 52nd Street, bebop caught his attention. During those formative years Jones kept his ears open to what was going on around him, yet he never lost touch with the swing traditions that provided his musical foundation.

Jones made his recording debut, with Page, in 1944. In the years that followed his reputation spread as a sideman of uncanny sensitivity. No other pianist has ever rivaled him in the critical but shadowy role of accompanist. He performed and recorded with practically every major player in jazz, from saxophone giants Lester Young, Ben Webster, and Coleman Hawkins through big band archivists like Artie Shaw to modernists like Dizzy Gillespie.

In much of this work Jones staked out a position that stood him apart from other piano innovators. One thing that Bud Powell and Thelonious Monk had in common was their perception of music as a provocation. Each, in his own way, created a personalized style that was as much about rejecting the past as charging toward some vision of the future. Jones was different. He heard what his peers were doing and found ways of honoring their innovations, along with the past that others of his time were trashing. Unlike most boppers, Jones interpreted even the newest music from respect more than from anger.

In the hands of Hank Jones, bebop came across as a supremely musical form, not just a performance art. His solos have an unforced quality; though not as exhibitionistic as a couple of choruses by Bud Powell, a Jones improvisation showed more reflection. Throughout the trio album *Bop Redux*, with bassist George Duvivier and drummer Ben Riley, he sounds extraordinarily relaxed. From one verse to the next on "Confirmation," "Yardbird Suite," and other staples of the repertoire, Jones rolls out right-hand lines that never repeat themselves. It's an elegant conception, based not on having to prove the validity of the form but on the acceptance of it as a culmination of a stylistic evolution.

On "The Song Is You," from Charlie Parker's *Now's the Time*, recorded in December 1952, with Teddy Kotick on bass and Max Roach on drums, Jones's line is broken up by spaces between phrases, but it speaks fluently, without any sense of momentum being interrupted. His solos on other cuts from this session are not built on fireworks but on coherent lines, even at fast tempos. Note placement, rather than momentum, is the key to his expression. The second chorus of his solo on take one of "Kim" is almost Basie-like: Playing very sparely, he doesn't race along with Roach but rather colors the rhythm section with teasing little chords. On the second take, he pushes harder, and it feels a little more forced; we hear Jones grunt out loud before going into the bridge, after which he spins out some outside harmonies in his line. It swings, but it isn't quite as eloquent as the more laid-back approach on the first version.

Eight years later, backing Milt Jackson and John Coltrane on their *Bags & Trane* session, Jones follows the saxophonist's challenging lines with instant responses in his chords, which are invariably played in the middle of the piano's range. During his own solo, as on "The Late Late Blues" after an explosive Coltrane performance, he keeps things fairly minimal, playing closer to Jackson's blues figurations than

Hank Jones was alone among pianists who could play one set with Benny Goodman and the next with Charlie Parker.

to Coltrane's cosmic abstractions. Always, there's a sense that Jones is working to not repeat himself or play the easy way out. When blues licks crop up, he places them in a context that doesn't extend the cliché element but rather bookends those licks with fresher twists and turns. By the time they get to "Three Little Words," he is comping very loosely behind the soloists, with stern-sounding chords that march toward resolution on boppish augmented voicings. This solo typifies his best work: economical, underplayed, strongly melodic yet not bound by tired harmonies.

The fact that he came to bop somewhat late, on moving to New York in 1944, explains his occasional practice of developing a motif in a solo. Where others let their ideas flow out as an unconscious and unchanneled stream, Jones could take a simple figure and work it through a few variations in something like the more conservative swing approach. However, he clearly understood the emotional nuances of bop, and as a result enjoyed a unique influence in being able to infuse it with subtle elements of tradition. By the same token, on some of the more harmonically adventurous ballads in the bebop canon, Jones could find disarmingly simple elements—a straightforward triad or even folk-like figuration in "'Round Midnight" or "Ruby, My Dear," a slightly corny quote from some chestnut here or there—where some of his peers might have trotted out something that conformed more to the modernist context.

Despite his relaxed feel, Jones generates a tension by playing a bit behind the beat and articulating less than crisply. On the medium-tempo "Algo Bueno," from *Groovin' High*, with Sam Jones on bass and Mickey Roker on drums, he hits every note in his line, but seems to fudge one or two slightly; the effect is to create a subtle kind of syncopation between the clean and blurred notes.

Accompanimental brilliance is evident in the title track from *Groovin' High*, a non-bass arrangement with brother Thad on cornet and Mickey Roker on whispery brush drums. Hank's solo picks up telepathically from the final phrase of Thad's solo and leads without a wrinkle from a complex but unobtrusive performance behind the cornet into the piano showcase. Every one of the gestures is underplayed, yet rhythmic and stimulating. Check out the echoes of the theme dropped into the final verse by Hank—a stunning display of wit and quick musical thinking.

In solo settings, the taste that characterizes his ensemble performances only clarifies. Jones never shows off but also resists the temptation to over-analyze a tune. His reharmonizations, as on his rendition of "In a Sentimental Mood," from *Hank Jones Solo Piano* on All Art Jazz, don't trumpet his brilliance as much as lay out insights into the tune. This is solo jazz piano at its sweetest, and all the more impressive for going down so easy.

During the heyday of bebop on 52nd Street, Jones worked extensively at the Onyx Club and elsewhere. For fifteen years, from 1958 through 1973, he punched the time clock at CBS as a staff musician, a testimony to his adaptability to the musical needs involved in playing for a network. Rather than gig endlessly with other 52nd Street veterans, he vamped for plate spinners and Bolshoi dancers on *The Ed Sullivan Show*. At the same time, he guested on countless albums, backing everyone from Billy Eckstine to Sammy Davis, Jr. For five years he accompanied Ella Fitzgerald on the road and in the studio—the supreme marriage of vocal improvisation and telepathic accompaniment. On more than one thousand sessions, Jones enhanced the artistry of featured performers. He was, for decades, the definitive session pianist, a player whose imprint, though unmistakable, never distracted from the headliner.

On these projects, as well as on those that he led, Jones was the responsible modernist. His gift was to see beyond whatever the trend happened to be and put its lessons into an informative context. Tradition hung on his boppish lines, and his nods toward Tatum and Waller felt fresh and new. He could play the most devilish passages without calling attention to himself. Gary Giddins got it right when he observed, in the *Village Voice*, that Jones had "refined his art to the point where his technique is almost invisible."

In later years he would play the piano part in the musical *Ain't Misbehavin'*, whose producers entrusted him with the inevitable final line of the show: "One never knows, do one?" In fact, musicians knew. They knew that Jones, the subtle, courtly presence, the guy in the shadows behind the keys, dapper and dark, represents a kind of artistry that flashier pianists can only emulate. It's not just about saying more with fewer notes; it's more a matter of spirit, of deference, of shining with a light that only a few can see but all can somehow feel.

20. JAKI BYARD

Born: June 6, 1922, Worcester, Massachusetts
Died: February 11, 1999, Queens, New York

Does scholarship necessarily equal solemnity? Not according to Jaki Byard, one of the most thorough students of jazz piano who ever lived—and at the same time, an irrepressible entertainer. There was precedent, of course, in the career of Fats Waller, but Byard picked up where Waller left off, with a style that goes back even further than stride yet is equally conversant with the most avant-garde exertions of Cecil Taylor. In his encyclopedic command of the entire tradition, Byard really was without equal.

And, again, he made it easy for audiences to appreciate this with a performance style that only a sourpuss—or some academic who takes himself way too seriously—could hate. I remember watching Byard one night in a duo performance with fellow piano giant Tommy Flanagan, at San Francisco's Keystone Korner. From his stage entrance to his final bow, Byard was "on"—his eyebrows soared in quizzical surprise when Flanagan pulled off an unexpected modulation, his left hand rose to his cheek in astonishment at some obscure musical pun executed by his right hand, and his high-watt smile warmed the audience throughout the night.

Byard was the son of enthusiastic musical amateurs; his mother played piano, and his father played baritone horn in a marching band. He began piano lessons at age seven with the neighborhood teacher, Grace Johnson Brown; over the next two or three years he would develop a facility for accessible pieces such as the Chopin *Waltz in C# Minor* and Chaminade's *Scarf Dance*. After a while, though, he started hanging out at local performances by Count Basie, Teddy Wilson, Earl Hines, and Fats Waller, then pecking out their licks by ear. He also started learning trumpet and by age 16 was playing it on gigs with local bands, while also working as house pianist at the Saxtrum Club in Worcester.

Induction into the Army in 1941 meant, to Byard, an opportunity to get into playing another instrument. As a *nouveau* trombonist, he won a chair in an Army band whose personnel included proto-bopper Kenny Clarke. After his discharge he went back to Boston and, briefly, stopped playing piano altogether, an all-too common response among pianists after their first sobering attendance of an Art Tatum performance. By the late forties Byard had recovered sufficiently to enjoy extended affiliations at the keys with Earl Bostic, trumpeter Herb Pomeroy, saxophonist Charlie Mariano, drummer Alan Dawson, and, beginning in 1959, Maynard Ferguson.

Much of Byard's best work conveys his spontaneous and playful nature. This is especially clear in his solo work: On "Hello Young Lovers," from *Jaki Byard at Maybeck*, he begins with ominous lines that stalk toward each other from the extreme ends of the keyboard—lovers headed, with some trepidation, toward their first encounter? From there he moves into a Chopinesque episode, stately if a little sloppy, then trips into a waltz tempo that brings Vince Guaraldi momentarily to mind. These and other segments of Byard's performance sometimes seem about to bog down, as lines blur or just miss running into each other. There's a sense, rightly or wrongly, that he's making everything up as he goes along, guided not by deep insight into the tune as much as an attitude that's equal parts respect and irreverence.

Certainly Byard did nothing to counteract that impression. There's no musical reason why he had to play "'Round Midnight," on *Maybeck*, with his left hand only—or to announce it to the room prior to performance—other than to entertain. (Perhaps he could have had his right hand tied behind his back.) At other times, though, his flamboyant gestures convey a complex beauty, as in his splashy but evocative short solo on "Portrait," from the Charles Mingus *Complete Town Hall Concert*.

Never an easy player to categorize, Byard had a rare ability to slip in and out of styles without disrupting the flow of his improvisation. So it was on "Doodle Oodle," an uptempo blowfest from the Al Cohn/Zoot Sims album *Body and Soul*, on which the pianist begins his first chorus with a band-like riff, then jumps into some delightfully oblique boppish lines. By the second chorus, he's taken us through bluesy repetition, pointed clusters, and, finally, a genial, deliberately clichéd turnaround at the end.

Byard's solo on "Good Bye Pork Pie Hat," from Charles Mingus's *The Great Concert, Paris 1964*, illustrates another example of his versatility, specifically in being able to unify traditional and modern references. The first choruses are spacious, with practically no left hand making it possible for a single lower-register stab to have a nearly percussive effect. As the solo unwinds, Byard explores bitonal ideas, then digs into the groove with funky piano figures and a more emphatic rhythm, building a titanic tremolo in the last chorus, similar in its effect to Art Blakey's massive press roles.

A sprightly spirit animates the opening of Byard's free extemporization on the following track, "Meditation for Integration." Pixie-like trills slow down into a more reflective, slow-motion sequence of suspended chords and simple dissonances, which provide a spare but compelling backdrop for Mingus's arco solo. At the same time, the eloquence of his long single-line solo through several choruses of "Orange was the Color of Her Dress," announced by Mingus as a substitute for the improvisation usually played by the trumpeter, is brilliantly focused, free of affectation yet shimmering with inventiveness; the high-register chords, and even the fist-pounding dissonances at the end of his performance, are an appropriate climax to the solo as a whole. And none could miss the irony in the "Yankee Doodle" quote, as well as the juxtaposition of sober triadic chords, bluesy licks, and twinkling little runs, on "Fable of Faubus."

With his encyclopedic command of the entire jazz piano tradition, Jaki Byard really was without equal.

Byard's association with Mingus began with the bassist's Town Hall concert in 1960 and lasted until 1969. It was his longest and most rewarding affiliation, perhaps because of the odd combination of clash and congruence that the job entailed. They shared an interest in music that was rich in unabashed emotion, and a tolerance for rough edges. The Mingus bands had a bull-like intensity, with a looseness in their charts that anticipated powerful spontaneous interaction between performers. So it was on *The Black Saint and the Sinner Lady*, recorded in 1963, in which Byard's performance within arranged sections roams through the changes, like a hungry cat set free. His solo moments are all about freedom and a kind of *noir* romanticism: The unaccompanied two-bar intro and subsequent arpeggios and splashes through a bluesy two-chord vamp at the start of "Duet Solo Dancers," and the longer, heavily pedaled tremolo-inflected thematic statement at the start of the following movement, "Group Dancers," though expressive, reflect an organic, almost biological vitality, far more than any sense of technical discipline.

On other sessions, Byard's unique buoyancy often comes through more clearly elsewhere than on the menacing beauty of Mingus recordings. From the opening moments of "Mrs. Parker of K.C. (Bird's Mother)," recorded in December 1960 for the Eric Dolphy album *Far Cry*, he proclaims his presence on this medium-tempo blues with highly unorthodox, off-beat, exuberant clusters as Dolphy and Booker Little play the head. Byard's playing here brings to mind a picture of a kid playing with blocks—building things up, letting them fall down, starting again. Even when the band settles into a swing pattern for the solos, the pianist is all over the keyboard, his chords getting even thicker without losing their lighter-than-air quality. (Nat Hentoff, in his liner notes to this disc, aptly describes the Byard style as "springy.") When he starts his own solo, Byard maintains a childlike exploratory sense, which leads him from an elementary opening lick into a few quizzical modes, a fractured montuño, and a resolution on a jagged, somewhat Middle Eastern chord destabilized by placing the third in the bass. After this bizarre beginning, he then dishes out a solo that oscillates between very simple bluesy lines and more enigmatic moments. Byard's willingness to jump from idea to unrelated idea here emphasizes that impulsiveness that Mingus recognized and employed so well in his own arrangements.

Also during the sixties, Byard led his own groups on sessions for Prestige, with Dolphy, bassist Ron Carter, and trumpeter Freddie Hubbard among his sidemen. Toward the end of the decade he began cutting down on gigs and concentrating on teaching, primarily at the New England Conservatory, to whose faculty he was appointed by Gunther Schuller in 1969. By all accounts an inspiring and enlightening pedagogue, Byard recruited his students into a 12-piece band that he called the Apollo Stompers, which offered budding jazzers and wide-eyed classical players experience in an ensemble whose mission was to ignore all barriers and discover the adventure of exploration through improvisation and Byard's own charts.

The adventure ended one night in 1999 when Byard was found dead from a gunshot wound to the head in the apartment that he shared with two daughters. He was 76 years old.

21. RED GARLAND

Born: May 13, 1923, Dallas, Texas
Died: April 23, 1985, Dallas, Texas

Not to deny what's due to the Monks and McCoys, the ones who broke things up and put them back together again, but it takes a more elusive talent to work within an existing structure, to leave the surface unchanged while transforming the stuff that holds it all in place. In the eyes of their colleagues, these more retiring masters are among the giants of their craft.

Red Garland is one such engineer. Listening to his best work now, it's easy to mistake just how significant it was, precisely because its impact among musicians was so great. Lots of people play today as Garland did then. To our ears, their approach is almost canonical: comp with the left hand, solo in single lines with the right, and build to a big finish with some fleshy two-handed chords.

Lots of pianists were following this approach in the bebop era as well, but it was players like Hank Jones and Red Garland who cooled their edgy energy a bit and adapted their practice to a more inviting, somewhat mainstream setting. The trick was that they did so without either pandering to commercial trends or calling a lot of attention to themselves.

Garland's impact was in many ways more notable even than that of Hank Jones, because of the almost radical restrictions he placed on himself. Single lines were to Garland what P-K4 was to Bobby Fischer: an opening to be followed with rigor. His resistance to flashy effects bordered on ascetic. The great majority of Garland's improvising was done in a narrow range of maybe three octaves, with his left hand taking exclusive possession of the lowest one. You could bank on his approach: From one tune to the next, he would accompany the soloists with irregular, thoughtful chords, then turn on a stream of melodic inventions in his own solos that would only grow more startling with more careful examination. Few pianists, including many who enjoyed greater prominence, could rival this consistency; unlike Monk, or even Bill Evans, Garland at his height never seemed to play an indifferent solo or get stuck for an idea.

Which, of course, makes it difficult to point to examples of his greatest work: For maybe ten years, *everything* he played was his best work. A fallow period followed, and after that came a disappointing coda as he tried to regain the form he had lost. Nothing, however, could tarnish his legacy as one of the greatest jazz section pianists of his time, or any other time.

There was no evidence of inherited talent in the Garland family. His father, an elevator operator in downtown Dallas, was perceptive enough to get William started on clarinet lessons as a kid. He worked his way up to playing alto sax with the Booker T. Washington High School, but it took a chance encounter as an 18-year-old to bring the piano into the picture. Garland was stationed at Fort Huachuca in Sierra Vista, Arizona, where he heard a fellow soldier, future Modern Jazz Quartet founder John Lewis, amusing himself at the canteen piano. They spoke, and soon Garland was studying, first with Lewis and later with another pianist in uniform, Lee Barnes.

Mustered out of the service in 1944 at age 22, Garland more or less drifted into the musician's life. He played his first gig at the keys in Fort Worth that year, working with local saxophonist Bill Blocker. Oran "Hot Lips" Page heard him perform; that's all it took for Page to offer him an audition to replace the touring pianist who had just given notice. To his own surprise, Garland got the nod, and with only an appropriate amount of apprehension he left right after that for several months on the road with the trumpeter's group.

Most of what Garland was listening to in those days meshed well with Page's straight-ahead swing style: He dug the Basie band, with whom Page had apprenticed, though he connected more with Nat Cole's smooth take on swing. After a couple of years, however, he was ready to stretch, so in 1946 Garland began looking for work in New York.

Work found him quickly, as silky singing star Billy Eckstine picked him up for a tour. The Eckstine band was one of the more progressive ensembles at the time, with a strong contingent of bebop pioneers. By the time he got back to New York six weeks later, Garland had embraced the new music, its feverish tempos and displaced melodies. He met Bud Powell at Minton's and hung out at his house, took some instruction from Art Tatum, gigged with the greats—Coleman Hawkins, Charlie Parker, Fats Navarro, Lester Young.

The pivotal moment came in 1955, when Miles Davis heard him play in Boston and invited him to join his new quintet. Although Davis couldn't get commitments from the players he wanted originally, including Sonny Rollins and Max Roach, the lineup turned out to be Olympian anyway, with Paul Chambers on bass, Philly Joe Jones on drums, and a young Philadelphia saxophonist whom Garland himself recommended: John Coltrane. Over a three-year period this group laid down a string of epochal albums—*Workin'* and *Steamin'*, *'Round Midnight*, *Milestones*—and provided a setting that allowed Garland to complete his own growth as an artist.

These were Garland's great years, from '55 through the mid-'60s. After leaving the Davis group due to amicable creative differences, Garland cut some solid albums of his own, though none sold as strongly as he would have liked. These recordings, and the many sessions he played for his friends, leave us with a picture of a thorough professional whose style could complement the work of the leader without losing its own unique feel.

It was a feel that appealed perhaps more to musicians than to the public. Yet discerning audiences could also sense something extraordinary in, for example, Garland's solo on "My Funny Valentine," recorded in 1956 for *Cookin' with Miles Davis*. Like most of his improvisations, it highlights a single line in the right hand, whose simplicity can distract from the fact of its uninterrupted coherence and elegant construction; only one awkward quote, from a Christmas tune, briefly diverts the flow.

This stream of ideas marked Garland as a modernist, even when he was playing dated material. On the 1957 album *Art Pepper Meets the Rhythm Section*, he tackles the New Orleans chestnut "Jazz Me Blues." The breaks at the end of each verse were used by traditional players to show off flashy licks and build momentum; here, Garland simply keeps blowing, with only one or two off-beat rests to keep things moving when the drums and bass drop out.

Garland seemed hesitant only when confronting certain harmonically challenging tunes. On the title track to the John Coltrane album *Lush Life*, from 1958, his runs skim the surface but don't sink into the Strayhorn changes. His habitual switch to chorded passagework doesn't illuminate the tune any better, and in the end the open fifths that support the Deco ascending chords at the end of his solo feel a little stark.

When his mother became ill in Dallas around 1968, Garland quit the music business and lapsed into a period of retirement. He started playing locally in 1976, and in '78, with encouragement from record producer Orrin Keepnews, he made a return of sorts with a trio date at San Francisco's Keystone Korner. This engagement, documented on the 32 Jazz release *I Left My Heart . . .*, captures the artist out of touch with whatever energies drove him to distinction 20-odd years earlier. Gone are the long, fascinating lines; in their place, on "Bye Bye Blackbird," his solo is either riddled by funk clichés or interrupted by dry moments, during which he finds nothing to offer but a few fractured fifths. His attempts to rediscover the eloquence of his chord work feel similarly forced.

Garland played his last gig at the Dallas Park Central Jazz Festival three years before his death by heart attack. Like some of his classic solos, his life had a quiet denouement, his exit underplayed yet his absence growing only more apparent with time's passing.

22. TOMMY FLANAGAN

Born: March 16, 1930, Detroit, Michigan
Died: November 16, 2001, New York, New York

I t's amazing that the city that spawned Ted Nugent, the Amboy Dukes, Mitch Ryder, and the MC5 was once known for the taste of its native jazz musicians. Pianists in particular reflected what was then Detroit's celebrated elegance. Where New York's rent parties produced a flamboyant breed of player, suited more to aggressive and competitive solo performances, Hank Jones, Sir Roland Hanna, Barry Harris, and Tommy Flanagan comported themselves with a deference that adapted easily to ensemble settings. They were nice guys who didn't shoot off their mouths or consider it their mission to draw blood in carving contests.

Flanagan and Jones are the greatest incarnations of these qualities. Unlike Fats Waller or Art Tatum, they kept their chops at bay and concentrated on making other musicians sound great. Bravura solo pianists were too busy, and too self-contained, to cultivate listening as a skill; for Flanagan and Jones, listening to and complementing other musicians was what jazz performance was all about.

This explains the attractions of Flanagan's playing. He is the most unruffled of pianists in jazz; never did he seem to lose control or be in a hurry. His rhythm section work and his solos represented the highest standards in mainstream group performance. As a vocal accompanist he had no peer in jazz; his insight with a tune, burnished through collaboration with Ella Fitzgerald and Tony Bennett, elevated his interactions with the great instrumentalists as well.

These talents are not always apparent to the casual fan. Anybody could appreciate the genius of Art Tatum alone at the keyboard; Flanagan's unmatched ability to extemporize beautiful lines, as crafted as the melodies of painstaking composers, rewarded the more discerning listener. Tatum's music was a spectacular, multi-course feast; Flanagan served perfect, gourmet-quality sweets.

He was born in the Conant Gardens neighborhood of Detroit, the son of a postman. From his mother he inherited some Native American lineage and a love for jazz. His first inspiration, though, was the music of Tatum, Waller, Teddy Wilson, Billie Holiday, and the other discs collected by his older brother, Johnson Junior. Like some other pianists of his generation, Tommy learned his way around the ivories on the family player piano, by pumping the pedals and watching the patterns dance across the keys. From the ages of five through ten, this was his main method of self-instruction.

His first formal lessons were on the clarinet that he received for Christmas at the age of six. Though this regimen helped him learn to read music, he had trouble connecting with the instrument. Everyone eventually got the message that the piano was his medium when, at age ten, Flanagan was taken to hear Fats Waller perform locally at the Paradise Room. The clarinet went back into its case, and piano lessons began with his brother's teacher, Gladys Dillard.

Flanagan was 12 when he first played in public; his parents, nervous that he was maybe a little too precocious for his own good, had grounded him, so naturally Tommy snuck out to make that first gig. Soon he was connecting with other emerging talents, including Barry Harris, who was also studying with Gladys Dillard, and Roland Hanna, a fellow student at Northern High School. By this time Flanagan's listening tastes had progressed to the more modern players favored by his friends; Bud Powell and Nat Cole replaced Tatum and Waller as his favorite pianists. Lucky Thompson, Milt Jackson, Pepper Adams, Joe Henderson, and Thad and Elvin Jones were among the locals with whom he explored the new ideas presented by bop, in a cooperative climate that would make each of these players a master of ensemble performance. They learned through practicing, stretching out on the bandstand, studying records, and hanging around outside clubs they were too young to enter, straining to hear Miles Davis, Charlie Parker, and other giants as they passed through town.

After graduating from high school Flanagan began a steady job at the Parrot Lounge and kept working elsewhere around town. On one date with Billy Mitchell, he even got to play with Charlie Parker, who made an unannounced guest appearance. Right around then Selective Service intervened; for a while Flanagan kept up a familiar routine even in uniform, as pianist with a revue at Fort Leonard Wood in Missouri. When that opportunity expired he shipped to South Korea and began two uneventful years as a movie projectionist.

Despite all the action in Detroit, Flanagan knew that New York was still the place to be if you were serious about playing jazz. So in 1956, after mustering out of the military movie business, he and his boyhood friend Kenny Burrell made the pilgrimage together. A few days after moving in with Burrell's aunt, Flanagan sat in with Oscar Pettiford at a loft jam session; a few days after that he performed with the bassist's big band at Town Hall. Days later he was called by Elvin Jones to sub for Bud Powell on a two-week stint at Birdland. Right after that, in March, he made his recording debut on a session with Thad Jones. Three days later he was in the studio again, this time with Miles Davis and Sonny Rollins, cutting "No Line," "In Your Own Sweet Way," and other memorable tracks.

You get the picture: New York took to Flanagan immediately, and vice versa. A few weeks after the Davis date he backed Sonny Rollins on *Saxophone Colossus*. By the summer of 1956 he was a member of J. J. Johnson's band, with whom he toured Europe. In the years that followed he would appear on other epochal discs, most notably John Coltrane's first Atlantic project, *Giant Steps*, in 1959 and Roland Kirk's *Out of the Afternoon* in 1962. He worked extensively with Coleman Hawkins beginning in 1958, and briefly with Lester Young in the late fifties at Gem's Paradise in Brooklyn. In 1962, following a South American package tour with Hawkins, Roy Eldridge, and Herbie Mann, Flanagan began his long association with Ella Fitzgerald, which would continue intermittently for some 16 years.

And so it was throughout the sixties and into the seventies, as Flanagan played with just about everyone who was anyone. Very gradually he slowed down, beginning with a move from New York to Los Angeles in 1966; in later years he would settle in Phoenix, Arizona. In March 1978, while on the road with Fitzgerald, Flanagan survived a minor heart attack, which he took as a hint to cut back a little more. That year he began playing solo piano more often, with engagements at Michael's Pub and Bradley's in New York; he also did some duo recordings with Hank Jones and Kenny Barron, duo concerts with Jaki Byard, Roland Hanna, Barry Harris, and Monty Alexander, a trio date with Barry Harris and Walter Davis at Carnegie Hall, and a memorable quartet appearance on a *Today Show* broadcast with Teddy Wilson, Marian McPartland, and Ellis Larkins.

Critics have taken greater notice of Flanagan since he began performing more on his own. His style, freed of the supportive function on which it was originally based, began to deepen, a process which Whitney Balliett noticed: "About five years ago," he writes in *Goodbyes and Other Messages*, "his work took on a new subtlety. He began to play with a delicacy and steadiness that infused everything—his ballads, his blues, and his uptempo numbers. He was continually refreshing, continually surprising."

In truth, rough edges began to appear in Flanagan's later work, but these were typically balanced by his lingering intelligence. On *Sunset and the Mockingbird*, a live trio CD cut at the Village Vanguard in 1998, he slips out of the pocket now and then, but there's plenty of authority in his unison articulation of the Thad Jones bop standard "Birdsong." From the "Woody Woodpecker" reference in the break after the first verse, he delivers a searing solo built on unexpected bitonal excursions and high points positioned at odd points within the 16-bar framework. Even with the occasional fudged run, Flanagan hits electrifying high points again and again. Call him the Reggie Jackson of postbop piano. And, like "Mr. October," the pianist picks up steam with time; on another Thad Jones number later in the set, "Let's," he lifts off from the treacherous syncopations of the opening motif into a solo fueled by truncated rhythmic motifs, outside harmonic implications, and a few pointed dissonances. Hard to believe the session marked his 67th birthday.

Flanagan's ability to come up with the unexpected twist in a line has been a hallmark of his style throughout his career. His solo on "This Time the Dream's On Me," from *Introducing Kenny Burrell*, recorded in 1956, is a gem in every respect: His touch is impeccable, with each note in his dotted-eighth phrasing skipped and skimmed over the groove laid down by Paul Chambers and Kenny Clarke. Though there are breaks in his phrases, Flanagan tends to keep his line very long, with perfectly positioned high and low points in the improvisation and a very spare use of repetition, serving to render these two choruses flawlessly. The fact that it is such a typical performance for Flanagan makes it that much more of a wonder.

Another example occurs on the medium-up original tune "Jes' Fine," from the 1960 *Tommy Flanagan Trio* session; he maintains a bluesy feel through his solo but without relying on either funk or bop devices. Instead, he concentrates on keeping his solo fresh: On the opening verse, starting in the middle range and leaving plenty of space in his line, Flanagan gradually raises the center of his improvisation by about an octave, through fluent expansions that transform a few blues licks into material for long melodic commentary. Only once or twice does he hit a note aggressively; the rest of the time Flanagan lets his ideas speak for themselves over the gently swinging backup of bassist Tommy Potter and drummer Roy Haynes.

On a medium-tempo "What a Difference a Day Makes," recorded in 1995 for the Sonny Rollins album *+3*, Flanagan offers an example of how to take a very familiar written melody and, with a nudge here and there, mold it into something new. References to the tune crop up throughout his solo, but Flanagan makes it a point to begin by inventing an alternate theme through the first eight bars, emphasizing a diminished second in his first variation of the opening motif as if to indicate that he's about to try out a few ideas. Having spread his alternate melody across the first verse, he begins the second with a direct quote from the tune, but even here he leads it through the changes, building his own peaks and releases along the way as if he were in fact reciting a familiar tune. All the way to the end of his solo, after the third verse, Flanagan makes it sound like creating a fully realized melody in real time is the simplest thing a musician could do—in fact, the only thing that's harder is making it sound as simple as Flanagan always does.

Without a rhythm section to support this sort of invention, Flanagan adds an expressive way with tempo to his resources. On Frank Morgan's 1992 album *You Must Believe in Spring* the pianist delivers a rendition of "With Malice Toward None," distinguished by a stately rubato, except for a few moments of gentle stride; the entire performance grows around an awareness of breath more characteristic of vocalists even than horn players, as if lyric was as much an element as melody. Flanagan's applications, on the chorus, of gospel voicings, simply spelled but powerfully inverted and separated from the body of the song by their quick skipping rhythm, are the final winning detail in a comprehensively conceived improvisation.

23. BARRY HARRIS

Born: December 15, 1929, Detroit, Michigan

Like fellow Detroit pianist Hank Jones, Barry Harris is regarded as a product of bebop. But, again like Jones, he is that and much more—an artist who has grown beyond the boundaries of the older style and settled into a way of playing marked by sophisticated interpretation and respect for the song form. In other words, Harris has lived long enough to achieve a maturity that represents a culmination of, rather than a contradiction to, his earlier work.

His latter-day activities—as a teacher, as a thoughtful spokesman for as well as critic of modern jazz—are indicators of his accomplishment. I still have a clear picture in my mind of Harris as he spoke to the young participants in the first Thelonious Monk International Jazz Piano Competition, backstage at the Smithsonian in Washington. Distinguished, with a brush of whitening hair, he was respectful yet candid in his assessment of their performances. In suggesting that they lacked Monk's insight into the relationship between tempo and dance, Harris was completely at home as an authority on what was correct performance practice, perhaps especially because of his personal ties to Monk, with whom he lived during the elder pianist's last years. Harris's audience, which included such future greats as Marcus Roberts and Joey DeFrancesco, listened in a state of something like awe.

This self-acceptance permeates Harris's style, though toward the beginning of his career he showed little evidence of ego or, for that matter, self-confidence. Though he began taking lessons from his mother, a church pianist, at the age of four, and was working regularly around Detroit by the time he reached high school, Harris admitted to being too intimidated to take his chances in the more competitive New York circuit until he was past the age of 30. Instead, throughout the fifties, he hung out with local talent, including Jones and his brothers Thad and Elvin, and worked in rhythm sections behind such visiting greats as Lester Young, Roy Eldridge, Ben Webster, Miles Davis, and, one memorable night at the Graystone Ballroom, Charlie Parker. After a few brief road trips with guitarist Emmett Slay and Max Roach, Harris finally made the plunge in 1959, when he joined Cannonball Adderley's band and disembarked in New York.

What he found proved disappointing—a relic of the halcyon 52nd Street era, with less apparently going on than there had been in Detroit. For much of his first few years in New York, Harris concentrated on practicing, taking only the occasional gig with Yusef Lateef, and dropping in now and then on jam sessions. Eventually he landed a steady position with Coleman Hawkins, whose lifelong inclination to explore new musical areas proved compatible with Harris's attitude.

As an improviser, Harris follows a measured, somewhat deliberate approach. More than most pianists, he absorbed the harmonic and rhythmic nuances of Bud Powell's style, then scaled it down to fit his more reflective temperament. The Harris solo on "Big Foot," from the Red Rodney album

Bird Lives, is a classic example of how to honor an influence without resorting to imitation: Harris plays fluently around the changes of the Charlie Parker tune, adhering strictly to the bop canon but infusing it with a relaxed phrasing that's totally his own. With his left hand nudging offbeats in the bass range, he shifts his right-hand phrasing back and forth from on to slightly behind the beat. This builds a tension against the pulse laid down by bassist Sam Jones and drummer Roy Brooks that's almost subliminal yet completely undeniable. The same tendency is clearer on medium-up performances: On "Western Style," from Sonny Stitt's 1981 album *In Style*, Harris swings by dragging consistently behind bassist George Duvivier and drummer Jimmy Cobb, with an introspective solo that's almost too muffled to hear.

Like John Lewis, Harris is capable of a sprightly treatment of rhythm but often prefers to create moody textures through methodical explorations. On the Dexter Gordon album *Gettin' Around*, he begins his solo on "Mahna de Carnaval" with a sensuous statement of the theme in the low, left-hand range, then floats it gradually up the keyboard; rather than demand attention, his performance conjures an atmosphere and draws listeners into it. (On the same session, Harris creates a marvelously unhurried solo through a string of dotted eighth-notes on "Heartaches," in which he strolls through the changes with a gentle but insistent bounce in his step. It's a great example of how a pianist can build momentum on his own without detracting from the efforts of the rhythm section.)

Barry Harris has achieved a maturity that represents a culmination of, rather than a contradiction to, his earlier work.

When playing unaccompanied on ballads, Harris shows the same atmospheric inclinations, but on up-tempo tunes he can sound somewhat out of his idiom. His left hand plays lightly and irregularly on a flag-waving version of "Cherokee," from *Live at Maybeck Recital Hall*, in the bop tradition, which leaves the right hand responsible for pushing the groove. While the pulse is certainly clear throughout this performance, Harris's disinterest in laying down any steady rhythm in the bass eventually creates an impression of the piece never quite taking off. His solo line burns, but there's little fuel to keep the fire alive up to the perfunctory ending.

On "Hocus-Pocus," from Lee Morgan's 1963 album *The Sidewinder*, Harris confirms his command of improvisational structure. After the opening verses, he leaps into the bridge with two quick sixteenth-note figures, which both define the transition into a new section and open the door for similar bursts over the next couple of choruses. It's notable that Harris doesn't hit the tonic, or root note of the song, on his way into the two bridges he plays in his solo; on the second, especially, he plays across the start of the bridge, delineating the section not with a cadence but with a change in the character of his solo.

Any pianist who has developed this mastery of form in improvisation will have high standards, for himself and for his peers as well. Often blunt in his comments about trends in jazz, and even in expressing his disappointment with uninformed audiences, Harris speaks always with a candor born of love for his art form. Only he, his boyhood friend Hank Jones, and a few other veterans seem at home these days on that plateau. Until the next masters come along, Harris is keeping the light on for them.

24. SIR ROLAND HANNA

Born February 10, 1932, Detroit, Michigan

As one of that line of stellar pianists who began pouring out of Detroit in the forties and fifties, Hanna possesses the technical assurance, ensemble sensibility, and bebop credentials that this pedigree demands. He was more of a prodigy than some of his colleagues, and no less respected by musicians who have had the pleasure of working with him.

He got his start very early—at all of two years old, when he was taught to read music by his father, a minister who doubled as a saxophonist. At age four he brought home a music book that he had found while playing in an alley, then started using it to teach himself the basics of the piano. A precocious reader of books as well, Hanna was admitted to Northern High School at eleven—the same age at which he finally began taking formal piano lessons, from Josephine Love.

In those days his instruction was classical all the way, with an emphasis on European drillmasters Bach, Clementi, Scarlatti, and Czerny, though he eventually developed a special attachment to Satie and Debussy. Jazz joined the party when Hanna, at 13, got to know a classmate and future piano giant, Tommy Flanagan. Through Flanagan he heard recordings of Art Tatum for the first time; the experience was sufficiently imposing to dissolve Hanna's previous resistance to jazz. It didn't take long for him to track down a local club, Freddie Guinyards', where Tatum would sit in whenever he was passing through town. During summers Hanna dug deeper into jazz and blues at Birdhurst, a community center where renowned bassist Major Holley worked as a counselor and informal teacher.

Over the next few years Hanna kept practicing, checked out the major artists as they performed in Detroit, and started playing at jam sessions with Flanagan, Barry Harris, and Hank Jones, among other hometown piano giants. The Army summoned him in 1950; two years later, he enrolled in the Eastman School of Music at Rutgers University. On learning of a school policy that banned students from playing jazz, Hanna bailed out and fled back to Detroit.

He found a more amenable climate at the Juilliard School in New York, where he began classes in 1955. The faculty there didn't mind when he started playing trio gigs on the side with George Tucker and Bobby Thomas, and even granted him time off in 1958 to join the Benny Goodman band for a European tour that included an appearance at the Brussels World Fair. The following year he worked for a short while as well with bassist Charles Mingus.

With a Juilliard degree in his pocket, Hanna went to work for three years as accompanist to the great singer Sarah Vaughan, then left in 1963 to alternate with Thelonious Monk at the Five Spot in New York. A year later he led a group that included trumpeter Thad Jones to Japan for a series of performances and to record a movie soundtrack; Jones returned the favor by inviting Hanna to join the jazz orchestra he formed with drummer Mel Lewis in 1966—an association that would last until 1974. The years since then Hanna has spent as leader of several forward-looking ensembles, including the New York Jazz Quartet, whose members have included bassists George Mraz and Ron Carter, drummers Ben Riley and Grady Tate, and saxophonist Frank Wess. He has also held various teaching positions and more recently served as pianist with the Lincoln Center Jazz Orchestra.

Though classical allusions often flavor Hanna's work, he is unhindered by any European affectations in his explorations of blues and postbop. His solo on "Slop," from the Mingus album *Shoes of*

On learning of a school policy that banned students from playing jazz,
Sir Roland Hanna bailed out of Rutgers and fled back to Detroit.

the Fisherman's Wife, was more churchy than most of what had been recorded by the funk school, with rocking riffs and, in the last chorus, brilliant off-tempo left-hand jabs beneath right-hand stabs, in a sizzling call-and-response variation.

Hanna's accompaniment behind the horn solos from this session, on "Things Ain't What They Used to Be," is a study of Monkish economy. His staccato chords provide the barest outlines of the blues changes, with each attack positioned to sting the momentum. Hanna's own solo begins and ends with his familiar quick waterfalls of fifths, again with only the barest gestures making maximum emotional impact.

Both of these elements—patient explorations of essential elements of a theme and a command of gospel devices—guide Hanna in his solo on "Summertime," from *The Sir Roland Hanna Quartet Plays Gershwin*, recorded in 1993. Over a parade-ground beat from drummer Ronnie Burrage the pianist kicks things off with a funky two-handed unison rumination on the theme, then drops behind Bill Easley's soprano sax to punch out barbed dissonances and open fifths. Hanna's own solo adheres to this same feel, with more heavily syncopated unison lines illuminated by pinwheel trills and framed by spacious silences. There's not much harmonic adventure here, but more than enough incendiary emotion.

On the other hand, Hanna was fully equipped to burn with the best technicians. He begins his solo on "Mood Indigo," from the Mingus album, with thoughtful, blues-inflected lines, including an unusual major-third figure. When Mingus kicks into a sauntering swing on the second chorus, Hanna digs into the groove with double-fisted tremolos and thick octave lines. The bassist, shouting encouragement, rips a double-time pattern on the third chorus, and suddenly Hanna is on fire, scattering a lengthy, fleet line across the upper middle register, weaving in and out of bitonality, and making it all sound easy.

Some of Hanna's original material posed interesting challenges to the soloist. On "The Night Before," recorded on August 2, 1991 and featured on the LRC album *Double Exposure*, he presents a tune based on the whole-tone scale. But where Monk made this form a trademark in his improvisations by imposing it against the eight-tone structure of standard tunes, Hanna makes it the critical element in his foundation. Accordingly, his solo has a circular feel as it flows easily over stacked major thirds in his harmonic accompaniment, creating a sense that playing pentatonic is as natural as riffing on the blues. He plays similarly pliant whole tones in his brief solo on the ballad "Manhattan Nocturne," from the same date.

Hanna's exuberant "Oleo," from the Maybeck recital recorded in 1994, kicks off with a tight two-handed octave statement of the theme, which leads into an unusual pedal-tone foundation for the start of the solo section. What follows is a rhythmic showpiece, with thumping low bass under lines that scamper around a diminished-fifth structure and lead to a mélange of broken stride, alternating left-hand octaves, and exotic-sounding modal chorded passages. It's not the perfect sort of performance one might expect from a Tatum or Peterson, but it does take the passion of postbop to a greater employment of both hands and independent rhythmic movement than one normally hears.

Hanna adopted the "Sir" honorific upon being knighted by the president of Liberia in 1969 for his activities in raising money for the education of children in Africa. For his accomplishments in adapting his comprehensive knowledge of European technical and harmonic theory to the interpretive and improvisational magic of jazz, Hanna is royalty several times over.

Brilliant Corners

25. THELONIOUS MONK

Born October 10, 1917, Rocky Mount, North Carolina
Died February 17, 1982, Weehawken, New Jersey

There was a time when Thelonious Sphere Monk was the best-kept secret in jazz. Musicians knew who he was—they didn't necessarily know what to think of him, but they knew him. The name alone was enough to fix the man in everyone's brain. Yet even after the public had memorized the hipster honor roll in the late forties—Bird, Diz, Fats (Navarro, of course)—they had only a shadowy impression of Monk, a dark presence behind the piano at Minton's, his 200-pound frame obscured by the smoke and his spare fills overwhelmed by one apoplectic bebop horn solo after another.

Later, of course, all that changed. Not only did Monk become well-known; he became a hot property. He won the *Down Beat* Critics Poll in 1958 and '59, signaling his acceptance in the jazz establishment. He even found himself on the cover of *Time* magazine in 1964. (He had been slated originally for the November 25, 1963, cover, but President Kennedy's assassination held the story up.)

By this time, the Monk legend had taken root. People who would never bother to seek out his music knew of his many hats, his little dances onstage, his long solitary walks, his elliptical ruminations and moody silences. But although he was finally playing concerts and even making television appearances, he was paying a price. He hadn't changed, neither to accommodate nor to spite his idolators, yet in this brighter glare it was still hard to see him for what he really was. In the eyes of the public, he remained an enigma.

And in his last days, Monk slipped back into the shadows. After only a few sporadic appearances in the seventies, he retired to the New Jersey home of his longtime friend, the Baroness Nica de Koenigswarter. There he rested in solitude and silence, sinking with a slow tragic grace into the realm of legend even before his death at age 64.

From start to finish, Thelonious Monk was a private man. He would rarely grant interviews, and when he did, as often as not, he would refuse to discuss his work; to one persistent writer, he repeatedly responded, "Get the records, sit down, and dig." Clearly, in his view, the answers to any questions about music were in the music itself. One gets the impression that Monk was irritated or amused, depending on his mood at the moment, with efforts to find the essence of his art in words rather than sounds.

Surely this is a sign of Monk's purity as an artist. Music occupies the center of most musicians' lives, but in Monk that center stretched nearly to the surface and dominated his view of the world, leaving practically everything else—excluding his ties to his wife Nellie and their family—incidental. As Charlie Rouse, who played sax for years in Monk's quartet, noted, "Monk thinks only of music." So absorbed was he in jazz that he would walk the New York streets for hours or stand still on a corner near his apartment on West 63rd Street, staring into his private landscape and running new songs and sounds through his mind. As he explained it, "I just walk and dig."

This kind of attitude affected his ways of communication; if music speaks for itself, what more is there to say? More subtly, it affected the way he played, leading him toward a highly individual flat-fingered technique on the keyboard. To get inside new doors, a new key had to be forged.

Audiences who were used to familiar runs and chords had a lot of trouble with Monk's coalescing style in the forties. Critic Paul Bacon was one of the few observers who could get past the perception of Monk as an eccentric who cultivated odd habits to make up for a deficient mechanism. Monk "has the most expressive feeling I can find in any musician playing now," he wrote in *Down Beat*, "but it has cost Monk something to play as he does. . . . fifty percent of his technique. He relies so much on absolute musical reflex that Horowitz's style might be unequal to the job."

Today there is little doubt that Monk had all the chops he needed, and more. Mary Lou Williams once looked back to her first encounter with a young Thelonious: "While Monk was in Kaycee [Kansas City], he jammed every night, really used to blow on piano, employing a lot more technique than he does today. Monk plays the way he does now because he got fed up. I *know* how Monk can play. He told me he was sick of having musicians play the same thing all the time."

We can look even further back to see early signs of Monk's now familiar style. As a boy, he practiced for hours each day behind the Steinway grand his family had gotten for him, not listening to the combinations he was working out on the keys, but watching the movements they required. A mirror had been mounted on the ceiling over the piano to reflect the rise and fall of the hammers, the shifting of the dampers, as he played. The visual balance, as well as the sounds, pleased him.

Monk's birthdate and place were for a while a matter of debate. When asked to clarify them by *Down Beat* in 1956, he replied, "When shall I be born? I'm just playing a game like everyone else." Subsequent research pinpointed the day—October 10, 1917—and place—Rocky Mount, North Carolina. He was named after his father; his mother, Barbara, was a former civil service employee, a Jehovah's Witness, and a strict disciplinarian.

Monk showed an early interest in music. A friend of the family had given them a player piano, and Thelonious was entranced by the sight of the keys magically rising and falling as the piano roll wound inside. At five or six he began picking melodies out on his own, and soon was teaching himself to read by watching over his older sister's shoulder as she took lessons.

In 1924 the Monks moved up to the San Juan Hill section of New York City, near the Hudson River. Shortly after that the father, suffering from a long illness, went back down south to recover, leaving his wife to raise their three children. By now Thelonious was showing great promise. At P.S. 141, and later at Stuyvesant High School, he excelled not only in music but in physics, math, and basketball as well. Despite his family's shallow finances, his mother somehow managed to bring a Steinway baby grand into the house, and when Thelonious was eleven years old she began paying for weekly piano lessons. Although musical scholarships were available to neighborhood kids and Monk's gifts were evident, the scholarship administrators deemed the child too musically unorthodox to invest in.

She also got him his first gig, accompanying the Baptist choir in which she sang. For two years Monk played organ and piano at the church for his mother; eventually she would return the favor by attending as many of his club dates as she could. By the end of his stint there, he had picked up some grounding in the gospel style, which stayed with him throughout his career. Many years later, when asked to bring a new Monk composition to a recording session, he showed up with his favorite old hymn, "Abide with Me," which, he solemnly pointed out, was composed by one William H. Monk. (Interestingly, "Abide with Me" was also the favorite hymn of Fats Waller.)

Soon a new musical love made its way into Monk's life. Jazz was alive in the city streets. One of the kings of New York's piano jazz scene, James P. Johnson, lived near the Monk household, and a number of clubs were in the area too. Thelonious absorbed the music, learned band arrangement at a local community center, and began playing with a trio at the age of 13, making his debut that summer in a New York bar and grill. At 14 he broke into the rent party circuit, where solo pianists matched themselves against competitors in festive musical combat. He also won at the Apollo Theater's famous weekly Wednesday amateur music contests; in fact, he won so many times that he was eventually banned from the event.

But it was gospel music that first took Monk on the road as a professional musician. At age 16 he left school to travel for a little more than a year with a woman evangelical faith healer and preacher; it was during a stopover with her in Kansas City that Monk met Mary Lou Williams. Even then, she later recalled, he was exploring new sounds on the piano, producing what she would characterize as "those frozen sounds."

On his return to New York, Monk began scuffling for work, first with non-union jobs. It was a tough regimen; soon he was playing seven nights a week and taking home $20 for the entire week's labor. He organized his first group in 1939, after working with a band at Kelly's Stable on 52nd Street. Not long after that, Monk landed a gig as resident pianist at a new club, but one that would prove to be more than just another jazz dungeon.

It was called Minton's, named after the owner, Harry Minton, a well-known figure on the city's music scene. Before opening this establishment, Minton had run the Rhythm Club, a popular hangout for an earlier generation of New York piano greats, including Fats Waller, Willie "the Lion" Smith, and the rest of the Harlem stride pianists. In the early forties he appointed bandleader Teddy Hill to manage Minton's, with instructions to find a house pianist. It was on the recommendation of drummer Kenny Clarke that Hill signed Monk.

Looking back on his stint at Minton's, Monk would recall, "I was just playing a gig, trying to play music. While I was at Minton's, anybody could sit in if he could play. I never bothered anybody." But others remember it differently. The early forties was a time of restless innovation. A group of young musicians who were dissatisfied with their work in swing bands began searching for new modes of expression in smaller groups and challenging themselves with a musical language they were defining as they went along in jam sessions and discussions that stretched past the far side of midnight. According to jazz folklore, the activity centered on Minton's, and as the house pianist there, Monk was at the eye of what would become the modern jazz hurricane.

Our earliest recordings of Monk stem from this period. In 1941 one Jerry Newman went down to Minton's to record the great guitarist Charlie Christian. Monk appears on two of the resulting cuts: "Topsy," later retitled "Swing to Bop," and "Stompin' at the Savoy." Subsequently released in 1947, they show the young pianist in a state of transition, with swinging single-note runs, especially on "Savoy," mixed with rhythmic exchanges between him and drummer Kenny Clarke that definitely reach beyond the conventions of swing.

More than anyone else in the Minton's crowd, Monk showed a knack for writing. Years before his piano work would be taken seriously, he would be known for his composing. In fact, most of the classic Monk tunes, such as "Blue Monk," "Epistrophy," and "'Round Midnight," were written during his gig at Minton's or before 1951.

Had he never played a note at the piano, Monk would still have left his mark on jazz players everywhere through these compositions. But though he frequently wrote away from the keyboard while strolling through his neighborhood, his piano playing and composing are tied closely together. This becomes clear when one listens to his treatments of other people's tunes. In his various recorded versions of "Smoke Gets in Your Eyes," for instance, his improvisations go beyond variations on the melody to alter the structure of the song, with his familiar minor ninths positioned around the theme as if it had been written for that purpose.

Monk's early bebop records make it clear that he stood apart from his peers. Gunther Schuller commented on this in the November 1958 issue of *Jazz Review*: "Monk was never the bopper so many people thought he was, and he was never 'cool' in the bop sense. One searches in vain for the atmosphere and clichés of the bop era . . . and one finds only Monk—original, daring, blunt, occasionally crude, and witty."

The most apparent difference, his avoidance of pyrotechnics, is obvious. On another level, the Harlem stride tradition, rejected as old-fashioned by many bop modernists, left a strong imprint on Monk, though he seemed at times to parody the stride style or use it to contrast with what the listener might expect. His minor ninths, voiced more frequently, starkly, and prominently than usual among bop pianists, may have stemmed, Schuller speculates, from Monk's childhood attempts to strike octaves with his smaller-than-average reach. Then there was his preoccupation with whole-tone runs, which first surfaced in four 78 rpm recordings he made in 1944 on the Joe Davis label with Coleman Hawkins, though this was a logical extension of the bopper's interest in diminished fifths.

In fact, Monk was ambivalent toward the bop style. In an interview with Nat Hentoff in the now defunct *Nugget* magazine, he lashed out as his compatriots: "They molest! They magnify! They exaggerate!" Later, he spoke more analytically: "They don't pay enough attention to swing [*i.e.,* the beat], and that goes for both the horns and the rhythm section. They don't know where to put those bops." When asked what the difference was between their style and his, Monk explained, "They think differently harmonically. They play mostly stuff that's based on chords of other things, like the blues and 'I Got Rhythm.' I like the whole song, melody and chord structure, to be different. I make up my own chords and melodies."

Yet it was the more extroverted bop players who stole the spotlight in the forties. For all the genius of Charlie Parker, the bop prototype, it proved easier to imitate his flashy and intricate runs than to duplicate the mysterious substance of Monk's simpler lines and chords. Bud Powell, not Monk, became the best-known pianist in that style. Ironically, Monk had helped Powell gain a foothold at Minton's, insisting that he be allowed to sit in when Clarke, Gillespie, and others had no interest in him. Later Powell returned the favor by persuading the popular trumpeter and Ellington alumnus Cootie Williams to record "'Round Midnight." Monk wrote the song at age 19, yet Williams demanded equal credit as a composer before recording it, a not unusual condition in those days.

Though reluctant to talk about personal matters—or, often, to talk at all—Monk allowed some bitterness to seep through in a 1960 interview with *Jazz* magazine. "Bud Powell? I'm the only one he

Monk would pass days in his room, staring for long hours at a picture of Billie Holiday taped to his ceiling.

really digs," he stated. "I brought Bud Powell around when he first started. That's never been in print. Doesn't worry; truth got to come out some time. . . . Oscar Peterson never gives me any credit. . . . George Shearing copies so much jive from me. He names everybody but who he *really* digs. I don't care who *I* mention, 'cause I don't envy anybody. . . . all you read today is how Miles followed Diz, Parker, Fats Navarro around like a puppy—everybody but me. Read everything but the truth. Miles never yet mentioned how much he learned from me. . . . Parker, Dizzy, they all came to hear me. Bird never excited me like he did the others. 'Bird is a god,' they said. He wasn't to me! No, and no one else was either!"

"He's a solitary man who, when he looks back, does not see his fellow travelers—who doesn't even know if he has fellow travelers."—Andre Hodeir, *Toward Jazz*

As the bop star blazed, Monk's career waned. In 1942 he played for a while with Lucky Millinder's big band, and in '44 he joined Coleman Hawkins, with whom he made his first studio recordings and went on his first extended jazz tour, playing in Chicago and on the West Coast as well as on New York's jazz club boulevard, 52nd Street.

But work began getting scarce. In 1946 he played briefly with Dizzy Gillespie's big band. The following year he made his first recording as leader of a combo, but from then through 1954 his record sessions were sporadic—two for the Blue Note label and five for Prestige. By 1948 he was doing only occasional nights at Birdland, and his days were often passed in his room, writing tunes, gazing silently at the television, or staring for long hours at a picture of Billie Holiday taped to his ceiling. Not much of that time involved getting paid. Nellie, his wife, helped keep food on the table with outside work during his spells of moody immobility.

Things weren't made any easier when, in 1951, Monk was arrested with Bud Powell on a charge of narcotics possession. He spent 60 days in jail, but more crucially, the New York State Liquor Authority rescinded his cabaret card, which in those days all club performers had to have in order to work. When he got out, Birdland wouldn't even offer him free admission, much less hire him. For the next several years he survived only with help from the Baroness de Koenigswarter.

Monk's fortunes didn't change until the mid-fifties. In 1954 he accepted an invitation to give a series of concerts in Paris. French journalists were perplexed at his refusal to discuss his music— "Let's not talk about it," he would remonstrate gently, "let's play it"—and reviews were mixed, but it was in Paris that Monk cut his first solo piano album, *Pure Monk*.

In 1955 he began his association with the Riverside label, catching some by surprise by focusing on other people's music on the first two LPs, *Thelonious Monk Plays Duke Ellington* and *The Unique Thelonious Monk*. With the release of *Brilliant Corners*, a stunning collection featuring Sonny Rollins on tenor sax, in 1956, his albums began to attract wider attention.

Meanwhile, the Baroness and Monk's manager, a high school English teacher named Harry Colomby, got his card restored, and word began to spread that he was back in action. The mystique also grew: Program notes for the Berkshire Music Barn Jazz Concert in 1955 read, "Monk is the Greta Garbo of jazz, and his appearance at any piano is regarded as a major event by serious followers of jazz."

Monk's television debut, on the CBS *Sound Of Jazz* in 1957, was a sign that something big was happening. A number of important jazz players shared the stage with him, but Monk, though still not widely known to the public, was perhaps the hit of the show. During a coffee break between rehearsals, he seated himself at the piano and began improvising. The other performers, including Count Basie, Billie Holiday, and saxophonist Lester Young, gathered around to listen. The scene moved the director to stage Monk's solo number with them assembled once more around the piano, the camera capturing their amazed expressions.

Though his TV appearance went well, it did create one problem. Three days before the telecast, Monk was scheduled to play at a recording session. He was there for each rehearsal, but when it came time to show at the studio, he was nowhere to be seen. At the last minute Mal Waldron was brought in as a substitute. It was later learned that Monk had fallen asleep; for days his anxiety over the TV gig had kept him wide awake.

His opening in the summer of 1957 at New York's Five Spot drew full houses, and the grateful management invited him to choose his own piano for the club and to stay as long as he wanted—he stayed for eight months. Fronting a powerful quartet there, with Shadow Wilson on drums, Wilbur Ware on bass, and a young saxophonist named John Coltrane, Monk found himself at the center of a cult. Audiences lined up to see his unpredictable performances, his quirky, quietly ecstatic dances during horn solos, his wanderings through the room. To the musically astute, however, there was much more than that going on, not the least of which being the first signs of genius in Coltrane's work. Coltrane himself laid much of the credit for his growth during this period on Monk, who, among other things, taught him how to blow more than one note at a time.

Monk's luck seemed to take one more turn for the worst in the fall of 1958, with another drug-related arrest. En route with the Baroness and Charlie Rouse from New York to Baltimore for a gig there at the Comedy Club, Monk decided to pull over for a glass of water at a hotel in Delaware. In the hotel, offended in some manner by the manager, he lapsed into a stony silence and began moving slowly back and forth through the lobby. His withering glare and massive presence frightened the manager into calling the police. By the time they arrived, Monk had returned to his car. They ordered him out, but he stared quietly ahead, not moving. Finally they dragged him out, prying his grip from the steering wheel, pulling him to their van, and beating him on the hands despite the Baroness's pleas. Meanwhile, some marijuana turned up in the trunk; the Baroness announced that it was hers. Charges against her were eventually dropped, but Monk was found guilty of disturbing the peace.

This was enough for the New York Liquor Authority to again withhold the pianist's cabaret license. Monk's manager, protesting that racism had been involved in the complaint and arrest, demanded a hearing, but when Monk refused to confirm that the hotel manager had called him a nigger, the appeal was denied.

Monk never enjoyed being far from his wife or from New York, so when this new exclusion from local clubs forced him to go on the road, the pressures of exile escalated, culminating in a strange episode during a job in Boston's Copley Square Hotel in the fall of 1959. Monk showed up late and ambled through the lobby, staring at the walls until the unnerved management refused to give him a room. At ten that evening he seated himself at the Storyville piano, played two songs with his band, and then left. At 11:30 he returned, did the same two songs, and then sat motionless for about eight minutes with the band looking uncomfortably on. Sensing that they weren't needed, the group then left the stage, and Monk remained, totally still, for more than twenty more minutes before finally getting up and leaving.

Later that night he was picked up at the Boston airport by the state police. He had taken a cab there in hopes of catching a flight back to New York, but finding that the last planes had already departed, he started pacing up and down through the terminal. The police took him to the Grafton State Hospital in Worcester, where he was held under observation for a week. No one knew where he had gone; his wife phoned the Boston police, not thinking to check the state force as well, and a telegram sent by the hospital to her never arrived. It wasn't until a friend in Boston heard where he was on the local news that Nellie was notified and he was released.

From that point on, when asked about his eccentricities, Monk would answer, "I can't be crazy, because they had me in one of those places and let me go."

After two years, deciding that Monk was no danger to audiences in New York, the Liquor Authority reinstated him once more, and finally he was able to play on his home turf. Most important, Nellie would go to work with him; on rare occasions when she couldn't, he phoned her during intermissions. Both of them believed that their marriage was literally made in heaven, or some similar department in the spiritual bureaucracy. They had first seen each other as children on a playground; though six months would pass before they actually met, both sensed a connection with that initial contact, and

Monk would later surprise her by recalling everything she was wearing that day. When she had to spend some time in a hospital, Monk composed one of his most beautiful tunes, "Crepuscule with Nellie," for her, taking a full month to get exactly the feeling he wanted with it.

Monk felt an obligation to provide for Nellie and their children, so he must have been especially grateful for his increasing good fortune in the early sixties. As late as 1958 he was charging $800 for his band; by 1960 his prices as risen to as high as $2,000 for week-long jobs, or $1,000 for one-nighters. In 1964 his earnings climbed to $50,000.

And better gigs were coming in. On a European tour in the early sixties he sold out the historic Concertgebouw in Amsterdam, and his concert in Sweden was nationally televised live. He delighted in bringing back souvenirs from these tours, including new additions to his ever-growing collection of hats and a beautiful opal ring purchased in Hong Kong. Monk always wore this ring along with one he had designed himself in New York during the fifties: a black onyx with the letters M-O, two large diamonds, and then the letters N-K.

But of all his concerts, the one staged in December '63 at New York's Philharmonic Hall may have been the most personally satisfying. Monk and his quartet—drummer Frankie Dunlop, bassist Butch Warren, and saxophonist Charlie Rouse—shared the stage with trumpeters Thad Jones and Nick Travis, saxophonists Steve Lacy, Phil Woods, and Gene Allen, and trombonist Eddie Bert in a big-band presentation of Monk material. This was not an entirely new setting for Monk; he had fronted a ten-piece band doing Hall Overton's arrangements of his tunes at Town Hall and the Randall's Island Jazz Festival, which won enthusiastic reviews in *The New York Times*. But Philharmonic Hall was special: It was within walking distance of his apartment, a part of the neighborhood he had crisscrossed on his long meditative strolls. After years of hassles with local clubs and unsympathetic critics, Monk had finally made it close to home.

"Thelonious is a very strange person."—Milt Jackson

Through feast and famine, one thing never changed: Monk himself. To the end he stuck to the technique he had begun exploring when Mary Lou Williams first heard him. Holding his fingers almost totally flat, he sacrificed accuracy in arpeggios and runs in order to get the sound he wanted, even playing with his elbows if necessary. His mood dictated his performances. After a hair-raising airplane ride to Detroit, he spent most of his concert that night jabbing the keys with his elbows for sharp, harsh clusters.

In rehearsals he could be exacting, leading his band over a one-minute segment of his music for two hours without telling them that they were practicing at a slow tempo. Since the band hadn't suffered any apprehensions about matching heavy technical demands with quick tempos, they could follow Monk's guidance up to full speed with almost no trouble once they had mastered their parts. At one rehearsal, when alto saxophonist Gigi Gryce protested that his part was impossible to play, Monk coolly replied, "You have an instrument, don't you? Either play it or throw it away," then walked off. Eventually Gryce played it.

The feeling of a piece, and its overall contours, were always more important to Monk than getting all the notes right. Not a strong sight-reader, he rarely looked at scores in rehearsal. "That way," he explained, "nothing distracts." He habitually gathered up the band's charts immediately after concerts and took them home, sometimes misplacing them there.

Needless to say, Monk remained personally, as well as musically, true to himself. He never moved from his apartment, a flat in the rear of an old tenement building near warehouses and public housing developments, with a tan baby grand nearly filling the main room; the keyboard almost reached the kitchen sink. His idiosyncrasies remained: He still went on long drives in his '56 Buick or traipsed the local streets lost in music, still broke into street-corner shuffles like a tranced-out jazz dervish. His brother recalls Thelonious whisking into his apartment one day with a collard leaf pinned to his label, dancing blissfully before a mirror for a few moments, then leaving without a word.

Neither did he escape his brooding quiet spells. Often he would keep his silence for days on end; strangers and loved ones alike could only watch and wait for the clouds to pass. Even Nellie, asking if he was worried, would sometimes only get him to say, "No."

It seems likely that music, that angel spirit that beat time for his joyful tap steps, might sometimes have doubled as demon. Monk's disinterest in talking about his art may have stemmed from the presumptions of his fans nearly as much as from their earlier indifference. Imagine the scene when, at a Columbia University seminar on his music, the professor asked Monk, "Would you play some of your weird chords for the class?" The pianist bristled: "What do you mean *weird?* They're perfectly logical chords!" Then there was his record company's request for him to pose for one album cover dressed as a monk in a pulpit. He refused, but he did consent to be photographed while sitting in a little red wagon in front of his house.

There's an important point here. What may seem to industry executives as another marketable Monk eccentricity in fact stemmed from the man's consistent view of integrity. He objected to wearing a cassock because monks did not sermonize from behind church podiums, but he saw no problem with the latter shot because in reality he had composed while seated in the front yard in his son's toy wagon. Truth, in representation as well as music, was the light in Monk's life. For a man who knew only how to be true to his muse, who had never learned to compromise his art, misplaced enthusiasm may have been harder to take than the anonymity of his earlier career.

Monk's last years were spent at the home of the Baroness de Koenigswarter, where he isolated himself from people who had at one time been his closest friends and colleagues. As at every other stage of his remarkable life, we as outsiders can only speculate on what led to his withdrawal. More than most people in music, Monk must remain a mystery, but in his work he left us echoes of that hidden world inside his mind—that sidewalk dance, midnight dream, love, and loneliness.

"All ways know, always night, all ways know—and dig the way I say 'all ways.'"—Thelonious Monk.

Hard Bop to Funk

26. HORACE SILVER

Born: September 2, 1928, Norwalk, Connecticut

Bop, in the late forties, was about moving forward. The message of the church was to go the other way—back toward values that were disdained, if not forgotten, by the modern vanguard. Bop fled from the hand-clapped beat of church music, shifting the rhythm toward the cymbal and only dropping irregular accents on the drums. Its improvisers burst past the pentatonic vocabulary of gospel into a language riddled with quizzical flatted fifths and "Chinese" dissonance.

It was Horace Silver's mission to bridge these opposed forms. The impact of his earthy style stretched beyond the piano into broader realms of pop music. Silver's performances set a precedent for Ray Charles, whose fusion of gospel vocals and secular lyrics defined much of the direction that rock and R&B would follow these past 40-odd years.

For all his importance, Silver shows none of the swagger of celebrity. He was unobtrusive, slight and quiet, almost a fragile figure in his early years. Later, as his world view developed along holistic spiritual lines, he would let his hair grow, devote himself to health foods, and switch from narrow ties and white shirts to colorful African finery. But even now Silver makes his impact gently, with soft voice and an inviting smile. His optimistic manner radiates an inner peace, tempered by the residual hipness of his jazzy argot.

You could say the same about his piano playing. Silver learned to generate heat through minimal gestures. In the context of bop, with its emphasis on long lines and high velocity, he created a style based on relatively limited chops and an empathy for the feel and phrasing of church music. This sound, quickly tagged as hard bop, scaled the innovations of Bud Powell, Charlie Parker, and Dizzy Gillespie down to a language that a broader range of players and listeners could embrace.

Much of Silver's originality traces to his family background. Along with services at the local Methodist church and jazz radio broadcasts, he was affected by the sensuous, bossa-like music of the Cape Verdean Islands, from where his parents had emigrated. His father played guitar and a bit of violin in a band with two of his brothers; young Horace was a regular at their gigs and at musical parties in his own home.

From the start, Silver appreciated the distinctions and common ground between a variety of rhythms. Raised as an only child, with one older brother gone from home by the time of his birth, Silver was a desultory saxophone student until around age 12, when he was inspired by a Jimmie Lunceford concert at a nearby amusement park to pick up the pace of his practice. His training on piano was sketchy, involving little more than some lessons in his teens from his church organist. But he listened carefully to records, which he would memorize while playing them slowly on a wind-up turntable.

Though saxophone was his first instrument throughout high school, Silver was forced to set it aside and switch full-time to piano right after graduation. A physical exam at age 19 revealed a curvature in his spine; within a year, a temporary deterioration in ability to control his arms made it difficult for him to play his horn. Chiropractic treatment prevented further damage, but there was no way to undo what had already been done.

Fate, then, led Silver to the piano bench. He was at the keys on a gig in Hartford when fate again made an appearance, in the form of tenor saxophonist Stan Getz. Silver and the rest of saxophonist Harold Holdt's rhythm section had been hired to back Getz at the Sundown Club. Apparently things went well, for Getz immediately offered Silver a job with his own group. With that, the pianist left on an extended road trip that ended with his relocation to New York.

Other opportunities followed quickly, as Silver landed bookings with Coleman Hawkins, Oscar Pettiford, Lester Young, and other major leaguers. Between these performances he continued to practice, often on the house piano at Birdland, working not just to build his technique but to develop that original sound.

Silver's star rose further in 1954, when *Down Beat* lauded him as a hot new talent and Minton's, the original bebop club up in Harlem, offered him a gig. At that engagement he fronted a quartet that featured trumpeter Kenny Dorham and saxophonist Hank Mobley. They stayed with Silver when he expanded to five pieces, with bassist Doug Watkins and drummer Art Blakey. This quintet built its arrangements around a jam-session model, which encouraged each member to look for and lock onto the groove in each tune. Their missionary zeal inspired Silver to call this group the Jazz Messengers.

From that point up to the present, Silver has recruited a long string of great players into his many bands. After letting Blakey appropriate the Jazz Messengers name for his own group in 1956, Silver and Mobley assembled a new quintet, with Art Farmer on trumpet. Others followed, most often paired in tenor sax/trumpet combinations: Junior Cook and Blue Mitchell, Joe Henderson and Woody Shaw, Stanley Turrentine and Charles Tolliver, Bennie Maupin and Randy Brecker.

For all these groups Silver wrote a prodigious amount of material. Typically, these tunes are straightforward blowing vehicles, built on catchy themes and seductive rhythms. The titles themselves reflect something of the process that Silver brings to his writing: "The Preacher," "Blowin' the Blues Away," "Soulville," "Cookin' at the Continental," and his other earlier works suggest images and characters that might have inspired the tenor of each tune. On later works, a lighter mentality seems evident, along with an enduring sense of humor: "The Hillbilly Bebopper," "The Hard-Bop Grandpop," "The Respiratory Story."

Despite its persistent amiability, Silver's later work doesn't compare well to his earliest output. His playing has settled into a familiar formula as well, with many of the elements but little of the urgency that made him so important in the late bop era. This is perhaps inevitable, given Silver's longevity. Plenty of artists have built careers for themselves based on abuse of his innovations; in the end, it is difficult to filter his work from 50 years of regurgitated gospel licks from his imitators.

Listen, for example, to "The Preacher," recorded in 1955 for *The Horace Silver Quintet, Vol. 2*, on which Silver devotes two choruses to a fairly conservative elaboration on the theme. Much of what he plays is in fact pretty close to the gospel figurations and repetitions that he played behind solos by Mobley and Dorham. There's heat in Silver's playing, but it comes more from his references to gospel phrases than from any incendiary display. Better than most funk pianists who followed him, Silver understood how not to beat a lick to death.

Silver was in his prime a very active rhythm section player. On "Room 608," recorded in 1953 for *The Horace Silver Quintet, Vol. 1*, he delivers a powerful solo, notable mainly for its unusually active

Horace Silver's impact stretched beyond the piano into broader realms of pop music.

left hand. Throughout two choruses the pianist jabs off-beat chords and clusters beneath the right-hand line. Because Silver plays quietly, and because he keeps his solo spare, there's no sense of clash between the two parts. On a later date, "Cookin' at the Continental," from the 1959 album *Finger Poppin'*, Silver tones down the left hand just a bit during his own two choruses, but as the rest of the band members take their turns, he lays down a remarkably busy interaction with bassist Gene Taylor and drummer Louis Hayes, with on- and off-beat chords dropping nonstop. He goes further still on the title cut from *Blowin' the Blues Away*, recorded in 1959, not only jabbing chords with hardly a break throughout everyone else's solos, but throwing in whippet-quick riffs and linear snippets for contrast. His solo, too, is built on insistent, rocking riffs, punctuated by clustered bursts in the bass register.

Even at more moderate tempos, Silver frequently built his improvisations on a restless, active left-hand foundation. In his solo for "Nica's Dream," from *Introducing Kenny Burrell*, the pianist constructs his right-hand improvisation with meticulous care, coming up with a spare but eloquent line. There's plenty of space between notes as Silver creates a vaguely modal statement, with a satisfying switch to a straight-ahead riff toward the end of the first chorus. What's notable, though less noticeable, is the way his left hand keeps feeding the momentum, sometimes with nothing more than an oddly positioned note or two. Without it, the skeletal frame of Silver's right-hand line would be deprived of a certain energy.

During very up-tempo tunes, Silver sometimes seemed overtaxed. On the supersonic "The Natives Are Restless Tonight," from the mid-sixties live album *Re-Entry*, he breaks his solo up into short gospel bits rather than challenge himself to construct a less fractured longer line. Too often during this solo he punctuates right-hand rests with closed-fisted thumps in the bass range, in what seems to be a turn toward effect when more substantial ideas run short.

There were times, too, when his somewhat narrow range seemed to thwart possibilities for a more revealing approach to a tune. Silver composed the beautiful "Song for My Father," yet his solo on the live version from *Re-Entry* feels uncomfortable: His left hand hits unchallenging chords with too much weight, even rushing the beat at times, while his right hand keeps hammering on octaves, fifths, and minor ninths, or tossing out gospel licks and other familiar devices. Undoubtedly he plays with energy, but there would seem to be much more that one could bring on this sort of a tune.

Never a harmonically sophisticated player, Silver in general either stayed within a simple blues framework or slipped into a bitonal setting. One clear example of this device is on "We've Got Silver at Six," from the 1996 album *The Hardbop Grandpop*, in which all but the last few bars of his solo are played one whole-step above the key. The effect does offer something beyond the traditional blues scale on the root chord of the song, but Silver's tendency in this and other songs to not explore the implications of tonal juxtaposition make it clear that he's playing more for effect than in pursuit of harmonic insight.

This relatively unadorned approach to harmony sometimes left Silver ill-equipped for ballads. On "Peace," from the 1959 album *Blowin' the Blues Away*, he hops his single-line solo into double-time over a very spare left hand; though finely conceived, with extended bitonal jaunts and a tasteful tremolo or two, it suggests a limitation in Silver's ability to pursue more than one avenue in slower tempos. But that path he explored with exquisite taste and inventiveness; his thoughtful solo on "I Married an Angel," a 1956 date for Donald Byrd featured on the Savoy Jazz release *The Birth of Hard Bop*, is a showcase of melodic invention.

In the end, Silver's most important contributions as a mature artist may be in his cultivation of young talent as sidemen. But it's his own youthful explorations that endure, and will maintain his prominence as a pivotal pianistic influence for generations to come.

27. WYNTON KELLY

Born: December 2, 1931, Jamaica
Died: April 12, 1971, Toronto, Ontario, Canada

He was, above all else, a pianist whose talent allowed him to grow past limitations that would have encumbered most other pianists. A technically competent but not exceptional player, with a background that included fundamental but not advanced instruction, Wynton Kelly flourished because of his wonderful ear and unparalleled feel for rhythm. He was, as Bill Evans once pointed out, one of the best accompanists in jazz, and like Herbie Hancock he was able to find delicacy and nuance buried in the roots of his blues.

Born in Jamaica to West Indian parents, Kelly was raised in Brooklyn. Though he took his first piano lessons at the age of four, his training was sketchy; as a student at Metropolitan Vocational and the Music and Art High School in Manhattan, Kelly concentrated on theory rather than performance, and even spent some time learning to play bass. Even so, he was playing gigs in Brooklyn at age 13. Two years later Kelly began doing local jobs with tenor saxophonist Ray Abrams; while still in his teens he worked with trumpeter Hot Lips Page, and then spent a year with Lockjaw Davis before taking a gig with the Three Blazes.

For several years Kelly went back and forth between Dizzy Gillespie's band and backup work with singer Dinah Washington. After a stretch in the Army, during which time he met and befriended fellow pianist Phineas Newborn, he played again with Gillespie from 1954 until leaving to form his own group in '57. When he replaced Bill Evans on the piano with the Miles Davis band in 1959 Kelly began to win widespread attention throughout and beyond the jazz community, in part because of the contrast between his soulful but satiny style and the more cerebral explorations of his predecessor.

Writer Gene Lees summarized Kelly's style in *Down Beat*, noting its "highly personal ease and lightness, an infectious, casually bouncing quality to which one rapidly becomes attached." Equally important was his strength within rhythm sections, where his discerning ears, generous willingness to feed the soloist, and aversion to overplaying made him an ideal component. Though he would record eleven albums as a leader, Kelly did some of his best work backing other artists throughout the fifties and sixties.

Conceptually, Kelly wasn't the most innovative player; his solos often followed the bop formula of left-hand comps and right-hand lines that built to percussive, two-fisted chorded climaxes. His rhythms, especially in the way he would divide phrases or syncopated chords against the beat, drew strongly from the churchy elements that influenced the funk or hard bop school. Soloing on "Blue 'n' Boogie," from the 1962 Wes Montgomery album, *Full House*, Kelly pops percolating chords in a way that suggests how Jimmy Smith would play the part on organ—thick in timbre, spicy around the edges.

Blues scales supplied most of the material for Kelly's solos. On "New Delhi," from the 1961 album *The Cannonball Adderley Quintet Plus*, to name but one of many sides, he extemporizes entirely within the pentatonic structure of the style. But Kelly also understood the importance of stepping outside those boundaries now and then. On "Harry's Last Stand," a medium-up blues from *Introducing Wayne Shorter* in 1959, Kelly begins his three choruses firmly latched onto the tonic (echoing the last notes of Lee Morgan's trumpet solo) and ends on a tonic as well. In the second verse, after a variation on the closing figure from the first verse that ends this time on the fifth, he builds his line up to an unidiomatic major seventh in the fourth bar, then follows with some unexpected movement in bar eight. Here, Kelly hits a diminished interval in his left hand—a flat-five, G-flat below C. Within the style, it's reasonable to expect him to hang onto it for another bar as the beginning of a VI–IIm–V–I progression back to the tonic. Instead, he takes it up a half-step, to G below E-flat, which leads his right-hand line into a brief but effective variation on an escalating figure. This is a small but significant touch, the kind of thing that separated him from far more predictable players.

Kelly's superbly inventive accompaniment is evident on "Bye Bye Blackbird," from the 1961 album *Miles Davis In Person Friday Night at the Blackhawk*. He opens for the band with a snappy eight-bar intro, quoting the first notes of the theme within a simple but effective reharmonization that emphasizes the sixth interval. When Davis makes his entrance, the trumpet plays only the first half of the first two lines, leaving out the "bye-bye, blackbird" part of the lyric. Kelly holds back during the silence in bars three and four, offering just one little fill, but then in bar eight he drops in a beautifully conceived bluesy lick, ending it on the last eighth-note pulse of the measure; this cues Jimmy Cobb to answer with a snare accent on the first beat of bar nine, which in turn gives the trumpeter an effective nudge into the bridge. Then, still pushing to give Davis inspiration, Kelly comes back in on the next eight bars with a few extended chords, emphasizing the flat-five, which allow Davis to take the theme up to a contrasting key for a few bars, after which Kelly hits a single articulated octave on the dominant as a final sendoff into the horn solo.

In his own solo on this track Kelly plays a balancing act between clear references to the melody in his verses and faster, slightly more outside lines on his bridges. He uses funk phrases here and there but doesn't rely on them to sustain melodic interest. Typical of Kelly, everything he plays swings hard—and, in this case, seems to push against Cobb and bassist Paul Chambers, who for some reason are noticeably dragging the tempo.

By far Kelly's most famous performance is on "Freddie Freeloader," the one cut from the Miles Davis *Kind of Blue* session on which he appears. For all the wondrous playing delivered by Bill Evans on the other tracks, Kelly is the perfect pianist for this medium-clip, groove tune. Right from the start, his fills find precisely the right spaces, with just enough movement to balance the languid horn theme. Taking the first solo, he plays with economy and elegance, using little more than the blues scale to concoct a simple opening motif, which in turn defines his direction through four subsequent verses. By referring to clichéd idiomatic figures without actually articulating them, Kelly makes his improvisation feel familiar and fresh at the same time. Each note is a gem, and each space between them speaks as well.

Even in the unusual context of Latin rhythm in session with Dizzy Gillespie and Stuff Smith on "Rio Pakistan," recorded on April 17, 1957, for *Dizzy Gillespie and Stuff Smith*, Kelly infuses a hard-bop feel in the unforced syncopations and resolute movement toward the tonic on modal-sounding runs. He manages to sound exotic and bluesy at the same time. For his solo, he maintains the straight sixteenth-note feel of his fills but falls back on more fundamental churchy figures, except for one delightful passage in the last verse, where he expands into rolled octaves. The effect of plucking a double-stringed instrument leads Kelly back into modalisms before he breaks back down to a single line and bluesy tonalities to end the improvisation.

At ballad tempos Kelly maintained his moody, after-hours feel, with expressive chords played in the spaces left by the soloist. A typical example can be heard on "Why Are We Afraid," recorded in 1960 and re-released most recently on the Art Pepper compilation *The Art of the Ballad*, in 1998. When taking his short solo on the bridge, Kelly nudges Paul Chambers and Jimmy Cobb into a brush-driven double-time pulse and makes his statement with a simple single line, again built entirely on a standard blues scale. Immediately after Pepper comes back in, Kelly drops back to a harmonic role, this time with popping staccato chords on the quarter-note beats and a gentle unpedaled smear down the keys, which serve to ease things down to a ballad tempo. In every respect this is a typical Kelly ballad performance, with its switch to double-time and single notes, yet within its limits it is a completely satisfying snippet.

Kelly died as a result of an epileptic seizure in Toronto, not long after recording a final session with saxophonist Joe Henderson.

28. RAY BRYANT

Born: December 24, 1931, Philadelphia, Pennsylvania

His family tree bears the fruit of jazz—brother Tommy was a highly regarded bass player, and nephews Kevin and Robin Eubanks would achieve distinction as a guitarist and trombonist, respectively, in the eighties. Yet blues is as much a part of Ray Bryant's style as bop and stride. Over the years he has allowed more emotion into his performance, a process that initially caused some skepticism among critics who couldn't get past their own prejudices about his R&B affiliation. Today, his odyssey marks Bryant as a pioneer, whose unapologetic embrace of boogie-woogie, New Orleans piano, and soul music paved the way for genre-hoppers of a later generation.

A late starter, Bryant began playing jazz piano around age 14. He learned quickly, though, and by the late forties was gigging with guitarist and frequent Art Tatum sideman Tiny Grimes. Beginning in the early fifties, Bryant made himself part of a popular local rhythm section that featured his brother Tommy on bass. Together they landed a gig in 1953 as house band at the Philadelphia Blue Note, where they backed an assortment of visiting stars, including Charlie Parker, Lester Young, Sonny Rollins, and Dizzy Gillespie.

In 1955 he made his recording debut on *Meet Betty Carter and Ray Bryant*. Working with bassist Wendell Marshall and drummer Philly Joe Jones behind Carter's smoky vocals, Bryant displayed the confident, understated style that's necessary for accompaniment. On the medium-tempo "I Could Write a Book," he slips a tasteful figure into the eighth bar of each verse, in which he follows Marshall down a descending line that leads through a V chord to a second-inversion I chord on the ninth bar. This sets the mood for Bryant to mix a gentle concoction of light, lounge-like runs and substitute changes. Nothing spectacular, but flawlessly conceived, without a single awkward note or pause.

On several instrumental cuts from the same album, such as "Sneaking Around," Bryant shows a somewhat more assertive side: His performances throughout these selections—on several original tunes, during the bridge sections of "Old Devil Moon," and on much of his solo during "What Is This Thing Called Love"—coast on a stream of straight eighth-notes that suggested a preference for R&B phrasing, with relatively few boppish triplet ornaments. On "No Moon at All" Bryant even breaks up this flow of straight eighths with a few beats of triplets on an open fourth, closer in spirit for a moment to Little Richard than to Bud Powell or even Horace Silver.

Following sessions for Miles Davis and Sonny Rollins, Bryant began working with Carmen McRae in 1957 while also accepting calls for projects with Art Blakey, Lee Morgan, and Clifford Jordan. Drummer Jo Jones signed Bryant to his trio in 1958. Featured prominently in this instrumental setting, the young Bryant played cautiously, even tentatively. His rendition of "Sweet Lorraine," recorded in 1957 for the album *Jo Jones Plus Two* and subsequently reissued on the Vanguard compilation *Key One Up*, emphasizes open, old-timey chords, complete with tremolos and turnarounds that seem lifted straight from the Earl Hines book, articulated with a finicky precision that's only made stiffer by Bryant's straight-eighth phrasing. Elsewhere on the same albums, however, Bryant, powered by his brother Tommy's nimble bass and Jones's irresistible brush drumming, shows a flash of his emerging ability to swing. His somewhat simplistic chords and sprightly arpeggios, along with some slightly overplayed left-hand comps on "Sometimes I'm Happy" and "Bicycle for Two" fail to derail the momentum Bryant establishes through his muscular, insistent lines.

It takes a more ambitious setting to inspire a more daring performance. Recorded the same year as the Jo Jones trio date, Bryant's solo on "Toffi," from Art Blakey's project *Orgy in Rhythm Vols. 1 & 2*, builds insightfully on the drummer's Pan-African concept for the album. Over a syncopated bass vamp and a hand-drum pattern, Bryant creates a compelling solo. He builds momentum and tension through the ease of his improvisation and the division of that flow into concise sections punctuated by articulations of the tonic. Aside from a couple of growling open fifths and two final licks before Herbie Mann comes in on flute, Bryant plays the whole thing in a silky string of single notes. The result is an intriguing simplicity, filled with harmonic and rhythmic implications.

Bryant also made his debut as a leader in 1958, on *Alone with the Blues*. He achieved a pop hit in 1959 with "Little Susie," followed shortly by "Madison Time." Throughout the sixties he scored several hit singles in a soulful vein, including "Cold Turkey," "Slow Freight," and "Gotta Travel On," on which he quickly achieved a consistently expressive level of performance within a relatively unadorned style.

It's easiest to appreciate this approach when he worked with more idiosyncratic artists. On *Sonny Rollins on Impulse!*, recorded in 1965, the saxophonist's sprawling solos characteristically spill across bar lines, with ballooning timbre and phrasing that slips in and out of tempo. This, of course, contrasts vividly with Bryant's meticulous, metrically tight approach. On "Blue Room," even Rollins's statement of the theme, with its unexpected inversions of the melody and capricious skipping rhythms, projects a restless urge to break into freer territory, but in the piano solo that follows this verse, Bryant keeps his improvisation rigidly symmetrical: The first half of each verse and of the bridge is played primarily with triplet phrasing, the last sections in largely unsyncopated eighth-notes. (Bassist Walter Booker highlights the contrast by anchoring the triplet sections with a quarter-note pulse on the dominant, then switching to walking patterns as Bryant changes his phrasing.)

With a sequence of highly touted live solo piano albums in the seventies, Bryant finally won recognition from critics and audiences. *Alone at Montreux*, recorded in 1972, showcases a mature style based on full-blooded, two-fisted blues. His aggressive attack and rhythmic figurations anticipate the work of Henry Butler, particularly on cuts like "Gotta Travel On" and "Little Susie"—with their sharp single notes and octaves in the bass riveted between right-hand runs, and their exuberantly executed, messily pedaled climaxes, these performances maintain the R&B connection that continues to feed Bryant, as it does Butler, to this day.

29. RAMSEY LEWIS

Born: May 27, 1935, Chicago, Illinois

He was the Erroll Garner of the sixties—the jazz pianist that everyone knew and loved. His formula for fame combined slimmed-down hard bop and a shrewd selection of pop repertoire. The momentum of his hits—"The 'In' Crowd," followed by "Hang On, Sloopy"—carried him through decades of albums and performances marked by variations on his commercial funk sound.

Did the success of Ramsey Lewis come with a price? As a pianist with a complete understanding of modern postbop, he was equipped to follow in the steps of Bud Powell toward areas of real innovation. Instead, he created an identity for himself as the most accessible of jazz pianists, with a rock-oriented, backbeat-driven rhythm and a solo vocabulary that seldom ventured beyond the limits of funk.

The son of a choirmaster, Lewis was six years old when he persuaded his parents to let him begin piano studies; it took a crying fit one day when his sister went off to her lesson for Ramsey to cinch the deal. For five years he worked with the same teacher, after which he pursued advanced studies at the Chicago Musical College and DePaul University.

Though he played with a local group called the Clefs during his high school years, Lewis was set on a career as a classical pianist. But when the act split up in 1955, Lewis, then at DePaul, put his first trio together, with Clefs bassist Eldee Young and drummer Butch McCann. After Isaac "Red" Holt replaced McCann, Chicago disc jockey Daddy-O Daylie set up an audition for the trio with the Chess label. This led to their debut album, *Ramsey Lewis and His Gentlemen of Swing*, in 1957. For several years after that, the threesome worked the jazz club circuit, winning modest notice until they scored their first hit album with *Sound of Christmas* in 1962. Two years later, their album *At the Bohemian Caverns* launched their first single, "Something You Got."

Ramsey Lewis created an identity for himself
as the most accessible of jazz pianists.

They cut "The 'In' Crowd" at the suggestion of Nettie Gray, a waitress at the Caverns in Washington, D.C., where they recorded it live on opening night. The performance is funk jazz redux: Practically everything Lewis plays involves a blue note, a "crushed" or elided minor/major third, or an articulation of the tonic above the melody. Lewis's solo is the antithesis of Bud Powell's long line; instead, it's assembled from fragmentary gospel figures, usually no more than two bars long and inevitably separated by another bar or two from the following figure. With the crowd chattering and clapping along, "The 'In' Crowd" is clearly a party disc, designed to be part of a festive ambience rather than studied analytically.

And so it goes through the entire album. On ballads Lewis sounds short of ideas: His "Love Theme from *Spartacus*" is little more than a lifeless recital theme until the trio kicks in with an undulating, ersatz Arabian beat, over which Lewis plays a sometimes awkwardly discordant funk solo. And his unaccompanied rendering of Ellington's "Come Sunday" is long on melodramatic rubato and flourishes, but short on more subtle, harmonically-based insights. Like everything else on this disc, it plays to the crowd.

Much of the Lewis catalog is tethered firmly to the party/soul genre. His best-known performances are short, seldom more than four minutes long, with concise improvisational passages tucked into clever arrangements. His treatment of "Carmen," based on the Bizet opera, makes effective use of a key change going into and out of the solo sections—but the solo itself is little more than syncopated versions of the theme; the last two verses consist largely of funk clichés and a sly quote from "Anything Goes." Anything, indeed.

Unlike every other jazz pianist in or out of this book, Lewis relied on the sound of a festive crowd as the critical ingredient in the sound of his most popular early records. To make sure that everyone clapped at the right place, he made sure his tempos were comfortable and that the snare beat hit clearly on the second and fourth beats of every bar. Invariably, the big applause comes when everybody can identify "High-Heeled Sneakers," "Hang On, Sloopy," or whatever R&B tune Lewis happens to be playing. Sad to say, the high point in these shows seems to be that moment of recognition. In effect, the pianist provides accompaniment to his listeners as they celebrate their own hipness.

More than a few moments in his catalog suggest that Lewis has consciously simplified his style over the years. He does have an ability to conjure a perfumed, hothouse atmosphere that is not at all inconsistent with his blues base. On "Delilah," from the compilation *Ramsey Lewis's Finest Hour*, Lewis plays an intoxicating introduction at a slow tempo that suggests a mirage in shimmering heat, with the bass hitting the first and third beat like the trudge of a caravan. Lewis's harmonies are simple, mostly straight minors, but his articulation is evocative and seductive, with the melody whispered in unison at the top and bottom of each chord. When the beat slides into a sensuous, swaying funk rhythm, followed by another verse in swing time, the piano turns up the heat with a bluesy reflection on the theme; he touches on the funk licks, but slithers beyond them with snake-like modal stretches. Obviously Lewis can turn in a tasty performance without falling back on obvious devices; for whatever reason it's his choice to walk a straighter and narrower path than necessary.

The trio format remained central to Lewis throughout his career. On many of these he attempted to move beyond his early persona, toward fusion in some projects, more in a mainstream direction on others. His 1999 album for Narada, *Appassionata*, typifies the latter approach. On these performances the pianist plays with unfailing taste, yet there's a shortage of fire, and an absence of any distinctive voice. He fills several choruses on "Song for Jan" with richly chorded passages and an echo or two of the soul/jazz devices he had helped to popularize, all without generating any real excitement.

It's instructive, perhaps, to compare Lewis to Herbie Hancock, in that both made their first impressions within the funk school of jazz. Hancock, however, had the brilliance to grow his artistry with time, while Lewis, aside from a few exceptional projects, has settled into a niche from which pleasant, somewhat incidental music and a sense of disappointment most frequently emanate.

30. LES McCANN

Born: September 23, 1936, Lexington, Kentucky

He has the common touch, with a style that fit the temper of his times by spanning the gap between hard bop and funk fusion. While self-appointed illuminati debated the aesthetics of electric jazz, the rest of the country danced to his gravelly vocals and raw, soulful piano.

At about the same time that Marvin Gaye asked "What's Goin' On," Les McCann rocked the house with another rhetorical question, "Compared to What." His was the rougher performance, textured by his own growls as he punched bluesy fills over a whacking cowbell beat. But in its sunny discontent and easy-to-groove feel, the song clearly measured the pulse of the people.

It's important to remember that "Compared to What" was recorded live, at the Montreux Jazz Festival. The presence of the crowd, real or implicit, was crucial to McCann's music. Miles Davis turned his back to his fans and dared them to stick with him. McCann, like Ramsey Lewis on his bigger hits, took an opposite approach by performing to the gallery. It is difficult to imagine his best work without the sound of listeners whooping and signifying in the background.

This is the strength and the weakness of Les McCann. The funk tradition, from which he and Lewis drew, was music with a strong social component—block party music, impossible to resist and stamped with feel-good authenticity. Mainstream audiences could listen to funky jazz without being challenged by it. And no one was funkier, and less challenging, within this school than McCann.

What lingers most, after listening to his catalog, is the degree to which minimal gestures prompted maximum reaction. Much of what he played was a simple distillation of gospel beat and blues phrasing. McCann wasn't a technically equipped pianist. Bebop was apparently beyond his reach. Instead, he built his performances on smeared thirds and church rhythms. Like lanterns in the darkness, he illuminated his works with pseudo-sanctified titles: "The Truth," "Gone On," and "Get That Church." In the latter, there is practically no melodic essence in multiple choruses of his piano solo; instead, McCann repeats rhythmic figures to whip up an intensity that would only have been tainted by any stain of sophistication.

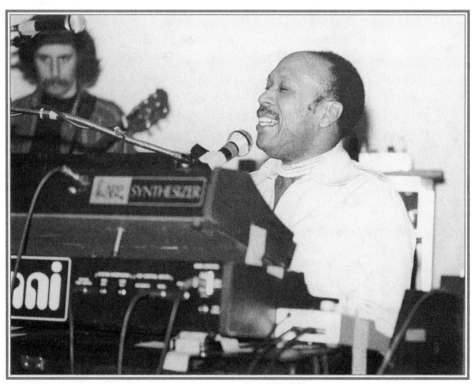

Les McCann whips up an intensity that would only be tainted by sophistication.

It isn't surprising that McCann is largely self-taught. His formal instruction ended after four lessons with a neighborhood teacher, although he played a variety of instruments, including tuba and guitar, in marching bands as a kid. Still, it took enlistment in the Navy at the age of 17 and a posting in the San Francisco area to inspire him to dream of a musical career. He worked as a doorman at the city's famous Black Hawk club, in part to be able to hear sets by headliners like Miles Davis and his idol Erroll Garner, whose music McCann first heard playing at a store on his base.

After his discharge, McCann moved to Los Angeles, where he took classes in music, drama, and radio and television broadcasting at the City College, and landed a position in Gene Daniels's band. A recommendation from Miles Davis led him to Cannonball Adderley, though he turned down an invitation from the saxophonist to join his band. Instead, McCann put his own group together, whose appealing combination of West Coast cool and sultry soul led him toward a deal with the Pacific Jazz label. Under its auspices, he released his solo debut, *Les McCann Plays the Truth*, in 1960.

The next several years swept McCann into the spotlight. He recorded on Pacific Jazz with singer Lou Rawls, tenor saxophonists Stanley Turrentine and Ben Webster, organist Groove Holmes, the Jazz Crusaders, and the Gerald Wilson Orchestra. In 1962 he shared top billing with Count Basie and Ray Charles at the Antibes Jazz Festival. A year later he toured Europe with saxophonist Zoot Sims and guitarist Charlie Byrd.

A contract with Atlantic Records in 1967 gave McCann access to a broader market and led to his breakthrough on the pop charts. That came through his partnership with saxophonist Eddie Harris, whom he met during the Montreux Jazz Festival. Their recording of "Compared to What" racked up platinum sales. The spirit of that performance cannot be denied, but neither can the fact that this was the last great gasp of funk-jazz. From this point on funk would slip through the fingers of jazz and into the grip of R&B and proto-rap.

Like organists such as Jimmy Smith who are associated with this same style, McCann plays with a sensual, bare-bones approach. When he tries to stretch out, as in "Something Special," he reverts too easily to the tired devices of blues thirds and sevenths, despite the more boppish context of the solo. His repetitions of one note, as on his unaccompanied chorus during "Baylor the Wailer," echo Smith even more directly. Often McCann has his bassists lock onto one note, which allows him to build tension without getting into more involved motivic development. He also breaks up his lines into call-and-response patterns, a variation on the Bobby Timmons approach in "Moanin'." McCann's rhythm is strong; his fiery, fragmented lines make up for the shortage of melodic material. But the limitations in his note choices reduce that rhythm to a commercial affectation.

McCann's voice-leading can be a little rugged. On "God Bless the Child," his harmony on the line "while the weak ones fade" steers Lou Rawls to an uncomfortable note and strands him there. And in his solo after the Rawls vocal in "Willow Weep for Me," McCann leaves himself dangling midway through the bridge; his chords don't suggest anywhere to go, so he escapes through a smokescreen of funky licks without bothering to develop any linear ideas.

A soft-spoken man, McCann harbors an upbeat attitude and a fondness for painting watercolors of flowers and photographing the hundreds of friends he has made throughout his career. Many of these rallied to his side when, shortly before playing the closing date on a German tour in January 1995, he suffered a diabetic stroke in his hotel. Though he made that final performance, he was unable to fly back home and wound up spending six weeks in a hospital, paralyzed on his right side.

But just nine months later McCann returned with his 44th album, *Listen Up!* Some of its material refers to his recovery, with bass lines drawn from exercises he had practiced to restore movement to his left hand. Since then he has continued recording, including a project with European jazz pianist Joja Wendt in 1997 and an appearance on Marian McPartland's *Piano Jazz*.

Few artists have disseminated good vibes as liberally as McCann. As dated as some of his work now seems, it still stirs memories of simpler musical pleasures and expectations of what major artists have to offer.

31. BOBBY TIMMONS

Born: December 19, 1935, Philadelphia, Pennsylvania
Died: March 1, 1974, New York, New York

He was the purest example of the funk permutation of hard bop. Throughout his brief career Timmons stayed faithful to the style. Certainly he felt the emotional pull of this music strongly—but so did Herbie Hancock, a player of superior technique and most likely greater natural gifts. Even Les McCann, whose schooling was more limited than that of Timmons, pushed himself into what were then new territories, where jazz and rock would join or collide as fusion.

Timmons, however, shook up the world and then stayed in the same place as his career and life sank into their long descent. This is not to diminish his considerable importance, but rather to put a sad story into context.

Timmons was raised by his grandfather, a minister at whose church Bobby made his debut during a Sunday service. Piano and organ lessons began when Timmons was six years old; his uncle, who had a master's degree in music, was his teacher. Eventually he pursued advanced study after receiving a scholarship to the Philadelphia Academy of Music.

At 17 he discovered jazz. Bud Powell, Art Tatum, Kenny Drew, and James Forman (who played with Dizzy Gillespie) were his first piano idols. He made his professional debut in Kenny Dorham's band in 1955. For a year he toured with trumpeter Chet Baker, and afterwards played for a while with saxophonist Sonny Stitt and trumpeter Maynard Ferguson before signing on for a year and a half with Art Blakey's Jazz Messengers. It was there that Timmons made his first impact, as the definitive funk-jazz pianist. His profile stayed high when he left Blakey in the fall of 1959 to join Cannonball Adderley's quintet, and on several successful solo albums as well.

Particularly on his early recordings, Timmons could sound a little young and unformed. His solo reading of "Lush Life," from his debut album *This Here Is Bobby Timmons*, takes an unadventurous approach: The tempo feels uncharacteristically hurried, and his rhythm on the bridge ungraceful, perhaps because the restrictive structure and Deco feeling of the tune don't fit his aesthetic. Another solo performance, a full two-verse, bridge, and verse intro to "My Funny Valentine," is built rather melodramatically around a swirling, Chopinesque ostinato; the contrived feeling is emphasized in the final verse, also played solo, with ostentatious alternating two-handed octaves and other classical affectations.

On the same album, his attempts at arrangement sometimes seem similarly unformed: The stumbling rhythm motif that kicks off "The Party's Over" only contributes to the pianist's tentative articulation of the theme. Only when they kick into their swing groove does Timmons relax and lay down a solo that will strike listeners raised on the *Peanuts* specials as remarkably Vince Guaraldi–like—perhaps because Guaraldi drew so much from Timmons's phrasing yet seldom played in his groove.

Because of his reliance on churchy phrasing and a fairly limited scale, a Timmons performance was heavily dependent on the moment—on how he was playing off the rhythm on any given night. His solo on the medium-tempo "Chuckin'," from the Kenny Burrell album *Blue Lights Volume 2*, offers a glimpse of how he sounded when not fully engaged. His solo, picking up on the last lick of the theme, never takes off. Throughout the performance Timmons uses a triplet ornament way too much, and his flat-five licks during the first verse of his solo, along with similar repetitions elsewhere, seem to stem more from a shortage of ideas than from any conscious use of repetition as a device. He even flubs the end of his improvisation, playing for a few beats into Burrell's guitar solo before cutting himself off. This is Timmons imitating Timmons, not an effective soloist digging into the material.

When just blowing within his idiom, Timmons was much more effective. On the title track of "Soul Time," over a quietly rocking 6/8 rhythm laid down by Art Blakey on brushes, the pianist characteristically takes his time, often falling back from his bluesy single line into a series of gospel figurations. None of it feels forced; all of it burns with a slow but steady heat. And on "S'posin'," from the same album, his boppish solo is breezy and free, rhythmically dynamic, and as fluent as the best of Bud Powell—thanks, no doubt in large part, to Blakey's irresistible momentum.

Within a couple of years, Timmons showed evidence of considerable development in his performance. Though "soul jazz" remained his foundation, he was also drawing deeply from Monk by the time he cut *Born to be Blue!* in 1963. His performance of "Sometimes I Feel Like a Motherless Child" is borderline derivative, in fact, from dissonant minor ninths to whole-tone runs, but delivered with an undeniable passion and urgency that had nothing to do with Monk's style. And on "Know Not One" he builds effectively against a clever theme that involves the addition of one extra beat in the last bar of the A section. The rhythmic destabilization makes Timmons' solo in the straight-four choruses that follow seem that much more rooted in the groove. He even takes a moment to quote from "Twisted," as if to emphasize the playful vibe written into the tune.

At its best, the Timmons style was centered pretty much in the midrange of the instrument, where he unfolded long melodic ideas and punched them into rhythmically emphatic sections. Bluesy licks played pivotal roles in his improvisations, such as the minor-seventh, out-of-rhythm motif that kicks off his solo on Benny Golson's "Along Came Betty," from the Art Blakey album *Moanin'*.

There was an unhurried quality to Timmons's solos. His playing simmered rather than blazed; he seldom attacked the keys, but rather played at an intimate volume. The heat came from his gospel phrasing. Even the awkward march groove on "Blues March" from the same Blakey album is loosened by Timmons's smeary minor-seventh blues licks and a bouncing left-hand comp that refers on occasion to stride rhythm.

A good example of his easygoing feel can be heard on "Spontaneous Combustion," from the Adderley album *In San Francisco*. His solo begins with an emphasis on the tonic, as if laying down the truth. It expands with ecstatic little bursts of blues, which resolve repeatedly on the I, almost like emphatic shouts of "Amen" scattered throughout a sermon. As the solo unfolds Timmons stretches out a bit, breaking his line where breath would be, falling back on familiar repetitive figures, but always moving things along. When he breaks into his two-handed finale, he conforms to his own pattern of building to a big finish; these sorts of passages encourage the rhythm section to lock onto a backbeat. While not an example of improvisational brilliance, it does nail the groove.

Equally representative is the Timmons solo on "The Chess Players," a Wayne Shorter tune recorded on March 6, 1960, for Blakey's *The Big Beat*. The pianist opens with a very idiomatic blues lick, which Blakey answers by kicking into a steady rim-shot backbeat. Timmons smoothly negotiates the song's contours, with a very relaxed, behind-the-beat line that shows no exertion in adapting its gospel elements to Shorter's alternations between major and minor and untraditional, fourths-based design.

The definitive Timmons solo is on "Moanin'" with Blakey. It builds on a repetition of gospel figures through the first two verses, then winds through the bridge with a sequence of lines, including one relatively outside variation going out of the bridge. The last two verses of the solo center on a motif of two chords, which Timmons presents and then extends in a simple but propulsive rhythmic variation. All of this is done without excess or flash; it works because of the economy and innate swing in the Timmons style.

A similar aesthetic guides his solo on "This Here," from *In San Francisco*. Everything he plays is based on gospel phrasing and blues runs, and always with a strong rhythmic push. We hear also his familiar minor-third smears, as well a repetitive two-beat figure set against the 6/8 groove, aggressive simultaneous two-handed chorded passages, and other familiar devices. It's not the most imaginative or challenging improvisation, but it says what needs to be said.

Timmons jabs out a two-handed solo in "Come Rain or Come Shine," from the Blakey *Moanin'* CD. The effect is more nervous than swinging—a rare example, perhaps, of his pushing too hard. That same quality surfaces during his long solo on "Broadway," recorded live in 1969 and available on the Dexter Gordon album *L.T.D.* His persistent use of a trilled figure turns into a repetitive device after a couple of choruses, but its uneven articulation and overuse eventually deflate the intended escalation of tension. In the following choruses, over a very spare left hand, Timmons seems to be playing as fast as he can in the upper range of the keys; this sense of pushing too hard, and for being a little too contrived in quoting from "Twisted," contrasts with the more deliberate, less frantic approach that marks his best work.

Disappointed perhaps in his career trajectory, with younger pianists who had once imitated his style now riding the charts and grabbing headlines, Timmons developed a drinking habit. His death, at age 38, is attributed to cirrhosis of the liver.

32. HERBIE HANCOCK

Born: April 12, 1940, Chicago, Illinois

What impresses most about Herbie Hancock isn't the multiplicity of his strengths but the absence of any weaknesses. Even the greatest players have left themselves open to criticism in one small area or another. But where is Hancock's flaw? The harmonic profundity of Bill Evans, the facility of a healthy Bud Powell, the down-home soul of Horace Silver, the carefree swing of Teddy Wilson, the overall musicianship of Art Tatum are all part of his package. And none of these progenitors could match his range; from the blank slate of free improvisation through the intricacies of classical interpretation and up to the challenge of making one chord dance through the maze of exotic technology, Hancock claims the complete panorama of jazz as his back yard.

Unlike many of his peers in jazz, Hancock came to music from a largely secular background. His first lessons, at age seven, were with a teacher at the Ebeneezer Baptist Church, but the regimen from the start was old-world European. A child prodigy, he made his concert debut at eleven, when he performed the first movement of a Mozart concerto during a young people's concert with the Chicago Symphony Orchestra. With ears attuned to the complexities of Impressionist and other twentieth-century repertoire, Hancock was able to approach jazz from both visceral and analytical perspectives. Beginning at Hyde Park High School, after hearing a fellow student improvising at the piano, he started transcribing performances from recordings by George Shearing and Oscar Peterson, and breaking down the arrangements of Clare Fischer and the vocal harmonies of the Hi-Lo's.

Though he was playing with his own jazz group by the time he had graduated from Hyde Park, Hancock declared an engineering major at Iowa's Grinnell College in 1956. After two years, however, he bowed to the unavoidable and switched to a music curriculum. By 1960 he had won a student award for composing a suite for woodwinds, written several charts for Grinnell's 17-piece jazz band, and absorbed even more information through supplementary courses at Roosevelt College in Chicago.

Fresh out of school, Hancock hit the ground running, beginning with a gig for several weeks behind saxophonist Coleman Hawkins at a Chicago club. In December 1960 he took a call from trumpeter Donald Byrd to sub for his pianist, who was stuck in a snowstorm en route to a gig. That's all it took for Byrd to offer Hancock a permanent position in his band, and with that the pianist, just 20 years old, left with his mentor for the big time in New York.

For two years Hancock worked there on a variety of freelance projects, including jobs with Oliver Nelson and Phil Woods, some accompaniment for assorted singers, and a little television work. Eventually he inked a deal with Blue Note, which released his debut album, *Takin' Off*, in 1962. The following year, while working with Clark Terry at the Village Vanguard, Hancock was heard by Miles Davis and Sonny Rollins. When each expressed interest in hiring him for their band, they agreed to set up a joint audition at Birdland. Hancock showed up and found himself face-to-face with another young pianist who was making an impression around town. After a brief discussion, he invited Paul Bley to play first; as a result, Bley got the first offer, to play with Rollins.

Davis, meanwhile, was having trouble with the piano chair in his band. Wynton Kelly had left in May 1963, and the British-born pianist Victor Feldman was filling in until a permanent successor could be found. It seemed clear to Davis that Hancock was the ideal candidate, but to be sure he first invited the young pianist to drop by his place for an informal jam session. Hancock showed up and found himself hanging out with an imposing little gathering of musicians: saxophonist George Coleman, bassist Ron Carter, and drummer Tony Williams. Rather informally, while waiting for their host, they started jamming, unaware that Davis was listening surreptitiously through an intercom system.

This routine went on for several days, all the while with Davis nowhere to be seen. Finally, after three or four days, the trumpeter made his entrance and asked him to join the group for a studio session the next day. That made it official, and when Wayne Shorter stepped in to replace Coleman, one of the most important bands in jazz history had taken final form.

In his autobiography *Miles*, Davis described his young pianist as saturated with talent. "Herbie was like a sponge," he wrote. "Anything you played was cool with him; he just soaked up everything." His only complaint was that Hancock tended to overplay, with chords too lush and a few too many notes. Under Davis's guidance, Hancock learned to pare down his style, so that with three or four notes he might imply his advanced harmonies. This was his last and greatest lesson, the one that completed him as a jazz player; though Hancock would continue to learn throughout his career, subsequent explorations would take him away from pure jazz toward the newer ground of fusion, funk, and techno.

After a powerful run with Davis, Hancock left the band in 1968 to form his own six-piece band, which featured saxophonist Bennie Maupin, trombonist Julian Priester, and trumpeter Eddie Henderson. His conversion to Nicherin Buddhism indirectly triggered Hancock's next musical step, when a session of chanting his mantra in 1973 stirred up memories of his early interest in R&B. This led to his Headhunters project, inhabited more by the spirit of Sly Stone than by Bud Powell. Critics, and some of Hancock's fellow pianists, expressed apprehension that the electric keyboards utilized in this band would erode his touch on the piano—but he would dispel all doubts by 1977 through a series of stupendous duo piano performances with Chick Corea, as well as in work with Davis alumni Shorter, Carter, and Williams in his V.S.O.P. quintet. (Freddie Hubbard played the role of Davis in the original lineup, with a very youthful Wynton Marsalis later taking Hubbard's place.)

Hancock's work since then has been extraordinarily varied. He has written film scores, and even debuted as an actor himself, in the 1986 approximate biography of Bud Powell, *'Round Midnight*. He has hosted a television show on modern technology, and used the latest music tools to shred any trace of his harmonic finery on the minimalist dance hit "Rockit."

There were hints from the beginning that Hancock would be too restless to confine himself to just one school of music, let alone medium of creative expression. In an interview with John Mehegan in *Jazz* magazine, he chafed against any attempt to pigeonhole his work even up to that point in the mid-sixties. "I would rather not classify myself," he demurred. "I have played in so many different styles that I could not categorize myself." For Hancock, this aversion wasn't based solely on retrospective self-analysis; it was essential to his work to not think of himself in terms of labels: "It isn't even important as to what period you belong to," he told Mehegan, "so long as the sound you are producing is good. . . . I don't think about this or that school, or this or that style, or this or that guy's technique. I [only] think about music as a sound."

For all the diversity in Hancock's work, certain essential qualities continue to tie it all together. In his earliest recordings, his roots seemed closer to hard bop rather than to the Bud Powell line. On "Watermelon Man," recorded in 1962 for *Takin' Off*, Hancock stays strictly within the lines set by Bobby Timmons: His solo is built on repeated riffs and trilled figurations, and his chords draw directly from the gospel tradition. Aside from an ambitious exploration of outside lines before falling back into the funk bag on "Driftin'" and some Bill Evans moments on "Alone and I," there isn't much of a hint on this disc—or on his sophomore release the following year, *My Point of View*—of the harmonic ideas that would guide Hancock's work in years to come, but, significantly, there's very clear presentiment of his Headhunters-era excursions into R&B fusion. (In the liner notes to this album, Hancock soberly reveals, "As a teen-ager, I went through my rhythm & blues days.")

More important than the somewhat formulaic funk on *My Point of View*, tracks such as "A Tribute to Somebody" allow Hancock to display a fully formed mastery of melodic improvisation that forecasts his potential in more sophisticated structures; occasional funk ornaments only complement the lyrical aspects of his creativity, from the extemporized opening motif at the start of his solo through exquisitely balanced ascending triplet figures at the beginning of the second verse and only the barest use of repetition without variation. As time passed Hancock grew stronger at this type of performance; his solo on "One Finger Snap," from the 1964 concept album *Empyrean Isles*, restricted to well-placed, evocative left-hand chords and a single line in the right hand, suggests an almost unprecedented expressiveness, with masterful placement of breath marks, beautifully conceived sub-rhythms and motivic alterations, and a boundless capacity to build and release tension. At age 24 Hancock was making a clear bid for the mantle left by Powell as the greatest melodic improviser of modern jazz piano—and in many respects he was already a superior composer.

As a composer, Hancock's specialty involved fresh changes on extended blowing sections; as his ear for arrangement developed, extended voicings became increasingly important at the written level. Significantly, he never lost his ability to stretch simpler material to the point of severing its connection to the feel of the tune. On *Speak Like a Child*, from 1968, the simplest track—"First Trip," a medium-up tune by bassist Ron Carter—is also the only non-Hancock piece. Yet through highly syncopated clusters and a typically sleek right-hand line, the pianist leaves an unmistakable imprimatur on his solo; as he winds his solo in and out of contact with Carter's basic changes, he attains that combination of bluesy feel, simmering rhythmic heat, and cerebral harmonic invention that had already become his trademark.

Few pianists could dig into the funk elements of jazz with the kind of urbanity brought by Hancock. There was never anything condescending about his blues excursions, yet his phenomenal harmonic vocabulary allowed him to bring out the emotional essence of these tunes. Examples are too numerous to mention: One can point to his quartet performance on Kenny Burrell's *Blues: The Common Ground*, recorded with Grady Tate and Ron Carter on February 19, 1968. From the loose but expressive comps behind Burrell's gritty solo to his own improvisation, Hancock refers to the clichés of the style—repetitive figurations, minor-seventh trills, bluesy hooks framed by churchy right-hand octaves—without getting impaled on them.

On his 1965 release *Maiden Voyage* Hancock toned down the funk and moved toward more challenging postbop settings. "The Eye of the Hurricane" follows essentially a minor blues form, but his emphasis on the sixth note of the scale in the first verse of his solo points toward how far he was willing to stretch within that structure. With Ron Carter and Tony Williams from the Miles band anchoring the rhythm, Hancock concentrates almost entirely on melody, which weaves through several verses, with only a few rests breaking its increasingly abstract trajectory. At no point does the young pianist exert himself, and only toward the last couple of verses does he smudge one attempted figure—but here he recovers quickly by intensifying the rhythmic placements in his line as the final chorus rushes past.

Later on the same album, Hancock creates one of his most beautiful improvisations, on "Dolphin Dance." At a relaxed, strolling tempo, he illuminates the many changes of the tune with spare left-hand comps that build in frequency during peak moments or drop out entirely during faster right-hand passages. A little minor-third trill turns into a device for ascending into the opening of his solo; a similar figure, played with delicate deliberation, elevates the line gently from the first verse into the second. At the end of the third verse Hancock shifts direction in his transitional figure, this time in arpeggiated triplets that cascade downward through spacious bitonal juxtapositions. Everything about this solo reflects Hancock's preference for eloquence over effect, from the hushed dynamics to the highly original harmonic language.

During the early sixties Hancock also began exploring freer improvisational settings. On *The Illinois Concert*, he joins Eric Dolphy, bassist Eddie Khan, and drummer J. C. Moses in a performance that is essentially unrecognizable as "Softly as in a Morning Sunrise." In his solo Hancock extemporizes with no reference to the theme; over economical clusters and open fifths, he slides between the I and ♭II chords of the verse, with lines divided alternately along four-beat and three-against-four-beat units. Perhaps because he was fairly new at this sort of invention, Hancock sounds less fully developed, and less engaged with the rhythm section, than on later projects, yet his patience at defining and building on fragmentary motifs over extended forms is evident.

On his third album, *Inventions & Dimensions*, Hancock lays down his own rules for free exploration. His method centers on an embrace rather than a rejection of structure; where Keith Jarrett in later years would devalue form in preference to spotlighting the process of creation at an almost germinal level, Hancock seems to be playing composed material even while working from scratch: Though based only on the barest instructions to his band, he repeatedly comes up with themes and variations as if spontaneous composition was the primary goal of improvisational excellence.

His experience with Miles Davis tremendously expanded Hancock's range. On the title track to the 1965 album *E.S.P.* he begins his solo with a conscious echo of the last lick in the trumpet solo, but then stretches into a bracing solo of his own, mixing freedom in his long melodic extemporization with a solid grounding in rhythmic subdivision and development. To this same combination of freedom and form he adds modal concepts on tracks such as "Freedom Jazz Dance." Here Hancock's embrace of unusual intervals, as well as the thoughtful pace of his improvisation, reflects an intention to reinforce the feel of the tune more than grab for spotlight time.

In all of jazz piano, no one has surpassed Hancock as a harmonic improviser. His performances carried a sense of breezy genius, with breathtaking chordal elaborations tossed off like so many seeds.

Yet seldom did these bits of bravura obscure the essence of his ideas; on Joe Henderson's 1995 album *Double Rainbow*, Hancock plays the basic changes on the opening verse of "Triste," then jacks up the energy on the second verse with a variation on a diminished voicing that startles, amuses, and inspires, all at once. And on the Wayne Shorter album *Adam's Apple*, from 1966, Hancock turns in several stunning performances, the most impressive being "502 Blues (Drinkin' and Drivin')." By the second verse of the tune he is already stretching the structure, with highly evocative harmonic extensions explored in complex, multi-layered rhythms. Just before starting his own solo, he answers a triplet line by Shorter with parallel chords that follow the saxophone's descent into the bass register. From this point Hancock creates a memorable improvisation, with gently ambiguous clusters supporting an improvised melody remarkable for its coherence and intelligence. In the second half of this performance he switches his emphasis to counter-rhythms, in a series of figures that spiral, swoop, and finally climb to a gentle peak, which Shorter, completing the circle of interactivity, answers in his return.

With a more idiosyncratic soloist, Hancock seldom had trouble finding the balance between providing a bedrock for experimentation and subsequent flights of fancy into the unknown. It was typical of Sonny Rollins to call an offbeat tune—"Winter Wonderland"—for a 1964 session with Hancock at the keys, and then to play it as a moody ballad. But the pianist was up to the challenge: In the last

Herbie Hancock claims the complete panorama of jazz as his backyard.

half of the first verse, with Rollins running the theme through a wringer of trills and exaggerated vibrato, Hancock finds a fresh angle on the descending chords ("traveling along, singing a song"). His quiet experiments with the tune continue into the second verse and on through an inspired whole-tone alteration of the final few bars before the saxophone solo officially begins. Musicians know that the most adventurous work in these sorts of settings is going on in the background, where the effect is almost subliminal and yet irresistible. The results can be heard on the RCA/Bluebird album *Sonny Rollins & Co. 1964.*

Perhaps the greatest evidence of Hancock's harmonic range comes in songs such as "Sister Cheryl," a Tony Williams composition on Wynton Marsalis's eponymous debut album. The feel of the tune is spacious and vaguely Arabian, which leads Hancock to base his performance on suspended chords, fifths, and broad bitonal chords. However, in his solo chorus, after adhering to this feel, he tackles the bridge with tighter dissonances, octave passages, and other devices that reflect his own sensibility—it could be any one of a number of pianists playing the first part of the solo, but Hancock comes through brilliantly in the middle before settling back into the tune's feel for the last few bars. (On the same album, during Marsalis's opening solo on "Who Can I Turn To," Hancock pushes the trumpeter with some extraordinary reharmonizations and counter-lines that stretch from an elegantly simple R&B fill to scattering runs that somehow don't crowd the melody.)

In accompaniment, as much as in his solos, Hancock displays a breathtaking harmonic profundity. On *The New Collection*, a Stan Getz compilation issued by Columbia, Hancock's velvety chords and cool hints of funk gently nudge saxophonist Getz and trombonist Bob Brookmeyer through their solos on "I've Grown Accustomed to Your Face." The piano intro takes a fragile paraphrase of the tune's opening notes and floats it through two chords that turn out to have little to do with the tonal center of the performance. Brookmeyer's statement of the theme balances the abstraction of Hancock's opening and brings the pianist down to earth. Even here, however, Hancock moves his cloudy harmonies around a bit before settling on the root at the end of the theme in the second bar; this sense of resolution is nonetheless balanced by the richness of the voicings. Always, with Hancock, the exotic and the straightforward seem perfectly in tune with one another.

As an accompanist, Hancock was brilliantly imaginative. His September 1994 duet with Joe Henderson on "Happy Madness," from *Double Rainbow*, casts the opening line and its reiteration in dazzling contrasts, first in slower suspended chords that let the saxophonist's articulation of the melody unfold, then with a descending counter-figure that matches the tune in a delicate, tumbling spiral. In his pedaling, his alteration of simple and lush voicings, and his ability to phrase through rubato, Hancock's performance is as spectacular as it is understated.

For all his problematic adventures into other idioms, Hancock repeatedly returns to jazz with all his powers undiminished. Given his prolific output, it is petty to argue that he has spread himself too thin; whatever caprices he may follow in the future, there is every likelihood that Hancock will remain the most vital jazz pianist of our time. (Remember, in 1974 he told Leonard Feather that he was thinking about getting into country music. Even now, there are worlds to conquer. . . .)

Everybody
Digs Bill Evans

33. BILL EVANS

Born: August 16, 1929, Plainfield, New Jersey
Died: September 15, 1980, New York, New York

Jazz has had no more unlikely revolutionary than Bill Evans. He had none of the swagger of Jelly Roll Morton or Earl Hines—indeed, in his introversion and self-deprecating wit, he was their antithesis. Musically, too, he was an opposite to both Art Tatum and Thelonious Monk, in avoiding the show-stopping virtuosity of the former and the quizzical eccentricities of the latter. And though he expanded prevailing notions of freedom in improvisation, he had neither tolerance nor understanding for the anarchic indulgences of Cecil Taylor.

His music, like his personality, had a questioning quality, visually represented by his posture at the piano: Hunched forward, his nose an inch or so above the keyboard, he even looked like a question mark. Whether playing standards or his own compositions, he sought the essence of the material in its harmonic implications. The kind of ecstasy that Tatum could induce through sheer virtuosity, or that Cecil Taylor unleashed in hurricanes of sound, Evans would find in the placement of one note within a shimmering, complex chord—and in finding ways of moving that note to an even more expressive position in the chords that followed, he pursued a fusion of the intellect and the spirit that was unique in jazz.

Other pianists played with thick harmonies. George Shearing, specifically, preceded Evans as a master of chordal movement. But there was something transcendent in the Evans approach, something that eluded Shearing and the many pianists who would attempt—misguidedly—to achieve it through imitation. Playing at a hushed volume, with delicate pedaling and extraordinarily subtle dynamics, the shy, bespectacled pianist spoke louder than almost all of his contemporaries.

With uncharacteristic bravado, he released his second album as a leader in 1959 under the title *Everybody Digs Bill Evans*. In fact, the name was dreamed up by his producer and friend Orrin Keepnews, but it also spoke the truth, or something close to it. Even in those early years of his career, Evans was recognized as a player without precedent. Or perhaps he represented a resurrection of an aesthetic first explored in jazz by Bix Beiderbecke, whose infatuation with Debussy, the lyrical line, and tonal purity anticipated aspects of what Evans would bring to the table some 30 years after the young cornetist's boozy death—which also, in a more poignant way, forecasted the pianist's tale.

As he was coming up in the jazz world, with blessings from Miles Davis and his band of visionaries, Evans was already drawing negativity from players and listeners who defined quality in jazz along racial lines. With his grad-student demeanor, he was a perfect target for these polemicists; as a free-thinking individual with unusually progressive views for his time, Evans felt every verbal blow from those for whom his skin color was reason enough for ridicule.

Looking back, it seems strange that all of this was triggered by someone whose music was so understated, and ultimately so beautiful. Yet even today, 20-odd years after his death, Evans polarizes musicians. His acolytes, some far too young to have known or seen him personally, revere him, while others resist his legacy, or simply ignore it, or even disdain it with a peculiar but righteous indignation. Consider the opinions of Stanley Crouch, the godfather of the "young lions" movement launched by Wynton Marsalis, who reportedly dismissed Evans as a "punk" and, in so many words, a fraud, as noted in Eric Nisenson's book *Blue: The Murder of Jazz*.

Though Crouch sees irreverence draped like kudzu from every suspended chord and gentle bi-tonality in the Evans catalog, it's still not easy to understand why his work is as "punk" as, say, that of Ornette Coleman within the jazz canon. In published comments about Coleman and other incendiary innovators from the fifties and sixties, Evans actually comes across as a conservative, not just in terms of preserving European aesthetics but with respect to such African-American innovators as Cecil Taylor, Ornette Coleman, and later John Coltrane, whose music would replace, or demolish, established notions of form.

As Evans saw it, this was more than a musical issue. "I'm scared, because art portends the future," he admitted in a *Jazz* magazine interview. "When I hear chaos in contemporary jazz, I worry about the future because it appears that perhaps we really are headed for chaos."

At the same time, Evans couldn't feel comfortable with the academic exercises being explored by Dave Brubeck. Playing in 9/8 or 7/4 had no particular meaning for Evans, unless it were done within a context where polyrhythmic tension might reflect some emotion. Thus, in "Five," a brilliantly constructed boppish original on *New Jazz Conceptions*, he elaborates on the title by performing five groups of four-note motifs in the theme, and yet the performance swings—one is tempted to say, despite this Evans-esque punnery.

There were many in his brief life who loved Bill Evans, or at least were fascinated by his sensitivities. His great champion was probably Miles Davis, who risked his own position in the jazz hierarchy by taking the young pianist into his group back in 1958. Years after Evans's death, one late night at the trumpeter's oceanside home in Malibu, I asked Davis to reflect on the great keyboard players who had worked with him over the years. After he had commented on Keith Jarrett, Chick Corea, and other giants whose paths had crossed his, Bill's name came up. He grew quiet, then said, "It's a drag he's dead. Now I'll never get to hear him play 'Alfie.'"

This was powerful, in that it mourned the loss of the music as much as the musician who made it. No one will ever stage a Broadway musical about Bill Evans because, unlike Jelly Roll Morton, he was much more about music than image. Morton played great piano in spite of himself; Evans played it because through his worst nights of drug abuse and depression, he had nothing else but music to lean on.

His father was born in Wales, then raised in Philadelphia. His mother's family name was Siroka, and her background was Ukrainian; though she was born in the U.S., she spoke Russian fluently and frequently around the house. Because of her devout Russian Orthodoxy, Bill was raised in a religious environment; Orthodox services, with their plangent polyphonic choirs, provided his first exposure to music. Some relatives on his mother's side were active in choral music, including a cousin who worked extensively under Toscanini. Through all of these influences, harmony, restraint, technique, and a cantabile feeling came to represent all the qualities that made music most expressive to him.

Bill's father wasn't the most responsible parent on the block. He was a drinker who would disappear for days at a time on binges and eventually exit this world as a result of his abuses, in 1965. Dad also dabbled in a variety of jobs, which ranged from running a bakery to operating a laundromat to managing a driving range for golfers. In the latter job, at least, he left an impact on his son, whom he employed to retrieve balls sent into orbit by errant customers. Because or in spite of this work, Bill developed an enduring love of golf, which he played through most of his adult life, until jazz and its attendant abuses eroded his enthusiasms.

Bill's biggest inspiration might have been his older brother Harry. A musical spirit himself, he probably provided stability in Bill's life, through the example of using music to find meaning and satisfaction. Because Harry was the first to take piano lessons, Bill began on violin. But the piano beckoned to him: When Harry's teacher would visit each week, Bill listened to the lesson while hiding out of sight, then came forward and played back everything he had heard. Harry eventually got the message that his brother was the real talent in the family, and stepped aside as Bill began piano instruction on his own.

Music, though, haunts the sensitive soul even as it enlightens. Though Harry went on to serve with distinction as superintendent of music in the Baton Rouge, Louisiana, school system, he reportedly harbored some resentment toward his brother's accomplishments as the years went on. Maybe this had something to do with Harry's decision to commit suicide just a year before Bill's own death— or maybe not.

At any event, Bill began absorbing every type of music he heard. He played through scores by modernist composers like Claude Debussy, Darius Milhaud, and Igor Stravinsky, while also digging into the antecedent disciplines of Bach; for a while he spent up to eight hours a day poring over written music and sharpening his reading. At the same time, he tuned into a variety of jazz influences on the radio. As he would later tell the French magazine *Jazz Times*, "From Nat 'King' Cole I'd take rhythm and sparsity, from Dave Brubeck a particular voicing, from George Shearing also a voicing but of another kind, from Oscar Peterson a powerful swing, from Earl Hines a sense of structure. Bud Powell has it all, but even from him I wouldn't take everything."

He was a quick learner, though initially he didn't distinguish between the literal elements of learning about music and the more intuitive aspects involved in creating jazz. For all his strength as a sight-reader, he didn't really improvise, at least not until he began subbing for his brother at the age of twelve on gigs with Buddy Valentino's band. One fateful night, a simple glitch on the keyboard turned itself into a revelation: While playing an arrangement of "Tuxedo Junction," he accidentally hit a minor third, rather than the major third written in the chart. Though technically a mistake, this imposition of a bluesy accidental against a major chord clued Evans in to the possibilities involved in inserting his own interpretations, whether errors or moments of inspiration, into a performance.

At that moment, an improviser was born—and the seeds were sown that grew to define Evans's artistry.

A year after that enlightenment, Evans began taking flute lessons. It was no surprise that he developed very quickly into a strong player; what wasn't apparent was the effect that playing that most ephemeral of wind instruments would have on his approach to the piano. The kind of ears it takes to manipulate air through the flute won't miss hearing the expressive potential of sound at the piano.

After graduating from Plainfield High School, Evans accepted a scholarship to study at Southeastern Louisiana University in Hammond, about a two-hour drive from New Orleans. There, he aced a double degree, in piano performance and music education, with honors in both, despite an admitted indifference to practicing, a willingness to skip class for a round or two of golf, and a growing infatuation with jazz. His formidable sight-reading gave him an advantage over harder-working students, but more important was his ability to take in the spirit and structure of a piece and more or less improvise a mature interpretation.

For Evans, memories of college would include a blur of gigs with his band, the Casuals. It must have been an awakening for this serious, retiring East Coaster to work in roadhouses behind a wall of protective chicken wire, taking breaks to let the occasional gunfight play itself out, or jam for dancers in the glow of campfires and the scent of bubbling jambalaya.

These years were also valuable in that Evans made his first important professional acquaintance. Mundell Lowe, an up-and-coming jazz guitarist, had also been a Southeastern student, a few years older than Evans. On hearing the pianist play one night in Hammond, he invited Evans to look him up sometime in New York. Which is exactly what Evans did, right after pocketing his degrees. The two formed a trio, with a New Jersey friend of Evans's named Red Mitchell on bass. Though they didn't work much, they did make some exciting music until a steadier gig won the pianist's attention.

For ten months Evans played with saxophonist Herbie Fields, an expressive player whose career would end tragically in suicide. For Evans, the most important lesson learned in the Fields band involved the art of accompaniment, something that would become a cornerstone of his subsequent trio work. In the years to come, Evans would not have been able to so dramatically alter the relationship between soloists and backup musicians without first fully grasping these roles in the traditional sense.

The draft board called in 1951, and Evans spent his three-year hitch at Fort Sheridan. Luckily, this post was within easy reach of Chicago, so in addition to serving his country he was able to keep up his chops in the city's clubs as well as through writing charts and playing piano, flute, and piccolo in the Fifth U.S. Army Band. By the time of his discharge in January 1954 he was ready for real action—at the front lines of jazz.

His first civilian gigs were in New York, where he played dance band dates with Tony Scott and Jerry Wald and made his recording debut with singer Lucy Reed. In 1956 he found more adventurous work with George Russell's group. Russell built his harmonic structures on the Lydian mode, which augmented, or raised, the fourth note of the scale by a half-step. This alteration was not incompatible with the pentatonic, or six-note, scale explored by Debussy and the Impressionist composers, who had already had a strong impact on Evans. Within a jazz context, then, Russell's ideas resonated strongly with the young pianist.

Evans was well into recording and working with Russell when Mundell Lowe made a critical phone call. The guitarist, who was as impressed by his friend's talent as he was frustrated by Evans's reluctance to seek exposure for himself, called the influential jazz producer Orrin Keepnews out on the West Coast. Lowe not only raved about Evans, he played a recording of the pianist into the phone. Through the scratchy connection from thousands of miles away, Keepnews recognized at once that there was something different about this new artist. He brought Bill Grauer, his partner at the Riverside label, over to listen as well. Together they decided to give Evans the break he deserved.

After undergoing the unnatural experience of having to persuade the artist that he actually was talented enough to merit being recorded, Keepnews got Evans into the studio in September 1956 with bassist Teddy Kotick, who had previously recorded with Charlie Parker and Stan Getz, and drummer Paul Motian, who Evans met while working with Jerry Wald. In just one day they recorded eleven selections, which included four Evans compositions. Released under the title *New Jazz Conceptions*, the album was a "sleeper," selling only eight hundred copies during its first year in the stores.

It was, however, a remarkable and tantalizing debut. *New Jazz Conceptions* clearly captures the pianist in his earliest stages of development. The trio sticks to the conventions of the time by keeping the pulse steady and responding only minimally to cues from the piano; by the same token, during bass solos Evans withdraws, playing occasional fills rather than interacting with the improvisation, and when Motian takes the spotlight, both Kotick and Evans stop playing entirely, in the old swing tradition of unaccompanied drum solos.

Evans's playing, though built on an unusually fertile harmonic base, was also transparently derivative. Given his later, more reflective work, it's surprising to hear how strong his connections are to Bud Powell, or even to the funky accentuations of Horace Silver. He even draws from Monk, in the minor seconds and stark attack used in his original tune "Five" and in the quick whole-tone descending runs, played in thirds, on "Speak Low."

In fact, Evans felt a kinship with bebop players. Powell and Silver, in his view, were important not so much for the superficialities of their style, but more for their coherent and comprehensive approach to improvisation, as well as their acute awareness of the song structure. This aspect of their playing surfaces in the Evans solo on "Easy Living," from *New Jazz Conceptions*, in which his line unfolds without any loss of integrity or ideas over and beyond entire verses—and when he reaches the end of the bridges, he momentarily expands to a series of chords that float the listener into the following verse. In what would eventually be acknowledged as typical for Evans, this performance is conceptually profound, yet so understated that it almost escapes attention.

Other premonitions occur in one of the unaccompanied piano pieces on *New Jazz Conceptions*. Partly because of the de-emphasis on the left hand precipitated by bebop, pianists in the fifties tended to not pay much attention to how the notes in the chords they played connected to the notes in the chords that followed. Just finding the right voicing was challenge enough, especially if they were improvising a line in the right hand too. There were, of course, exceptions to this rule, most notably George Shearing and Dave Brubeck. But their performances often leaned toward the academic, sometimes at the expense of emotion.

If Evans had one single mission, it was to stir the greatest possible emotion through the most advanced harmonic movement. Already we can hear this on "My Romance": The bass line, from the opening moment, reflects a mirrored image of the melody, at times staggering the rhythm of the theme but mostly tracking it note-for-note. On the last phrase of the first verse, Evans hits a pedal tone, one of his favorite anchoring devices after a harmonic exploration, but then dissolves it into a transition into another key, where an even more probing examination of the song's harmonic and rhythmic implications begins. As the beauty of the sound stirs the heart, the symmetry of the internal movement, with the notes in one chord each leading to those in the next, touches the intellect. Here, in first blossom, is the genius of Evans.

There was lots to keep Evans occupied through the rest of 1956, including sessions with trombonist Bob Brookmeyer, trumpeter Art Farmer, saxophonists Lee Konitz, and Jimmy Giuffre, vibraphonist Eddie Costa, and George Russell. Most important was his first encounter with Scott LaFaro, a prodigiously gifted bassist, during auditions being conducted by Evans for trumpeter Chet Baker's band. Their meeting would, in the near future, lead to the greatest epiphany in Evans's career, with an impact that would last far beyond their brief and tragic association.

Despite positive reviews for *New Jazz Conceptions* in *Down Beat* and *Metronome*, Evans didn't win much attention until 1957, thanks to his showcase solo on "All About Rosie" with George Russell's ensemble. This was part of an early experiment in finding common ground between classical music and jazz, conducted as part of a program at Brandeis University that also included Gunther Schuller, Charles Mingus, Cannonball Adderley, and the composers Milton Babbitt and Harold Shapiro. The premise obviously made sense to Evans, who passed it along to students during a short stint at the School of Jazz in Lenox, Massachusetts, and began digging a little deeper into it through his own postgraduate studies at the Mannes School of Music in New York.

Then, in 1958, came an offer that could not be refused. Miles Davis, whose explorations of "cool" jazz reflected a similar interest in jazz/classical fusion, had just been given notice by his pianist, Red Garland, and had asked George Russell for help in finding a replacement. Russell introduced him to Evans, and by February he was brought into the band. They performed over the radio from the Café Bohemia in May and, shortly afterward, hit the studio together. Davis, intrigued by the pianist's unique style, gave him extended solo space on their recording of "On Green Dolphin Street," both in the introduction and at the end. The contrast between Evans's poetic style and Garland's more mainstream approach could not have been made stronger.

Musically, Evans's stint with Davis was a transformative experience, as each musician fed the other's curiosities. The basis of their work was the trumpeter's fascination with improvisation based on modal frameworks that were often stretched out over single chords. With his taste of modal improvisation under George Russell's tutelage, as well as his preoccupation with harmony, Evans sensed something exciting in Davis's idea—something that might enhance or even supplant the structural foundation of popular songs.

Yet his tenure with Davis would also cast a shadow over Evans and his career. In the company of musicians like John Coltrane, Cannonball Adderley, Philly Joe Jones, and Davis himself, he had to wrestle with his lifelong feelings of inadequacy. The fact that he was the only white member of the group only exacerbated the problem. In the book *Miles Davis*, drummer Jimmy Cobb told writer Ian Carr, "We'd be talking, and Bill would say something, and Miles would tell him, 'Man, cool it. We don't want no white opinions.' That kind of shook him because he didn't know how to take that, and Miles would be giggling behind him."

Davis actually had a great personal affection as well as respect for Evans. But nothing he said could shield the sensitive young pianist from the abuse hurled his way by those black jazz fans who found his presence in the band offensive. This wasn't the first time Davis had dared to cross the racial line. "I remember when I hired Lee Konitz," he told one interviewer. "Some colored cats bitched a lot about me hiring an ofay in my band when Negroes didn't have work. I said if a cat could play like Lee, I would hire him. I didn't give a damn if he was green and had red breath."

Still, the comments stung Evans, and though he got paid a solid $200 a week with the band, their intense touring schedule deepened his sense of isolation. The solution to dealing with all this was only too easy: Chambers and Jones were using heroin at the time, and Evans quickly made it his habit as well.

By November that year, Evans had had enough. He quit the band and fled down to Ormond Beach, Florida, where his parents had retired. For three weeks he rested, played golf, and tried to recapture a sense of stability. Then, feeling a little better, he went back to New York to record his second album as a leader—one that marked a big step forward in his creative development.

As on the first album, the rhythm section on *Everybody Digs Bill Evans*—in this case, bassist Sam Jones and, from the Davis band, drummer Philly Joe Jones—pretty much follows the conventional formula by laying the groove down behind piano solos. Evans, however, is clearly looking for something new to say. Somewhat atypically, he shies away from thick, romantic chords; instead, his voicings are spare, often stripped down to prominent open fourths or fifths. On "Lucky to Be Me" the folky turnaround at the end of the first verse has almost a Windham Hill vibe.

The ending of this performance, as well as the parallel fourths and sixths in the very brief "Epilogue" for solo piano and "What Is There to Say?," all lead to the improvisation titled "Peace Piece." A hypnotic ostinato, conceived (and later recorded, in the same session) as the basis for an arrangement of the song "Some Other Time," repeats dreamily in the left hand, while apparently aimless figurations drift overhead. But this impression of formlessness is as misleading here as in, say, the more familiar works of Erik Satie. One of Evans's closest musical associates, bassist Chuck Israels, explained the method behind this miniature gem:

"Polytonalities and cross rhythms increase in density as the ostinato undulates gently," he wrote in *Musical Quarterly*, "providing a central rhythmic and tonal reference. The improvisation becomes increasingly complex against the unrelenting simplicity of the accompaniment. . . . This effective use of form to communicate abstract feelings and ideas is one of the strongest aspects of Evans's work."

That's true, but it's tempting to also hear "Peace Piece" as a release of tensions induced by the gig with Miles Davis, or even as a search for something more free than the Impressionistic complexities that guided Evans's discipline up to that point. At any event, it is unusual, a momentary escape or a brush with some timeless, koan-like truth.

Just a couple of months later, as Evans was just starting to put a more permanent trio together, Miles Davis called again for one more gig. Wynton Kelly had taken over the piano chair in the band, but Davis had conceived this particular project as a final, pure manifestation of his interactions with Evans. Somewhat reluctantly, Evans agreed to rejoin the band; the result, completed over a two-day period in late March and early April 1959, was one of the greatest achievements in all the history of recorded jazz.

With *Kind of Blue*, Davis and Evans created a near-perfect example of modal improvisation and its harmonic extensions. (Kelly does play on one track; his restrained but buoyant blues inflections on "Freddie Freeloader" complement rather than clash with the Evans aesthetic.) Fully confident of his band's abilities—Coltrane, in particular, was playing with exquisite focus and originality after shak-

Bill Evans could find ecstasy in the placement of one note within a shimmering, complex chord.

ing off some of his heroin burn—Davis brought only the most skeletal sketches of each tune to the studio. There were no rehearsals, and practically no direction. And, as Davis himself would remember it, every one of these performances was a first take.

"It must have been made in heaven," drummer Jimmy Cobb insisted to Ian Carr. "All Miles did was tell each musician, 'You play like this up to here, and then you modulate to here, and then you come back to this. Okay, let's do it.' And we just went ahead and did it."

The spontaneity of this approach was actually the source of some dispute in the future between Davis and Evans, each of whom would claim authorship of the most delicate piece on the album. "Blue in Green" is dominated by Evans, from the gentle, open voicings in the introduction, with its dreamlike, vaguely Spanish insinuations, throughout his wonderfully constructed accompaniment; you can practically hear Evans thinking as he stretches each chord to its next extension, as if improvising on a harmonic theme behind Davis' minimalist solo.

"Actually, it's my tune," Evans would later tell an interviewer, "even though Miles is credited as co-writer for reasons only he understands. One day at Miles's apartment, he wrote on some manuscript paper the symbols for G minor and A augmented, and he said, 'What would you do with that?' I didn't really know, but I went home and wrote 'Blue in Green.'"

No matter how it happened, this performance, and all the others involving Evans, pinpoint the moment of his maturity on disc. What would follow over the next twenty years was an unfolding of all he had realized on *Kind of Blue*, like constellations illuminating after a gentle big bang.

The brightest among all the stars in Evans's heaven was his first permanent trio, which he assembled after *Kind of Blue*. Over a short period of time he ran through a succession of bassists and drummers, beginning with Jimmy Garrison and Kenny Dennis during a dismal stint opposite Benny Goodman at Basin Street East. Philly Joe Jones took over on drums for a while, and then Paul Motian returned. While all this was going on, Scott LaFaro began showing up and sitting in. With that, the lineup was complete; everybody in the band felt it, and soon the world would know it too.

This combination of talent and temperaments clicked immediately. As with the Davis band, they considered rehearsals unnecessary and concentrated on letting things develop through interaction onstage. Motian was happy to abandon the drummer's burden of articulating the beat, and LaFaro proved uniquely capable of holding the flow together even while joining his colleagues in their improvisational fancies. This was an entirely new dynamic in jazz, as Terry Teachout noted in an article for *Commentary*: "Prior to 1959, bassists and drummers had played a straightforward and largely subordinate role in jazz rhythm sections. . . . Evans, by contrast, encouraged his sidemen to abandon the regular timekeeping patterns of bebop, preferring a conversational approach in which the underlying meter was not so much stated as implied."

They recorded four albums, two in the studio and two before an audience at the Village Vanguard in New York. Even now, their performances are a revelation. On *Sunday at the Village Vanguard*, for example, LaFaro's improvisations around the piano part on "Gloria's Step" target and bring out the strongest parts of Evans's imagination by encouraging him to focus on harmony, rather than rhythm, as the source of his "groove." In response, Evans plays more texturally, and with more rhythmic and melodic restraint, than he did with more conservative bassists. Similarly, when LaFaro moves out for his own solos, Evans outlines extended textural suggestions for him, rather than dropping formulaic chords here and there.

This approach clarifies in the opening of "Solar," where all three players drift into what seem like private meditations which nonetheless intersect and even swing. Evans plays his solo in octaves, replacing his old practice of spelling out harmonies with attempts at more economical telepathy with his colleagues. Eventually they settle into a clear 4/4 pulse, but even here each musician spends more time letting the beat breathe than locking it down.

That set of performances at the Vanguard was recorded on June 25, 1961. Just ten days later, LaFaro was killed in an automobile accident. His death at age 25 was a cruel theft of what would surely have been many memorable hours of music. For Evans, it was a personal as well as artistic blow that devastated him for months. As colleagues and as friends, they shared an extraordinary communication; the fact that LaFaro was also one of the few musicians who was persistently pushing Evans to get off of drugs made the event that much more tragic.

For six months he secluded himself. When he began playing again, it was sporadic at first, with nothing but solo piano appearances. His business affairs grew increasingly tangled. At one point he found himself legally bound to two separate managers, one of whom was Louis Armstrong's longtime associate Joe Glaser, and neither of whom had much tolerance for the other. Getting out from this mess took a lot of energy, but in the end Evans emerged with Helen Keane, a smart and sympathetic manager whose other clients had included Marlon Brando and Harry Belafonte. Keane had met Evans through their mutual friend, the jazz journalist and lyricist Gene Lees, who took her to the Vanguard to hear the pianist perform. Keane's response said volumes about both Evans's expressiveness and her own respect for his gifts: "Oh, no, not this one!" she cried to Lees. "This is the one that could break my heart!"

And the heroin use stepped up, so that by 1962 both Bill and his wife Elaine were fully addicted. To be sure, Evans didn't fit the junkie stereotype: He continued to play, often exquisitely, and to maintain a reasonable façade. But his earnings went up his arm, and gradually his world fell into tatters. He began putting the touch on his friends for drug money—never in desperate or threatening tones, but with an uncommon and apologetic civility that was hard to turn down. When his phone was disconnected, he shifted to pleading for cash from a public phone on the street outside his apartment.

In his book *Meet Me at Jim and Andy's*, Gene Lees tells wrenching stories about Evans during those dark, abysmal years. He writes about visiting his apartment one night and finding that the electricity had been shut off; Evans was providing light for himself by running an extension cord to an outlet in the hall outside his front door. He relates how Evans had once borrowed a wad of cash for his next purchase, only to lose it when another addict saw him, reached into the taxi, and snatched it from the pianist's hands. And there were lonely stories of shooting up in basements and other forlorn retreats.

These days, those people who repeatedly handed money over to Evans would be called enablers. But something persisted in his personality that encouraged trust and a belief that he would eventually survive. Indeed, unlike most other addicts, Evans made it his mission to pay his friends back, once he was able to. After receiving an advance from producer Creed Taylor for a contract with his Verve label, Evans called Gene Lees, and together drove through New York, settling all of his debts. At the end of their ride, the pianist made his last payment by handing $200 to Lees, who had pawned his record player and some of his albums on a loan to Evans.

None of this distracted Evans from his calling. In fact, he won a Grammy Award—his second—in 1963 for a groundbreaking album, *Conversations with Myself*, in which he overdubbed himself on two tracks of solo piano. He would follow this in 1967 with *Further Conversations* and in 1978 with *New Conversations*. Most of the material in this series doesn't hold up that well; there's a hesitancy to many of his rhythms, and some of his improvised elaborations on the melodies tend to meander. The important point, though, was that Evans was still restless, still looking for something new to explore.

By the mid sixties Evans had returned to trio work, first with Paul Motian back on drums and Chuck Israels on bass; their solid performance at the Village Vanguard in July 1962 persuaded Evans that he was ready to return to his favorite format. Israels soon left, with Gary Peacock taking his place in 1963, Eddie Gomez coming in for an extended stay from 1966 through '77, and Marc Johnson taking over from 1978 through '80. Motian gave up the drum position due to family problems and a few musical disagreements with Evans; he was followed on drums by Philly Joe Jones in 1967, Jack DeJohnette in '68, Marty Morrell from 1969 through '75, Eliot Zigmund from 1975 through '78, and Joe LaBarbera from 1979 through '80.

There was more than trio work to challenge Evans, including an orchestral project with conductor and arranger Claus Ogerman in 1965. Invariably, though, he was most satisfying in smaller formats, especially in two duo albums with guitarist Jim Hall, one each with Eddie Gomez and harmonica virtuoso Toots Thielemans, and two surprisingly successful projects with singer Tony Bennett. And he delivered intriguing solo piano discs, though some, such as the erratic *Solo Sessions* of 1963, raise questions as well: Long gaps between notes, unresolved phrases, and other anomalies leave the listener wondering whether something is eluding Evans, or even if he simply gets lost now and then, due to the distractions, perhaps, in his personal life.

And problems did persist for Evans, culminating in the suicide of his wife Elaine, who threw herself in front of a subway train in 1970. Relations with his label at the time, Columbia, were strained; Clive Davis, who never bothered to meet Evans in person, passed along a message that he ought to consider boosting sales by switching from jazz to rock. For a while Evans lapsed back into his heroin habit, but after checking himself into a methadone program he managed to escape drugs—for a while. He married again, and dedicated songs to his wife ("For Nenette") and their son ("Letter to Evan"). But when that marriage broke up, he left his home in the Bronx for a small apartment in Fort Lee, close to the George Washington Bridge, and once again got into drugs—cocaine this time, which he considered "safer" than heroin.

Ironically, Evans died just as his career seemed to be picking up a new momentum. Despite what some saw as a fallow period through much of the seventies, he was playing at full strength on some of his final releases, including an electrifying set of performances with Marc Johnson and Joe LaBarbera that were recorded at the Village Vanguard in June 1980. Just three months later, while riding around New York with LaBarbera, he suddenly complained of stomach pains and asked his drummer to take him to Mount Sinai Hospital; even in his agony, he managed to correct LaBarbera's directions when they got lost. Hours after checking in, Evans, emaciated, fragile, and exhausted, passed away, on September 15.

Echoes of Evans persist to this day. Lots of pianists emulate his wistful voicings—the harmonies that made the budding pianist Alan Broadbent weep when he heard his first recording of Evans at age fifteen, and moved Glenn Gould to laud him as "the Scriabin of jazz." On a tribute album to Evans, released in 1983, some of the most distinguished pianists in jazz offered their interpretations of his material, or in some cases echoed his sound.

There is, if anything, an epidemic of Evans sound-alikes among certain young pianists—those who have inherited his view of classical music as a reference for jazz improvisation. But Evans himself recognized that reliance on European tradition could inhibit as well as enhance jazz performance. In the liner notes he wrote for the Thelonious Monk album *Monk*, which was recorded for Columbia in 1964, Evans described Monk as "uncorrupted" by classical music: "Because he lacks, perhaps fortunately, exposure to the Western classical music tradition or, for that matter, comprehensive exposure to any music other than jazz and American popular music, his reflections of formal superficialities and their replacement with fundamental structure has [*sic*] resulted in a unique and astoundingly pure music."

Reading between these lines, one can assume that Evans envied that purity, that absence of distraction from the task of developing a personal voice as a musician. "Sometimes," he told Jean-Louis

Ginibre in an interview for *Jazz Times*, "I feel like I'm living two hundred years behind, back in the eighteenth century, not the twentieth." This admission sounds like regret, or even an apology, more than a boast.

To his friend Gene Lees in *Down Beat*, Evans went further in questioning whether his classical training helped or hindered his artistry: "You try to express a simple emotion—love, excitement, sadness—and often your technique gets in the way. It becomes an end in itself when it should really be only the funnel through which your feelings and ideas are communicated. The great artist gets right to the heart of the matter. His technique is so natural it's invisible or unhearable. I've always had good facility, and that worries me. I hope it doesn't get in the way."

Critics today, particularly those from the Stanley Crouch school, might agree with this self-criticism. From their standpoint, Evans did more to thwart than encourage the development of jazz, through his fidelity to harmony as a means of expression. Truthfully, harmony is somewhat out of fashion these days. To a pop culture enamored with the power-chord clangor of rock and hip-hop's nearly ideological rejection of chords themselves, Evans might be considered a reactionary.

Parallel to this attitude is the tendency to see Evans as deficient in the essential discipline of playing the blues or knowing how to work effectively with rhythm. But examples abound that contradict these perceptions: On many of his trio performances Evans does seem to stumble off of the beat, but obviously for reasons that have more to do with a curiosity about juxtaposed rhythms than with any lack of feeling. His touch also has a lot to do with it; though he was capable of digging into the keys, he preferred letting his syncopations speak for themselves, without having to underscore them with a jabbing attack. And even when playing with emphasis, Evans did so with a legato mentality that reflected his interest in exploring the long flow of melody rather than breaking a phrase into bits.

And he could play the blues when he wanted to. "No Cover, No Minimum," from *New Jazz Conceptions*, was one of his indulgences in the style, with repetitions of funky figures that are intrinsic to the idiom. But he also pushes beyond convention, with long improvised lines and a willingness to stretch past the limits of the blues scale, all without losing the feel.

If we view Bill Evans through the prism of modern preconceptions, he must be seen as a servant of two irreconcilable masters. Emotion, above all, was paramount in his music, but the level of intellect that he possessed made it impossible for him to unleash feeling for its own sake. By any standard, he had an exceptional mind: The jazz educator John Mehegan was astonished when Evans recalled their first encounter nine years earlier, at a party where Mehegan was playing the piano—Evans could recall not only the song he was doing, but the key as well. Away from the keyboard, he was equally inquisitive, with a literate appetite that guided him through the works of Plato, Freud, and Sartre, and turned him into an amateur authority on Thomas Hardy. Sophisticated wordplay entertained him as well; his love for anagrams surfaces in the titles he chose for his musical tributes to Orrin Keepnews ("Re: Person I Knew") and Sonny Clark ("N.Y.C.'s No Lark").

His attempts to harmonize these aspects of his personality, like his almost graceful descent into the junkie's life, reflects in the simultaneous intricacies and delicacies of the harmonies he played. Perhaps Oscar Peterson had it right when, on learning from Gene Lees of Evans's death, he commented quietly, "Maybe he found what he was looking for."

The Sophisticates

34. GEORGE SHEARING

Born: August 13, 1919, London, England

There's a passage from *On the Road* in which Jack Kerouac describes a performance by George Shearing in language that would surely perplex the modern reader. The sweaty intensity of Kerouac's prose suggests that he had burned one too many herbs that night, or that there was some early incarnation of Shearing that has nothing to do with the civilized, orderly approach to jazz piano that he represents today.

Probably the truth was, as truth tends to be, somewhere in the middle, though most likely closer to the reality rather than the perception of Shearing's performance. Even now, traces of something feverish linger in the most recent examples of his prolific output. It is a buttoned-down fever, to be sure, but with sultry overtones perfuming his hypnotic chord movement. An hour or so of those sophisticated yet steamy harmonies, and it's easier to see how some young kid with a skinny tie loosened around his neck, a blonde on his arm, and another martini in his hand could be seduced by this music.

In fact, Shearing's piano style connects the work of several distinctly funky players. Milt Buckner, in particular, was a direct antecedent: Though best known now as a pioneering R&B organist, he represented something subtle to the young Shearing. With his style of moving block chords in parallel fashion up and down the keys, Buckner provided the main inspiration for the sleek salon insinuations that now define the Shearing sound. Not only that: Bebop, even with its emphasis on single lines and breakneck tempos, left a mark that would endure, though in distinct and idiosyncratic ways, throughout his career.

Perhaps his disability facilitated Shearing's empathy with the emotional intensity of the bop school. Blind from birth, he found solace practically from infancy with music. At the age of three he began memorizing popular tunes from radio broadcasts, which cued his parents to get him started on piano instruction. By the time he started taking lessons at the Linden Lodge School for the Blind, he was already showing a flair for improvising with a distinctively American feel drawn from Art Tatum, Teddy Wilson, Earl Hines, and Bob Zurke.

During the war years Shearing performed throughout England, first on piano and accordion with a band of blind musicians led by Claude Bampton. Later, during a two-year stretch with Bert Ambrose, he rose to dominate the jazz piano category in the annual *Melody Maker* poll. As G.I. musicians flooded into London, Shearing met and impressed some of the leading lights of jazz—Mel Powell, Peanuts Hucko, Glenn Miller, Coleman Hawkins, and the inimitable Fats Waller.

Critics, too, took notice of the promising young pianist. As far back as 1938 a reporter for *The Star*, a daily paper in London, extolled "Mr. George Shearing, a remarkable blind pianist of some nineteen years [who] plays in the discordant style of Negro pianists known as boojie-woojie [*sic*]. Boojie-woojie baffles our crack jazz pianists, but Mr. Shearing sits at the piano in happy ecstasy, swaying to and fro, crashing his feet on the pedals and his hands on the keys, playing pure boojie. Swingmen say he has a big future."

That future beckoned from the boojie-woojie clubs of faraway New York. A fellow Brit, Leonard Feather, brought him to the States in December 1946 to take part in a record date for the Savoy label. Shearing went back to London once that was done, mainly to work with French violinist *nonpareil* Stephane Grappelli, but at the end of '47 he gave in to the inevitable and returned to New York, this time to stay.

Immediately he plunged into the city's jazz scene, which was ruled at that point by bebop. After sitting in with everyone he could in the clubs on 52nd Street, Shearing was hired for his first steady gig at the Three Deuces, where bassist Oscar Pettiford and drummer J. C. Heard rounded out his trio. From there, early in 1949, he moved to an engagement at the Clique Club, later christened Birdland, with clarinetist Buddy DeFranco. By this time Shearing was as much a bopper as he ever would be, and fully at home within the hottest American rhythm sections.

The big break for Shearing came in February 1949, when DeFranco had to bow out from a session with his own band for the Discovery label, due to his affiliation with Capitol. Leonard Feather, who was producing the date, called vibraphonist Marge Hyams and guitarist Chuck Wayne to substitute. With John Levy on bass and Denzil Best on drums, the quintet worked out a formula based on a combination of unison lines articulated by the vibes and guitar, supplemented by the same line played by Shearing in octaves, using the thumb of his left hand and the little finger of his right. Cushioned by rich chords moving parallel to the melody on piano, this became the basis for what is now described as a "locked-hands" technique. In truth, this approach didn't signal any harmonic breakthroughs; Shearing seldom fills the inner space with anything more daring than harmonies derived from swing or the more mainstream aspects of European orchestral tradition. Yet it was, unmistakably, a new approach to texture, and a sound that Shearing could claim as his own.

The sound is very clearly recreated on the 1994 Telarc release *That Shearing Sound*. Using his classic quintet lineup, Shearing breezes through intricate chord sequences, most of them built fairly close to the written changes of the song but sometimes more cleverly conceived. The group's rendition of "Girl Talk" does feature some elegant harmonic substitutions, and Shearing's solo is quite characteristic: Beginning with a variation on the last lick from guitarist Louis Stewart's preceding chorus, the pianist extemporizes a relaxed line against unobtrusive but steady quarter-note chords in his left hand. On his second chorus, while adhering to the same dotted-eighth phrasing, he switches to a more linear conception, with figures tossed from hand to hand in a gentle but infectious sequence of rhythmic fragments. The most impressive thing about this performance is the fact that Shearing generally maintains his trademark octave articulation of the improvised melody, through broken as well as locked chords. Though he makes it sound easy, it's actually no simple feat to adhere to that line while varying his approach to framing it every couple of bars.

It's often forgotten that Shearing can be a powerfully swinging player. Among the ample evidence is his performance of "Oleo," from the Shearing-Mel Tormé album *Top Drawer*. Buoyed by Don Thompson's assertive bass, Shearing blows through the opening chorus, kicking off with a bit of "Sailor's Hornpipe" and sailing from there with a long solo line, crisp in execution and pearly in tone. Shearing's melodic imagination is matched by his rhythmic vitality, which is evident as he shifts to a driving chorded solo in the second verse. On the same album, he laces a reflective waltz treatment of "Away in a Manger" with boppish lines that in no way disrupt the fragile fabric of the arrangement, demonstrating his fascination with juxtaposing jazz and Romantic aspects of music.

Shearing would revert back to pure bebop throughout his long career, though even on such stylistically pure performances as "Birdfeathers" and "Wail," from his 1992 live trio album *I Hear a Rhapsody*, he retained an almost aristocratic perspective on the idiom. From the antiseptic unison statement of the theme through his solos and on to the elegant sustain applied to the chords that cap his call-and-response segments with drummer Grady Tate toward the end, there's nothing abrupt or urgent in Shearing's execution. The minor seconds that end his first chorus on "Wail" are deliberate, where such glitches in Bud Powell performances were more likely byproducts of an escalating intensity. On the other hand, Shearing's lines on the bridge leading into the Neil Swainson bass solo show a deep understanding of the bop harmonic canon. And on a stunning performance in "Subconscious Lee," recorded at the same Blue Note date but released on *Walkin'*, he slips with uncanny ease from a rapid-fire linear concept in the first chorus of his solo into a strict locked-hands variation on the second, then brings the two approaches together over some Django-like rolled left-hand comps in the third verse.

Pedaling and touch are hallmarks of Shearing's solo work. It's instructive to compare the solo turns that he and Marian McPartland take on their duo album, *Alone Together*, recorded in 1981. Where McPartland's sound on Shearing's tune "To Bill Evans" is somewhat harder, with perhaps more dynamic range and heavier pedaling, Shearing purrs throughout his unaccompanied track, on the McPartland composition "There'll Be Other Times." His tempo follows the contours of the tune, with impeccably nuanced pedalwork highlighting its romantic structure and bluesy melodic touches. A few repeated notes and unexpected fourths allow Shearing to inject a hint of exotic modality into the hothouse ambience.

When playing unaccompanied, Shearing usually keeps improvisation minimal or leans toward a miniaturist, classical aesthetic. His reading of "My Favorite Things," from the 1996 album *Favorite*

Things, perhaps draws consciously from a music box reference, typical of the literal connections that Shearing often made in his solo performances. The ending, certainly, owes more to Lawrence Welk than to Bud Powell.

On earlier solo recordings, though still guided by a European structural aesthetic, Shearing could push himself a little harder. His performance of "Yesterdays," from the 1974 album *My Ship*, sparkles with rich chordal movement in the rubato opening verse, followed by three choruses of dazzling improvisation marked by kaleidoscopic shifts of style, unexpected rapid passagework, solid internal voice movement, and a burning propulsion. Shearing balances this display with a more structured second verse, built on a trilled motif riding a cascade of descending IIm–V figures. By the time he slows down for the finale at the end of the third verse, he's left us with yet another reminder of how, in the right hands, a polished technique and informed harmonic sense can enhance more fundamental elements of rhythm and swing.

There are few better vocal accompanists in jazz than Shearing. His successful partnership with Mel Tormé began in 1977, when they appeared together at Carnegie Hall as part of the Newport Jazz Festival. On and away from the stage they discovered that they had a lot in common, including an interest in such English composers as Grainger and Delius; as a result, they would treat audiences for decades to come to more than a few impeccable interpretations of standard and jazz repertoire. Shearing has also done lovely work with Peggy Lee; their duo reading of "Don't Ever Leave Me," added as a bonus track to *Beauty and the Beat!*, offers a highly satisfying example of rubato, appropriate voicing, and a tasteful modulation down a major third for the piano break. In this solo, Shearing simply plays the melody over restrained arpeggiation in the left hand, modifying it slightly to get back to the original key for Lee's entrance on the bridge. Not a note is misplaced in this wonderful performance.

It's not a long slide, however, from these moments of excellence into the realm of silky lounge sound. On "Sweet Lorraine," from his trio album *Paper Moon: Music of Nat King Cole*, after spelling out the tune with single lines, a tremolo or two, and a couple of quick runs in the first verse, the pianist devotes a few choruses to a facile solo that flits across the bass-and-guitar groove without either pushing or anchoring onto the rhythm. Shearing's execution is impeccable; no rough edges are exposed, no risks taken. Other chord-oriented players, such as Bill Evans or even Dave Brubeck, push themselves as a matter of course; Shearing seems content to ruffle the surface now and then. Much of his work sank even further into the ambient well, with sweet strings and nothing more than a soft pulse from the rhythm section. This formula helped him sell his *Black Satin* album in 1957 and, three years later, the follow-up, *White Satin*. In these settings his locked-hands style fit neatly into the gauzy mix to create almost a celeste effect in the midrange of the piano.

Shearing's career is one of the longest and most consistently excellent in jazz history. Nearly half a century would pass between 1952, when he wrote "Lullaby of Birdland," on commission from the club, to 1999, when he celebrated his eightieth birthday by taping a concert for BBC, followed later by a performance and tribute at Carnegie Hall. The years between were filled with innumerable solo recitals, duo performances with Brian Torff and other outstanding bassists, and symphony engagements. In the late forties and early fifties his group repeatedly won best combo honors in the *Down*

Beat Reader Poll. Future giants of jazz apprenticed at one time or another in his bands: Cal Tjader, Gary Burton, and Joe Pass cut their teeth on his deceptively demanding arrangements.

In the end, Shearing represents the apotheosis of the conservative aesthetic, in that his work celebrates the maintenance of established standards. In a revealing article that he wrote for *Down Beat* on the state of piano technique, Shearing declared, "I know that a number of people criticize young pianists because they sound like others. And some feel that almost any kind of original is better than a copy. But I believe—and this may be the result of my plebian taste in food, meat and potatoes—a good copy is better than a bad original."

That's the paradox, considering that these words come from one of the most original pianists that jazz has yet produced.

35. MARIAN McPARTLAND

Born: March 20, 1920, Slough, Buckinghamshire, England

Harmony is the essence of Marian McPartland. She enjoys nothing more than casting a classic tune in a new light. It's light, after all, more than the shadows, that plays in her performances. Each note that she plays illuminates a thread as it weaves through the fabric of her chords. More than this, though, the emotion behind these solid conceptions defines her work. Buoyant at medium tempos, reflective on ballads, the McPartland style has a near-universal appeal to the casual and the critical listener.

Chalk it up, perhaps, to her upbringing in the European classics. Born with the name Margaret Marian Turner, she was raised in comfortable circumstances by a family with a pretty clear picture of what culture means. Of course, there was no place for jazz in this picture, so when Margaret began showing signs of talent at the age of three or four, she was given a violin and subjected to classical lessons. When her teacher died, she switched to the piano and eventually began studying at the Guildhall School of Music and Drama in London.

An exceptional student, she worked hard on classical repertoire, took violin lessons as well, and won a school prize in composition. But Guildhall was also where she first heard recordings of Duke Ellington, Benny Goodman, Fats Waller, Sidney Bechet, and other jazz pioneers. Soon she was playing at London pubs and billing herself by her middle name to avoid detection by the school's arbiters of musical propriety. Eventually, to the alarm of her parents, she abandoned the classroom for the vaudeville hall, as a member of a touring quartet of pianists that tinkled through arrangements of pop trivialities.

With the outbreak of World War II, Marian signed up as an entertainer for British troops near the European front. At one gig, not far from the front, she met Jimmy McPartland, an American cornetist with a lovable, extroverted personality. They were married before the war had ended, and early in 1946 they were on their way to the States. They settled first in Chicago, Jimmy's hometown. As the guy who had taken Bix Beiderbecke's place in the Wolverines more than twenty years earlier, he had impeccable local credentials, so finding work was no problem. This meant work as well for Marian.

It also meant a growing restlessness. Jimmy's style was traditional jazz, but as Marian played along on "Royal Garden Blues" and the other dusty numbers in his book, she was running Charlie Parker changes through her mind and feeling more and more that her musical destiny lay elsewhere. After a few years of frustration, she persuaded her husband to join her as she sought new challenges in New York.

Following a few short engagements and a couple of years behind the keys at the Embers, Marian began a two-week stint at the Hickory House in 1953 that stretched into ten years. There wasn't a better gig in the world for a pianist in those days. The world's greatest jazz players made it a habit to catch her trio whenever they weren't on their own bandstands. She relished the opportunity of learning through letting them sit in, as well as from listening to their critiques of her playing. Duke Ellington, on hearing her for the first time, remarked, "You certainly play a lot of notes!" After thinking this over, she decoded his message and began concentrating on making more music with less embellishment.

By the end of her residency at the Hickory House, McPartland was a bona fide headliner. She accepted an invitation to tour with Benny Goodman, then left when she decided that he wasn't modern enough for her. For decades she has led her own trio, recorded prolifically, and written plenty of wonderful songs; several have been covered by singers such as Peggy Lee and Tony Bennett and ensembles like the Thad Jones/Mel Lewis band. She founded her own record label, Halcyon, in the seventies, and inspired women musicians, not through speechifying but through defining and attaining her goals. She has also educated generations of jazz fans through appearances at grade schools and for more than twenty years as host of the weekly radio program *Piano Jazz*.

And, of course, she continues to play, in the harmony-based style forecast as far back as her Chicago dates with Jimmy. In fact, her brilliance in this area can distract from other aspects of her style. On "Willow Weep for Me," from *Live at Maybeck Recital Hall*, she drops a few blues licks into her richly patterned exploration of the tune; it feels unnatural, a bit like slumming. Her rhythm, too, seems forced, with shifts from walking bass to stiff attempts at swing. But then she comes out of her first solo bridge with a spectacular sequence of chords that illuminate the theme in unexpected colors. These harmonic explosions, vivid and spontaneous, are clearly where she is most comfortable and in communion with her repertoire.

Not to suggest that McPartland doesn't have a rhythmic side—it just has to be the right kind of rhythm. On "Twilight World," an original tune from her trio album *In My Life*, she plays with a sensual, swaying groove, somewhere in the ballpark of bossa nova. In this feel, she can build lines on thick chromatic chords; in a more traditional straight-ahead beat, she can fall back on single lines, with less satisfactory results. But when doing a medium-tempo blues, such as Ornette Coleman's "Turn Around" from *Maybeck*, without a quick pace to test her, she can take a hint from the slightest outside gesture in the theme and follow it into some prickly patches of dissonance without losing the blues feel.

Whether doing a basic blues or a standard tune, the song is important to McPartland. On the title track to *In My Life*, unlike most of her interpretations of older titles, her solo seems somewhat unfocused. Her statement in the opening verse is insightful, with a nice balance of simplicity and bass placement. When she begins improvising, though, she wanders across the surface of the song, as if looking for landmarks to follow toward a more probing improvisation. She plays a few "Chinese" fourths below a fragment of the melody, skims for a while, quotes the theme again. Though pleasant to the ear, this performance confirms McPartland's preference for older works or more modern ones that lend themselves to harmonic extension, such as Stevie Wonder's "All in Love is Fair," a highlight from her superb solo album *Willow Creek and Other Ballads*.

Yet even the simplest morsel can inspire McPartland to create a memorable reading. She closes *Just Friends*, an album of duets with other pianists, by playing a solo version of "When the Saints Go Marching In" as a tribute to her late husband Jimmy. On paper, it reads sentimental: an opening that consists of a simple, unharmonized quote from "Blue Bells of Scotland," followed by an examination of that grizzliest of jazz hymns. But it's safe to say that nobody has played "Saints" this way, with an introspective and, yes, sentimental approach that taps equally into the spirits of Bill Evans and folk balladry. If anyone has the experience in life and music to play with this kind of wistful affection, and if anyone can do so and make it work, it is McPartland.

Above all, through her music and her example, McPartland epitomizes class—in the best, New World sense of the word. Never a chops machine, she has learned that lesson given to her by Duke Ellington years ago. Similarly, on her radio show, she furthers the cause of her music by letting her guests speak for themselves, while prodding them along with only the occasional question. As a player, and as an advocate for jazz, she chooses her notes and words carefully and with something that feels like love.

Duke Ellington, on hearing Marian McPartland for the first time, remarked, "You certainly play a lot of notes!"

36. JOHN LEWIS

Born: May 3, 1920, La Grange, Illinois
Died: March 29, 2001, New York, New York

John Lewis was the anti-bop pianist, the product and yet the reverse image of the Bud Powell school. His approach to performing came directly from pure bebop, with his emphasis on right-hand lines weaving through intermittent light chords in the left. But what Lewis did with that formula challenged its fixation on speed and dexterity—not in the same way that Monk did, with deliberately primitivist elements, but through an antithetical strategy that emphasized understatement and dignity.

No other pianist—in fact, no other instrumentalist of his time, other than Miles Davis—stuck so rigorously for so long to this sort of minimal approach. But where Miles let his style lead him toward a career marked by controversy and radical experimentation, Lewis applied his arid gestures toward efforts of a conservative nature. Davis ultimately rejected, and Lewis embraced, the European aesthetic; as a result, one produced *Bitches Brew*, and the other created the apotheosis of classical/jazz fusion, the Modern Jazz Quartet.

The MJQ was Lewis's great achievement. Of course the individual talents of each member were critical to the group's longevity and artistic accomplishments. But even more important was the vision that defined how those talents would be employed, and that vision was entirely Lewis's. One need only listen to vibraphonist Milt Jackson in other settings, where his fiery style was allowed to burn hotter, or to drummer Connie Kay, whose playing was almost never as stark as it was within the quartet arrangements. Indeed, Lewis went so far as to dictate Kay's choice of cymbals for MJQ sessions, in order to achieve precisely the timbres demanded by the pianist's discerning ear.

Lewis, however, played pretty much the same in every setting, whether backing Charlie Parker on sizzling tracks from the forties or performing in his own chamber and orchestral works in the nineties. Never a showman, always an advocate of the highest standards in all areas of the arts, Lewis took his work seriously and never compromised, going so far as to acquiesce in the dissolution of the MJQ when it seemed to have overstayed its welcome.

These dry aspects of his performing and composing may owe something to his upbringing in Albuquerque, New Mexico, where his family moved shortly after his birth in Illinois. Their lineage was African-American, with Creole and Native American strains. John was assured of a comfortable and cultured upbringing, with his father working as an optometrist and his mother trained as a classical vocalist. But his circumstances changed when his parents divorced; he lived with his mother only briefly, as he was four years old when she died. He was then sent to live in a hotel owned by her father, who shortly afterward also died, from tetanus that resulted from a hunting accident. From that point John was raised by his grandmother and great-grandmother.

A studious and quiet child, Lewis was a reluctant novice when his piano lessons began at age six; within a year, however, he had developed more enthusiasm for practicing. While digging into his lessons, John also cultivated an interest in jazz, which he first encountered on a Louis Armstrong recording. Soon after that he discovered the Grand Terrace Ballroom performances of Earl Hines on the radio; subsequent broadcasts by Fletcher Henderson, Jimmie Lunceford, and especially Duke Ellington, added to his listening regimen. Among pianists his early favorites included Fats Waller, Art Tatum, and the Chicago masters of boogie-woogie.

Lewis was quite young when he began playing in public. At ten he joined a band made up of his fellow Boy Scouts; his work with them, at a club that kept them onstage from nine until midnight for a dollar each and all the food they could eat, earned him a merit badge. By the time he was fifteen Lewis was gigging steadily around Albuquerque. His fascination with music competed with a concern over the changing racial complexions of American life. These twin interests led Lewis to declare two majors, music and anthropology, as an undergraduate at the University of New Mexico; despite his heavy academic load, he somehow found the time to put together his own group and book them at dances and nightclubs.

Just six months before graduation, Lewis was drafted, but even this couldn't keep him from making music. He went to Europe in an Army band in 1944 that included Kenny Clarke, an early giant of bebop drumming. Because there were already plenty of pianists and drummers in Special Services, both musicians managed to quickly learn enough about playing trombone to stay with the group. Their encounter gave rise to a friendship that would eventually lead to the formation of the MJQ.

Mustered out in 1945, Lewis returned to Albuquerque and the University of New Mexico. His experiences in the Army had changed his career plans, though, and he dropped the anthropology major to concentrate exclusively on music. Drawn by performances on the radio from the likes of Charlie Parker and Dizzy Gillespie, and encouraged by teachers who knew better than to tie him to his desk, Lewis left school for New York to find a place for himself in the city's turbulent new music scene.

Opportunities arose quickly for the determined young pianist. While taking classes at the Manhattan School of Music, he found work with trumpeter Hot Lips Page in assorted clubs along 52nd Street. Then, in June 1946, his Army friend Kenny Clarke invited him to a Gillespie rehearsal. Lewis had the foresight to bring along one of his arrangements, which the band read through, with Lewis playing his own piano part. A month later, as Thelonious Monk prepared to leave the Gillespie band, Lewis was invited to take his place. Though he would eventually earn two degrees from the Manhattan School, he once more put his studies on hold and hit the road. Impressed by his sober intelligence as well as his music, Gillespie hired Lewis to work as his manager as well as his keyboard ace.

He stayed with Gillespie through 1948 and wrote some of his band's most successful charts, including "Two Bass Hit," "Stay On It," "Emanon," and an ambitious *Toccata for Trumpet and Orchestra*, which they premiered at Carnegie Hall. But Lewis was earning plenty of notoriety as a player too, with his unique variations on bebop piano. In addition to working with Illinois Jacquet, Lester Young, Coleman Hawkins, and Ella Fitzgerald, he was involved with two historic sessions, playing with Charlie Parker on "Parker's Mood" and with Miles Davis on his *Birth of the Cool* project, whose innovative arrangements were especially in tune with Lewis's style.

Still, it was the Gillespie band that would provide the foundation for the most important project of Lewis's career. On some of their concerts, when the horn section would tire out, Lewis and the rest of the rhythm section would offer small-group performances as a kind of interlude. With Clarke on drums, Ray Brown on bass, and Milt Jackson on vibes, this foursome became the first incarnation of the Modern Jazz Quartet. They cut their first sides as the Milt Jackson Quartet on Gillespie's Dee Gee label, but it soon became apparent that Lewis was the defining personality of the group. By 1952 Brown gave notice in order to work with his wife Ella Fitzgerald; Lewis replaced him with Percy Heath and officially changed their name to the Modern Jazz Quartet. When Clarke, feeling confined by the pianist's meticulous instructions, left in 1955, Connie Kay came in from Lester Young's band to take over the drum throne, and the classic lineup of the group was complete.

The MJQ made its debut in 1952 at Chantilly on West Fourth Street in New York. The music world took immediate notice as the group, in its quiet way, revolutionized small ensemble performance. With their formal, funeral-director attire and their integration of blues with counterpoint and other classical devices, Lewis and company stood as kin to Bach as well as bop. As jazz writer Francis Davis saw it, "With the advent of bop, the soloist reigned supreme, and the ensemble had some catching up to do. John Lewis was one of the musicians who set out to restore that balance."

They had a long run, all the way up to 1974, when Jackson, professing disgust with aspects of the music business, quit. The inevitable reunion gigs began in 1981 with a Japanese tour and continued into the nineties, even past the death of Connie Kay and the arrival of Percy Heath's brother Albert on drums. Still, over the past several decades Lewis was concerned mainly with an almost bewildering variety of solo projects: solo piano recordings of works by Bach, teaching engagements at Harvard and CCNY, affiliations with classical ensembles in Bellingham, Washington, and at the Manhattan School of Music. He scored a number of films, including Roger Vadim's *No Sun in Venice*, which was recorded by the MJQ, and *Odds Against Tomorrow*, which mixed written horn parts with passages improvised by Milt Jackson, Jim Hall, and Bill Evans. Other ambitious compositions throughout his career range from a ballet, *Original Sin*, created in 1961 for the San Francisco Ballet, to a suite, *The Comedy*, which blends complementary improvisational techniques from jazz and *commedia dell'arte*.

He kept performing in other settings as well. Whether recording Bach solo pieces, standards, or his own works, Lewis maintained one of the most recognizable piano styles in all annals of jazz. It takes a poet among critics to describe the beauty that lives in the simplicities of his improvisations, and so in various pieces for *The New Yorker* Whitney Balliett has extolled the art of Lewis the pianist: "Although his playing—simple, single-note melodic lines that have a dogged, crystalline quality—has a deceptive, amateur air, he often puts together, from combinations of nearly childish figures, solos that take on the ring of classic improvisations. He is an emotional pianist—in a transcendental way— and he succeeds where most pianists fail, in transmitting his emotion. Lewis's best solos develop an irresistible rhythmic momentum, and when he rises into the upper registers, where he often ends his solos, he seems to tap the sky. He is probably the most undervalued pianist of his generation."

The elegance of Lewis's approach, as well as its emotional reserve, is apparent in the spare, on-the-beat chords of "Boplicity," from the April 29, 1949, *Birth of the Cool* sessions, as well as in his brief solo break, with its impeccable placement and economy. His accompaniment is slightly more active on "Israel," yet there's still an objective, detached quality to the way he drops tidy little figures, the bare minimum to nudge the beat and add a dash of flavor, to the flow. In the solo on his own tune, "Rouge," Lewis again sticks to the midrange, playing consistently behind the beat; it's an approach that reflects an analytical rather than an incendiary aesthetic, as if to explore how tension might be built through putting the brakes on, rather than accelerating, the momentum.

John Lewis challenged bop's fixation on speed and dexterity through a strategy of understatement and dignity

This approach brought out the best from many of the giants with whom Lewis recorded during the bop era. On a 1947 session with Charlie Parker, Miles Davis, bassist Nelson Boyd, and drummer Max Roach, Lewis improvises 16 bars in "Milestones" that make real melodic invention sound as easy as breathing. Faster tracks, such as "Little Willie Leaps," give Lewis a chance to drop perfectly positioned chords behind the horn soloists; like Basie, he could be busier as an accompanist than as a soloist, and his chorus on this tune sounds as unhurried as if it were recorded in half-time. This approach complemented and encouraged Parker's performance—which, contrasted with Lewis's economy, made the saxophonist sound more technically as well as melodically brilliant.

Even when working with a barn-burning soloist like saxophonist Illinois Jacquet, Lewis maintained his spare style. Between exploding drum fills and growling horn passages in "Black Velvet," recorded in 1949 and available on the Bluebird album *Flying Home*, he plays a piano bridge remarkable for its sobriety, economy, and restraint—a two-handed chord motif, repeated with slight variation, repeated again as the chords change, and ending with a simple resolution of the melody to the dominant. Lewis hits that final note on the first beat of the last bar and, rather than throw in a lick that might stir up a bit of a breeze and lead to the horn section's entrance, lets it sit there and fade through the remaining three beats. This is even drier playing than Basie's, but Lewis already understood two things: that his goal was to serve the arrangement, and that the contrast he provided in these sorts of settings could speak louder than two roaring choruses from Jacquet.

Lewis's symmetrical aesthetic, and his gift for deriving maximum swing and eloquence from the fewest notes, is evident on "La Ronde Suite," from the 1953 Modern Jazz Quartet album *Django*. With a medium-up bop accompaniment from Percy Heath and Kenny Clarke, Lewis begins his non-caloric solo with a simple descending scale below minimal figurations. In the solo choruses that follow he barely plays anything with his left hand, while laying down an incredibly minimalist line in the upper middle range. He picks each note carefully, almost fussily, with a soft, Teddy Wilson–like intonation. Even so, the performance is thrilling, like an intimate whisper.

An even more striking example of Lewis's economy can be heard on "A Social Call," from the MJQ performance of his film score, *Music from Odds Against Tomorrow*, recorded in 1959. His solo here is as bare as a jazz solo can be, at times consisting of only the three notes of a basic triad, or the first three notes of the scale, played in varying order. As usual, Lewis plays them quietly, with virtually no left hand. This is simplicity taken to an extreme, closer to the childlike side of Vince Guaraldi than to bebop. And by working to establish this kind of an atmosphere, rather than indulge in splashy display, Lewis proves himself a composer, more than a performer, by temperament.

Within expanded arrangements, Lewis stuck with his practice of making every note count—notice how much mileage he gets from single repeated notes within the ensemble chart for "Django" and in his ebullient solo on "Lyonhead," both from the 1982 sextet album *Kansas City Breaks*. (On this disc it's easy to hear where much of Chick Corea's writing for small groups derives.)

Not surprisingly, all of these traits show up most clearly in Lewis's relatively infrequent unaccompanied work. On his 1999 album *Evolution* he maintains an almost puritanical approach to a set of standards and original tunes. As on his MJQ and other group projects, Lewis plays quietly, with no sense of being rushed and no inclination to fill the empty spaces in his lines. He sketches out the barest outlines of each song. In this context, the blue notes that crop up in his arid rendition of "Willow Weep for Me" seem more intriguing and out of place than in more consistently idiomatic interpretations.

In Lewis's hands, minimal gestures go a long way. It's instructive to compare his take on "Cherokee," from the same album, with the rendition discussed in the Barry Harris chapter. Though both pianists emerged from the bop movement, and each avoids laying down a steady beat with his left hand, Lewis has been able to move further, into a style that allows him to generate greater propulsion with far fewer notes and practically no apparent exertion.

The lesson of Lewis is that if one measures eloquence by the power invested in each single note, then his notes are among the most persuasive in all of improvised music.

37. DAVE BRUBECK

Born: December 6, 1920, Concord, California

D ave Brubeck was once modernism incarnate. In 1954 his face—quintessentially fifties, with thick-framed glasses and a smile that broadcast optimism and adventure—graced the cover of *Time*, which feted him as the herald of "a new kind of jazz age." For many listeners, this era began with the fulfillment of a dream that had intrigued musicians as far back as Scott Joplin, which was to bring jazz and European music into concord. Many had tried and failed; Brubeck, like the rocket scientists celebrated in the emerging space age, found the formula that made the dream possible.

His quartet was his medium. Its sound was smooth, sleek, and cerebral—jet-age jazz. They transformed rhythm, once the sweat and blood of this music, into abstraction, something to contemplate and savor, like a painting or a martini. Brubeck's harmonies had little to do with funky sevenths or flat fives. Producer George Avakian, in his liner notes to the 1954 album *Jazz Goes to College*, portrayed the pianist as a radical of near-Dada extremism. "Brubeck's piano solos are sometimes so far removed from the melody and harmony of the number he is playing that one sometimes doubts that any return is ever possible," he wrote. "Harmonically, [he] is more frequently in the camp of the longhair atonalists than jazz. . . . He employs melodic intervals which are more common among the atonalists."

Of course, Brubeck's aesthetic is anything but atonal. Perhaps his harmonies sounded chaotic even to ears as educated as Avakian's in the fifties, but from our perspective his music has more in common with progressive rather than subversive composers; there's more Bartók, or even Beethoven, than Schoenberg in his chords. Avakian is on the right track, though, in citing classical tradition as a context in which to assess Brubeck: Jazz elements guide his playing, yet his appreciation for them, though unmistakable, feels detached. Theoretical aspects of their application, more than any sense of urgency, guided Brubeck's explorations.

Today those elements of his music that once thrilled collegians now seem somehow dusty. Yet Brubeck enjoys near-universal reverence from his peers and younger generations, who recognize him as an artist of complete originality. By his own admission he is not and never has been a virtuoso pianist, but his style is one of the easiest to recognize in the jazz catalog, with its distinctive blend of intelligence, playfulness, occasional heavy-handedness, and transparent love for the blues.

The qualities that define Brubeck derive from a background unlike that of any jazz artist of comparable stature. He was a farm boy, the son of a cattle rancher who had also made a name for himself as roper on the rodeo circuit. From the start, cows and music were his life; though he was already composing and playing his own works by age four, Dave assumed that his siblings would wind up working as musicians while he followed his dad into the livestock trade. In fact, he loved his rural life as much as making music; as a teenager in Ione, a tiny burg at the foot of the Sierra, Dave relished doing his chores by day and then playing in funky clubs throughout mining country.

He was still playing dance gigs, six nights a week, when he entered the College of the Pacific, but as a major in veterinary medicine he seemed ambivalent about committing himself to music. That began to change when he met Iola Whitlock, a fellow student and director of a music show on the campus radio station. Two weeks after their introduction Dave proposed to her. It was Iola's inspiration and talent that would help launch Brubeck's career in music and sustain it for more than five decades to follow.

After graduating in 1942 and doing postgrad work with French composer Darius Milhaud at Mills College in Oakland, Brubeck took a little diversionary trip to Europe, where he saw action as an infantryman under General George S. Patton. He returned intact to begin playing jazz around the San Francisco area. From the start Brubeck kept looking for something new in the music, something beyond swing but distinct from bebop. A meeting in 1947 with Paul Desmond during a job at the Geary Cellar laid the foundation for an initially tempestuous but ultimately rewarding partnership. Desmond hired Brubeck for his trio in Palo Alto in '49; within two weeks an argument led to the pianist's departure. Returning to Oakland, Brubeck founded his own three-piece in November, with Norman Bates on bass and Cal Tjader on drums; inevitably, Desmond started dropping by their gigs and sitting in. The musical fit—a milky, sophisticated saxophone flowing through Brubeck's fissured harmonies—was a natural.

A little earlier, Brubeck put an experimental octet together. Tjader, Desmond, and clarinetist Bill Smith were among the players in this group, which won plaudits from both *Down Beat* and *Metronome* as the best new instrumental group. Already, Brubeck was showing a fascination with alternate time signatures, in works for the octet such as his "Schizophrenic Scherzo" and in the 7/4 bridge he wrote in their arrangement of "What Is This Thing Called Love?" The octet only lasted on an occasional basis into 1949.

After having some success with his trio, in 1951 Brubeck suffered a crippling back injury while swimming in Hawaii. After three weeks in traction he went through a long period of recovery before picking up his performing career again, this time with his first quartet. Composed originally of Desmond, bassist Bob Bates, and drummer Joe Dodge, the group switched to drummer Joe Morello in 1956 and bassist Eugene Wright in '58. It was this lineup that would capture the public's imagination with one of the most celebrated albums in the catalog, *Time Out*, featuring Desmond's "Take Five," the first single recording in jazz to sell more than a million copies.

From that point Brubeck would blossom in a dozen directions. A prolific writer, he has signed his name to several ballets, beginning in 1960 with *Points on Jazz*, four cantatas, an oratorio, and an ambitious fusion of Broadway with jazz, *The Real Ambassadors*, premiered at the Monterey Jazz Festival in 1962. He has performed at the White House, entertained the Gorbachevs at a Moscow soiree, and filled a house with trophies that include a BMI Jazz Pioneer Award, the National Music Council's American Eagle Award, a National Medal of the Arts presented by President Bill Clinton in 1994, and four honorary doctorates.

He has also established a unique and somewhat contradictory identity as a jazz pianist. In one chorus Brubeck can begin a complex extemporization, then pull the rug from under it with an unsubtle paraphrase or fixate indelicately on a simple polyrhythmic riff. In everything he plays there's a persistent "what if?" quality, as in, "What if I repeat this bitonal blues figure again and again?" He did so during his solo on "Pennies from Heaven," from *The Dave Brubeck Quartet at Carnegie Hall*—not, one senses, to push the beat but just to see how it sounds. When he does lock into the rhythm on this solo, with the thick two-handed chords that are one of his trademarks, the effect was heavy, almost ponderous; Joe Morello's airy cymbal work keeps things from bogging down, and his mirror of another obsessively repeated piano motif plays well to the crowd.

If anything, much of Brubeck's classic work now sounds rather conservative, with strong roots in swing. The rhythm of his chorded solo in the quartet's muted version of "Balcony Rock," recorded at the University of Michigan for *Jazz Goes to College*, recalls big-band riffs, though his harmonies flee further from the idiom with each verse, as old-timey inner voice movement and corny song quotes alternate with brow-furrowing dissonances. He digs even further back on "Bru's Boogie Woogie," from *Time Further Out*, a 4/4 evocation of rolling-eighths in the Jimmy Yancey style. These traits survive in his more recent work as well: Nothing in his solo on "In a Shanty in Old Shanty-Town," from the 1998 album *40th Anniversary Tour of the U.K.*, from the spelling of the harmony to the rhythmic phrasing, betrays any modernistic taint.

Brubeck often enjoys taking plenty of time to develop his ideas. On "Like Someone in Love," from *The Dave Brubeck Quartet in Europe*, he plays a surprisingly restrained and conservative solo over several verses, essentially outlining the melody at a leisurely pace, completely without fireworks, polyrhythmic distractions, or dissonances. It is, in fact, almost an accompaniment, as if to prove that not every tune has to be approached as an excuse for working out one's musical fixations.

At times Brubeck seemed to embrace his reputation for not swinging: The opening moments of "Take the 'A' Train" feature his statement of the familiar theme, with a brief but ponderous smear inelegantly marking the end of the first phrase. None of this prepares the listener for his solo, which Brubeck begins with a simple swinging line, which in the second verse traces the tune's whole-tone motif into an ingenious minor-key section. This, in turn, sets up an angular, ear-twisting exploration of parallel fourths in the third verse, followed by moments of two-line Baroque contrapuntal movement. On through the end of the tune, Brubeck draws fragments from different styles, much as Tatum might have quoted themes from different tunes; in its curiosity, heavy execution, literacy, and humor, it is one of the classic improvisations from the Quartet catalog.

Brubeck was aware of the tension built into contrast between heavy chords and wispy single lines. Thus, on his beautiful "Strange Meadow Lark," from *Time Out*, he plays in thick voicings, sliding out of rubato for a surging bridge built over an altered left-hand pedal-rooted chord and contrasting harmonic movement in the right hand, then back into it toward the end, complete with the occasional quick upward arpeggio at cadences, as a lead-in to the band's medium-tempo entrance. Yet after Paul Desmond's solo, Brubeck plays an almost ephemeral improvisation, beginning with an extension of the saxophonist's final phrase and continuing in a restrained, thoughtful single line. As in his unaccompanied intro, Brubeck emphasizes a pedal-tone in the bridge, though he plays it this time in his right hand; the rest of the solo is remarkable for its spaciousness and unhurried feel. Only at the end does he slip into a chorded sequence, though he preserves the reflective, gently dissonant feel created through his more sparse construction earlier.

Contrast between fundamental blues elements and more advanced rhythmic experiments also animated Brubeck's playing. The ambitious alteration between two bars of three and two bars of four in "Three to Get Ready," from *Time Out*, is made clearer by Brubeck's decision to begin his solo with very basic and repetitive figures, which lead quickly from a simplistic child-like motif into a starkly rudimentary pentatonic blues line. Had he gone outside too quickly, the innovative aspect of the structure wouldn't have been so apparent. The same is true of his solo on "It's a Raggy Waltz," from *Time Further Out*, in which his repetition of a simple triplet blues lick provides the essential motif of a two-fisted, tremolo-animated chorus.

His choruses in "It's Déjà Vu All Over Again," from the 1998 album *So What's New*, are about as typical a solo as he's ever played. Its inexorable climb from a single-line form to octave doubling to massive chorded dissonances, two against three, two-handed thumping rhythms, and final ear-twisting tremolos reflect the Brubeck aesthetic fully in just a couple of choruses. It seems impossible for Brubeck to comp sparely behind Bobby Militello's solos; each chord is a ten-fingered cluster, each

Dave Brubeck's sound was smooth, sleek, and cerebral— jet-age jazz.

placement as emphatic as a flat-footed stomp. Like it or not, it is pure Brubeck. At times he almost parodies this style, as in the banging climax to his remake of "Blue Rondo à la Turk," from the 1987 *Blue Rondo* album.

In a ballad context, Brubeck often left the gimmicks of his up-tempo playing behind. With no obligation to swing—or to develop not swinging into a statement—he could spell out compelling harmonies and develop melodic ideas more freely. His solo in "Easy as You Go," from the 1987 quartet album *Blue Rondo*, is a masterpiece of development; in one chorus he makes an insightful examination of the theme, with a few quick rushes enhancing rather than interrupting the topography of his statement.

This aspect of his playing emerges even more in solo settings. On "That Old Feeling," from *One Alone* in 2000, he slides in and out of bitonalism, his right hand slipping occasionally to a minor third above the left. What's surprising is how smooth he makes it sound; with delicate, reflective phrasing, Brubeck transforms the resulting dissonances into a poetic language of interpretation. It's the voice of a lion in winter, but if we look past his white mane and ignore the prophet-like smile lines that map eighty years of delight with life, it still projects the enthusiasm of youth, in its quest for adventure and bottomless optimism.

38. ROGER KELLAWAY

Born November 1, 1939, Waban, Massachusetts

Put Roger Kellaway on your list of pianists who deserve more attention than they've gotten. Of course, in this peculiar business, the kind of technique and erudition he possesses can act as a liability. He can play with a hard bop feel, or nose around in free territory, or blow a chorus or two of Dixieland. But that, of course, is part of the problem: The pianists who are easiest to pigeon-hole are the ones whose styles are the least ambiguous and, therefore, most widely appreciated.

Kellaway does cut a high profile. Tall and rangy, with a scruff of beard and a whimsical wit, he comes across as a well-adjusted academic. Being an eclectic, he is that—and far more. But the fact that Kellaway can write a vexatious chamber piece or a popular television theme, and play the blues in between, has made him sort of a blurry figure, and diminished the recognition that he deserves in all the areas of his endeavor.

The piano was Kellaway's love from his first moments in music. He began taking lessons at age seven, with a completely classical regimen until exposure to the music of George Shearing at age 12 kindled his interest in jazz. For a long while, however, Kellaway concentrated primarily on the bass, an instrument he taught himself to play in order to get into the student orchestra at Newton High School. He never abandoned the piano, though: At one high school concert, at which he was scheduled to conduct an original composition for piano and orchestra, he did so from the keyboard while playing the piano part as well when the intended pianist failed at the last minute to show up.

For two years he attended the New England Conservatory, first as a piano major with a bass performance minor, then as a composition major with a minor in piano, while playing some eclectic gigs on the side—one night under the baton of Charles Munch in the school chorus, the next jamming on trad jazz at the Hotel Buckminster. By the time he reached his third year, in 1959, Kellaway dropped both major and minor to hit the road for three months as bassist with cornetist Jimmy McPartland. Over the following years he played some more bass, with the Ralph Marterie big band, for which he also wrote his first professional charts, and for pianist Phil Ruedy at Jilly's in Manhattan. But he also began edging back toward the keyboard, taking the place of Peter Nero when he quit as house pianist at Jilly's during Ruedy's off-nights. After a short stint with Kai Winding at Birdland, Kellaway was hired in May 1963 by trumpeter Clark Terry and trombonist Bob Brookmeyer to work with their band at the Half Note.

With that, Kellaway's reputation spread quickly. He began picking up ever more unusual assignments—to play at a gospel service, to join émigré musicians in the Russian Jazz Quartet, even to be the butt of insult comic Jack E. Leonard in a nightclub routine. His curiosity is even broader than the stretch of his hands, a fact that gives his recordings a sense of vast reach and, on occasion, an absence of focus.

This was especially true early in his career. On his debut album, *The Roger Kellaway Trio* from 1965, he joins bassist Russell George and drummer Dave Bailey on a rendition of "Sweet and Lovely" that he builds to peak moments with idiomatic two-handed tremolos and smears, only to follow by alternating funky riffs with somewhat disruptive left-hand thumps and, on one bridge, an aimless atonal section; these passages seem to betray more of an analytical temperament than any full commitment to swing. On the next track, a 6/8 workout called "Signa: O.N.," Kellaway again draws energy from the collision of funk licks and bizarre dissonant moments. While his diminished-fifth glisses in the first two verses do provide reference for off-kilter trills and more atonal flurries later in the solo, the performance leaves a sense of disjointedness, of the parts, intriguing though they are, not quite coming together to form a satisfying whole.

His playing is tighter on "Breadwinner," recorded that same year for Kenny Burrell's *Guitar Forms*, Kellaway plays a restless rhythm accompaniment with drummer Grady Tate, bassist Joe Benjamin, and conga player Willie Rodriguez. His solo is crisp and precise; a few smears are dropped into the second verse, but only as a motivic device designed to contrast with the clarity of his line. Like much of Kellaway's playing, it is coherent and well-balanced, yet somewhat short of emotionally compelling.

More effective is his solo on "Alfie's Theme," from the Sonny Rollins score for *Alfie*. Kellaway offers an opening lick based on the rhythm of guitarist Kenny Burrell's last one in the preceding solo. This sets a funky tone, which the pianist maintains for two choruses, the first adhering to the requisite minor thirds and sevenths, the second stretching just a bit with a neat echo of an arrhythmic figure just before it on the tonic. This leads to a trilled minor third, which swells over the next chorus to a swirling two-handed tremolo and a semi-smeared ascending figure that serves as an emphatic finale. All of this is played at a muted dynamic; it's Kellaway's conception, rather than an ear-grabbing crescendo, that builds the tension and sets the stage for the saxophonist's understated entrance.

He gets more adventurous during "Transition Theme for Minor Blues, or Little Malcolm Loves His Dad," also from *Alfie*. His approach here is conceptually simple: After an opening figure that begins and ends on the second, Kellaway edges into a bitonal moment, ends the statement with another cadence on the second at the end of the first verse, then lets his line run far into another key center for the second verse before dropping it snugly into the main key with a few bars of conservative, blues-drenched, and very satisfying resolution.

Years later, on *Roger Kellaway Meets the Duo*, from 1992, he pulls Gene Bertoncini's "Soflee" way past the limits implied by its riff-driven, postbop opening. Following Bertoncini's swinging but conventional guitar solo, Kellaway takes the droning, rubbery repetition of the dominant by bassist Michael Moore as a cue to immediately invent a Bartókian motif built on a minor ninth and use it to bounce between boppish lines and stinging minor seconds. What strikes the listener here, aside from Kellaway's electrifying hand independence and sharp technique, is his refusal to acknowledge any borders between mainstream blowing and references to a cerebral European modernism.

In solo performance, Kellaway allows himself even more freedom to develop the harmonic implications of his material. On *Roger Kellaway Live at Maybeck Recital Hall*, he wanders through "Close Your Eyes" like a kid down a toy store aisle. At the end of the second verse, after settling with unexpected decisiveness on the I chord, he can't resist following with a completely unrelated series of bell-like descending II-V-I changes in the upper range. It is lovely, but its effect is subverted only a few bars later with trilled thirds that sink heavily into the bass register. Nobody can question the intelligence behind Kellaway's improvising, but its breadth makes it difficult to think of him as having a singular influence or even identity—which makes *Maybeck* perhaps Kellaway's clearest representation of his strengths as well as his shortcomings.

The Neo-Traditionalists

39. JIMMY ROWLES

Born: August 19, 1918, Spokane, Washington
Died: May 28, 1996, Los Angeles, California

Dapper and wry—not a vaudeville team or a law firm, but a description of Jimmy Rowles. In his later years he spoke with a gravelly rasp, the product of more than a few mixed drinks and cigarettes during a long career that established him as a completely reliable accompanist and rhythm section player. His style at the piano reflected his apprenticeship in the swing era, with an easy, sauntering rhythm and a fondness for saying as much as possible with the fewest gestures. In this love for economy, he was a disciple of Thelonious Monk, yet as the years went by this trait became part of a mellow, somewhat nostalgic sound, devoid of affectation, and always thoroughly musical.

It's not surprising that Rowles was essentially self-taught; his technique would develop only far enough to allow him to pour his personality into interpretations of standard tunes. Far from the action in New York, he didn't get hip to his main influence, Teddy Wilson, until a fellow student at Gonzaga College lent him a couple of records. As surely as mother's milk leads to hard drugs, Wilson steered Rowles into a lifetime of admiration for Earl Hines, Fats Waller, Art Tatum, and especially the writing and keyboard styling of Duke Ellington.

While Eastern and Midwestern jazz players made their treks to New York, Rowles journeyed down the West Coast to the next best thing. Shortly after arriving in Los Angeles he landed a gig there with saxophonist Lester Young. This led to regular opportunities to accompany Billie Holiday, who frequently performed with Young—which in turn inspired Rowles to explore the art of vocal accompaniment. In long associations with Holiday and Peggy Lee in the fifties, and for several years with Ella Fitzgerald in the eighties, Rowles earned a renown that would rival Tommy Flanagan's for making the greatest singers sound greater still.

He worked with big bands, including those of Benny Goodman and Woody Herman. After moving to New York in 1974, he began playing sessions with assorted headliners, including Zoot Sims, Charles Mingus, Stan Getz, Stephane Grappelli, and Lee Konitz. It's in smaller groups that his imprimatur comes through most clearly, especially on recordings of familiar repertoire. Rowles loved the classic tunes, and his interpretations reflect what a great time he had playing them. His range was broader than one might expect, from traditional to postbop; in every setting he played with a relaxed rhythm and an expressive harmonic sense. His adaptation of a Dvořák "Humoresque," on *Subtle Legend, Vol. 1*, has his characteristic loose and carefree feel. From a jaunty bounce to free tempo and back again, Rowles tosses off some tongue-in-cheek classical figurations; in this context only, he allows himself a few seconds of technical bravura, though only to add to the humor behind these references.

This was a rare bit of exhibitionism, for in truth no one could accuse Rowles of terrifying audiences with his chops. His pedaling could be heavy, and it was a rare Rowles performance that didn't include a few smudged passages. His duo performance of "Skylark" with saxophonist Stan Getz, heard on the Getz compilation *The New Collection*, is wet with sustain, but through the wash and the occasional fudged notes a vigorous, even iconoclastic, creativity permeates Rowles's performance. Odd minor substitutions, murky clashes in the low register, some whole-step movement in the bass where none was written by Hoagy Carmichael, a nice twist from a diminished chord at the top of the second verse—all conspire to reveal Rowles as an individualist with a distinctive way of taking a tune apart.

Like Monk, he found ways of rummaging amongst his limitations and coming up with a highly personal perspective. In fact, Rowles often sounded like a somewhat looser version of Monk, with disjointed chords and unexpected accents. His playing behind bassist Monty Budwig's choruses on "Isn't This a Night for Love," on the 1972 sessions for *Subtle Legend, Vol. 2*, echoes Monk in the opening

Like Monk, Jimmy Rowles found ways of rummaging amongst his limitations and coming up with a highly personal perspective.

chord and in the turnaround at the end of the first verse, but then Rowles adds a methodical delicacy in his own tiptoed solo, with meticulous delineations of the theme dropped between jagged passages (including an apparent quote from "'Round Midnight") and sudden smears or clusters.

The Monkish flavor of Rowles' style, as well as significant areas of difference, are evident also on his version of Fats Waller's "Jitterbug Waltz," from *Subtle Legend, Vol. 1*. At a moderate up tempo, he playfully varies his articulation of the written theme in the last half of each verse, and wraps it all up in ribbons of quick runs and, especially in the last half of the performance, propulsive left-hand jabs. Monk's spirit lives in the stark dissonance of his comps, though the open and relatively conservative bluesy language of his upper-register lines reflect a more traditional aesthetic. (The ultimate tribute is his "Ballad of Thelonious Monk," a playful ditty in which Rowles credits his hero with saving him from a life of listening to country music.)

No mere Monk imitator, Rowles blends very nicely into the ensemble behind saxophonist/composer Benny Carter on a stealthy version of "A Walkin' Thing," from the 1958 album *Jazz Giant*. His piano here works within the beat laid down by bassist Leroy Vinnegar and drummer Shelly Manne; a silky unison lick animates the intro to the tune without dominating the texture, and staccato triplet figures just before the first bridge give the beat an unusual but agreeable skipping feel. When he solos on a subsequent bridge and verse, Rowles picks his notes very carefully, placing them at first within a slowed-down triplet sequence that creates a delicious anticipation of the swing that he gradually generates. Notice Rowles's canny note selection at the end of the solo, with a blues run that manages to resolve without actually hitting the tonic on the way down.

But Rowles always sounded best when kicking back with material that allowed him to express his sly humor and crafty way with a melody. And when given a tune that was close to his heart, he regularly responded with a reading that brought out the magic he recognized in the writing. In duet performance with bassist Ray Brown on the 1980 album *Tasty!*, he handles the ballads "Come Sunday" and "Nancy (with the Laughing Face)" as one would a snifter of choice cognac after hours in one of the more posh saloons. Brown plays the bass with a smile on its face, conversing with the piano in low, intimate tones. And when the bass takes its solos, Rowles nods back from the piano, adding a feathery phrase here and there. The magic isn't just in the tune; it's in the spaces that the piano leaves, and in the dialog that he and Brown recognize as the key to playing jazz.

40. DICK HYMAN

Born March 18, 1927, New York, New York

The word "chameleon" has been applied to Dick Hyman, and not always as a compliment. His incredible command of multiple jazz piano traditions inspired this characterization; a superlative technician, Hyman can tear through a stride performance with complete fidelity to the style—and, not only that, break it down to an evocation of Willie "the Lion" Smith on one chorus and James P. Johnson on the next. Or he can deliver an equally convincing bebop set, or an understated harmonic *tour de force* that uncannily replicates Bill Evans.

All of this is admirable, but in the world of jazz, where originality and innovation are the most laudable goals, being the best musical mimic in the business isn't necessarily the greatest of distinctions. Hyman's music is the product of a boundless curiosity enhanced by intelligence and technique. He can play almost anything—even, for a few minutes at least, the whirling furies of Cecil Taylor. While this has certainly opened a variety of doors for him, it can't be said that Hyman has inspired any school of imitators, except for those who dream of becoming imitators themselves.

After acquainting himself with the basics of the piano, Hyman began taking lessons as a child from his uncle, Anton Rovinsky, a concert artist with an old-world approach to instruction. This classical regimen, enhanced by exposure to his older brother's jazz record collection, had instilled a determination by age ten to develop a swing style based on the work of his first hero, Teddy Wilson. Within a couple of years, though, Hyman began getting interested in older forms of jazz—the New Orleans school, Bix Beiderbecke and the Chicago sound, and New York stride piano. In addition to transcribing performances by Jelly Roll Morton and other pioneers, the young pianist read every book he could find on their lives; everything, from the notes they played to the quirks of their personalities, became critical information for Hyman in his formative years. For the rest of his career, no matter how broadly he would extend his range, these early innovators would define the direction of all his explorations.

By the time of his admission to Columbia University, Hyman had earned a lot of mileage in New York's club circuit. Except for a brief hiatus working for Uncle Sam at the Navy Yard in Vallejo, California, he spent his academic years juggling studies and music in and out of the classroom; as an undergraduate he scored the school's annual Varsity Show, and in his senior year his performance in a talent contest earned him a series of 12 private lessons with Teddy Wilson—Wilson, along with Mary Lou Williams and producer John Hammond, were among the jury members who gave first prize to Hyman.

From alternate fingerings to extended harmonic concepts, Hyman absorbed what his teacher had to offer. At the same time he prowled through the nightspots of Greenwich Village, where he caught repeated performances by James P. Johnson and Willie "the Lion" Smith. He began gigging more frequently as well; his first regular job after graduation was at the Wells Music Bar in Harlem, where he was paired with Wild Bill Davis, Charlie Stewart, and other jazz organists. More engagements soon followed, with clarinetist Tony Scott at Café Society Downtown, vibraphonist Red Norvo at Bop City, and Max Kaminsky and his Dixielanders at Birdland; when Kaminsky's stint ended, Hyman stayed on at Birdland as the house pianist behind Lester Young, Flip Philips, and other headliners, including one memorable evening as a sub for Bud Powell with Charlie Parker and Miles Davis. Aside from short tours with Victor Lombardo and Mundell Lowe, Hyman performed exclusively in New York.

Like Teddy Wilson and Billy Taylor, Hyman also worked outside of jazz circles, as a studio musician. He played with the staff orchestra at WMCA radio and hosted his own show for a while on the Dumont network. Through work as a bandleader for Morey Amsterdam's morning television show, he was hired as staff pianist and organist for NBC; from heart-tugging Hammond swells on soap operas to a five-year run doing music for *Beat the Clock* and on to a gig as musical director for Arthur Godfrey's radio and TV shows from 1959 through '62, Hyman became a fixture in the broadcast world.

If there was a downside to all this professional success, it was the time lost doing straight jazz. Though he had ample opportunity to work with artists such as Benny Goodman and Erroll Garner on the Godfrey show, the television studio was hardly comparable to the kinds of venues in which jazz players were encouraged and allowed to experiment and stretch out. For a while, Hyman filled his spare time recording tasteless ersatz ragtime dates for Enoch Light's Grand Award and Command labels. These performances, at reckless tempos on pianos whose strings were studded with thumbtacks for that "honky-tonk" effect, had little to do with real ragtime and less to do with jazz. Frankly, few pure jazz pianists would have taken that kind of work—maybe because few could have played this material with Hyman's panache. Whatever the reasons, by the time he was cutting a version of "Jingle Bells" with sampled dog barks providing the melody, Hyman had apparently accepted his position as a skillful emulator rather than a true innovator.

This becomes especially clear in the seventies, as he began composing nostalgic soundtracks for Woody Allen films and touring the Soviet Union and elsewhere with the New York Jazz Repertory Company Orchestra. In terms of performance, the most impressive of his later projects is the series of tributes to early jazz composers for the piano. Recorded solo on a Bösendorfer Imperial grand piano, each of these albums reflects the highest audiophile standards, with an elegant reverberation some might consider too ponderous for the material. Hyman's performance, though, is worthy of this royal treatment. His approach is, in fact, closer in spirit to a classical recital than to the rent parties and nightclubs where much of this repertoire took form; he keeps the listener focused more on the work than on his improvisational caprices.

For example, in his lavish rubato introduction to "Sophisticated Lady," from *Dick Hyman Plays Duke Ellington*, he exposes the architecture of the composition, drapes it in velvety harmonizations, and then strolls through the balance of the tune as a medium-tempo waltz. Every note—and there are many of them, from intricate chordal extensions to sprightly runs—brings us deeper into the tune. This selflessness typifies Hyman's interpretive style: insightful, reverent, and ultimately revealing.

Among the most tasteful of pianists in ensemble situations, Hyman makes the difficult sound simple, as in his solo on "As Long as I Live," from *Bob Wilber & Kenny Davern: Summit Reunion*. The entire solo is played in a single right-hand line, so unforced that its inventiveness almost passes notice. Hyman's mastery of rhythm is amazing: Only when he briefly trips into a triplet figure toward the end do we notice that the entire performance is structured as dotted eighth-notes, since the fluency of Hyman's melodic invention exists quite easily within this self-imposed limitation.

Equally important here is that Hyman doesn't need to fire up his chops to make an impression. On the following cut, "Lover Come Back to Me," he begins with a liquid-quick ascending run, again apparently effortless, that twists and spins through moments of stride, a counter-line in the left hand, a syncopated two-hand dancing descent in the bridge, and so on. One has to go back to Tatum to find a match for this marriage of breezy virtuosity and propulsion.

Hyman actually shows much more ease within a rhythm section than Tatum ever did, especially in his willingness to grant responsibility to the bass and drums for holding down the pulse. And when working with a partner, he never overplays or creates that sense of literalism that sometimes gives his unaccompanied work a formal air. His duet with Ruby Braff on the ballad "I've Grown Accustomed to Her Face," recently reissued on *Ruby Braff: The Concord Heritage Series*, seems to float on a steady but delicate current. The spaces he leaves in his accompaniment buffet Braff's elegant trumpet, and on his own Hyman plays with a difficult mix of sentiment, humor, and swing—which, in his hands, sounds anything but difficult.

This facility may be Hyman's weakness as well as his greatest strength. In everything he plays, he uncovers the essence of the style, whatever it may be. From stride to bop, his method adheres to conventions; his challenge is to perfect his mastery of historic elements, without any disruptions or distractions. Imagine a painter capable of reproducing the pointillistic technique of Impressionism, the angular abstractions of Cubism, and the suggestive shadows of the Dutch masters, while never crossing borders or shaking preconceptions. That same impression of never exerting himself contributes to a sense of dispassion, though certainly not a lack of humor or spirit, in Hyman's work. The only surprises he brings are when he exceeds our already high expectations of his impeccable execution.

What moments of exotica there are in his work draw from the early jazz practice of superficial reference. Whether playing an ersatz Latin groove in "I'll See You in C-U-B-A" (over a modified stride rather than a montuño) or nodding toward some vaguely Asian modality in a crisp intro to "Hindustan," both from the album *Summit Reunion: Yellow Dog Blues*, Hyman keeps these gestures light and momentary, in the fashion of the Fats Waller era.

This approach confirms that Hyman is in spirit an interpreter first and foremost; his artistry involves cultivating a relationship with the music of, say, Fats Waller that would be analogous to that of Horowitz and the music of Scarlatti. If jazz, like classical music, can allow as much honor for the archivist as for the cutting-edge innovator, then Hyman has his place in the pantheon. The chameleon is, after all, a survivor.

41. DICK WELLSTOOD

Born: November 25, 1927, Greenwich, Connecticut
Died: September 24, 1987, Palo Alto, California

He looked like a stride piano player, especially in his later years, with a stocky build and pugnacious face. He had the voice to go with the appearance, too—a sandpaper rasp, with a blue-collar, saloon-friendly accent best articulated through jaws clamped around a cigar. But looks and elocution, in his case at least, were deceiving, for Dick Wellstood was a scholar, and not just of the music with which he would be identified. He could play a lot more than stride, from the classics to somewhere in the neighborhood of postbop modernism; he even told one interviewer that he enjoyed playing with a polka band in his earlier years as much as any of the jazz gigs that would follow, and promised another that he hoped to someday play electric piano in a rock and roll band— a *good* rock and roll band.

He was an attorney as well. Or he could have been. On a lark Wellstood decided in the late fifties to enter the prelaw program at NYU, where he packed three years worth of study into two and served as president of the Student Bar Association, then dashed through the graduate program at the New York Law School with the same furious virtuosity. Unlike many of the customers who would clamor for another Fats Waller tune in the bars where he would entertain, Wellstood spoke Latin, played chess, and nearly qualified in his more slender days for the Olympic cycling team. In his spare time he had also taught himself German, just because he wanted to read Nietzsche in the original language. The erudite William F. Buckley was one of his great friends and admirers.

Fortunately, none of this got in his way when it came to playing the piano. For all of his eclecticism, it was stride that spoke to him most persuasively, and he played it with an authenticity that had not been heard since its heyday.

He was the son of a realtor. Just three years old when his father died, Dick was brought up by his mother's earnings as a church organist, piano teacher, and landlady. He entertained fellow students at the Wooster School in 1944 by thumping through boogie-woogie numbers during lunches in the cafeteria, which led to his first gigs at some YMCA teen club dances, which in turn somehow earned him an invitation to sit in with and subsequently play full-time with Bob Wilber's band. That same year, Wellstood heard two of his idols, stride pioneers Willie "the Lion" Smith and James P. Johnson, at the Pied Piper, as well as other legends—Donald Lambert, Marlowe Morris, Willie Gant, the Beetle, and the incomparable Art Tatum—at the Hollywood Café.

This wave of pianistic inspiration washed Wellstood into a lifelong whirl of musical work. There were long associations—three years with Gene Krupa's quartet, seven with trombonist Conrad Janis, two with Wild Bill Davison at Nick's in New York. Some of the shorter gigs were even more memorable, including an engagement in Chicago with Wilber's teacher, the definitive traditional jazz clarinetist and soprano saxophonist Sidney Bechet. The leading contemporary traditional clarinetist Kenny Davern was a longtime partner, as were Dick Hyman and Ralph Sutton; the three pianists would often pair off on four-hands sessions under the Barnumesque rubric "Stride Monster." Many other musicians shared the bandstand with Wellstood—189 of them, by his own reckoning in a list he compiled once for *Jazz Review* magazine, ranging from New Orleans drum pioneer Baby Dodds to latter-day bass experimentalist Buell Neidlinger.

Whitney Balliett touched on this almost unprecedented eclecticism in *The New Yorker*, where he suggested that Wellstood "has no verifiable style of his own. . . . He is a pianistic actor who slips inside other men's styles and brings them, with help of his own considerable improvisational energies, startlingly to life." In fact, this misses the mark somewhat; he came closer in observing that "Wellstood regarded himself as 'a contemporary musician who uses tools that are out of fashion,' and he was right."

The key here is that he played stride with no archival intention. The music was as real and immediate to him as it had been to Fats Waller, James P. Johnson, and the others who had originated the style. Unlike Dick Hyman, whose diverse discography includes performances with bebop icon Charlie Parker, early Moog synthesizer experiments, and a recording of "Jingle Bells" assembled from samples of barking dogs, Wellstood stood alone among modern stride pianists in his determination to build his every musical gesture on the bedrock of this form. He was 100 percent a stride pianist.

Even so, Wellstood differed from contemporaries such as Ralph Sutton and Mike Lipskin in his willingness to apply the form to highly unlikely material, from classical arrangements to John Coltrane's "Giant Steps." In all of the jazz catalog, "Giant Steps" must be considered one of the works least suited for stride treatment—which may be exactly why Wellstood accepted the challenge. With its maze of II-V-I changes, it seems written to discourage regular left-hand movement, yet on his live album *A Night in Dublin* Wellstood shows how to do it. By the third verse, at medium tempo, his rolling left-hand figure is opening up to allow some genuine boom-chuck action in the bass. A verse or so after that, Wellstood is grabbing octaves and quoting playfully from "Twisted" with his right hand. Shortly after that, damned if he doesn't pick up the tempo, shift his left hand into a roaring overdrive, and cascade ragtime-like alternating octave/interval figures through the changes as smoothly as water rushing through rapids. It's a conceptual *tour de force*, and more than a little cheeky. His stomping assault on "I Concentrate on You," which follows a few minutes later, is more ill-advised but certainly not unexpected.

(The same quote from "Twisted," incidentally, crops up on his swaggering rendition of "There Is No Greater Love," as heard on another exuberant nightclub performance, *Live at the Sticky Wicket*.)

Consistent with retro stride practitioners, Wellstood maintained a generally upbeat feel in his performances, down to playful paraphrases from other tunes. His technical authority in non-stride genres was neither as broad nor as academic as Hyman's. When playing traditional repertoire for the genre, Wellstood was somewhat more improvisational and less pristine than Hyman. And whether stretching a bit beyond the style or adhering to it, he played from the gut, with expression higher on the list of priorities than stylistic correctness; no one could slam out a bass pattern on the first and third beats of a bar with the gavel-like authority of Dick Wellstood.

On his solo album *Live at Hanratty's* Wellstood makes this clear with a set marked by its variety but unified by its fidelity to the spirit and form of stride. There is plenty of material here that fits the old form, including Sidney Bechet's "Quincy Street Stomp," which Wellstood wolfs down with hungry delight. He also wanders afield now and then, as with "Cha Cha for Charlie," despite the title a mournful original tune, with a trudging tempo and deep blue shadings. Yet even here Wellstood slips in and out of an idiomatic pulse that beats beneath sometimes enigmatic improvisations. There's almost a free-form element in the opening half of this tune, until he trips into a stride pulse with a hint of tango. It's an odd performance, very spur-of-the-moment and unconcerned about fidelity to other people's ideas of what's proper for someone in Wellstood's position.

Then there's the Wellstood wink—quick musical asides that seemed designed to tease the purists. No other pianist would have thought to throw a passage from "Tijuana Taxi" into "Ain't Misbehavin'," as he does on *Live at Hanratty's*. Few would have been able to see the ingenious structural connection, and maybe only Fats Waller himself would have had the impishness to piece them together, had he only been up on his Herb Alpert catalog.

Wellstood was an indefatigable performer; from 1959 onward his life could be measured on page after calendar page of one-nighters, quick tours, and steady gigs that included a long run at Hanratty's in Manhattan. It all came to an end one night in Palo Alto, where Wellstood died of a heart attack in his hotel room shortly before he was supposed to play at the annual Peninsula Jazz Party with Sutton, Davern, Flip Phillips, Milt Hinton, and others who admired his playing nearly as much as they loved the player.

42. DAVE McKENNA

Born May 30, 1930, Woonsocket, Rhode Island

With his rumpled jacket and weary-salesman demeanor, Dave McKenna looks like he might be more at home in the old Carnegie Tavern than in Carnegie Hall. In fact, he has played at the finest concert venues as well as in more than a few dives. Yet after more than 50 years behind the keys, his real musical home is in the intimacy and informality of the saloon.

There's nothing pretentious about McKenna's music. In his own words, he is a barroom pianist. He plays the old songs, the Gershwin and Harold Arlen and Arthur Schwartz catalogs. His straightforward way with a melody works best in a setting that's alive with conversation or the tinkle of ice against glass. It is, in the end, background music—except to those who might gather around the piano and pay attention. Then it reveals itself as something greater: a sound that's too elusive to invite imitation.

Swing is the essence of McKenna. No other pianist can match the momentum he builds through his baffling overlay of walking bass, rhythmic chording, and melody. By dividing these three functions between his two hands, he defines a system that players of greater technique have failed to master. The fourth and fifth fingers of his left hand lay down a mean and steady bass, both thumbs and second fingers thump out four-to-the-bar or syncopated chords, and the fourth and fifth fingers of his right hand blow saxophone-like solos; the third finger on each hand is kept in reserve for use wherever needed.

Fireworks are absent here. In fact, fancy runs would derail his propulsive motion. McKenna's got the chops to play fast and flashy, but he prefers sticking close to the middle range of the keyboard and letting the rhythm build without interruption in each tune. Sometimes his tempo gets out of control; "Margie," from his 1987 album *My Friend the Piano*, is typical of many McKenna performances that start off at a finger-popping saunter and end in an Olympic sprint. But who's keeping track of the time? What matters most is that drive, that locomotive beat, that has nothing to do with metronomes or click tracks.

The real testimony to his talent is that where most groove-oriented pianists are strongest when playing off of bass and/or drums, McKenna excels when working alone. He has recorded with other musicians, and often to good effect: When he starts trading fours with guitarist Gray Sargent during "Look for the Silver Lining," in *No More Ouzo for Puzo*, his right-hand line erupts into a spurt of self-

No other pianist can match the momentum Dave McKenna builds through his baffling overlay of walking bass, rhythmic chording, and melody.

contained, compact explosions. But Monty Budwig's bass in this quartet setting just doesn't burn the way that McKenna does when laying down the rhythm on his own.

Shy, a little awkward in front of a crowd, he was a late bloomer in music. His father drove a parcel post truck and played drums in amateur military bands; his mother played piano and violin. As a kid, Dave was more interested in following his beloved Boston Red Sox than practicing the piano lessons his mother gave him. But when he started paying attention to jazz programs on the radio, he got more into playing. Being somewhat solitary, he developed his command of bass lines by trying to do what it usually takes an entire rhythm section to do.

At age 12 he played his first gigs, at local weddings. He joined the musicians' union at 15; a year later he was working with Boots Mussulli around Milford, Massachusetts. Other gigs followed—with Charlie Ventura in 1949 in a band that included Red Mitchell on bass and Ed Shaughnessy on drums, followed by two years with the Woody Herman Herd in 1950 and '51. After a stretch in Japan and Korea with the Army, McKenna returned to Ventura, then moved on to jobs with Stan Getz and artists who came more from swing or even traditional jazz: the Gene Krupa sextet, cornetist Bobby Hackett at Eddie Condon's New York club in the sixties, and Bob Wilber in the seventies.

Mostly, however, he worked solo. Piano bars around Boston and Cape Cod were his preference; during one period in the seventies, he played duos with Teddy Wilson at the Columns in West Dennis, and for most of the eighties he worked six nights a week at Boston's Copley Plaza Hotel. He recorded frequently, making his debut on ABC in 1955, moving through a series of labels for several decades, then settling down with Concord Jazz in 1979.

The legacy left by McKenna on these discs, and in countless appearances on "jazz party" gigs and club dates, is one of consistency. Never an experimenter, he keeps faithful to the song and to the gospel of swing. In a sense, this is a modest mission, yet it also reflects a purity of intention. If we must accept him on his terms, as a saloon pianist, then it surely follows that he is the best of that breed.

43. GENE HARRIS

Born September 1, 1933, Benton Harbor, Michigan
Died: January 16, 2000, Boise, Idaho

He wasn't an innovator, and he wasn't exactly the greatest technician to ever command the keyboard. But Gene Harris deserves his place among jazz piano giants for one big reason— you feel better after listening to him than you did before.

The reason is self-evident. Practically anything that he's ever recorded conveys an uncomplicated and undeniable joy. His solos—most of the time—galloped like stallions, and when he played the blues there was nothing morose about the experience. While other pianists engaged in press polemics or exhumed old styles from the ancient graveyards of jazz, Harris and his audiences were having too much fun to notice.

Unlike most of his peers, Harris was completely self-taught, with a style derived mainly from his collection of boogie-woogie records. By the time of his induction in 1951 he was playing well enough to get into the Army band, where he befriended bassist Andy Simpkins. In 1956, with Simpkins and drummer Bill Dowdy, Harris formed the trio that would shortly become known as the Three Sounds. Based initially in South Bend, Indiana, they would relocate briefly to Washington, D.C., before moving to New York in 1958. An instant hit in local clubs, they were signed by Blue Note, for whom they recorded *Introducing the Three Sounds*.

Throughout the sixties and into the seventies the trio recorded and performed prolifically. In a little more than three years they would release 11 albums, including one with Lou Donaldson, titled *LD+3*, and *Blue Hour* with Stanley Turrentine. Beginning in 1962 they hopped a bit between labels, spending time at Verve, Mercury, and Limelight before returning to Blue Note in '66. Their popularity declined in the seventies, and Harris sought refuge in Boise, Idaho, beginning in 1977. After a few years, though, his friend Ray Brown persuaded to come back as a member of his own trio. Harris once again became quite active, as leader of his own trio and in guest appearances with Benny Carter and other artists.

The key to Harris's success is in his ability to add a bluesy dimension to an otherwise upbeat sound. Even on slow tunes, such as "Willow Weep for Me," from the 1958 album *Introducing the Three Sounds*, or the original blues "Down the Track," recorded in 1959 for *Down the Track*, his scrambling licks make his playing more accessible; for Harris, the blues season rather than define his playing.

Much in the Harris style embraces the obvious. As Erroll Garner had done, Harris catered to a broad audience; unlike Garner, he had no affectations that would lend strong distinctive qualities to his playing. His chords reflect a mainstream mentality, his high-register solos either spell out the tune or scatter easily absorbed bits. It's all agreeable, but little of it shows any probing intellectual orientation. And sometimes, especially when stuck on a funk rut, it can get more than a bit monotonous: It's hard to understand how the audience stayed attentive through his regurgitation of soul-jazz licks over an endless I–IV vamp in "I'm Still Sad," from the 1970 album *Live at the It Club*.

Still, there aren't many pianists who can play with the bouncy swing that defines the Harris style, especially at medium tempos. "Don't Be That Way," the Benny Goodman classic, proves an ideal fit for Harris on *Listen Here!*, his quartet album from 1989. Following Ron Eschete's short guitar solo, the pianist tears into several choruses of his own. His verses are dominated by blues licks, with bridges building to two-fisted climaxes that drive back to the following verses. On his last chorus Harris puts his big-band hat on and pounds rocking riffs with all the power and sparkle of the entire Goodman horn section.

The same can be said for his robust solo on "For Once in My Life," from the 1991 quartet album *Brotherhood*. This one practically jumps off the disc, with rippling two-handed tremolos, swooping glissandi, and runs sparked by quick trills that pop like fireworks over a footrace. Stylistically it's somewhat old-fashioned, but its show-stopping razzle-dazzle, especially in the massively extended coda, can't be missed.

Harris's approach to the blues involves a gleeful manipulation of familiar devices. He plays textbook runs, using flatted seventh and fifths, and ripples triplets on the high keys against a smoky low-tempo drag. It's completely predictable, yet Harris makes it impossible to resist. He doesn't pretend to seek new ground; rather, he trots out all the clichés and scatters them with blissful nonchalance.

Practically anything Gene Harris recorded conveys an uncomplicated and undeniable joy.

Even when playing show-type tunes, Harris draws heavily from the blues. His solo on "Just in Time," from *The Complete Sessions: Stanley Turrentine & the Three Sounds*, recorded in 1960, jogs along with jaunty dotted eighth-notes, smears a few funky thirds, and lands emphatically on the tonic with a down-home lick at the end of the first verse. Harris seems to get so carried away in the solo that he kicks off a coda prematurely.

In ballads Harris is restless, chafing against the beat with double-time passages and rapid repeated figures on key notes of the melody. On "That's All," from Ray Brown's 1974 album *Soular Energy*, the pianist plays spare lines in the upper notes, with minimal left hand. Though capable of inventing interesting lines, as in the last bridge section of this tune, Harris prefers staying close to the theme and high on the keyboard, as if to feed from the power of familiar ornamentation rather than to push for something untested.

On reflection, it is no small accomplishment to sustain the kind of enthusiasm that carried Harris through nearly fifty years at the piano. With those untrained chops and indefatigable spirit, Harris was a positive example for pianists of every style and generation.

The Endurance of Postbop

BILLY TAYLOR

Born: July 21, 1924, Greenville, North Carolina

O n balance Billy Taylor is probably the finest ambassador jazz ever had. Sure, he doesn't have quite the charisma that made Louis Armstrong an international phenomenon. Of course, no one else did either, but Taylor has a unique self-assured presence, enhanced by his warm manner and relaxed but articulate way with words. Wynton Marsalis will likely inherit this role, but at least for now it's doubtful whether he'll achieve the kind of credibility that allows Taylor to speak for and about musicians of all styles.

Let us not forget, though, that music, as well as personality, helped Taylor achieve this distinction. It didn't take long after his arrival in New York for word to get around that he was a nice guy, a thoughtful and respectful student and colleague. Less time than that was needed for Taylor to broadcast that he was also a formidable piano player, with an unusually mature sound for one so young.

With the passing years, as his presence broadens across the firmament of our culture, Taylor has grown a little less vital as a pianist. This is perhaps inevitable for any artist who makes it out of the trenches and into the Kennedy Center pantheon. Urbane and approachable, he is universally respected, if not revered. If that comes at the price of abdicating a position he once claimed as heir to Art Tatum's legacy as the definitive virtuoso of jazz piano, it's a fair trade, given the benefits Taylor has bestowed on music through his gracious and persuasive proselytizing.

There was always music in the air, from the moment Billy Taylor was old enough to hear it. His father, a dentist, led a church choir, though his view of sacred music regarded thorough European training as a prerequisite. Billy began taking piano lessons at the age of seven, desultorily at first. This attitude changed four years later, when he first heard Fats Waller and Art Tatum on disc. Inspired by their integration of classical technique and spirited improvisation, Taylor stepped up his piano study.

By the time his family moved to Washington, D.C., and took him to hear the bands of Chick Webb, Jimmie Lunceford, Count Basie, and Duke Ellington one memorable day at the Howard Theater, his destiny was sealed.

With a music diploma in hand from Virginia State University, Taylor left Washington to try his luck in New York. Just two days after his arrival, the 19-year-old pianist sat in with saxophone legend Ben Webster at the Three Deuces on 52nd Street—and was promptly invited to join the band. Over the following years he worked around town with other artists. He also developed a close friendship with Art Tatum, who became the young pianist's most important mentor. Taylor's first recording date came in 1944; two years after that he spent two months working with the Cuban percussionist Machito, an experience that would leave a lasting impression on his musicianship.

In 1949 Taylor formed his own quartet, which eventually evolved into the Gramercy Five when Artie Shaw took over the group. That same year he played for the first time with Charlie Parker, which led to his being hired as house pianist at Birdland. Dizzy Gillespie, Miles Davis, Lee Konitz, Gerry Mulligan, Roy Eldridge, Art Blakey, and dozens of other headliners benefited from his accompaniment during his three years on that gig. On off-hours Taylor pursued advanced piano instruction from Richard McLanahan, who imparted a technical regimen based on the teachings of Tobias Matthay. Its main effect was to impart a way of maintaining hand relaxation at high velocity and impact—an invaluable asset when battling crowd noise with a bunch of bebop players.

By 1951, with the end of the Birdland residency, Taylor was leading his own trio, beginning with Charles Mingus on bass and Charlie Smith on drums. His early recordings in this format capture him as a facile improviser with a leaning toward the hard bop school. Rather than play with the sweaty intensity of a Horace Silver, however, he adopted a lighter approach, one which skimmed rather than plowed into the beat. On *Billy Taylor Trio*, featuring recordings from 1952 and '53, his playing projects an irresistible upbeat feel, nurtured by an unusually balanced technique and a full grasp of jazz theory. Backed by Earl May on bass and Charlie Smith on drums, he romps through "They Can't Take That Away from Me," over precise off-beat comps in the left hand. After the opening verse, Taylor has a ball, popping truncated lines against the rhythm, gearing up to sixteenth-notes, quoting slyly from "Louise," and, in what would become a characteristic of sorts, jumping through several different keys. On this and many other tracks, Taylor moderates his bop influence into a song-driven format, in which dashing improvisations mingle with Shearing-like chorded passages. Even when blowing for blowing's sake, as in a blinding rendition of "Lover" marked by supersonic runs and playful altered arpeggios, this combination of elements, infectious as well as informed, made him one of the most listenable pianists of the fifties among both casual and discerning audiences.

By the end of the decade, though, Taylor seemed to lose a bit of that buoyancy, perhaps by spreading himself too thin. On *Uptown*, a live trio set recorded at the Prelude in New York on February 4, 1960, he tackles Bobby Timmons's "Moanin'" with an almost languid reading of the theme on the first verse, then begins his solo in an offhand manner, complete with a lightly tripping triplet run up to the tonic at the end of the first bridge. Though he restricts himself to the blues scale, especially during the first three verses, Taylor conveys an impression that he does so consciously in order to adhere to the style. A two-handed chorded passage makes the point that his resources are deeper than most of his solo would suggest—yet there isn't enough compensatory heat to make up for the funk limitations he respects throughout most of his solo. He confirms his impression later in the same set, with a clean but hardly incendiary reading of an original medium-up blues, "Cu-Blu."

Significantly, on the last track, "'S Wonderful," taken at a quicker clip and more in bop fashion, Taylor finally digs in. His dotted-eighth lines fit more smoothly into the rhythm here than on the funkier stuff. With bassist Henry Grimes and drummer Ray Mosca keeping the heat on in the background, Taylor spins very long, impeccably crafted lines through the Gershwin changes. He breaks his pace in the first bridge with a two-note motif derived from the tune, repeats the figure, then develops it in call-and-answer fashion through the next verse. The second bridge gets a similar treatment, this time with repetition of a two-note figure adding fuel to his fire. A key change after that heats things up even more, but Taylor resists breaking the impetus too soon, with more solid boppish blowing up to another effective bridge, this one powered by a string of accented dominant notes in the bass range. It takes a while to get there, but this cut confirms that when not pushing too hard in areas where he was less than comfortable, Taylor could burn.

He also excels within Latin settings, thanks to his apprenticeship with Machito. A set of original mambos, recorded on May 7, 1953, with a band that combined his trio with Machito's rhythm section, shows Taylor confident in executing unison lines, rhythmic chorded passages played on the beat, and in straight-eighth-note phrasing—fundamentally different from his bop-derived trio work, and appropriate to the groove. This sort of playing marked Taylor as one of the first jazz pianists to find something fresh from a serious study of Latin conventions. On "Candido Mambo," available on his album *Cross Section*, he uses the up-and-down approach to rhythmic phrasing represented by Latin piano to dish out some examples of hand independence that straight-ahead jazz piano seldom allows, with rhythmically and thematically independent lines twining together at several points in his solo over the sultry mambo groove before falling into a classic montuño passage. On a subsequent session, *The Billy Taylor Trio with Candido*, the pianist slides even more smoothly into a stylistic synthesis, as the Cuban percussionist sits in with Taylor, Earl May, and drummer Percy Brice on a series of tunes that waver between Latin and mainstream jazz.

Taylor possesses a rare command of harmonic language. When backing other soloists, he dishes out thicker chords than most pianists, often hitting them fully with both hands rather than dividing parts between them. His unaccompanied introduction to "I'll Remember April," from the 1993 album *Dr. T*, states the first two bars of the theme over a tonic pedal, with Impressionistic harmonies in parallel movement toward a diminished chord. In the next two bars, however, Taylor thickens the texture and shifts the bass, with the tension resolved through a graceful simplification back to the A major seventh in the eighth bar. And during Stanley Turrentine's solo on "At La Carousel," from Taylor's 1994 album *It's a Matter of Pride*, the pianist plays practically nothing but massive comps, in sprawling ten-fingered voicings. Though not as identifiable as the chording of Bill Evans or Herbie Hancock, Taylor's approach reveals a sophisticated understanding of traditional voice-leading and harmonic architecture.

For all of his superb taste and intelligence, Taylor isn't the strongest melodic improviser. Compared especially with some younger players, he keeps his lines close to the chords. This becomes apparent in the same performance of "I'll Remember April," as Taylor begins his solo with sequences of sixteenth-notes that contain somewhat repetitive figures and motifs. The absence of rhythmic variety or adventurous melodic ideas is apparent only because of the strength that Taylor brings to the denser passages in the opening verse. Elsewhere, on the more up-tempo "You're Mine," his frequent arpeggiated runs create an uncomfortably simplistic effect.

On his own material, including the *Homage* written for his trio and the Turtle Island String Quartet and recorded in 1990, Taylor shows a similar disengagement from vital melodic improvisation. His solo on "Homage, Part II," to name but one track from this ambitious work, follows the chord changes faithfully but consists almost entirely of a long stream of eighth-notes; the lack of rhythmic vitality, aside from the occasional triplet or quarter-note, leaves that same sing-song aftertaste noted in many of his solos on standards.

We are, of course, talking about the later stages of a remarkable career on these recent releases. Over the past several decades Taylor has arguably accomplished more for jazz away from the stage than on it. His Jazzmobile program, inaugurated in 1965, was an inspired device for bringing America's music back to the streets and neighborhoods where it had once thrived. In the seventies he served for three years as musical director on *The David Frost Show*, one of the more popular variations on the *Tonight Show* idea. Taylor also developed his own presence as host of an early National Public Radio program, *Jazz Alive*, as well as a thirteen-part series called *Taylor Made Piano* and, most recently, *Billy Taylor's Jazz at the Kennedy Center*.

Taylor also enjoyed high visibility as a cultural correspondent for 14 years on the CBS *Sunday Morning* television show. His position on the boards of the Rockefeller Foundation and ASCAP, his two Peabody Awards and his Emmy, his 12 honorary degrees, and all the other recognition he has received have lifted him above what any jazz artist might reasonably expect from life. Taylor has handled it all well; whatever reviews one may offer of his later piano work, it's easy to see why Stan Kenton once described Taylor as the most important jazz musician of our time.

45. TOSHIKO AKIYOSHI

Born: December 12, 1929, Darien, Manchuria

E ven after years of the stylistic shotgun marriage represented by world music, Toshiko Akiyoshi stands out for her nuanced application of international elements to a mainstream jazz framework. It is possible to detect what might be characterized as Japanese aromas in some of her work—for example, in her theme from "The Village," which reflects aspects of Ryuichi Sakamoto's "Good Morning, Mr. Lawrence." But these play a small role in a composition that is otherwise rich in hip chords and blues licks, and driven by a punchy left-hand ostinato that doesn't remotely evoke any Asian provincialism. The result is a style that sounds much more personal, and far less gimmicky, than what passes for multicultural music today.

Setting aside the additional issue of her arrival at a time when there were few pianists and no female bandleaders on the scene, Akiyoshi's playing demanded to be judged on its own merits from the moment of her exposure to some visiting North American heavyweights. If anything has stood in the way of her recognition as a formidable instrumentalist, it is her own success as a composer and head of one of the most innovative big bands of the later twentieth century. Fortunately, her performance is a matter of extensive record—enough to establish her, without qualification, as one of the more inventive pianists to emerge from the early postbop era.

An émigré from birth, she was the youngest of four daughters of a Japanese textile and steel mill owner settled in the Manchurian province of China. They stayed through the difficult war years, returning to Japan in 1945 when Communists started pouring into the area. By that time Toshiko was already playing a lot of piano, having begun lessons at the age of four and taken advanced instruction at the Darien Conservatory.

In Japan, jazz entered into the picture as well. Akiyoshi was 16, about to ship off to medical school, when she visited a cousin in Beppu, who told her of a local band that needed a piano player. In short order she became "one of the guys" and started performing around Tokyo, primarily for American servicemen. She had never played jazz up to that point, but she read music well, and for the first year or so with the band she concentrated on playing the charts in the band's book. At no point during this period did she take a solo, or even worry that much about improvising at all.

Her enlightenment began when a Teddy Wilson solo on a recording of "Sweet Lorraine" caught her attention. The first thing that struck her was the extent to which Wilson departed from what she knew as the correct version of the tune. Carefully she studied his performance, transcribing what he played and examining its relationship to the written melody. Soon she was transcribing other solos, and taking her first steps toward improvising by writing out her own solos in advance of her gigs.

Where other pianists might just patch segments together, Toshiko Akiyoshi's lines retain their logic throughout the entire solo.

Inspired now primarily by Bud Powell, Akiyoshi began playing extensively in Tokyo. Whitney Balliett, in his *Collected Works, 1954-2000*, noted some of the bands with whom she worked: the Blue Coast Orchestra, the Gay Stars Orchestra, and the Tokyo Jive Combo. Without a lot of competition from the local talent, she had little trouble attracting attention. By 1951 Akiyoshi was working with the outstanding saxophonist Sadao Watanabe. A few years after that she formed her own band, which she called the Coy Quartet. It was at a gig with this band that she would win a sudden entrée into the big time.

Norman Granz was in Japan at the time, leading one of his barn-burning Jazz at the Philharmonic all-star tours. Oscar Peterson, the headliner on that JATP bill, decided to visit some of the local clubs during one night off in Tokyo. By chance he wound up hearing Akiyoshi and her band. Recognizing her ability, Peterson made sure that Granz came down to catch the act as well. A quick introduction, and two weeks later Akiyoshi was in the recording studio, with Granz at the console and Peterson's rhythm section providing the backup as she cut her first record.

Aside from time taken to study at the Berklee School in Boston from 1956 to '59, Akiyoshi has worked steadily since then. In 1959, after her marriage to saxophonist Charlie Mariano, she joined her husband, bassist Gene Cherico, and drummer Eddie Marshall in quartet jobs at the Half Note and Birdland in New York, the Birdhouse in Chicago, and other American venues. In 1969, after her divorce, Akiyoshi married another saxophonist, Lew Tabackin; three years later, relocated to Los Angeles, they assembled some of the best studio musicians into a 16-piece group, whose vibrant swing and vivid arrangements established it from the seventies onward as arguably the top big band in jazz.

As a pianist, Akiyoshi reflects the kind of structural thinking required to arrange and compose for large groups. Her solo on "My Search," from the Charles Mingus *Complete Town Hall Concert* of 1962, takes off on the wings of a powerful ensemble blast, with a funky right-hand lick that drops at once into an exploration based on movement in thirds. This is followed by some whole-tone movement juxtaposed against the changes, most of which are identical to those of "I Can't Get Started." Where Mingus alters the last eight bars of the Vernon Duke tune, and the last chord going out of the bridge, Akiyoshi incorporates the changes to create a statement based entirely on Mingus's, rather than Duke's, vision. This is the performance of a pianist who understands composition, and how to make the smallest details critical in improvisation.

Her language in small group settings derives largely from bop, with restless left-hand accents prodding long right-hand lines. Akiyoshi's melodic conceptions are large-scale: Where other pianists might just patch segments together, her lines retain their logic throughout the entire solo. When stretching toward other styles, she can sometimes lose a bit of the swing she shows while sticking closer to pure bebop settings. In her arrangement of Cole Porter's "So in Love," from the 1987 album *Interlude*, moments of hesitation, starts and stops in the flow of her ideas, interrupt her line as she seems to struggle against the Latin groove laid down by bassist Dennis Irwin and drummer Eddie Marshall. Her left hand in particular loses some focus, at times see-sawing mechanically between the I and IV in a somewhat heavy reflection of the bass.

As a solo pianist Akiyoshi usually holds herself back from the fireworks of which she is capable. At times she projects a sober formality, as on her rendition of Duke Ellington's "Come Sunday," from *Toshiko Akiyoshi at Maybeck*. Though Satie obviously inspires the intro and ending, the somber stride, fixed inflexibly on root chords, and the softly jarring harmonies and whole-tone movement of thirds in her right hand bring Marcus Roberts to mind. Akiyoshi's stride is, like that of Monk, a variation on the classic approach: intentionally spare and irregular, with single notes or fifths rather than tenths in the bass. She plays off listener familiarity with the style by using adventurous, even cryptic, runs and chords to simultaneously acknowledge and move past the tradition.

Playing in the pocket is not one of Akiyoshi's strengths, especially when working alone. Perhaps her compositional sense led her toward the ostinato figures of "Con Alma" and her own piece, "The Bridge," or the thundering arpeggios and thumping fifths that support her dramatic treatment of "It Was a Very Good Year," as performed on *Maybeck*; her note choices, not always evenly articulated, are more interesting than electrifying. The likely point is that Akiyoshi, for all her professed bebop roots, is at heart as much a big band pianist as Ellington and Basie; her considerable strengths as a pianist derive more from numbers than from solitude.

46. CEDAR WALTON

Born: January 17, 1934, Dallas, Texas

Consistency is the hallmark of Cedar Walton's performances. Never flashy, he generally stays close to the piano's midrange, where he works well within postbop conventions. Yet his mastery of the idiom is so complete, and his rhythmic feel so natural, that he virtually never misses the mark. Listeners as well as his fellow musicians would be challenged to find any examples in which Walton's playing disappoints.

This dependability, better recognized as professionalism, owes something to Walton's very extensive sideman credits, as well as to his conditioning in that boot camp of jazz survivalism, Art Blakey's Jazz Messengers. The upshot was the reputation he earned for the contradictory act of developing his own sound and being able to apply it to virtually any type of jazz setting.

Walton's story has a familiar beginning, in which the mother plays the role of the first piano teacher. Both she and his father loved jazz, so there was no hesitation when their son indicated at age six that he was ready to learn everything they had to teach. This being Dallas in the forties, however, there wasn't any of the community feeling that nurtured jazz musicians and their acolytes along, say, Swing Street in New York. Instead, as Walton would remember it, racial restrictions made it difficult for Duke Ellington and other black bandleaders to find a venue for their groups in the Big D.

There was a positive spin, though: People like the Waltons made up for the shortage on concert halls by donating their homes to visiting musicians for more intimate performances. More than once a very young Cedar was lulled to sleep—or, more likely, kept awake—in his room by the sound of a jazz session and an enthusiastic crowd just down the hall.

The local gigs began in high school, as Walton rushed through clarinet lessons and out to roadhouses to lay down R&B grooves with David "Fathead" Newman and other up-and-coming players. He kept his calendar full at Dillard University in New Orleans as well, where his colleagues included saxophonist Plas Johnson and a fellow pianist and future dynasty sire, Ellis Marsalis. When not on the bandstand or bent over classroom assignments, Walton was paying close attention to recorded performances by his favorite player at the time, Art Tatum.

After earning his degree at Dillard, Walton pursued postgraduate music study for three years at the University of Denver. Still in his teens when he arrived, he maintained his double life in the classrooms and in the clubs. It was in one Denver nightspot that he began hearing the greats of jazz first-hand—Dizzy Gillespie, John Coltrane, Johnny Hodges, and Charlie Parker.

Finally, in 1955, Walton was ready for New York. It was an instructive encounter; to the musicians working there at that time, Bud Powell was the definitive innovator on the piano, so for the first time Walton was immersed in his influence. When Lou Donaldson told him, after they had played together one night, that Walton and Powell used their left hand in similar ways, no greater compliment could have been given to the young pianist.

From 1956 through '58 Walton was a guest of Uncle Sam in the U.S. Army. On his discharge he rushed back to New York to pick up where he had left off. Opportunities came thick and fast, as he gigged with Donaldson and Gigi Gryce, then got called to replace Tommy Flanagan in J. J. Johnson's band. After two years with the great bop trombonist, Walton inherited McCoy Tyner's piano gig with the Art Farmer/Benny Golson Sextet, then left after a little more than a year to accept an invitation in August 1961 from Art Blakey to follow Bobby Timmons in the Jazz Messengers.

This was perhaps the most prized gig for up-and-coming jazz players—a hard-swinging ensemble driven by a drummer known both for the intensity of his performance and his ability to nurture young musicians. Blakey's band at the time included several exciting new arrivals, saxophonist Wayne Shorter and trumpeter Freddie Hubbard among them. Everyone had room to develop his solo chops and to contribute material to the band's repertoire. Equally important, there were plenty of opportunities to guest on other projects. Walton pursued them enthusiastically and clocked studio time as sideman to the likes of Joe Henderson, Jackie McLean, Lee Morgan, and. Donald Byrd.

After three years with Blakey, Walton struck out on his own, a fully equipped artist whose consistent excellence became his trademark. Because of this relentless excellence, it's easy to pick out recordings that typify his steady, swinging style, and a bit harder to cite any dramatic departures above or below his high standards. On *Cedar!*, recorded in 1967, Walton turns Duke Ellington's "Come Sunday" into an infectious medium-tempo finger-snapper. His comps behind trumpeter Kenny Dorham and tenor saxophonist Junior Cook are repetitive only where he's building a rhythm motif in response to something in the solo; the rest of the time he plays freely and inventively, always pushing the beat and supporting the horn. Notice, in particular, his offbeat accents and angular voicings at the end of Dorham's solo, and his switch to a contrasting counter-rhythm as Cook kicks off his improvisation with a circular triplet figure; this is interactive jazz accompaniment at its best. In his own solo, Walton opens in the pocket, with a three-note motif that he recaps slightly off the beat, then builds into a beautifully balanced extemporization, flavored but not dominated by blues elements, and laced by fleet lines that break back down to elemental slower passages in order to stay connected to the groove.

On very rare occasions, particularly when attempting to conform to formulaic funk rhythms, Walton could sound clumsy within a rhythm section, as on "Higgins Holler," recorded in 1968 for his album *Spectrum*. Despite Jack DeJohnette's best efforts, the rhythm section sounds slightly out of sync throughout this track, for which Walton tries to compensate with heavy-handed chords that repeat far too frequently and stretch out far too long throughout the song; after just a few choruses of this, the piano part starts to sound positively annoying. Yet there are many more examples of Walton laying down a superb accompaniment. Listen to the opening chorus of "The Shadow of Your Smile," from the Eddie Harris album *The In Sound*, in which the nuances of his rhythmic placement and chord spelling are easy to appreciate. The unresolved bitonality at the end of the first phrase in bar four, the gently arpeggiated chord at the equivalent position in bar eight, the decision to play the last chord of the bridge on the beat rather than to syncopate it—all of these details contribute mightily to the breezy swing achieved by bassist Ron Carter and drummer Billy Higgins.

His early recordings showed great promise as a melodic improviser as well. Again with Eddie Harris, on *The Tender Storm*, Walton takes two choruses of "On a Clear Day (You Can See Forever)" and turns them into a solo whose proportions match the inventiveness of its content. After playing Latin-type comps and even a bit of montuño at the end of the sax solo, Walton delivers a highly swinging yet wonderfully restrained solo. He opens with one emphatic chord, as final punctuation to the Harris performance, then constructs a highly original melody, in which he avoids ending phrases on the root or right on the first beat of a bar; this subtle exercise keeps audiences from anticipating where he's going, without resorting to gratuitous eccentricities. At the fifth bar, Walton suddenly rockets a triplet chromatic run into a higher octave. There, he creates another ascending figure, this one syncopated in a three-against-four feel that builds to some exuberant gospel chording. He takes another verse as well, but that first one is all you need to get his message.

These characteristics are particularly evident when Walton plays in swing rather than funk settings. His solo on "Turquoise Twice," from *Cedar!*, again features a buoyant left hand and exquisitely realized lines in the right. Aside from a few quick runs, this performance is played with moderate velocity; its strength derives from Walton's developmental sense—notice his variation on a little riff he comes up with toward the end of his second improvised chorus—and irresistible rhythmic phrasing. And, again, his phrases tend to end on notes other than the obvious roots or tonics, including the second that he hits in the very last moment of the solo. The same can be said for an invigorating Walton performance of "Wee Dot," from *Bambino*, a 1994 live set at Sweet Basil's, as well as a simmering medium-tempo performance of "Little Jazz," from the 1994 Benny Carter *Elegy in Blue*—with one addition: Unlike almost every other pianist who attempts to build intensity in an improvisation by rapidly repeating one note, Walton does so in these two performances within the rhythm rather than with sloppy velocity, a reminder of the fact that precision and swinging are more important to him than effect.

Walton has always been an expressive ballad player, though not in the Evans sense of speaking through harmonies. Backed by bassist Sam Jones and drummer Louis Hayes on "All the Way," from a 1973 live date released on the album *Naima*, he uses quick lines in and out of tempo to maintain a sense of emotional urgency. Walton's churchy ornamentations and harmonic adventurousness are kept in balance through compelling use of ascending and descending repeated figures; it's outside and inside at the same time, and powerfully balanced throughout the five-minute performance. Repetitions of extemporized fragmentary motifs guide Walton as well through his improvisation on "A Nightingale Sang in Berkeley Square," from the 2000 Jackie McLean album *Nature Boy,* especially on his way out of his first chorus; because he moves these motifs freely through the chord changes, so that they function essentially as single notes, these figures ornament, rather than detract from, the melodic conception. By comparison, Walton's solo on "If I Had You" puts long strings of speedy sixteenth-notes into context by frequent referrals in slower passages to the written theme and, in the last half of the bridge, some full chordal movement that turns into a harmonic motif for the first half of the following verse—again, symmetry and balance, tension and release.

First and foremost an ensemble player, Walton was more than capable of extemporizing rich song interpretations as a solo pianist. *Cedar Walton at Maybeck* offers rock-solid performances, each one dedicated to bringing out the highlights of a classic tune. On his reading of "Darn That Dream," Walton begins with a free-tempo verse, always illuminating the melody yet adding just enough elaboration to keep the colors shifting. At the end of the first bridge he does play a minor gem of a fill, springing off from a short figure of mirrored descent and ascent to a contraction of this movement in padded harmonies that eventually nestle on a gentle pedal tone. From here Walton moves into another verse, which ends with a very similar sequence of chords, this one descending in parallel movement rather than contracting but settling nonetheless on another pedal. Only now does the performance slip into tempo, with a spry single line supported by the lightest possible rhythmic suggestions in the left hand.

There are flashier pianists than Walton in jazz—always were, always will be. Often, though, their performances are more erratic, marked perhaps by higher peaks as well as murkier depths. Professionalism is Walton's legacy, based on hard work in his student years and sustained by an unusual discipline and self-respect. As his colleagues know well, he is no less brilliant than the brightest stars.

47. STEVE KUHN

Born: March 24, 1938, New York, New York

There are few holes in the fabric of Steve Kuhn's music. Since breaking into jazz in the late fifties he has juggled the intellectual, the technical, and the essential elements of improvisation with a rare dexterity. His solos can sound premeditated, so balanced is the flow of his ideas. Yet there's a playfulness as well in his lines, and sometimes an almost existential moodiness. What's missing is angst or fatalism; Kuhn is too caught up in the pleasures of creation to waste his energies on that kind of posturing.

Kuhn was appreciated initially by musicians in two camps whose separation was clear and potentially contentious. He was an Ivy Leaguer, with thick-framed specs and a literary demeanor that served as badges for the Brubeck crowd. And he performed as well, though briefly, with John Coltrane, whose eruptive passions threatened to demolish the European foundations of cerebral jazz. Not many musicians could move from one to the other side of that divide and emerge with reputations enhanced.

The son of a former violin teacher, Kuhn showed very early signs of talent; reportedly he knew by the age of five that he would become a musician. More specifically, he would become a *jazz* musician: The only way to get him to practice the humdrum drills of classical instruction was to promise him an opportunity to read through transcriptions that his teacher had written from boogie-woogie piano discs.

After moving to Chicago in 1947, the Kuhn family settled in Boston three years later. There, barely in his teens, the young pianist began working at local nightspots while taking advanced lessons for more than two years from Margaret Chaloff—a rare figure in classical music, at least for the times, given her enthusiasm and love for jazz. Under her guidance, and through informal sessions with her son, the budding baritone saxophone great Serge Chaloff, Kuhn began digging into the music of contemporary modern pianists. His heroes at the time were Bud Powell and Lennie Tristano, with an appreciation of Bill Evans following a few years later. By the time he graduated from Harvard with a music degree, Kuhn was as well-rounded and technically equipped as any other young player trying to make himself heard.

Two years after that Kuhn left a gig with Kenny Dorham to join John Coltrane's quartet. The saxophonist had just departed from the Miles Davis *Kind of Blue* band and was interested in checking out freer formats. He and Kuhn hit it off personally, but after two months they both sensed that they weren't really meshing. As Kuhn recalled in a *Down Beat* interview with Martin Williams, "With the freedom I was allowed, I ran too much of the spectrum. . . . I was not supporting him, really. In a sense I was competing." Coltrane found his perfect accompanist in another stunning young pianist, McCoy Tyner; Kuhn departed the quartet on friendly terms.

Following that intense little interlude, Kuhn played for longer hauls with Stan Getz and Art Farmer before putting his first trio together, featuring drummer Pete LaRoca and bassist Steve Swallow. Other small groups would occupy him over the next several decades, including a period of émigré romanticism in Europe before returning to New York in 1971. Kuhn also spent some time doing duet work, most often with vocalist Sheila Jordan, though he also performed twofer gigs with bassist Ron Carter for a while at the Knickerbocker in New York. He and Jordan also co-led a quartet, with bassist Harvie Swartz and drummer Bob Moses.

At up-tempo tunes, Kuhn can invest his solos with a vigorous momentum drawn from attentive interaction with the rhythm section. With intuitive players like bassist Eddie Gomez and drummer Al Foster on "Tadd's Delight," from the 1989 album *Porgy*, Kuhn begins with a classic reduction of the theme, a simple but volatile quarter-note motif; in its third iteration, Gomez bounces it back with a quick sixteenth-note variation. Kuhn draws from the energy of this lick gradually; rather than kick at once into high gear or double-time, he continues to develop his opening motif through the second verse before finally turning up the heat with a few more repeated notes. However, when he does accelerate into a sixteenth-note passage, Kuhn keeps the heat on simmer by keeping to the middle register and then actually dropping down by an octave or more.

Eventually Kuhn does climb to the higher range of the keys, but not until building tension even more by dividing his solo into irregular and highly rhythmic subdivisions. By not shooting off fireworks too quickly, he sustains and increases intensity throughout the performance; more than a tutorial on how patience and taste can work better than undisciplined exhibitionism, Kuhn's solo on "Tadd's Delight" is a visceral thrill as well.

These sorts of performances reflect only one side of Kuhn's identity. On another trio date, *Remembering Tomorrow*, recorded for ECM in 1995, the pianist joins bassist David Finck and drummer Joey Baron on a series of improvisations that represent an antithesis to the emphatic swing of *Porgy*. Kuhn feels natural in both settings: The conventional left-hand comping and rhythmic single lines give way here to spacious, textural work, either in free tempos marked by an organic rubato, or in regular meters in which the beat is broadly implied rather than clearly laid out. On these original tunes Kuhn speaks mainly in minor keys, in which the timbre, more than the rhythm, is emphasized through twinkling or clustered tremolos. With these devices, and in the icy, glistening material, *Remembering Tomorrow* is a perfect representation of the ECM aesthetic—and a tribute, then, to Kuhn's expressive range.

On the solo album *Steve Kuhn Live at Maybeck Recital Hall*, these contrasting approaches prove to be complementary, as Kuhn opens the Miles Davis composition "Solar" with a stark open fifth in the left hand supporting a vaguely Celtic line in the right. Gradually the tempo slows, stops for a moment as Kuhn expands to parallel fourths and fifths in the right hand, then unfolds to more conventional postbop voicings in a free swing feel. He even plays some Dave McKenna-like walking bass and tosses a snippet from "As Time Goes By" into the mix—an irreverence that would border on heresy on an ECM release.

While Kuhn may not have met the career expectations that some observers held for him in the early sixties, he has been among the more consistently satisfying soloists in the idiom, with no sign of slowing down yet apparent.

48. CHICK COREA

Born: June 12, 1941, Chelsea, Massachusetts

This is the paradox of Chick Corea: Throughout the years of his greatest exposure, he was, at the same time, one of the most challenging and accessible of pianists. His work bristled with thorny dissonances and sizzled with rhythmic energy. He drew from an eclectic well of inspirations, from Bartók to salsa, cerebral now, and then burning with montuño spice.

His adventurousness couldn't be denied, but neither could his listenability. No matter how far he roamed in his reharmonizations, Corea never left the listener behind. Though the tune wasn't always apparent in his solos, a fidelity to the idea of melody persisted. For all the polyrhythms and sharp staccato attacks, something in his playing invited audiences to create their own melodies around his fragmented improvisations. His music was musical, and he brought out the best in his listeners.

From the first moments of his career as a pianist, Corea's formidable talents were evident. But for quite a few years, he affiliated himself with the avant-garde; on his early work with the iconoclastic first incarnation of Circle, he seemed unconcerned with catering toward the mainstream. It is a tribute to his artistry that he was able to find a way to extend his reach as an artist without significant compromise.

In the beginning, Corea drew almost exclusively from the postbop tradition. He was born with the name Armando, after his father, who worked in the Boston area as a trumpeter and bandleader. Chick was just four years old when he started picking out familiar tunes on the piano. By that time, he had already demonstrated an enthusiasm for percussion instruments. In later interviews, Corea would insist that all pianists should learn how to play the drums; in his case, the connection between rhythm and melody proved central to his creativity.

There were plenty of influences in the air as he was growing up. Spirits of Bud Powell, Lester Young, Charlie Parker, and Dizzy Gillespie mingled with those of Beethoven and Mozart. Piano lessons with Salvatore Sulo encouraged his appreciation for divergent traditions, as Corea applied his education to gigs with jazz and Latin dance bands and meticulous transcriptions of solos by Horace Silver during high school.

Eventually Corea knew he was equipped sufficiently to work professionally. He won admission to Columbia University in 1959, then dropped out to start playing in New York clubs. Like Miles Davis, he attended the Juilliard School of Music briefly; years later he would remember Peter Schickele, known for his P.D.Q. Bach parodies, as a favorite teacher. Though he had practiced intensively to get into that supreme school for virtuosos, Corea bailed out in 1960, moved into a flat on 71st Street, and committed himself fully to the musician's life.

Opportunities presented themselves immediately, as word of the young pianist spread. He spent 1962 and '63 backing up Willie Bobo and Mongo Santamaria. From 1964 through '66 he worked with Blue Mitchell, who was the first artist to record something written by Corea—"Chick's Tune," on *A Thing to Do*. He made his debut as a leader in 1966, with *Tones for Joan's Bones*, accompanied by saxophonist Joe Farrell, trumpeter Woody Shaw, bassist Steve Swallow, and drummer Joe Chambers. For a year he toured as Sarah Vaughan's accompanist. Then, in 1968, he produced his second album, *Now He Sings, Now He Sobs*, backed by bassist Miroslav Vitous and drummer Roy Haynes.

Corea's break came that same year, when he accepted an invitation to follow Herbie Hancock in the keyboard chair with Miles Davis. His tenure marked a crucial period in Davis's movement from postbop to collective improvisation, and on such albums as *Filles de Kilimanjaro*, *Bitches Brew*, *Miles Davis at the Fillmore*, and *In a Silent Way*, Corea occupied ground zero during an explosive period of jazz exploration. The lessons he learned on these projects, about listening to his colleagues at a higher level of perception and with fewer preconceptions, would affect him musically and philosophically as the era of fusion jazz began.

With Davis and, following short stints with his experimental ensemble Circle and with Stan Getz, as leader of Return to Forever, Corea rode the crest of technological change in keyboard music, and led the rush of young jazz artists who were willing to turn to rock music for a different kind of inspiration. On electric piano and synthesizer, he rode volcanic crescendos over Stanley Clarke's bass guitar and Lenny White's crackling backbeats on albums like *Hymn to the Seventh Galaxy*. Jazz purists and his former allies in the avant-garde were offended by what they saw as his commercial sellout; what they didn't understand was that Corea was building a bridge for the public to cross from the obscurities of Miles Davis and the accessibility of Wynton Marsalis.

Whether playing solo, doing duos with simpatico artists, or mentoring young guns in the Elektric Band, the Akoustic Band, and Origin, Corea made profound improvisation sound as easy as a 12-bar blues guitar break. Listen, for example, to his performance of "Bessie's Blues," on the *Akoustic Band* album from 1989. Corea's solo takes the form to a heady harmonic level, but what's most impressive is the relentless swing he generates on his own and in interaction with the bassist John Patitucci and drummer Dave Weckl. Particularly instructive is his listening. With Patitucci charging into adventurous territory during his solo, Corea follows very closely in minimal but very perceptive responses; he amplifies

Chick Corea's music is musical; it brings out the best in his listeners.

on each critical lick and, with just a couple of notes, feeds something back. The same can be heard in his comping behind Gary Burton's solo on "Country Roads," from the 1997 all-star release *Like Minds*: He slips into blues or even gospel figures where he senses a funky or rustic turn coming up; similarly, when a Burton line seems to be rising toward an unusual peak note, Corea anticipates it with a thick voicing that happens to include and embrace that note.

The connection in Corea's performance between classical and jazz is apparent on his second duo album with Burton. Many of the performances on *Native Sense* are more like recitals, which capture Corea's craftsmanship as a composer and mark his tendency to blur the lines between improvising and playing the written material. At the same time, this album delineates the connections between his preference in classical (Bartók), jazz (Monk's "Four in One"), and improvisatory language: Monk's and Bartók's angularities relate strongly to Corea's prickly, lightly pedaled approach. His performance on "Four in One," with its references to Monk's whole-tone scale and minor seconds and ninths, seeks and finds the lyrical essence of dissonance as surely as his literal renditions of Bartók repertoire. Here, as in most of his performances, Corea pushes toward the most adventurous tonal harmonies while preserving the pulse and keeping the music listenable.

In terms of jazz piano tradition, Corea bases his work on a respect for his audience's discernment. His approach to rhythm in solo settings is tempered by ample experience at playing within rhythm sections; he keeps the momentum flowing through free interaction between his hands, rather than through articulation of any pulse. The bebop element is very strong in his left-hand comps; one can imagine bass and drums laying down a pattern without significantly changing Corea's performance. He hears a rhythm section in his mind, and because of his own lively sense of pulse, the listener hears it too. His interpretation of the ballad "My Ship," on the 1994 solo album *Expressions*, shows how Corea's harmonic sensibility extends to the fullest possible range of intricacy without ever abandoning the melodic and accessible essence of the tune. The rhythm, unlike melody, is be implied rather than articulated; it is Corea's nature to suggest the beat through allusions to the piano's role within a rhythm section, with full chords and breathing rubato.

The argument has been made that Corea's virtuosity is more brilliant than profound. While there's tremendous facility and imagination in his approaches to familiar tunes, a sense of depth or even real connection to the material is sometimes lacking. His stunning improvisations emphasize craft more than spirit; while it is hard to quantify this impression, it seems apparent to listeners who find clever alternate harmonies less impressive than revelation uncovered in songs as they were conceived.

Even so, the furor over Corea's fusion experiments is long past. And in recent years, as upcoming all-stars like Joshua Redman and Christian McBride jostle to share the stage with him, Corea proves that his vision was correct after all. His lesson is that one can achieve greatness without alienating the public. Musicians and audiences alike are in his debt.

49. JOANNE BRACKEEN

Born: July 26, 1938, Ventura, California

She was once, by critical consensus, the most promising young player on the block. The scribes who had clout used it to knock her name to the highest and brightest row on the marquee. Whitney Balliett declared her "a brilliant, close-textured pianist. Her solos have the insistence and intensity of Coltrane." And Leonard Feather put his reputation on the line for her: "Beyond question, the pianist to watch for in the eighties is JoAnne Brackeen."

While it can be debated whether time has confirmed these assessments, the fact remains that Brackeen is the definitive mainstream modern jazz pianist. Her chords, her voice movement, her scampering right-hand lines, and her lively way with rhythm reflect a command of all the essential elements. All of these she applies strictly within the rules and regulations of postbop performance. The only surprise she brings is in the persistence of the spirit that never fails to animate her playing.

Her background was sunny Californian. Her Irish-American family—she was born with the surname Grogan—was by all accounts normal, except perhaps in how well they all got along. There weren't any musicians at home, but there was an appreciation of music; one of JoAnne's earlier memories involves hearing her father sing as he gave his kids their baths. She started piano lessons at the age of nine, with only middling success. Her mind wandered from the dreary regimen, then settled into a period of fascination with Frankie Carle—an unlikely early hero, until one considers the shortage of alternatives in white-bread Ventura.

She managed to connect with jazz anyway, by making her own way down to Los Angeles at age 16 and meeting people who knew more about what was happening than she did. JoAnne caught on fast: She was just 18 when she heard Ornette Coleman working at the Hillcrest Country Club with pianist Paul Bley, trumpeter Don Cherry, bassist Charlie Haden, and drummer Billy Higgins. Within days, it seemed, she was discovering and devouring the work of the most vital players of the time: John Coltrane, Elvin Jones, Art Blakey. A few pianists, including Bud Powell, Art Tatum, and Monk, also made her list.

Pretty soon she was performing around L.A. The top local players noticed her right away; some of her first gigs were with Dexter Gordon, Charles Lloyd, Bobby Hutcherson, and Harold Land. Yet even then she wasn't taking things too seriously. She spent all of three days as a student at the Los Angeles Conservatory of Music, married saxophonist Charles Brackeen, and started cutting down on work in order to raise their four children. For a few years she kept her horizons close to home, though she never stopped writing music and rather soon started dreaming about committing more fully to a performing career.

That happened in 1965, when the Brackeens, fed up with their California idyll, packed up and moved to New York. After getting settled, she began lining up work, beginning with a few jobs behind vibraphonist Freddy McCoy in 1966 and leading to her recruitment in 1969 into Art Blakey's Jazz Messengers—the only woman to join its long line of luminaries. This was followed in 1972 by the christening of an enduring musical relationship with Joe Henderson, and a two-year stint replacing Albert Dailey in Stan Getz's band, all of which led up to her decision to launch her solo career in 1977.

In her own projects, and in her previous work with other headliners, Brackeen's playing conveys a stimulating spontaneity. Unlike more theoretically inclined pianists, she seldom sounds like she's playing an arrangement; mostly she seems to wing it. In general that's all it takes for her to deliver a solid performance, except when she pushes a little too hard. When playing unaccompanied she implies the rhythm: Her irregular left-hand accents bounce off what perhaps the absent bassist and drummer lay down in her imagination. As a result, there's often a feeling that the groove is always just about to kick in. Listen, for example, to Brackeen's rendering of "It Could Happen to You," from her 1990 performance on Concord's *Live at Maybeck Hall* series: For all her activity on the keys, she never really spells out the groove. Had she locked onto a Dave McKenna-like bass line in the third or fourth verse, she might have resolved that unfulfilled anticipation.

On ballads Brackeen follows exactly the same path. "My Foolish Heart," also from *Maybeck*, begins reflectively but races quickly into some bravura reharmonizations, ascending right-hand chord movements, and booming proclamations of the theme amidst impulsive crescendos and diminuendos. The performance is of questionable taste and, at least, oblivious to the interpretive potential offered by the material.

Brackeen's style blossoms more often in group settings. Her nature is to play off of a rhythm section, with a masterful ability to draw energy and feed it back. On the opening verses of the Latinesque "Recado Bossa Nova," from the 1994 album *Take a Chance*, she radiates heat from the first notes, so that when Eddie Gomez comes in he's already caught fire. Much of the intensity of his bass solo comes directly from the fuel being fed to him from the piano over the previous several verses. And Brackeen doesn't have to dig in to make her presence known; her feather-light touch in the opening verses of "Frevo," from the same album, especially in the ascending passages of the first bridge, are as electrifying as any loudly pounded accents could be.

On more ambitious efforts, Brackeen can stun both in her vision and its realization. On her 7/4 treatment of "If I Were a Bell," from the 1999 album *Popsicle Illusion*, she starts with a dazzling juxtaposition of the truncated theme in her right hand over a steady stride in her left. This is followed by simmering interactions between her hands and some ingeniously crafted phrases that slide past the seventh beat in each bar with grace and guile. Once or twice she hits a pothole, most likely because it's hard to avoid falling into a familiar rocking 4/4. And she does bang a bit on the last verse. But the feeling on this and other later material is that Brackeen has matured to a point that's comfortable for her, her audiences, and those supportive critics as well.

50. KENNY BARRON

Born: June 9, 1943, Philadelphia, Pennsylvania

Hank Jones and Cedar Walton cleared the path for Kenny Barron's arrival in the sixties. They were his predecessors in the low-profile yet demanding discipline of studio pianist. Each would, in his own way, become known for being able to adapt to practically any kind of jazz session; each would use this reputation to build a solo career. Yet none would abandon the sideman role, and Barron is still taking calls, with credits for literally hundreds of albums in his résumé.

As the youngest in this line, Barron reflects the character of jazz in his era. Much of his work, with others and as leader of his own projects, draws from the kind of funk that led from Bobby Timmons to Les McCann. Where older pianists could seem a little out of place on long one-chord vamps and steady backbeats, Barron is able to keep the vibe fresh; the condescension that pure bop players could show toward this idiom is absent in his work. A more unusual twist is his occasional echo of pastoral or even new age elements. Yet he knows his jazz tradition, and is as capable of blowing through "Rhythm" changes as brilliantly as anyone else on any given night.

There was music all around Kenny Barron from the day he came into this world. A piano stood in his family's living room, and almost everyone there—his mother and four siblings, but not his father—played it. He was five years old when his mother started him on piano lessons; his teachers would include Vera Bryant Eubanks, mother of Kevin and Robin Eubanks and sister of another piano giant, Ray Bryant. His regimen was purely classical, but when the jazz bug bit there was no stopping him. With help from his older brother Bill, a working saxophonist, he began working on jazz improvisation at around age 12, and a few years after that was playing dance and club jobs around Philadelphia with Sonny Fortune, Andy Aaron, Don Moore, Jimmy Vast, Jimmy Heath, and other local heavyweights.

Plans to go to college at the Philadelphia Academy of Music were shelved when, only a few days after graduating from high school, Kenny got a call from Yusef Lateef to catch the next Greyhound to Detroit and join his quartet in the midst of a national tour. They had played together already, when Lateef needed a pianist at the last minute for a week-long appearance at the Showboat in Philadelphia; that was enough to convince the multi-reed innovator that Barron, all of 17 years old, was ready for the road. After two years of playing a highly varied book with Lateef, he decided to join his brother in New York and shoot for the moon.

It was 1961. Bill put him up at his flat in an East Village building whose residents included Pepper Adams and Elvin Jones, and started introducing him around town. It took no time for Kenny to pick up work: An opportunity to sit in with James Moody at the Five Spot opened the door to a plentitude of gigs. Purely on Moody's recommendation, without even having to audition, Barron was hired by Dizzy Gillespie to replace Lalo Schifrin as his piano player. Just 19 years old now, he began four years of touring with the trumpet master. This experience put food on the table and valuable knowledge into his head and hands—all of which he would expand upon through years more of steady work with Freddie Hubbard and shorter spells with Stanley Turrentine, Stan Getz as a replacement for Chick Corea, Lateef again, two months in a sextet with Buddy Rich, Ron Carter, and dozens of other major players. Additionally he has led more than a few provocative bands of his own.

As if he had time to spare, Barron was also looking into other areas where he could apply his creativity. He has composed copiously, producing material that's ranged from straight-ahead to dodecaphonic, for instrumentation that ranges from bass and drum duo through string quartets to orchestral. Armed with a degree in real life, he was appointed to a faculty position at Rutgers University in 1973, where he taught jazz piano, improvisation, composition, and arrangement; several of his students, including Geri Allen, Terence Blanchard, and David Sanchez, have since made their own marks in the business. In the eighties he resumed working with Getz on a few summer tours and European engagements, and joined former Thelonious Monk sidemen Buster Williams, Ben Riley, and Charlie Rouse in putting together Sphere, a band dedicated to the spirit as much to the letter of Monk's music. (In an impressive bit of synchronicity, Barron came up with the name of the band before learning that Sphere was Monk's actual middle name.)

But it's mainly at the keys that Barron continues to impress. His playing in recent years has in no way diminished; he continues to push his limits in performances that range from a daring Ornette Coleman project at Lincoln Center to remarkable trio work with bassist Charlie Haden and drummer Roy Haynes. Later recordings as well are packed with his pianistic feats. Barron plays brilliantly off the riff that drives his "Spirit Song," from the 1999 album of the same name. Following Russell Malone's guitar solo, he kicks off his improvisation with a crisp funk-inflected descending line, which is capped by his left-hand statement of the riff. From that point, in flowing even sixteenth-notes that wind in and out of the two-chord vamp structure, he builds a thrilling solo based on funk phrasing without the harmonic limitations. His long line includes intricate sub-rhythms, defined not as gaps between phrases but as quick note repetitions; the effect is to push the beat without losing the broad contours of his concept.

Another sparkling Barron solo surfaces on "Youthful Bliss," recorded in 1995 for the Christian McBride album *Number Two Express*. It begins with a three-note motif, then develops smoothly through the alternating swing and Latin rhythms written into the piece. Barron's approach is meticulous but never cerebral, especially in his interactions with the rest of the band: During the first Latin section, he pops a string of brisk triplet figures against the groove before resolving the rhythmic tension with two emphatic chords that lead back to the swing section. On the following verse, as Barron works with a variation on a three-note figure introduced in the first verse, drummer Jack DeJohnette responds with some powerful accents to underscore the figure and feed back to the piano some of the energy he had drawn from it earlier. The point here is to illustrate how two masters such as Barron and DeJohnette make interplay one of the most exciting aspects of ensemble jazz performance.

In intimate circumstances Barron has repeatedly proven his mastery of moody, introspective expression. His duo album with bassist Charlie Haden, *Night and the City*, recorded live at the Iridium in New York in 1996, is filled with tasteful piano, as Barron coaxes a chorus of emotions from a set of classic tunes. On "Spring Is Here," phrased like a cross between a half-time bossa and a Vince Guaraldi groove, Barron constructs a careful improvisation from transparent parts—open-sounding thirds and fifths, simple but evocative sixteenth-note lines, and a breath-like rise and fall in the trajectory of the solo. Though not a milestone solo by any means, it does illustrate Barron's ability to transfer characteristics shown in his "Spirit Song" to very different kinds of settings, which in turn gives us a glimpse of the adaptability that has become legend among his peers.

In solo settings Barron displays a pleasing blend of sprightly rhythm and thoughtful patience. His unaccompanied piece "A Flower," on his 1990 album *Sunset to Dawn*, nurtures a relatively simple figure through nearly seven minutes of rubato examination: He pedals lightly but effectively, and extends a reflective feel throughout most of the performance, with suspended voicings and other harmonic devices common to both new age and post-fusion jazz. Just before the final section, though, Barron switches to more jagged, Tyner-like chords, hit sharply to signal the high point of the performance. In its balance of quick figures and meditative silences, as well as in the overall contour of tension and release, "A Flower" is in fact a gem.

New age elements surface also in his solo reading of "Here's That Rainy Day," from the 1974 album *Peruvian Blue*. His opening lick, in fact, foreshadows what would become one of George Winston's favorite devices. However, once he digs into the tune, Barron becomes more aggressive, with plenty of pinpoint, stinging runs and a characteristic aversion to steady tempo.

Barron's nine-minute unaccompanied examination of "Darn That Dream," from his 1980 album *Golden Lotus*, follows a similar pathway. He plays most of the piece out of tempo, rushing for a moment or two toward breathless little pauses, many of them underscored by a tiny, zipping run. As the third verse begins, Barron toys with playing in tempo, then abandons the idea and falls back to a bracing exhibition of lightly pedaled, lickety-split flourishes and quizzical bursts. When he finally does settle into a rhythm, it's with a left-hand stride so dry and perfunctory as to barely qualify as a source of momentum. In fact, the push here comes from his right hand, with its long string of staccato double-time dotted sixteenth-notes. With the left hand on the verge of lurching to a stop, Barron keeps popping little right-hand fireworks; there is humor in this approach, but a kind of nervous beauty as well.

Later, in "Al-Kifha," as his quintet burns at a sizzling clip, Barron delivers a stunning solo, centered around a long single line that's built on a series of four-note ascending and descending figures. While these feel somewhat repetitive after a while, Barron never stops riding the tempo or finding ways to stretch his motif through intricate polyrhythmic hurdles. (These four-note runs are also heard in Barron's exhilarating unaccompanied sprint through Sonny Rollins's "Oleo," on the 1975 album *Lucifer*, more recently on *First Half Highlights*.)

This same exuberant invention, as well as precise articulation in runs and splashes, colors Barron's performance on the title track to his 1980 album *Golden Lotus*. Equally apparent is the ease with which he shifts in and out of an ersatz montuño pattern, never losing the essentially funky feeling of the piece. For Barron, anything that grooves is natural.

Yet as the ultimate jazz session pianist, Barron has no problem adjusting his style, if that's what the leader wants. While between takes on *Nini Green*, a 1997 album by saxophonist Virginia Mayhew, Barron took a few moments to come up with a solo intro to her tune "Time Alone." Only one lively note a few bars before the bridge alludes to the pianist's familiar style; the rest of his performance, with its gently reflective tempo, elegant yet simple chord substitutions, and muted tone, inevitably recalls Bill Evans's "Peace Piece," conceived also as an introduction to another tune. Equally exquisite is his solo on the langorous "Blue Green and Brown," from the same album. Here are Barron's usual quick flurries and bristling two-handed trills. More important is the contour of his solo, beginning with an ephemeral opening motif, wandering in and out of rhythm, emphasizing a shift from minor to major in the B section, then moving and thickening sharp-edged chords toward a final downward gliss that leads back to the horns' entrance. Understated, yet impeccable—just like Barron himself.

51. RICHIE BEIRACH

Born: May 23, 1947, Brooklyn, New York

A s a native of New York, Beirach makes full use of the attendant privileges. In the best possible sense of the word, he's a little cocky—a blunt-talking guy with Big Apple attitude. As a musician, he knows how good he is, and at times has seemed a little exasperated that this insight hasn't become universal. In one conversation a few years ago, I mentioned a new release by a colleague of his, adding that I thought she played pretty well on it.

He bristled, just a bit. Then, with one eyebrow raised, he replied, "Well, you know, she was a student of mine. I taught her a lot of what she's doing now."

On another day, in another discussion, Beirach recalled a heated talk that he and another nameless pianist had several years earlier. Let it be said only that Pianist X was, like Beirach, an ECM artist at the time, and, most emphatically unlike Beirach, a recent convert to Scientology. From his reconstruction of their debate, it appeared that Beirach had taken exception to his friend's decision to end his free-form improvisations and flirtations with the avant-garde, in order to follow L. Ron Hubbard's instructions to always communicate as clearly as possible.

The point here is that making music palatable meant less to Beirach than playing the way that one, as an artist, must play. If people listen, fine. If not, well, then at least no one can accuse the artist of not being true to his or her instincts.

These attitudes abound in Beirach's work. He is a superbly equipped pianist, with no limitation at the keys other than the encumbrance of having small hands. (Beirach demonstrated the irrelevance of his condition for me by pressing his thumb and first finger against a tabletop and flattening the stretch between them into a straight line—a flexibility he developed as a kid precisely to increase his reach.) His improvisations are tonal, though infused with a heady mix of freedom and technique; when he's on, it seems as if there is literally nothing he is incapable of playing.

Yet somehow he has yet to win the recognition he deserves. It may be because his playing lacks a certain humor and warmth; even when generating tremendous rhythmic heat, he seems to be holding something back. Within a rhythm section, among his peers in jazz, Beirach is known as a player of great empathy. It's only the broader public that has yet to give him his full due.

His foundation as a performer is entirely classical. Piano study began at age five and intensified within a year under the tutelage of James Palmieri. The young student showed an unusual interest in modern repertoire—Berg, Webern, Takemitsu—as well as the standard-fare, nineteenth-century romantics. After a few years he became aware of jazz—again, the most conceptually advanced jazz. Manhattan was a musical wonderland, and Beirach reveled in its bounty: On one memorable week he dashed each day from school to Birdland, where the two most critical bands of the mid-sixties, led by Miles Davis and John Coltrane, were sharing the bill.

Around age 15 he started to gig around New York. He began on the wedding and bar mitzvah track, but ramped up to jazz by the time he was admitted to the Berklee School in Boston; as early as 1968 he was earning real-world experience as a member of saxophonist Stan Getz's band. His pianistic influences widened to embrace Lennie Tristano, Bill Evans, Thelonious Monk, Wynton Kelly, Bud Powell—and, of course, Franz Liszt. In 1972, right after earning his graduate degree in musicology at the Manhattan School of Music, Beirach and saxophonist Dave Liebman joined forces to form Lookout Farm, remembered now as one of the few fusion bands that avoided melting down into a kind of fast-note mutation of rock and roll.

For Beirach the years since then have become a blur of albums and performances, with just about every jazz label and in every jazz club on the planet. He has backed Chet Baker, Lee Konitz, Freddie Hubbard, Joe Henderson, and countless others, and partnered with George Coleman, John Abercrombie, and other giants as well. In all these sessions and performances, in every format, Beirach drives himself to play at the highest level; on a pretty good night, his level of execution is astonishing.

Take his work in rhythm sections: From his earliest recordings this has been an area of special expertise for Beirach. As a young quartet member behind Stan Getz on *My Foolish Heart: 'Live' from the Left Bank*, he jolted bassist Dave Holland and drummer Jack DeJohnette with stinging fills and syncopated, popping chords. One has the sense from this exhibition that Beirach is entirely in the present, even when deciding to sit out, during the long sax solo on "Untitled." When he does play, nothing is extraneous; nothing detracts from the group's momentum. This is bravura listening, as well as evidence of uncanny ear/brain/finger communication.

As for Beirach's solo, as DeJohnette tones down and shifts to brushes, it's about feeding and drawing from Holland's lines. The piano line is springy yet guided by a sense of breath; Beirach leaves the kinds of holes in his phrases that one would expect from a horn player. All of this transpires over a dynamic left hand, which constantly tweaks and adjusts its chords. When Beirach punctuates with a low accent on the fifth in the bass register, the gesture carries finality and authority, as if each line were being conceived as an author would write a sentence, with that kind of reflection and craft, though done at a strong uptempo.

If anything, Beirach tops himself with his solo on "Litha," from the same performance. From a half-time introduction, garnished by an impeccable, graceful run up the keys, he follows DeJohnette and Holland into an extended bout of blowing. Beirach's line is extraordinarily long, with very little riffing or repetition, aside from one ascending four-note figure he uses to kick off certain passages. When he breaks into a bit of staggered call-and-response between his left hand, which thumps out alternate tonics and dominants, and his right, DeJohnette doesn't just follow—he's there as Beirach locks onto the counter-rhythm.

It's typical of Beirach to begin his hard-swinging solos with detached considerations of the theme. On "Moonlight in Vermont," from bassist George Mraz's 1995 album *Mraz Jazz*, he starts off by fragmenting the theme to establish a tie with the written tune. The meaty chords in his left hand expand clearly but provocatively on the written changes as his solo line builds through an exceptional blend of emotional escalation and analytical insight. Particularly noteworthy is Beirach's ability to suggest the theme without being anchored to it, through creative manipulation of its elements. Though delivered in segments rather than a continuous, Jarrett-like line, this solo hangs together over its entire length.

The approach is similar in "Alice in Wonderland," from Mraz's trio date *My Foolish Heart*, with a three-note motif cementing the entire Beirach solo through subtle paraphrases all the way to the end of the improvisation, when it recurs as a segue to the Mraz bass solo. This deep grasp of structure serves Beirach as well on ballads, though more than most jazz pianists, he displays a distinct difference in his treatments of uptempo and slower works. In the latter, his ideas move in slow motion, in uncluttered pastoral textures. On *My Foolish Heart* he opens his own "Sunday Song" over a pedal tone, with a quiet presentation of the theme to create a fragile, even reverent atmosphere.

Every aspect of Beirach's artistry shines on *Richie Beirach at Maybeck*, recorded in 1992. The opening cut is an extraordinary examination of "All the Things You Are," cast in gauzy bitonal textures over a sensuous, slinking tempo. And his rendition of "Elm" confirms his gentle profundity, with an improvisation over softly arpeggiated chords. Few moments in his catalog so vividly capture Beirach's distinctive ballad persona.

Not everything succeeds here. The pianist attacks "All Blues" with a roadhouse riff that substitutes a raw beat for the more reflective textures of the Miles Davis original version. Beirach even breaks into a very uncharacteristic accelerando, as if to dispel doubts of his ability to swing. In the end, he gives an impression of trying too hard, with blues quotes that sound more affected than natural. Clearly, Beirach thrives best within a rhythm section when chasing a brisk tempo; in solo settings, his strengths are more introverted.

Perhaps the problem with Beirach is that he has never been fashionable. Like Brad Mehldau, he follows a difficult and obscure path, through an unlikely overgrowth of classical and jazz in their more academic manifestations. Only musicians, and listeners who take the time to listen, will know the truth that lives in his music.

Old World/New Flavors

52. JOE ZAWINUL

Born: July 7, 1932, Vienna, Austria

I n the ruins left behind by the fusion upheaval of the late sixties and seventies, Joe Zawinul is one of the few still standing with credibility intact. With his menacing mustache and desert-merchant skull cap, he embodied the mysterious possibilities anticipated by the early collisions between rock and jazz. Most of those possibilities were lost in a welter of guitar and synth licks, executed at twice the speed and with half the substance of your typical bebop solo. Only Zawinul and a handful of compatriots survived all that tribulation, because what they were doing bore only a misleading and superficial resemblance to the musical mayhem being committed around them.

Zawinul was, in fact, the Thelonious Monk of fusion. These two visionary artists shared a suspicion of velocity for its own sake. Each sought to create a language in which a single note might speak more eloquently than a full chorus of "Rhythm" changes. For Monk, the piano provided an adequate medium through which to pursue that vision. For Zawinul, the piano would prove insufficient; he would have to wait for technology to equip him with a set of new tools before being able to chisel his sound sculptures.

For this reason, the period that Zawinul spent on the piano has to be considered transitional. Before electronic keyboards began sprouting across the musical landscape, he tried to anticipate their effect through arrangements that emphasized droning textures and shimmering spaces. He came closer during his association with Miles Davis, who was as much his soul brother as Monk had been; their collaboration on *In a Silent Way* opened a crack in the universe of improvisational technique, through which a silvery light beckoned momentarily. There were other keyboardists on that session: Herbie Hancock would follow the muse of Sly Stone into a dalliance with techno-funk at some cost to his harmonic subtlety and free linear spirit, while Chick Corea abandoned early free experiments and unleashed Return To Forever as a fast-notes monster. Both Hancock and Corea would also return, eventually, to the fountainhead, to the piano.

Zawinul, by comparison, would never look back. After working with Miles, he would devote himself primarily to the formation and preservation of Weather Report. Through all its incarnations, this band was the apotheosis of fusion, driven by the Davis gospel of listening a lot and playing nothing more than it took to breathe life into a new idea. As captain of this brave ship, Zawinul mixed and matched the wizardries of its wondrous crew: Wayne Shorter, Miroslav Vitous, Alphonso Johnson, Omar Hakim, and the incomparable Jaco Pastorius—names as seductive as the stars that guided them through *Mysterious Traveler*, *Heavy Weather*, *Black Market*, and other ports of call.

The piano, then, was only one station along Zawinul's way—yet it was a crucial place for him to spend his early years, where he could map out his path for making a music he knew would one day no longer be beyond his reach.

One of the great multiculturalists of jazz, Zawinul came into the world with a twin brother who did not survive birth—a premonition of difficulties that lay not far ahead. He started taking piano lessons at age 11 at a rural school for gifted children, under the tutelage of Valery Zschorney, a second-generation Liszt student. As a result of a talent search by Nazi cultural authorities, he was conscripted to sing in the celebrated Vienna Boys Choir—an honor he declined, though he did eventually accept a scholarship to study briefly at the Vienna Conservatory.

Life grew tougher, though, as World War II wound down. When not working on his piano and composition studies, or developing his chops as well on accordion and various wind instruments, Zawinul resorted to shoplifting to help his family survive. Once hostilities had ceased he was able to investigate jazz as well. Ideologically suspect under Nazi rule, it became a way to earn some quick income from Allied soldiers milling around town. For several years, in Czechoslovakia and then back in Vienna, Zawinul sharpened his understanding of the new music by playing servicemen's clubs, writing band arrangements inspired largely by Woody Herman and Dizzy Gillespie, and breaking the music down through lessons with the classical virtuoso and fellow jazz lover Friedrich Gulda.

In 1959, with a scholarship to the Boston's Berklee School in hand, Zawinul made his first visit to the States. Almost instantly he forgot about the classroom and dove into a frenzied series of gigs, beginning with 18 months in the Maynard Ferguson Orchestra—Wayne Shorter, his future partner in Weather Report, was in the reed section. This was followed by a 19-month engagement as accompanist to Dinah Washington, during which time he first got his hands on an electric piano. Following a hiatus in New York, Zawinul accepted an offer to join saxophonist Cannonball Adderley's quintet in April 1961; his original tune "Mercy, Mercy, Mercy" became the most popular number in the saxophonist's repertoire.

By 1969, when he recorded with Davis on *In a Silent Way* and *Bitches Brew*, Zawinul was listening enthusiastically to the avant-gardisms of Milton Babbitt, Morton Subotnick, and John Cage, taking synthesizer lessons from Roger Powell, and talking with Shorter about putting together a really unusual band. The piano, in other words, had served its purpose; aside from appearing as one color in a rainbow of electronic hues, it bore little importance in Zawinul's new scheme. Yet it is instructive to look back on his work when he was just establishing himself as a musician on the edge of making some serious history, though surprisingly uncomfortable on what was assumed to be his instrument.

He was in fact an imaginative if somewhat rigid improviser on his earlier recordings. His solo on "The Governor," recorded in 1963 and available on the Zawinul/Ben Webster album *Soulmates*, unfolds along clear conceptual lines, as the pianist shows off his understanding of bop harmonic and melodic conventions. In just one chorus, however, his unremitting dotted-eighth phrasing, over somewhat wooden and predictable left-hand accompaniment, suggests a formulaic, non-instinctive approach to swing. One track later, on a bouncy medium-up blues titled "Frog Legs," Zawinul again displays solid if unremarkable melodic gifts, as well as an awkward, choppy approach to dropping left-hand chords and difficulty at locking into a rhythmic groove, through three solo choruses. These same qualities are evident on the ballad "Trav'lin' Light," on which Zawinul's generally expressive harmonies are undermined by his placement of chords square on each quarter-note.

In his later "third stream" projects, Zawinul sounds similarly ill at ease. "Money in the Pocket," the title track from his 1965 album, is the kind of project that seems vaguely embarrassing when heard today. Over a humdrum soul-jazz riff, with Roy McCurdy going through the motions rather sleepily on drums, Zawinul fills two choruses with funk figures that were already clichés at that time. Later, in an unaccompanied rendition of "My One and Only Love," he plays the opening three verses and bridge in free tempo, with hurried flurries of superfluous arpeggios, runs, ascending repeated notes, somewhat pretentious ornaments, and sudden melodic jumps that distract from the tune. When he settles into a regular tempo and falls back on articulating the theme, hope arises that a more focused interpretation is at hand—but Zawinul seems to be pulling impatiently at the harness. It takes only a couple of verses for him to escape into another free section marked by florid filigree. Whether playing in a group or on his own, then, Zawinul comes off as unsettled and unformed. And in a trio setting on "Sharon's Waltz," Zawinul's stiffness, particularly in his heavy left hand, can only be contrasted unfavorably with that of Vince Guaraldi.

Two years later, on *The Rise & Fall of the Third Stream*, Zawinul begins to show signs of discovering a more original voice. His obvious influence is with the Coltrane school of free jazz, especially in the impact made by McCoy Tyner on his playing. By moving toward a modal language and exploring the timbral aspects of clustered chords, on such tracks as "Baptismal" and "The Fifth Canto," Zawinul trades a traditional view of harmonic movement for more compelling modern ambiguities, in which chord progression meant less than abstract textural shifts. Equally important, though perhaps not so apparent at the time, is the pianist's expanded cultural range. Rather than ape bebop convention, Zawinul is now drawing from exotic sources, in the fashion of Third Stream composers, with the greatest emphasis on his own Eastern European heritage, as heard in the plaintive violins and cellos, drone techniques, and unusual orchestration, including a hammered *cymbalom*, in "The Soul of a Village, Parts I and II." Significantly, Zawinul plays electric piano on "Part II," foreshadowing his upcoming work with Miles Davis and, in its pursuit of adventurous texture, Weather Report.

In the years that followed, as Zawinul fled toward the seductive songs of synthesizers and electronica, it is tempting to look back on his early years in mainstream jazz as little more than a rehearsal for his true calling as a world music and high-tech pioneer.

ADAM MAKOWICZ

Born: August 18, 1940, Gnojnik, Czechoslovakia

Adam Makowicz can be considered the legitimate heir to the Tatum mantle, which makes him part of a tradition of unaccompanied, virtuosic solo piano that stretches back to James P. Johnson. It's an imposing position for any pianist—and all the more so for Makowicz, who spent his formative years about as far from the wellspring of his style as a player could be.

Born in the middle of World War II, Makowicz was raised by his Polish parents in Katowice, first under Nazi domination and then, for the rest of his youth, in the Cold War variety of Communism. His mother began teaching him piano when he was nine years old, and he pursued advanced studies in Rybnik, Katowice, and Krakow. A big talent with a determined work ethic, he was bound for a career in classical music, the only path kept open to musicians of his caliber in Poland.

But destiny intruded, in the form of Willis Conover, the host of *Music USA*. This program, broadcast throughout the world over Voice of America, did nearly as much as diplomacy and war itself to weaken the grip of Stalinism in Eastern Europe. Like many of his peers, Makowicz sensed that freedom was essential in the jazz records that Conover featured on his program. To improvise, an artist had to respect his or her own judgment. In a climate where individualism was discouraged, the implications of this process went far beyond the practice of playing music.

Despite official discouragement and the ever-present threat of more active persecution, Makowicz began playing jazz in public at the age of seventeen. With no commercial clubs available to them, Poland's young jazz artists performed at student venues or at each other's apartments—not unlike the rent parties that spawned stride piano in New York. As the political climate warmed up a bit during the Khrushchev thaw, more opportunities to play presented themselves, and by the seventies Makowicz was testing the waters of fusion music as electric pianist with violinist Michal Urbaniak and his wife, singer Urszula Dudziak.

It was, of all people, Benny Goodman who made it possible for Makowicz to escape to a life of greater possibilities. After hearing rumors of a stupendous young pianist working in Poland, John Hammond, the A&R legend whose discoveries ranged from Bessie Smith to Bruce Springsteen, asked Goodman to check him out during an upcoming concert tour. The clarinetist returned with raves for Makowicz and an armful of his records. This was enough to persuade Hammond to pull the right strings and, in 1977, bring the pianist to New York for his American album debut. Makowicz arrived amidst a serious press buzz, decided to stay, and did not disappoint.

His kinship to the Tatum line is evident immediately in his steady pulse, whose swinging quality he emphasizes by darting from it and back again with lightning-quick lines. These he plays with equal facility in either hand—again, in keeping with the idea of evolution, he follows Tatum's lead by implying rather than articulating the stride rhythm most of the time. His performance of Cole Porter's "Get Out of Town," from *Adam Makowicz at Maybeck*, begins with a rather flamboyant left-hand ostinato that seems to have less to do with the tune than with the idea of technique as an arrangement tool—but then he begins moving through a series of classic rhythmic devices, most prominently some

Adam Makowicz plays exactly as a pianist of his caliber would have done fifty years ago.

elegant walking tenths. That feel is almost always there with Makowicz, even when his facility leads him toward dubious technical display.

Like Tatum, but unlike Oscar Peterson, Makowicz absorbs all the implications of the written material into his improvisations. He doesn't just blow through the chord changes or ignore the theme; it's easy to identify what song he's playing even if you drop into the middle of his most aggressive moments of a Makowicz solo. This stems from his thorough command of theory; his harmonic explorations, as in "I Get a Kick Out of You" from the *Maybeck* album, are far more illuminating than his fastest, flashiest single lines, and the unforced virtuosity of his key shifts on such tunes as "The Song is You," from *The Music of Jerome Kern*, reveal his understanding of how the way a song is written can lead to epiphanies in arrangement.

In a trio context, Makowicz does adapt and tone it down. With bassist George Mraz and drummer Alan Dawson carrying the rhythm on *Kern*, he offers an unhurried chord-based examination of "All the Things You Are" and a relatively understated long ramble through "The Way You Look Tonight," on which he proves his ability to swing hard with a less cluttered line. The presence of the bass alone, in the duo album *Adam Makowicz/George Mraz*, is sufficient to allow the pianist to move from quiet but ear-opening displays of hand independence to a carefully placed bit of exhibitionism within four minutes on "Where Is Love?"

Though profound, Makowicz's intellect is fundamentally conservative. He draws from no classical influence more recent than Impressionism. His touchstones are Mozart, Chopin, and—much more so than Brad Mehldau—Brahms; one listens in vain for any of the jagged bitonality or modal references that pianists like Chick Corea draw from Bartók. He is also untouched by Latin or other non-European cultural references. This, in the early twenty-first century, gives his music an odd detachment. Even his reflection of the Tatum school creates an archival impression. Where Marcus Roberts uncovers modern, post-Monk implications in his adaptations of stride piano, Makowicz plays exactly as a pianist of his caliber would have done fifty years ago.

In the end, the Tatum school, from Peterson through to Makowicz, stands or falls on its addiction to speed. Not just the ability to play fast notes, but the inevitability of playing them, is essential. At some point, they're going to happen. Other pianists have massive technique but keep it in reserve; whether Keith Jarrett or Gonzalo Rubalcaba, they've found ways of holding back in the interests of a different kind of expression. The question posed years ago and kept alive by Makowicz is why the Tatum disciples are so wedded to velocity—and whether, in the long run, this style serves or thwarts their artistry.

54. MICHEL PETRUCCIANI

Born: December 28, 1962, Orange, France
Died: January 6, 1999, New York, New York

In the end, it was all about the music. When Michel Petrucciani played, none of the other stuff mattered. Of course, everyone knew about the stuff—specifically, the osteogenesis imperfecta, the "glass bones" disease that capped his growth at somewhere around three feet tall and fifty pounds and led to his early demise. But his solo performances sprawled across canvas as massive as that employed by Keith Jarrett, though never bogged down by the fixations that could rivet Jarrett to a single phrase for minutes at a time.

Petrucciani's playing was a marvel of juxtaposition—hard percussive tone against milky legato, aching romanticism studded with barbed bits of the blues—and of scale. No other pianist except Jarrett could match his command of both the long and the miniature forms. Petrucciani, more the traditionalist, was far more often than Jarrett guilty of self-indulgence, in the form of gimmicky horse-race tempos or old-timey quotes from standard tunes. But these excesses rose from a joy that was absent from Jarrett's solemn marathons and much of the rest of jazz piano as well.

Raised in sunny southern France, Petrucciani was the son of a French mother and a Sicilian father who played jazz guitar. Jazz was in the air; reportedly Michel began talking and humming Wes Montgomery solos around the same time. At the age of four he received a pink toy piano for Christmas, which his father shortly upgraded to a full-scale upright. He learned the classics through eight years of lessons, with daily practice sessions that stretched to six or seven hours, through which he developed a special love for Debussy. By the age of nine he was gigging with his father and his two older brothers. His first exposure to the music of Bill Evans, at age ten, hastened the growth of a style based on rich harmonies and sharp articulation of the melody.

Michel moved to Paris, where he formed a trio with his brother Louis, a bassist, and performed with bebop expatriate legend Kenny "Klook" Clarke, all at age 16. He made his recording debut, as a sideman, in August 1980; his first appearance as a leader came on an eponymous trio date the following year. Stardom came swiftly, especially following a duo tour with saxophonist Lee Konitz. Before long, even the City of Lights wasn't big enough for the young pianist, and at age 18, accompanied by a friend, he left France to take on New York.

It didn't take long for Petrucciani to conquer the new world as well. After playing for a while on the East Coast, he left for California, where he inspired saxophonist Charles Lloyd to come out of retirement and put together a new quartet. With this group, he toured Europe, where they received the Prix d'Excellence at the Montreux Festival and recorded *Montreux '82*. After living for a while near Lloyd in the redwood wonderland around Big Sur, Petrucciani returned to New York and launched his solo career.

It was, from the start, a string of triumphs. He played his first American gig as a soloist at the Kool Jazz Festival in 1983, and followed with a headline appearance at the Village Vanguard. These led to further recitals, at the Kennedy Center and Carnegie Hall, and a parade of awards—from the governments of France and Italy, not to mention assorted publications better known for staying on top of developments in jazz. For 17-plus years, he would record with stellar artists—Joe Henderson, Jim Hall, Bobby McFerrin, Joe Lovano, Wayne Shorter—and lead projects that ranged from traditional quartets to piano/synthesizer duets with Adam Holzman.

In everything he played, Petrucciani exhibited a uniquely playful virtuosity. On *Flamingo*, an all-star quartet date from 1995, he feeds from the ebullience of Stephane Grappelli's solo for his own exquisitely constructed improvisation. After trading fours with drummer Roy Haynes in a stripped-down, Monkish approach, Petrucciani amplifies on this spare feel, with freely flowing lines and a beautifully articulated triplet sixteenth-note flurry at the end of the bridge. It's simple, but flawlessly executed and designed.

Within a rhythm section, Petrucciani was loose and spontaneous. His improvisations adhered to traditional theme-and-variations approach, with phrases delineated by carefully placed accents. His solo on the unusual bossa arrangement of "You Go to My Head," from the 1998 session for *Steve Grossman with Michel Petrucciani*, shows how he could make use of a particularly strong melody. From the opening notes he probes the tune, moving up an octave in the second verse, adding a few funky figures going into and out of the bridge, and finally breaking into a long burst of sixteenth-notes in an electrifying run that darts through the following two verses. This is typical of his style in playing standards with a group: an ecstatic spirit, a surging stream of ideas, and a judicious use—never an overuse—of his emphatic chops.

In unaccompanied performance, Petrucciani allowed himself greater freedom. On the Grossman album he plays a full verse, bridge, and verse lead-in to "Body and Soul," all the while supporting his reflections on the theme with a feathery rubato. His escalating chordal movement out of the bridge leads to a moment of romantic dissonance, with harmonic alterations that crystallize the mood of the improvisation and give Grossman a gorgeous opening for his entrance.

In duo combinations, this same emotional intensity could feed Petrucciani's partner. On "Petite Louise," from the 1997 *Both Worlds* session, the pianist's organic tempos, the tidal rise and fall of his dynamics, the shifts between solid and arpeggiated chords, prod saxophonist Stefano Di Battista into a

Michel Petrucciani's playing was a marvel of juxtaposition: percussive tone against milky legato, romanticism studded with bits of the blues.

performance of memorable expressiveness. Similarly, in his free-tempo "One Night in the Hotel," from the solo album *Promenade with Duke*, Petrucciani displays his characteristic skill at laying punchy, jabbed right-hand lines over intricate implied rhythms and legato phrases in the left, all of it tied together with tasteful blues devices and an unmatched cantabile touch.

In the blazing solo in his own "35 Seconds of Music and More," from *Both Worlds*, other elements of Petrucciani surface: the escalating rhythmic motifs as a device to build momentum in a solo, an implication of sophisticated voicings through an eloquent single line (also evident in his examination of "These Foolish Things," from *Au Théatre des Champs-Élysées*), deft two-hand unisons, the use of modal fragments as a coloristic device. What makes this performance and the entire album important as well is its showcase of Petrucciani's compositions in tight, small-group charts by Bob Brookmeyer. The message of this material is that there was clearly much more that Petrucciani could have contributed to the repertoire, had time allowed.

An unapologetic entertainer, Petrucciani usually exceeded his own standards when playing live. It's instructive to compare his studio performance of Duke Ellington's "Caravan" on *Promenade with Duke* to the version performed before an audience in Frankfurt in 1997, captured on *Live Solo*. Here Petrucciani launches his improvisation not just by examining the exotic implications of the theme, but by building the concept of his introduction on a volcanic rumble in the low end of the piano. Once he moves into the tune, the steady rhythm feels almost quaint—which is probably why it gives way quickly to eccentric truncations and extensions, a simplistic one-octave imitation of stride, dizzy accelerandos, a mosquito-like flight through the theme in the upper range of the keyboard, gnarly clustered approximations of the tune, and so on. He pulls it off with a panache that brings the crowd to its feet more than once. While one could question its taste, this performance is undeniably electrifying.

Above all, Petrucciani was a sensualist. His tone was lustrous and silky. His tempo swooned and sighed as his lines slithered and soared. At the high points in his phrases, especially when playing unaccompanied, Petrucciani would often pause, as if to admire the visions he saw from these peaks, then tumble down again to the place where his phrase had begun.

The flip side is that Petrucciani was one of the least cerebral players of his time. Emotion trumped intellect in his performances. His arrangements of standard tunes betrayed no sense of premeditation. Though a strong harmonic player, Petrucciani never gave the appearance of reharmonizing songs—maybe he did, but he never sounded like it. Players like Andy LaVerne, for whom chordal surgery was a fundamental practice, were his temperamental opposite. They were arrangers who played; Petrucciani lived entirely in the present, a tactile, vibrant master of the moment.

Maybe this was understandable, for Petrucciani knew that his time would be short. He was an extrovert, a joker, a ladies' man with a somewhat tangled romantic history. Only a week before his death he was up until daylight, celebrating the New Year with friends at the Vanguard. A lung infection was what officially took him out, although his disability contributed to health problems that made his exit unavoidable.

His legacy is a style too personal to launch any new movements in jazz. One cannot play like Petrucciani without his unique blend of wicked humor and tragic circumstance. But his intoxication with life is a lesson that can benefit anyone, artist or not, in whatever we do with the opportunities we've been given.

Outside Looking In

55. SUN RA

Born May 14, 1914, Birmingham, Alabama
Died May 30, 1993, Birmingham, Alabama

Herman "Sunny" Blount was never "normal," yet his persona masked the fact that he was a traditionalist at heart. More than Cecil Taylor or Muhal Richard Abrams or just about any pianist saddled with a reputation as an avant-gardist, the artist who would teach the world to call him Sun Ra preserved unmistakable ties to familiar aspects of jazz. The robes, the mysterious headgear, the multimedia spectacle of his concerts, the inscrutable names attached to his assorted ensembles, his cryptic and cosmic theology—in the end, they did more to contradict than to explain his music. He would proclaim that "Space is the Place," yet his music was rooted in the well-trod earth of blues and big-band swing.

Years before hallucinating rockers started crashing on each other's couches and staring into strobe lights, Ra was presiding over living communes and evolving a complex performance aesthetic. Showmanship was always a part of jazz—even Miles Davis's decision to play with his back to the audience was a performance gesture of a sort. But nobody had ever done anything like Sun Ra onstage. Novelist and jazz writer LeRoi Jones, a.k.a. Amiri Baraka, understood exactly what these shows were about: Writing in *Down Beat*, Jones reduced the band's outfits, lighting effects, massed percussion, hymns to elusive deities, and hypnotic chants to byproducts of Ra's search for "a music that will reflect a life-sense lost in the West—a music full of Africa."

Others saw something more insidious in Ra's search for music that depicted what Ra himself targeted as "the natural infinity of the eternal universe." In a *Down Beat* article ominously titled "Toms and Tomming," Brooks Johnson accuses the bandleader of "helping and encouraging the very thing he abhors: the closed clique of power that controls his musical life. . . . Sun Ra, in attempting to alienate from his work the white man, stunts his own growth and potential. In short, he Toms away part of his contribution to jazz."

Ra would insist that his concerns were more universal—in the most literal sense. "I want *everybody* to have immortality," he emphasized in a *Down Beat* interview. "It's too big for one nation, one people, or even one planet."

If there is an ironic postscript to this laudable thought, it is that Ra ultimately based his quest on musical forms that were long established as the foundations of jazz, mainstream as well as avant-garde. The universal language he sought was always within reach in his own—and America's—back yard.

When asked about his own life, Ra would sometimes insist that he had come into the world without a mother, and that he would never die. Though it seems churlish to dispel this mythology, Ra's background did include a period of mundane apprenticeship. He was 16 years old when he started transcribing recorded performances by Fletcher Henderson, who would emerge as one of his most important influences; eventually Ra would write arrangements for Henderson while they were sharing a gig at the Club De Lisa in Chicago, and for nearly a year in the late forties would play piano in one of Henderson's last bands.

He led his own groups in high school and at Alabama A&M University, where he studied music education and took piano lessons from Willa Randolph. Guided by the dolorous, triumphant vocals of Bessie Smith and Ethel Waters, Ra dedicated himself to harmonizing extreme elements of feeling and technique. Relocated to Chicago in 1946, he went on tour with Wynonie Harris and Lil Green, performed informally with Coleman Hawkins, and worked for a while with the Dukes of Swing, led by future Dave Brubeck bassist Gene Wright.

It was in the mid fifties that the prototypical Sun Ra began to take shape. He legally changed his name to Le Sony'r Ra, and would later insist that he couldn't remember ever having the name Blount. Much of what Ra was doing in those days was much closer to R&B than to jazz. *The Singles*, an outstanding collection of early Ra recordings on Evidence, documents his forays into doo-wop as pianist and arranger with a group called the Cosmic Rays, as well as Little Richard-style rave-ups, complete with honking tenor sax, on tracks like "Muck Muck," from 1957. These elements blend neatly into a jazz ballad form on a rehearsal tape of Ra's "October," recorded in 1958 or '59 and also featured on *The Singles*; here Ra takes a solo on one bridge that evokes both Charles Brown in its intimacy and deep blues feel, with a flat-five chord at the end of the second bar adding a hint of Monk as well. On a later track, a slow-drag blues titled "The Blue Set" from 1960, Ra digs even deeper into the Brown pocket, with "crushed" major/minor thirds and high-register triplets that come from somewhere closer to the downhome than to any outer galaxies.

Around this same time Ra was planting the seeds of the ensembles that would come to represent his musical and metaphysical vision for decades to come. They would bear exotic names: the Myth-Science, Solar, or Heliocentric Arkestra. Yet each was defined by Ra's fidelity to jazz tradition, and specifically in the discipline of song interpretation. His version of "Can This Be Love?" recorded in his Chicago apartment in 1955 as a duo with bassist Wilbur Ware, brings this connection to light. In many respects this performance bears evidence of a Monk influence, or at least of a communion of the two pianists on some common plane: As Monk would often do, Ra lets his solo amble into the piano's higher

The universal language Sun Ra sought was always within reach in his own—and America's—backyard.

range, where he can plink out a line or repeated notes in minor ninths; his occasional triplet ornaments also have a Monkish flavor. But Ra plays much of the early half of his solo in chords that splash against frequent major sevenths in the melody; this is Erroll Garner territory, far even from early bebop in spirit. And in his languorous rhythmic phrasing, which constantly trails the beat, he betrays the romantic inclination that would soften the edges of his more free-form adventures.

"Can This Be Love?" is featured on the album *Standards*, from the 1201 Music label. Also from this intriguing collection is his performance of "But Not for Me," recorded in late 1962 or early 1963. Ra's melodic language pushes far beyond where it had been only seven years before; the four-bar intro, an atonal meandering anchored only by bassist Ronnie Boykins' firm articulations on the first and third beat of each measure, offers no clue as to where it's leading. When the horns come in to surprise us with the familiar theme, Ra lapses into a more conventional supportive role—or perhaps it just seems more conventional with the song now spelled out. Certainly when his piano solo begins, the ties between the tune and his stream-of-conscious lines almost immediately dissolve: He opens with two notes that delineate Gershwin's written opening motif, then elbows against the structure by reiterating the same figure, this time on the flatted sixth and the third of the I chord. That's enough to send Ra off on a flight through passages with no tonal reference at all. On this chorus, and several others taken by Ra later in the tune, he returns now and then to the tune, like an explorer scanning for land before being drawn back to uncharted waters. Eventually Ra does find his way home, though by a route that less adventurous improvisers left undiscovered.

In the sprawling settings provided by his larger ensembles, Ra played piano with an arranger's sensibility, doubling or complementing the horn parts, providing segues between sections. Orchestral color was always foremost for Ra in these contexts—which may explain his eager acquisitions of electric pianos, Clavinets, synthesizers, and other early timbral tools. But this also took him a step away from his roots in piano—specifically, its well-established role as a component in big-band tonalities. His introductory work on "Images," from the 1972 album *Space Is the Place*, recalls nothing so much as Duke Ellington, in how the instrument is used to set both tempo and feel. The opening chord—again, Ra's favorite major seventh—has a thorny Monk quality, and the moody variations that follow evoke McCoy Tyner. But in establishing a mood, and subsequently in filling the spaces that thread through the Arkestra charts, Ra stands revealed as an unrepentant Ellingtonian. He pushes the beat, slides in rhythm through written triplet passages, and feeds his soloists from an ever-changing stream of voicings and rhythmic placements. On his own solo, the little downward runs and pointed chords illuminate the similarities between Duke and Monk, as well as the place that Ra could claim for himself in this line of succession.

The Monk influence can easily be overstated. Paradoxically, for all the multimedia effects and spacey affectations, Ra is held back to a degree by his respect for tradition. His playing on the title track from "Blue Delight" begins as a pure jump blues, right out of Kansas City; it could just as easily been cut in the thirties as in the late eighties. When Ra switches to octaves to articulate his right-hand part during the second verse, he edges right up to the fringes of stride piano. It makes a certain sense to move from there into more of a Monkish feel, with staccato minor ninths, and off-beat accents on individual notes. But one thing keeps Ra from pushing any further in that direction: his sense of swing. What's often missed about Ra is that he could swing harder than most pianists, with or without the sartorial affectations. For all that Monk accomplished, he was not a *swinging* pianist. If anything, he offered an escape from old swing formulas—and that was one trip that Ra chose never to take.

Eventually the piano would take a backseat to the electronic keyboards. In the book *Outcats*, Francis Davis saw these instruments as a perfect match for the artist's goals, in their ability to allow him to "evoke Ellington, Basie, Garner, Monk, and Meade Lux Lewis, often simultaneously." Ra certainly seemed to agree; his prediction, reported by *Down Beat*, was that synthesizers "may galvanize musicians into harmony and harmony units, and they will become exponents of harmonic brotherhoods, banded together at last to achieve ensemble presence and worth according to the greater standards of the universe."

Whether electronic instruments would indeed turn the universe of music upside down, they did have an undeniable effect on Ra's piano work. "Quest," a solo improvisation from 1982 included on *The Singles*, makes this clear: Recorded on an upright piano, it opens with a Morse-code-like staccato pattern on the dominant note, played over a stern, almost angry march of open fifths in the left hand. This rhythm stutters into a modified triplet pattern, then opens into an alternating sequence of adjacent open fifths as Ra slowly expands the right-hand pattern across a widening range of notes. Eventually a solo line emerges, which teases the left-hand pattern into more constricted clusters and, with the damper pedal down, murky blurs. With its tight development and adherence to a motivic idea, "Quest" exemplifies Ra's ability to reflect his big-picture vision in an economical, miniature scale.

As with Ellington, Basie, and other big-band pianists, Ra's accomplishments as a writer, and his willingness to play parts within his arrangements, distract from the prominence he might have otherwise achieved as a pianist alone. Of course, the joyful weight of his responsibilities as an intergalactic prophet didn't make this sort of assessment any easier. If it is possible to isolate his keyboard performances, through attention to unaccompanied piano recordings such as *Monorails and Satellites* or through the solos he allowed himself in more extravagant presentations, what emerges is a picture of an artist for whom adventure is enhanced by self-awareness. It takes someone with roots in Alabama, Fletcher Henderson, and Bessie Smith to find a style that might actually be appreciated and understood in the stars.

56. LENNIE TRISTANO

Born: March 19, 1919, Chicago, Illinois
Died: November 18, 1978, New York, New York

Lennie Tristano was one of those rare figures in jazz who was able to take something familiar and do something with it that had no precedent. He was a pianist of rigorous intellect, whose cerebral interpolations of bebop and blues concealed—and, in their unique way, transmitted—an almost intimidating intensity of feeling. His solos were streams of eighth- or sixteenth-notes, often played straight on the beat rather than with syncopation; for chorus after chorus he would unfold these long lines, bending them into ever more daring elaborations on the chords, until it seemed unavoidable that he would repeat himself somehow, or resort to some show-stopping vamps and riffs. Yet somehow he would keep going, playing the piano as a chess master plays the board, in endless combinations and with a quiet, frightening brilliance.

He had charisma, born in part from a tendency toward seclusion that added mystery to his rare public appearances. His blindness didn't make him any less enigmatic. When he spoke to the press or to his many students, his language was terse, his opinions blunt, and his insights often illuminating. He scattered barbed *bon mots* like the seeds of bitter apples: "In 1944 . . . I could rifle off anything of Tatum's—and with scandalous efficiency. . . . I can count on one hand the great improvisers. . . . Ninety-nine percent of the words written about jazz in the last forty years are garbage. . . ." And, in a briefly famous letter to *Down Beat*, "I think Diana Ross is the greatest jazz singer since Billie Holiday."

Critics were, of course, transfixed by Tristano. Len Lyons and Don Perlo saw him as a revolutionary whose assault on swing-era approaches to rhythm made it necessary for him to instruct his bassists and drummers to play without accents. A broader appraisal of his playing prompted Gunther Schuller, in his book *The Swing Era*, to challenge the cheap-shot dismissals of the pianist as a cold-blooded intellect: "Tristano's early work pulsates with the vitality of invention, luxuriates in warm sensuous harmonies, revels in a richly varied pianistic touch, and pleasures in the contrapuntal independence of his two hands. If that be mere intellectualism, so be it."

Long before fists pounded podiums in support or dismay over his contributions, Tristano was busy mixing music with a losing struggle against blindness—influenza suffered at birth darkened his world gradually and left him sightless by the age of eight. He musical gifts were prodigious; at age four he began picking out tunes on the piano, with formal lessons commencing three years later, followed by parallel work on cello, guitar, clarinet, drums, trumpet, and saxophone. Tristano was 12 years old when he made his jazz debut at a saloon gig. An excellent student, he earned a bachelor's degree in composition at the American Conservatory. Immediately after graduation he plunged into a routine of teaching at the Christiansen School of Popular Music and playing around Chicago: On any given night he might be playing clarinet licks with his own trad jazz band, squeezing accordion at society gigs, or stirring up consternation with more experimental performances.

Bassist Chubby Jackson talked Tristano into moving to New York in 1945. He arrived toward the end of the year, started hanging around the clubs on 52nd Street, and found himself steady work with guitarist Billy Bauer and bassist Arnold Fishkin at a place called Al B. White's in Freeport. His first records, dating from 1946, bore evidence of unorthodox ideas about the relationship between meter and the improvised line. People started listening; by the late forties, though already slipping away from the mainstream through his explorations of mixed time signatures and atonal improvisation, Tristano had been voted into the annual Metronome All-Stars recording session.

Lennie Tristano played the piano as a chess master plays the board, in endless combinations and with a quiet, frightening brilliance.

In the April 1979 issue of *Music Quarterly*, Barry Ulanov recalled just how adventurous Tristano's concepts were during these productive years. At the core was the old clash of freedom versus form: "The thinking . . . always preceded the playing, so that when he played his feeling could be given absolutely free rein. . . . [Yet he also recognized] that improvisation must have a vertebrate center—a set of familiar chords, a tonal base, a chorus length, the assiduously pursued finger-line exercises." In attempting to reconcile these elements, Ulanov concluded, Tristano accomplished "an opening even larger than that provided by the earlier masters of jazz to human feeling."

Paradoxically, Tristano's pursuit of this goal led him toward a style in which he seemed to defy any temptation to swing. His comping behind the soloists on "Ear Conditioning" and "I Never Knew," both recorded in 1956 for *Intuition*, is astonishingly stolid, with both hands playing resolutely on the occasional beat, never between with any syncopation. These chords tended to be voiced traditionally, with the root in the bottom and not much complexity in the middle. The effect suggests nothing revolutionary—to the contrary, it seems pedestrian. His solo does lock onto the rhythm section's momentum, but even here, on both tracks, his left hand punctuates several times with a rather deliberate single note on the fifth of the root chord, not so much to push the beat as to punctuate—or, perhaps, suggest removing a sheet of paper from the typewriter before a new one is inserted.

A different side of Tristano emerges in his solos, which swing despite their objective quality. On "Crosscurrent," recorded in 1949 and available on *Intuition*, he comps more freely as his right-hand line darts through the changes. His phrasing is confident and fluid, his note choices stimulating. And, not untypically, he ends with an emphatic left-hand punctuation on the lower fifth.

In a similar sense, Tristano's antiseptic approach to playing the blues conveys a unique fusion of charm and foreboding. On the unaccompanied "Requiem," from his 1956 album *Lennie Tristano*, the pianist follows a somber introduction, built from a simple minor figure into a moody and murky meditation, with a straight blues. It is, in fact, almost painfully straight, with a bone-dry line strung methodically over the heavy tread of dark quarter-note chords. Tristano's note selections draw completely from blues tradition, but his emphases are wildly unconventional, particularly in his preoccupation with a sharply enunciated flatted fifth. On the last verse, just before the piece fades out, a trilled fifth and minor seventh appears as an overdubbed third hand. There's no discernible reason why Tristano would add this puzzling detail, except in that it accomplishes his likely goal of submitting the blues to a different type of examination.

Tristano creates a similar impression on "Progression," recorded in 1949 and available on saxophonist Lee Konitz's album *Subconscious-Lee*. Over a breezy bop rhythm from guitarist Billy Bauer, bassist Arnold Fishkin, and drummer Shelly Manne, Tristano solos several times. His first chorus, following the opening verse, is played mainly in a straight-eighth rhythm, supported by more syncopated chords in the left hand. The pianist sculpts his improvisation into cleanly delineated four-bar phrases, some of which end with runs through distinctively un-idiomatic major triads. It's almost a "square" approach, yet Tristano makes it work on the strength of his originality. Notice, as well, his complex interactions with Bauer behind Konitz's first solo, after which Tristano kicks off a chorus of trading fours with a cleanly executed triplet run in 32nd-notes. While not exactly textbook swing, this playing is in no way lacking in rhythm or deficient in pushing the groove.

When the song has a more challenging structure, Tristano's harmonic innovations clarify, with appropriate reflection in his right-hand line. The opening moments of "Yesterdays," from *Intuition*, directly echo "'Round Midnight." Indeed, much of the performance reflects Monk's focus on minor ninths, though Tristano shows more fluidity in a few left-hand counter lines and a greater willingness to underscore his harmonic language with unexpected pure triads. Throughout "Yesterdays" Tristano displays an arresting depth of improvisational resources; his line stretches virtually without break, and stays within a leisurely sixteenth-note pace, yet never fails to engage the listener.

Tristano's distinctive harmonic language emerges in his solo on "Lover Man." Again, the playing avoids rhythmic grooves, but at the same time its complex voicings have little to do with the more Romantic harmonies of Shearing or Tatum. On the B-section of the first verse he lets a unison line lead him into some crowded bitonal dissonances built on juxtaposed triads on the root and minor third of the I chord. It isn't easy to listen to, even now, but it does cast light on an imagination not easily distracted by standard practice in the fringes as well as the mainstream of jazz. Similarly, his solo on "These Foolish Things," recorded live with saxophonist Lee Konitz, bassist Gene Ramey, and drummer Art Taylor for the album *Lennie Tristano*, is built on thick chords threaded by occasional unison lines. Particularly on the bridge, Tristano uncovers complex harmonic implications that, played with rigid two-handed formulations, manage to sidestep any conventional emotional expression.

Even more extreme is Tristano's unaccompanied reading of "You Don't Know What Love Is," from the 1962 album *The New Tristano*. Throughout this piece, Tristano draws inspiration from a sober muse: Though he plays the first bridge and other passages over a cautious walking left-hand bass, most of his improvisation involves distending the harmony as much as possible. As a result, we hear the melody altered here and there to accommodate Tristano's harmonic explorations. His efforts lead to an astonishing last verse that opens with a highly unstable bitonality based on the diminished fifth, which Tristano quickly resolves only to move into a minefield of clustered melody and a brief nod back to the flat five before closing unexpectedly without a final recapitulation of the verse. Few solos sound so interesting and, at least in conventional terms, so unengaging at the same time.

The movement toward free improvisation, outlined in Tristano's elliptical solo introductions to the title track and to "Digression" on *Intuition*, is based on a rigorous conception of structure. Even with the harmonic movement delineated here, and in the interactions that follow with the other musicians, Tristano creates a legitimately atonal impression; the elusiveness of a tonal center is achieved through pursuit of intricate linear improvisations in real time, rather than through the less demanding paths indicated by clusters. There's a greater emphasis on vertical harmony in "Digression," but even here Tristano works ambivalence into the chord sequence, so that expectations of traditional voice-leading are thwarted. It is a more serious and profound exploration of modern European applications in jazz than anything being done by Brubeck.

In the last ten years of his life, Tristano played no public concerts. He continued to teach until shortly before his death. His influence on young players today is difficult to gauge—perhaps because of the difficulties involved in the contradictory art of expressing emotion through something mistaken too often for detachment.

PAUL BLEY

Born: November 10, 1932, Montreal, Quebec

An icy blue aura envelops the music of Paul Bley. In this respect he is the definitive ECM pianist—the perfect realization of producer Manfred Eicher's glacial aesthetic. Emotions stir inside this music, though it can take a bit of effort to identify them. Fundamentally Bley's improvisations are driven by a kind of dispassionate analysis of passion, a search for how form and space can produce something—beauty, insight—from nothing.

Bley's style is based on an affection for mixing freedom and form, a perennial inquisitiveness, and an intoxication with pure sound. While this would lead him, with mixed results, into a dalliance with synthesizers, the piano is the enduring object of his interest. Very much in the fashion of Monk, Bley cultivated a keyboard technique that could objectively be described as primitive, for the purpose of weaning his imagination and the ears of his listeners from the distractions that technique can bring. In this respect Bley has proven to be a highly underestimated influence; Keith Jarrett in particular has credited him for pointing out how to use the silences between notes to speak as persuasively as the notes themselves, by offering mute views into the act of creation.

Because of his emphasis on openness, Bley was an ideal sideman for adventurous musicians; his quick ear allowed him to complement Chet Baker, Sonny Rollins, Lee Konitz, Archie Shepp, Steve Lacy, and other artists unified only by their idiosyncratic and unpredictable styles. Few pianists listened as deeply as Bley, whose intelligence allowed him to develop a deep understanding of improvisation, and to subsequently attempt to put that understanding into words.

His ruminations often read like the writings of an unusually prescient critic: "Most of the young jazzmen today are listening hard to the schools of the past . . . and assimilate them into their own playing," he mused in a 1955 issue of *Down Beat*—six full years before Wynton Marsalis's birth. At other times Bley could be elusive—a hep-cat Yoda: "I'm against freedom in the wide sense. If freedom means free improvisation rather than free jazz, that's where I draw the line" . . . "The avant-garde starts when you throw chord progressions away" . . . "We live in a 72-minute world, soon to be a 72-minute world accompanied by visuals" . . . "I hope eventually to destroy the prejudice of the means and to be more concerned with the content."

Speaking more universally, Bley suggested in a later *Down Beat* interview that "to be a complete human being, one must understand one's childhood." That would take him back approximately to age five, when Bley began taking violin lessons before switching three years later to piano. A precocious student, he was 11 years old when he earned his "junior diploma" from McGill University.

In 1950 Bley left for four years of off-and-on study at Juilliard in New York. He began recording during this period, in a trio date with bassist Oscar Pettiford and drummer Kenny Clarke. While still in his teens Bley also got involved with launching the Jazz Workshop of Montreal, a group of restless players whose activities included early attempts to fuse music to video, and a series of concerts that featured artists such as Sonny Rollins, Jackie McLean, Al Haig, and Kai Winding. The Workshop brought Charlie Parker back to Montreal in 1953, the same year that Bley recorded a semi-free improvisational project with Charles Mingus and Art Blakey for the bassist's Debut label. A few years later he moved to Los Angeles with his own group, bassist Hal Gaylor and drummer Lennie McBrowne; following a series of personnel changes, the trio evolved briefly into a visionary group that included bassist Charlie Haden, drummer Billy Higgins, trumpeter Don Cherry, and the groundbreaking saxophonist Ornette Coleman.

Coleman, who generally found the piano uncongenial to his free and linear style, established a unique relationship with Bley. As Len Lyons and Don Perlo observed in *Jazz Portraits*, "Bley's spare melodic lines, involving minimal harmonic constraints, accommodated Coleman's aversion to chord changes and enabled him to work with the controversial saxophonist, who was then nearly ready to abandon harmony altogether." On two albums, *Live at the Hillcrest* and *Something Else!*, Bley would be the only pianist with whom Coleman would consent to record for quite a few decades.

In 1962 Bley and his wife Carla left Los Angeles and drove to New York, where he accepted an invitation from Jimmy Giuffre to join with him and Steve Swallow in a melody-based improvisational threesome. This group led Bley to organize another trio, featuring Swallow on bass and Pete LaRoca on drums, whose work challenged the traditional relationships between structure and solos. Only a year later he recruited bassist Gary Peacock and drummer Paul Motian for another trio, with Swallow returning and Barry Altschul taking over on drums in 1965. Though Bley would perform frequent duo, quintet, and solo gigs, the three-piece would long remain his preferred format.

Shortly afterwards, intrigued by early reports of the synthesizer as a musical tool, he obtained one of the early electronic instruments from inventor Bob Moog. He started using it in duo concerts with vocalist Annette Peacock, and in 1969 performed the first synthesizer concert ever held at Philharmonic Hall in New York. During the early seventies, seduced by this new muse, Bley hardly touched the piano at all.

But with the release in 1972 of *Open, to Love*, Bley reclaimed the piano and revisited his practice of stimulating the arts through ambitious organizations. In 1976 he and Carol Goss co-founded Improvising Artists, Inc. to encourage non-commercial, experimental jazz; Sam Rivers, Dave Holland, Jimmy Giuffre, and Sun Ra would record for the IAI label. In the nineties, while reconnecting with Giuffre, Swallow, and other early collaborators, Bley kept pushing after new ideas as well, including adaptations of 12-tone classical theory in the context of free improvisation.

Bley's style stands most exposed in his solo recordings. For all his movement through these past 50 years, his unaccompanied work has changed mainly in overt aspects of performance. Rarely today does he unleash the fervent dynamic contrasts displayed on his performance of "Ida Lupino," from *Open, to Love*. Written by Carla Bley—who, like Annette Peacock, contributed some very intriguing material to his repertoire when married to him—this piece, with its tango references and compelling theme, inspires Bley in one of his most riveting presentations. The opening figure, based on a somewhat unstable augmented fifth, leads him into an extemporization in which sharp dissonances alternate with cantabile lines, all of it deepened by the blues and shaded by bursts of tonal obscurity. Above all, "Ida Lupino" offers an outstanding example of freedom built on form, and of the possibilities suggested when romanticism and abstraction find each other.

Jump forward a quarter-century, and discover a slightly different Bley on his 2000 album *Hands On*. In place of the cerebral melodramas evident on "Ida Lupino," we find here a more reflective temperament, though just as strongly drawn by the intellectual side of improvising. Where his spiritual descendant Keith Jarrett took the lessons of Bley and extended them through forty-minute soliloquies, Bley does his free invention in smaller scale. The "man at work" aspect of witnessing the improviser in the act of creation is equally important in each of their output, but Bley's process is more densely displayed—not in sheer numbers of notes, but in the trickle of ideas that never abates or strays off course. On "Points" Bley opens with a sequence that wanders from an atonal drip-drop to a few bluesy riffs and then back again. He stops for a moment to juxtapose some polyrhythmic figures, much as one might pause on the street to consider an enigmatic sculpture or a busy urban vista, then moves on. He ends this enigmatic passage with a single bass note, hung out in silence as a reminder of the pianist's appreciation for naked sound, then proceeds, essentially in a 6/8 meter that dissolves in isolated and unresolved intervals to mark the end of the piece. There's almost no sense of beginning and end, but there is evident a maturity—a mastery, in fact—in Bley's measured, courageous approach.

When not working with space and sustain, Bley tends to splatter, rather than dash, across the keys. Just as often he fixates on figures that might have been drawn from the primers of beginning piano students, with sing-song motifs. His performance of "Told You So," an original tune on his 2000 solo album *Basics*, actually scatters bits of a familiar chant—"it's raining, it's pouring"—into a disturbing soundscape, at one moment as innocent as the tinkle of a music box, then suddenly as ominous as a dangerous stranger in a playground. Bley's performance is rhythmically elusive, with repeated notes, chords, and edgy intervals randomly articulated over ragged left-hand pulses before knotting into a messy contrapuntal tangle.

The legacy in this material is that Bley is as unusual an artist as any in jazz. He is avant-garde and listenable, distant and intimate, settled in his ways yet driven by ceaseless curiosity.

58. RAN BLAKE

Born: April 20, 1935, Springfield, Massachusetts

The "Third Stream" label that has affixed itself to Ran Blake ultimately fails to provide insight into this unique pianist's work. He still uses the term himself, to describe the underpinnings of his elusive style. But the meaning that "Third Stream" once had is no longer clear; if anything, it is an artifact now in jazz terminology, with a vague beatnik association.

None of this has helped Blake much, especially given his retiring nature. His recordings are hard to come by; his performances, rare as they are, tend to go unnoticed by Ken Burns trendies. Yet he is still among us, working in the kind of self-imposed isolation that one might expect from his threadbare academic nature and lifelong devotion to Thelonious Monk.

In their book *Jazz Portraits*, Len Lyons and Don Perlo note that Blake's "playing has been called, fairly enough, 'oddball,' 'quirky,' and 'surreal.' But at the same time, it is humorous, imaginative, and artful." This comes close, but Michael Ullman comes closer in this passage from *Jazz Lives*: "Blake's piano style has been called pianistic rather than hornlike. . . . One of his pieces begins before we hear anything: Blake depresses silently several keys so the first notes he hits will set up the overtones he desires."

Blake is, in fact, a kind of transcendentalist bopper. His highly improvisational music conveys both intelligence and reflectiveness, with little sense of urgency. It seems to work better in, say, museum auditorium recitals than in jazz saloons, with a cerebral appeal that almost discourages applause. He is, more than any other pianist, a true student, in that from listening to his master, Monk, he has gone beyond imitation into essence, and used what he found to attain real originality.

He was a lonely child. The son of a paper manufacturer, Blake was only three years old when he began picking out tunes on the piano. More than music, movies provided solace; young Ran spent far more time staring at the screen at nearby theaters than practicing the keyboard at home. "I'm nutty about Buñel and Hitchcock," he told Art Lange in *Down Beat*, "and have been hung up on *film noir* since childhood. I've seen *The Spiral Staircase* 18 times." Even now he maintains an omnivorous interest in art films, and often expresses himself on musical matters through cinematic references and metaphors.

Still, music proved his truest muse. His took lessons from a number of local teachers; by the time he started advanced instruction in Hartford at age 14 with Ray Cassarino, a onetime member of Woody Herman's band, Blake was already enmeshed in a web of strange and conflicting influences. From the radio he acquired a fascination for Prokofiev and, a couple of years later, Bartók. At the same time Blake was infatuated with gospel music, which he first heard at a black Pentecostal church—his public debut, in fact, was during services at the Holy Trinity Church of God in Christ in Hartford.

Blake entered Bard College at Annandale, New York, in 1956. During a break in classes, while working as a guard at the Newport Jazz Festival, he became acquainted with Gunther Schuller, the renowned composer and jazz instructor. At his invitation Blake began attending workshops at the Lenox School of Music, where he took classes from Schuller and Modern Jazz Quartet pianist/composer John Lewis. (Other reports suggest that Blake met Lewis first, and through him became friendly with Schuller.) Eagerly he sought out members of the Lenox faculty for private lessons; his teachers ranged from bop trombonist J. J. Johnson to Oscar Peterson, who gave Blake five sessions free of charge.

In 1960 Blake graduated from Bard with a music degree. Yet he felt unsatisfied with his accomplishment—like, as he told Michael Ullman, "a fish on a land garden." Without a real plan in mind, he moved to New York and began taking odd jobs—slicing cheese, bagging groceries, doing the night shift as a hotel clerk. While working as a waiter at the Jazz Gallery he became friendly with the Baroness Nica de Koenigswarter, a regal expatriate whose relationship with New York's jazz community was comparable to that of Gertrude Stein and the Lost Generation writers of Paris. Through the Baroness Blake was introduced to Thelonious Monk, who would become in many respects the younger pianist's guru—a source not so much of specific musical knowledge as philosophical perspective.

While taking more traditional lessons from Schuller, Mary Lou Williams, and Mal Waldron, Blake began playing gigs around town. After running into Jeanne Lee, a singer and fellow Bard alumnus, he started working with her as a duo, beginning with an unlikely victory during an amateur night ap-

Ran Blake works in a self-imposed isolation that one might expect from his threadbare academic nature.

pearance in 1961 at the Apollo Theater. Following a successful set at the Monterey Jazz Festival the following year, they built a professional relationship that would sustain, on and off, for decades to come. He made his recording debut with Lee as well, before cutting his first solo album, for the ESP label, in 1965. This was followed in 1969 by *Blue Potato and Other Outrages*, a politically charged project in which Blake set original music to writings by Malcolm X, Eldridge Cleaver, Regis Debray and Che Guevara.

By this time Blake was working for Schuller at the New England Conservatory. From his first position there in the mailroom, he moved up to teach improvisation and help lead community service projects. By 1974 Blake had made enough of a mark to be appointed chairman of the school's Third Stream department. His goal in that position was to apply his interest in combining classical music and improvisatory jazz to the growing field of popular and what would later be called world music.

But there was more to it than even that. "His third stream is also a stream of consciousness," notes Frank Davis in his book *In the Moment: Jazz in the Eighties*, "enveloping not only a body of music but whatever impressions of politics, literature, film, philosophy, and nature happen to be floating through his mind when he sits down to play or compose." There was a loose group of musicians who circled around this concept, with Ralph Towner, Paul Winter, and Don Cherry among them. Yet the breadth of its mission, and the difficulty involved in making these components come together as recognizable elements in a new sound, made it a tough label to sell to the public.

Whatever the label, Blake's music has maintained its integrity and high standards. Highlights include *A Memory of Vienna*, a set of standard tunes interpreted with somber deliberation by Blake and Anthony Braxton. Recorded on the spur of the moment during a few hours in November 1988, these performances use the mainstream nature of the material to point both musicians toward exploring the tensions between form and freedom. On "'Round Midnight," after several choruses of backing the saxophonist with intriguing clusters, unexpected chord movements in and out of rhythm, and occasional echoes of the theme, Blake takes his solo at a measured tread. With his left hand very discretely articulating just enough of a pulse to keep things moving, he slips in and out of other keys, hits dissonances that refer to Monk's style without mimicking it, and alternates dense clusters and delicate single notes. But unlike Braxton, Blake plays all of this in constant touch with the written theme. Abstraction is a tool, not a goal, in his examination of the titles in this set.

So it is as well on *Something to Live For*, where Blake delivers a reading of "Mood Indigo" that preserves the languorous romanticism of the Ellington composition while nudging it through a concept based on an augmented reharmonizations and sudden textural changes. None of this disrupts the continuity of Blake's conception; as on the *Vienna* set, he unifies his vision by keeping the tempo steady even while altering his enunciation of the beat, and by preserving a fragile, Satie-like ambience from start to finish. More surprising is his take on "A Night in Tunisia," from the same album: This one is delivered completely out of tempo, with only the barest references to the harmonic structure. Instead, Blake concentrates on the exotic character of the theme, which he plays at extreme rubato, leaving certain tones to hang dimly in resonant space, and pedaling after sharply hammered notes to emphasize his asymmetrical view of the tune. Indeed, he ends the piece quizzically, in the middle of the familiar opening motif, to create simultaneous senses of irresolution, mystery, and beauty.

Blake continues to follow his own path, as a highly original teacher at the New England Conservatory, and through musical projects as unexpected as *Horace Is Blue: A Silver Noir*, his tribute to the music of Horace Silver. But even his ghostly evocations of Silver's prototypical funk, when put into context, aren't such a surprise after all, for Blake once devoted a full-semester class to the music of Silver, as he had done for Monk, and had in fact written liner notes for one Silver album. In these notes he suggested that "the energy with which Silver erupts is often greater than the content of his ideas"— an odd tribute, perhaps, but also an insight into the fact that Blake represents precisely the opposite aesthetic, with all the golden moments in his catalog and career difficulties that this implies.

Order Within Chaos

59. CECIL TAYLOR

Born: March 15, 1930, Long Island City, New York

M usic seems to swirl around Cecil Taylor. When he walks, he steps gingerly, his dancer's body keeping time to the invisible orchestras that surround him. He keeps one ear cocked to the silent chorus; when the wind catches its voice, he stops himself in mid-sentence, a smile creasing his face. His eyes close, his head nods, following the angels' melody. At the coda, he laughs, a deep private hiss of delight, then returns to the room, to the friends who have learned to wait patiently for his communion to end.

The room is in Cecil's new house, a brownstone in Brooklyn. After years of frustration within an industry that was at best disinterested in his personal and passionate music, he has finally been able to find, buy, and settle into a place of his own. For years he washed dishes, took welfare, and otherwise paid the price for refusing to compromise his art. Even while listeners in Europe and Japan clamored for him, he found himself playing mostly in his own home, more palatable performers having scored the concert and club gigs. Characteristically, Taylor was able to turn this situation into a process of solidifying himself as a jazz visionary; his home became a haven, his piano a spiritual well from which he watered his ideas and grew them into events so powerful that he knew they would inevitably burst out into the world and be heard.

"Obviously, to me, the stool upon which I sit when I'm playing could be considered an altar," he told a *Down Beat* reporter in 1975, "a tripod upon which Isis or the Pythoness sits containing the closed calabash, the Iqua Odu, the seed, the beginning, the water, the sea of divinity from which my heritage speaks."

As recently as the seventies, mainstream critics and listeners took note as Taylor made his enigmatic declamations, or sat through his marathon piano performances, shaking their heads in befuddlement. When he spoke, he seemed to be spinning playful webs around his interviewers, inwardly smiling as they struggled to rearrange the poetry of his images into "sensible" patterns. When he played, he assaulted the public's expectations more forcefully. For hours at a single setting he would rage at the keyboard, disintegrating tonality, traditional structure, and rhythmic convention with a piledriver assault. His fingers would stiffen and fuse into pointed weapons with which he would jab out clustered spirals, one on the black keys, the other on the white. Complex themes would blur within a savage fury of sound, exhausting in sheer sonic dimension as well as emotional and intellectual breadth.

Taylor still plays this way; what has changed is the world's acceptance of him. Years ago he gave a duo performance with the late Mary Lou Williams; their brief encounter succeeded more in exposing the gaps between the new and the old than in bridging those gaps. By way of contrast, Taylor was able to share a concert billing with Oscar Peterson in New York partly because they played sequentially rather than together, partly because of their strong mutual respect, but even more because greater numbers of listeners had come to recognize Taylor's contributions, they were able to do what Williams and Taylor had failed to do: harmonize two diverse styles and celebrate their common lineage.

Yet there is still resistance. Taylor's unwillingness to cater to prevailing tastes has created a mixed impression over the years. Because his music is tied so closely to his interest in non-Western cultures, the Western (read: white) musical establishment extends only a wary appreciation. Though acknowledged now as a vital force in jazz, he is kept at arm's length. Even the *Village Voice*, for all the editorial support it extended to Taylor, dismissed his work at one point as "violent folk music of the sort one would expect from any bunch of pretentious illiterates." More succinct, notorious, and surprising is Miles Davis's dismissal of the Taylor catalog: "That shit ain't nothing."

Though personally courteous, Taylor has at times been as blunt as his detractors in interviews. In *Keyboard* magazine's January '79 encounter with him, he decried the provincialism that he sees as smothering the spirit of Third World art in America. He railed at the "myth of social progress" propagated by white observers of the black American artist, and accused writer Len Lyons of "trying to defend . . . the disease." In a tense and testy dialog, *Keyboard*'s questions were deflected, evaded, and ridiculed by the pianist. Yet in his enigmatic responses Taylor did in fact offer answers, leaving it up to the reader to see beyond the surface of the conversation:

What do you mean by musical expression?
What do *you* mean by it?
The realization or creation of what you hear in your mind.
If you hear it, why is there any need to play it? Isn't it enough that it exists in your head?
. . . Do you have a view on the usefulness of musical notation?
Now, who'd be interested in that?
People who are interested in your music.
Who would they be? They aren't responsible for me making any money all these years . . .
Are you dissatisfied with your own records?
Of course, I like 98 percent of the records I've made, but that doesn't alter the fact that the engineers don't know how to record the music.
How could they improve their work?
If I had a part of their salary I might tell you.
. . . What's your concept of technique?
I don't know what language you speak, or what you're prepared to hear. You might write anything. How do I know? If we're going to talk, I need some idea of who you are.

Clearly Taylor chooses to not play by the accepted rules, either in journalistic exchange or in music. Yet he is a master of sound and word, schooled enough in Western traditions to responsibly reject them. He was in grade school when he began composing and playing piano. His mother, an acquaintance of Duke Ellington's longtime drummer Sonny Greer, encouraged him to listen to the big bands and to blues singer Bessie Smith. For four years during the early fifties he studied at the New England Conservatory of Music, where he acquainted himself with Stravinsky, Schoenberg, Bartók, and other European iconoclasts whose music had created nearly as much of a scandal in their idiom as Taylor's would in his. Yet he developed a distaste for their approach; the formalistic roots of their innovations stifled his sense of expression. While he would borrow certain elements of the classical heritage in his own work—theme and variation, retrogrades, rondo form, and the piano itself among them—he fled quickly from their drawing room atmosphere.

"To feel is perhaps the most terrifying thing in this society," he has said. With that in mind, Taylor honed his style along the patterns of his passion. He gained a valuable foothold on traditional jazz by backing trumpeter Hot Lips Page from 1953 through '55, spending a week working with saxophonist Johnny Hodges, and gigging with other swing veterans, including trombonist Lawrence Brown. Then, in the mid-fifties, he began leading his own groups in New York. With saxophonist Steve Lacy, whom he lifted from Dick Wellstood's trad jazz band, bassist Buell Neidlinger, and drummer Dennis Charles, Taylor inaugurated the jazz policy at the Five Spot in 1956.

Throughout this period Taylor's debts to earlier jazz styles were evident. As writer Len Lyons has pointed out, his polyphonic skills found early inspiration in Dave Brubeck, though percussive pianists like Thelonious Monk, Bud Powell, and Horace Silver would more decisively influence his touch by the end of the decade. His growing explorations of the African side of the African-American cultural lineage catalyzed this movement: "In white music the most admired touch among pianists is light," he stated in Valerie Wilmer's book *As Serious as Your Life*. "We in black music think of the piano as a percussive instrument. We beat the keyboard, we get inside the instrument. Europeans admire Bill Evans for his touch. But the physical force going into the making of black music—if that is misunderstood, it leads to screaming."

By the sixties, Taylor's music had structured itself along this line. Occasionally he would still play from the standard repertoire—*New York City R&B*, a Taylor date from early in 1961, included Ellington's "Things Ain't What They Used to Be" and a couple of blues tunes. But his treatment of these titles was revolutionary. Without Neidlinger's bass and Charles's drums to delineate the sequence of chords and bars, his piano would seem divorced from the song except for tenuous thematic references. Indeed, if one concentrates only on the piano, blocking out the bass and drum patterns, one hears the modern Taylor: conceptually vigorous, disturbing, and ultimately thrilling.

Taylor's quartet, which at that time included tenor saxophonist Archie Shepp, performed at the Five Spot that year and provided music for a play, *The Connection*. In 1961 alto saxophonist Jimmy Lyons began his long association with Taylor. After a European tour with drummer Sunny Murray, capped by a live album date at Copenhagen's Café Montmartre, Taylor and Lyons recorded their first group album: *Nefertiti, the Beautiful One Has Come*. They worked together for years after that, with drummer Andrew Cyrille a regular colleague from 1964 into the early eighties. Taylor helped organize the Jazz Composers' Guild in 1964 and '65, and played a set at the 1965 Newport Jazz Festival. Saxophonist/pianist Sam Rivers, an old acquaintance from Boston, joined the group for a European tour in 1969, playing for the Maeght Foundation in France and elsewhere.

Subsequent highlights include a controversial teaching assignment at the University of Wisconsin in 1970–71, a group performance at New York's metropolitan Museum of Art in 1972, solo piano concerts at the 1972 Newport and 1974 Montreux festivals, a Guggenheim Fellowship in 1973, his first solo piano album in 1974, a return stint at the Five Spot in 1975, piano duo concerts with Mary Lou Williams and Friedrich Gulda in 1977, a stunning collaboration with dancer Dianne McIntyre at the Studio Museum in 1978, a live broadcast performance from Columbia University in 1979, a mind-expanding teaching experience with his group at the Creative Music Studio in December 1979 and January '80, collaborations with drummer Max Roach and dancer Mikhail Baryshnikov, and, in October 1974, a monumental concert with Steve Lacy and other innovative players at the Cologne Opera House in West Germany. [Since the original publication of this interview in the January 1965 issue of *Keyboard,* Taylor continued to challenge himself in an ever-broadening range of artistic disciplines, from scoring and directing plays to composing new works for dance. The presentation of a "genius grant" from the MacArthur Foundation represented a long-overdue recognition by the American cultural establishment of Taylor's unique accomplishments.]

Taylor never stopped experimenting. He tried playing in trio settings without a bassist (*Café Montmartre*) and supplemented his group with a second bass player (Alan Silva, in *Conquistador*). He worked with large ensembles (*The Jazz Composers Orchestra*) and explored the limits of solo piano improvisation/composition (*Spring of Two Blue-J's, Indent, Silent Tongues,* etc.). In every format he worked at monumental scale to build contemplative as well as cathartic sculptures through a vast dynamic range, thematic inventiveness, symmetrical manipulations, and above all a mastery of movement. Taylor found his stillness in motion, and audiences discovered a peculiar stability in his turbulent excursions.

At home in Brooklyn, Taylor is anything but restless. His house is elegant, peaceful, with spare furnishings, high ceilings, a wisp of incense always in the air, and in the music room, a Yamaha concert grand. Though it has obviously been played more than a few times, it seems solid, a match for its master. Sheet music blankets it—Taylor's own hand-written scores, each one done in his hieroglyphic system, covered with letters and arrows, devoid of staves. Downstairs, books line the walls—books on music, politics, philosophy, the African-American renaissance. Throughout the place there's a reflective air, suggesting a seriousness tempered by moments of ecstasy.

In his rooms, near the shrine of his piano, Taylor moves on his own time. Our interview begins more than four hours after our arrival. During that time friends drop in, bringing wine to warm him in his new home. Taylor blossoms in their company, dancing quick steps of welcome, embracing, laughing. He talks and listens, the center of attention, shorter than you might expect, but wiry as a cat, his mind and body nimble. Finally, as shadows stretch across his bare floors, he invites us downstairs. There, perched cross-legged on a cushioned stool, caressed by smoke from his cigarette, he listens to questions while gazing off to a far corner of the room, then takes time—his own timeless time—to answer.

You've said that you play most of your gigs at home these days. I suppose that makes the process of selecting a house that much more important. What did you find in this house that let you choose it as the center for you and your music?

It doesn't really matter where you're living. After finally understanding the challenge that my aesthetic point of view means to musicians, and also to business people, it became incumbent upon me, not having gigs, to fight for my own development. The place you fight best is in your own home, wherever that is. So you practice at home.

What sort of practice do you do?

It really begins with the breath of one note, with hearing and experiencing that, and the separation of that note from all the notes that you play.

You view each note in your practice as a separate event?

I think it's all about finally making clear to oneself the kind of form that you want, and using that to make the one note sing.

Do you practice the connection of the notes, the phrasing, after addressing the notes in their singularity?

I think it begins with the attempt to make the one note in itself . . . a universe.

In actual performances, though, are the notes that you play as important as the overall texture or contour?

I don't make a separation. You begin with the first note, and the aesthetic processes that shape the touch and the hearing and the breath of the first note determine the accumulation of the pulsations, the contour of the notes.

In A. B. Spellman's book Black Music: Four Lives, *Buell Neidlinger said that singing was an important part of your practice. "He'll sing a phrase, and then he'll harmonize it at the piano, and then he'll sing it again," Neidlinger said, "always striving to get the piano to sing." Is your voice in fact an important part of your practice at the piano?*

What happens is that one hears oneself sing at the same time that one strikes a note. There is no separation.

How do you settle your space in order to begin playing or practicing?

The thing we understand now is that before music, there is the word, the voice, the drum. But the thing that makes the voice, the word, the drum say the specific cultural thing that they do is the spiritual essence of the culture that produces whatever process it is that identifies specifically the language in the music. Once you understand that, then you try to investigate and discover what has been shepherding you in your ignorance.

How should people listen to your music—analytically, or through a surrender to the effect of what you do without trying to figure it out in musical or historical terms?

I really have no demand that I can put on the listener. At this point, however, I think those people who do come to my performances have an idea of what they're going to be in for, in terms of the totality of the experience that they may receive. They may not *comprehend*, in which case they have the option of leaving, and you don't worry about that.

You're not offended if somebody walks out?

Oh, no! Actually, I'm amused [*laughs*].

I've read that you began as a non-improvising musician.

No, that's not true.

Well, when you started playing, then, did you begin with your music or with pieces written by somebody else?

Mother gave me the first piano lesson that I had, so there was a certain lesson that I had to learn, but she always allowed Sunday for me to do whatever I wanted to do.

How different were those Sundays for you?

It was about what I wanted to hear, getting in touch with a particular spirit of the universe that informed my particular thrust, and I was allowed to do that.

Were you aware even as a child that you had a very unusual musical thrust?

In retrospect, one becomes aware of it. But fortunately, the home environment allowed me that one day to do that. The catechism had to be dealt with during the other six days of the week.

Did your teachers find you a frustrating student?

Yeah, I was, of course. I never practiced. I always had a problem with any authority, outside of my mother's. You know, life depended upon genuflection. It really does depend on that. I'm very fortunate that certain spirits have chosen this body as a vessel to pass through, and that allows me to do what I do. I realize that maybe it's easier to say that at times than to live with it, but it has nothing to do with my ego. It's something that makes stones stones, trees trees, plants plants, and my cat a cat. The life force inhabits all of this, and music to me at this point is really the celebration of the life force. And practice, which I still believe in, is the preparation to celebrate one's entrance into the temple of invention.

What impact has the business of music had on that element of celebration in music?

The reality is that there's a commercial margin which we must find, and choices we must make to perhaps go beyond that. It's a question of whether we can develop suitable options in terms of areas in which we might express ourselves.

When you spoke about playing most of your gigs in your living room, were you saying that, given those commercial realities, it might be better for you to not play at all in public than to play in a way that didn't feel right to you?

Oh, that was a choice I dealt with years ago. However, what one chooses to deal with as years go by becomes easier when one understands the limitations placed on one. And then one deals within those limits to create temples, pyramids.

How did you deal with that choice?

Not very well. But I've been fortunate in that I'm still alive, and that I've had opportunities to grow wiser. That's what I mean when I say that I'm having more fun now than ever. All things are possible, but one must be centered, and one must believe totally in the spiritual essence of the music and then make the necessary adaptations, because a society is always changing. The machine that is the force determining whether the music we play is heard, it too is alive, and it too is doing investigations. Finally it becomes easier because one no longer confuses absolutes or morality. One begins to understand reality, and then one makes a choice. So I can enjoy Michael Jackson, but I enjoyed Michael Jackson eight, nine years ago.

Or go see A Chorus Line, *as you did the other night.*

And learn!

Yet at some point in your development, there must have come a moment when you began to realize that you were speaking with a different musical voice.

The thing about that is, that didn't happen until I had made my first record. Upon hearing me, it took me at least three years to get over the shock, because I had always considered myself as paying homage to the great geniuses who had preceded me. What that first record made very clear to me was that what I had done with Ellington, Waller, and Monk was very personal.

That was the first time that you had heard your music from an audience's perspective, hearing your creation after it had been finished rather than from the middle of the creation process.

Yes! The internal process is always different from what you objectify when you hear, because when you hear from outside it's always as though someone else is doing it.

Did it change the way you wanted to play?

No.

You really weren't aware of your sound relative to what else was happening in jazz. You were just making music.

Yes. Maybe it's hateful to use the term, but when one hears, one must objectify. Then there is a whole process of thought patterns that comes out of that, which is startling and disturbing.

What exactly was the difference in what you heard and how you had thought you sounded?

I think what happens is that you imagine you are sounding much closer to the people that you would most love to emulate. From outside you hear all the other ingredients that make you sound the way you really sound. You can hear the people that you emulate, but you also hear other forces that make you . . . an individual voice.

Specifically, did you hear non-Western elements in your playing that you hadn't consciously assimilated?

I think I heard everything I'd ever imagined I had heard.

How were you able to absorb these elements into your work on the piano, with its very Western tonality?

The limitations of the instrument always strike you. The surprise is that, given the limitations, you begin to hear these other things that you thought you had digested invisibly before.

In the early stages of your career, you played with some traditional swing-type players. Did you ever feel a dissonance between your obligations to back them up and your own developing style at the piano?

No, I never felt that. I felt that I was privileged to play with them, because it seemed to me that they recognized something in me, and they *informed* me in a way that made me attempt to do things that I would later develop on my own. They gave me the information I needed. It was always a positive experience with Hot Lips Page and Johnny Hodges.

Is it still important for young musicians to develop themselves by playing the standard repertoire you played with those artists?

No, because times have changed now. You play your own repertoire now, and then you get validation of your own repertoire. If you are really into your own repertoire, the nature of that will make you go back and perhaps investigate the repertoire of that which preceded you.

How do musicians discover their own repertoire?

Well, the problem that I've been thinking about is that so many pianists repeat the mistakes of teachers who have themselves been molded by similar teachers, so that the attitude and the shaping of the style is with a language that is commonly accepted as being the piano language, rather than seeing the piano as just one instrument that makes a sound, on which you attempt to imitate the sound of nature.

For hours at a single sitting Taylor would rage at the keyboard, disintegrating tonality, traditional structure, and rhythmic convention with a piledriver assault.

Do you strive for sounds that are beyond the limits of the piano?

Well, of course, I understood that you could always hear the great people who inspired me on the piano sing when they played. Then if you hear the Kabuki or the Bunraku [schools of Japanese music and theater], if you hear the Mabuti or the Azuma, you understand that these are part of the voice that they didn't understand in the West. You understand the connection of Louis Armstrong to it, and the universality that the music *they* labeled jazz, which I might call something else, was in touch with. So now, for instance, we do use our voice in performance. The idea of limits can be better described as a process of better understanding the nature of what one's life work is about. One works always to move beyond the limits that one is very aware of one year. You work at it, and then a year later you've moved maybe an inch further. You remember John Coltrane's piece, called "The Inch Worm"? By *inching*, you make music your life's work.

So the process is as important as the product.

The process is the magic of it [*giggles delightedly*]! Yes!

You've described music-making as a spiritual experience. To what extent is it also a physical experience?

Well, I am a dancer. But playing the drums is a physical manifestation. Obviously, the Third World musicians—the Kabuki, the Azuma, the Bunraku—dance, sing, *and* play.

You've said that one reason electronic music doesn't attract you is that it is a non-physical music. Presumably the point is that the body comes more into play with the mechanics of the piano than with the keyboard triggers of the synthesizer. Do you still feel that division between body and spirit in electronic music?

See, that's the philosophy that the spiritual essence determines the extent of involvement of the body. If it should happen that I come into a position where I become perhaps more commercially successful, and those companies decide to lay these electronic instruments upon me, then I would have the chance to enact some of the things I believe about that but don't necessarily hear. But what can one say? I mean, the rock groups and the rhythm and blues groups use electronics today, and the best of these groups are magical.

Have you ever looked at synthesizers or tried them out?

No. In Paris, though, when I went through the Pompidou [Center], I spent some time with [composer and former jazz trombonist] George Lewis and David Wessell [director of pedagogy at IRCAM, the French electronic music research institute], who were both working for [composer Pierre] Boulez. David has been interested in what I do for a long time, and George is into electronic reproduction of human sounds. I had an opportunity to see what George was working on at the time, and I spoke with David. I'm looking forward to working with both of them sometime in the future.

You've worked with a very wide range of artists. How do you go about choosing and doing collaborations with these different people?

Well, there is a surrendering of the ego to try to enter into a holistic combination of spirits.

A process of adjustment?

You could say that.

What about the members of your band? How do you choose which musicians you'll be working with over an extended period?

You do not choose the people who play with you. They choose you. Maybe the most important aspect of being a leader is to understand the human aspect. We all know of talented people who might want to play, but the human quotient becomes an anomaly to the overall thrust.

In other words, you've come across many musicians whose music would have been compatible with yours, but who you couldn't work with for other reasons.

You could phrase it that way.

You've had to deal with a problem that most artists never confront, which is to get very long performances onto LP discs. You've had to release many package albums, sometimes with six sides devoted to performances of a single uninterrupted piece. This means five interruptions.

Oh, sure, that's a problem, but it's a problem that can be dealt with. Then there's the artificiality of recording. But Miles Davis did it, Duke Ellington did it, so our job is to do it in terms of all that we bring. It may be in excess of what they brought, but naturally it would be, because it comes from the riches that they gave us. I'm contemplating certain new things now—being able to play a complete musical thought in two minutes. It's a challenge that must be met.

Because of the process, or because of the commercial pressures?

The process is the magic. If you understand the higher magic, and all of the commercial entities that one deals with, they are two separate things until one understands that one does not control the reality under which one pays the mortgage of the house. Then one can deal with all that in most affable terms.

And, again, that is part of the process.

Yes! That becomes a part of the process. The difference is that when one is young, one is emotionally enraged because one sees the inequity of justice being perhaps the *ice*, with the *just* as the prefix.

You learn to adapt.

It isn't even about adapting, *i.e.*, compromising. It's about knowing that one has a spiritual opportunity to express oneself, as opposed to the methodical process of doing a job.

Are you interested in exploring what some people might perceive as a more consonant style of playing?

But I've always *loved* Billie Holiday! And I've always been trying to be able to make that one note sing!

Your piano lines sing to a more jarring effect than most listeners are used to, though. When an artist on the ECM label, for instance, might play a melody line in single notes, you often play your melodies in minor seconds, which many people would recognize as dissonance.

No comment on ECM [*laughs*]—no, that was a joke. The point is that I have recorded very clear pieces that would be called ballads, but because of my history, they're simply not heard as that.

Yet after listening to much of your work, I get a reflective feeling that isn't dissimilar from the feeling induced by certain ECM artists, which seems surprising because of the constant activity in your playing. Why have you apparently rejected static and long sustained sounds in favor of busier lines and flurries of notes?

I know that one's conception of what one does becomes enriched the more that one does it. One may think at a certain time in one's life that vertical structure is stationary within the boundaries of the weight applied by the piling of tones upon one another, but as one grows one sees those innards breaking apart and standing independent of the verticalism.

Early in your career you did play blues progressions with vertical chord structures. Why doesn't that structure work for you now?

What happens is that one adds to one's experience. All work is built upon the continuing aesthetic experience. One adds to the body of the work; the forms change in themselves by themselves.

Do you find that trained pianists and teachers have trouble comprehending what you do because your technique is so far outside their tradition?

Well, the other thing is that most piano teachers would appear to lack courage, because I don't hear that from them.

Have you taught many students yourself?

Very few, actually. I rather shy away from teaching pianists, because the piano to me is in itself an orchestra.

You've talked in the past about Western tradition representing a separation of the musical process and the intellectual perception of that process. Today you also spoke about the intellectual phenomenon of perceiving unanticipated elements upon listening to your own records. So you see a similarity somehow between recording and notating music?

See, it is an intellectual process to understand that there was that separation on my records. But when you're doing what it is to record, you do the best you can, although you are forced into an artificial environment in the recording studio. The intellectual doesn't have anything to do with it; the weight of what you respond to is one of the prime forces. The emotional fact of all that makes human beings human beings. My contention is that the emotional thoughts are the basic determinant, and the intellectual selective thought process determines which aspects you have chosen from the world view. The blood of my family does not encompass only one thing; it encompasses maybe three or four different cultural manifestations.

So from the very beginning you saw that there were many cultural paths open to you?

As an only child, brought up in a special, *i.e.*, precious way, I was not aware of anything except what I was allowed to do. At that point one is dealing with the opportunity that the immediate environment of home allows one to do. As one begins to venture forth, it's at that point that you discover how to let the self-protective armament, which could be translated as ego, protect yourself.

If that ego compels some musicians to struggle to master conventional modes of musical expression in order to win recognition through competition with their peers, then your music seems extremely free of ego.

Well, since I was involved in track, basketball, softball, and baseball, I've always been competitive. But when one gets older, one understands that for all the grace of the gymnasts, or of Willie Mays or Joe DiMaggio, athletes usually leave their careers behind them at 35. The truly great poets are maybe reaching their first period of greatness at 35. That's how Lena Horne, approaching 70, is for me far greater now than ever. [Bandleader/composer] Gil Evans, to me, has continued to develop.

What bridges these two worlds—the athletic world of youth, and the poetic world that emerges later in life?

I appreciate the athletic world, but the world of poetry is another level of human development. Young gymnasts can inspire, but great poets can really excite.

You were working on a book at one point, titled Mysteries. *How is that going?*

That's probably turning out to be a life work. A lot that I have written is an attempt to analyze the cultural process that gives birth to the individual art. Other statements I would align side by side with musical instruments, the sources of musical inspiration, but they may be directed to questions of human experiences as such.

You've noted that Mysteries *will focus specifically on the phenomenon of black music in America. What is the greatest misconception that white America still has about black music?*

Ignorance of the magic of rhythm.

Can this eventually be rectified? Or is there a permanent misunderstanding?

[*Smiles.*] One likes to be . . . optimistic.

Back to the Fountain

60. RANDY WESTON

Born: April 6, 1926, Brooklyn, New York

I n his music and appearance, Randy Weston is a giant. At nearly six feet and eight inches in height, he towers over the piano, with a stretch in his hands capable of spanning sixteen notes on the keyboard. The music he makes is vast as well—bigger in some ways than jazz itself. It sprawls beyond the familiar borders and beckons back toward a wellspring that most of his peers have forgotten, in the African cultures from which the blues was born.

More than just echo African elements, Weston has devoted most of his career to bringing them back to the heart of his own performance as well as jazz in general. In his embrace Weston gathers indigenous instrumentation—not only percussion, but strings and wind—and forms that antedate even the earliest jazz. He is not, however, an archivist, nor even an artist who finds comfort only in tradition. The key to Weston's importance is in his search beyond both past and present, for a new language that honors forgotten ancestors and today's innovators. His performances are timeless because he is pushing toward a time that has yet to arrive, when faraway African and immediate American aspects of improvisation will find their common ground.

He got a good head start on his mission as a kid in Brooklyn. His home was shelter in a rough neighborhood; there he read books on African culture collected by his father, Frank Edward Weston, a Panamanian-born barber of Jamaican lineage and an enthusiastic student of Pan-African history. Once a week he would emerge with his mother to absorb the primal holy energies of gospel church services. His father pushed Randy into three years of classical piano lessons, an experience that the young student resisted. Even in high school, with Max Roach, Duke Jordan, and Ray Copeland among his classmates, Weston maintained a casual interest at best in music. His taste in jazz was good but conventional—Ellington, Basie, the big bands—and not, in any event, that fervent.

After graduation, during his domestic military service, Weston started spending down time in the clubs along 52nd Street in Manhattan. The unprecedented abundance of piano talent there couldn't help but kindle a response, as Weston attended performances by Art Tatum, Willie "the Lion" Smith, Herbie Nichols, Red Garland, Elmo Hope . . .

. . . and Monk, playing piano at a Coleman Hawkins date. Here, at last, was an approach to the piano that spoke strongly to Weston. The two pianists soon became acquainted, and Weston began hanging out at Monk's house, listening to him play for hours at a time. For two years, from 1947 through '49, they had an almost Zen-like master/pupil relationship; Weston absorbed all that he could from Monk, stirring it into the appreciation of older forms that his father had already passed down. This process was almost entirely silent and internal, facilitated through only minimal contact with the keyboard.

Finally, at age 23, Weston felt ready to step out and start playing in public. He kept his day jobs at first, which included managing a luncheonette that his father had opened, and also took classes in theory and composition at the Parkway Music Institute. Performance, however, grew more important in his life. His first steady gig was with Bull Moose Jackson, a gut-bucket rhythm-and-blues shouter and saxophonist; Connie Kay, later of the exquisitely tasteful Modern Jazz Quartet, was the unlikely drummer in the band.

Weston's solo career traces to an encounter with producer Marshall Stearns in the early fifties. Stearns was running the jazz program at Music Inn, a club about two miles down the road from the Windsor Mountain School at Lenox, Massachusetts, where Weston had taken a summer job as a cook. Their meeting led to a trio gig for Weston at Music Inn over eight consecutive summers. Far from the club district, in the rolling Berkshires, Weston began to build a following. One early fan was Bill Grauer, president of the Riverside label, who hired Weston to work in the company mailroom and, in 1954, put him in the studio to make his recording debut with an album of Cole Porter songs. When Weston was selected best new pianist in the 1955 *Down Beat* Critics Poll, he was able to give notice in the mailroom and commit full-time to the piano.

As his career grew over the next few years, Weston took steps to pursue his interest in African music. He visited there for the first time in 1961 as part of a tour to Lagos, Nigeria, sponsored by the American Society of African Culture; on his return to the States Weston commemorated the event by composing an ambitious multi-movement work, *Uhuru Afrika*. Since then he has visited the continent numerous times: During a short return trip to Nigeria in 1963 he worked with future Afro-beat superstar Fela Kuti, and in 1967 Weston and his family moved to Rabat, Morocco, where he eagerly introduced jazz to village musicians while learning as well from their traditions. In 1974 he returned to New York and, after a triumphant appearance at the Montreux Jazz Festival, began investigating the possibilities of solo piano performance while continuing to write for and perform with large ensembles and trios.

When working solo Weston reflects a compelling mixture of experimentation, awareness of tradition, and deep feeling. A poetic current flows through his improvisations, to convey an almost pictorial quality. When he reiterates the theme from "Over There" throughout his performance of "Where," on the 1991 solo piano album *Marrakech in the Cool of the Evening*, the effect is not so much hu-

Randy Weston's performances are timeless because he is pushing toward a time that has yet to arrive.

morous as mournful, similar to the discordant trumpet fanfare that recurs throughout Charles Ives' *The Unanswered Question*.

On the same album we hear a superb example of Weston's ability to create a thoroughly contemporary interpretation of period-specific, older material. "The Jitterbug Waltz," as played by Weston, recalls Monk far more than its author, Fats Waller, especially in reharmonization of the descending theme as a cascade of major thirds over a stark and stumbling left-hand part. Each time he plays the theme, he staggers the cross-rhythms in different ways, evoking the skip of a limping rabbit, or the tumbling of a stream, or even, for a moment, Waller's own ornamentation. Like very few other pianists, Weston can connect with the spirits that tie superficially disparate schools of jazz together, and offer an exciting bit of enlightenment in demonstrating that connection.

Weston's worldliness guides his ensemble playing as well. "Tangier Bay," from the 1995 album *African Rhythms*, opens with a Monk-like, free-tempo piano extemporization over Alex Blake's bowed bass and some atmospheric cymbal work from Billy Higgins. After Weston floats this intro up to a filmy finish at the top of the keyboard, the band lays down an Afro/Latin groove, behind which Weston switches between evocative chords, bitonal counter-figures, and bits of montuño. His solo begins with an idiomatic Latin between-the-beats motif, but then moves to a faster line placed on the beat in more straight-ahead jazz fashion. Toward the end of the first verse Weston switches back to Latin phrasing, then continues alternating between the two up to the bridge. There, he jumps full-bore into Monkish dissonances for four bars, slips back to a Latin feel for the next four, tries some Arabic modalities over a growling open fifth in the left hand for four bars after that . . . and continues to mix diverse flavors in equally precise measurements through the rest of the solo, all without losing any sense of unity.

Weston's great contribution has been to demonstrate how to remove Monk's pointed, stark sound from contexts where it might be critiqued as short of the European standards of tone and execution, and transfer it to a neo-African setting that fully justifies Monk's aesthetic. On "Anu Anu," from the 1998 album *Khepera*, Weston improvises a line entirely in the bass range, over a sensuous 3/4 pattern laid down by African and American percussion. Beginning with an extended triplet rhythm, it flows down to a tonic cadence on the third bar, then wanders through a forest of rainstick and other ambient sounds, along a path carved from exotic modal material. Despite his deviation from the blues pentatonic scale, Weston saturates this brief solo with blues feeling through his adaptation of Monk's technique and phrasing; the results make obvious the bridge between continents and traditions.

When playing in more of a jazz style, with less emphasis on African modalities, Weston still often enjoys expressing himself in the lower range of the keyboard. His unaccompanied performance "African Village Bedford-Stuyvesant 1," from the 1991 double-album *The Spirits of Our Ancestors*, is essentially a swinging blues, with the right hand never rising higher than the midrange (except for one prickly dissonance at the end of the piece). The left hand sticks mainly to an eighth-note walk, at times sinking to the bottom notes on the 96-key Bösendorfer Imperial Grand. The rumble of these lowest notes doubtless appeals to Weston's fascination with blurring the line between percussive effects and tonality.

Of course Weston also made the entire keyboard his playground. On "African Cookbook," a 6/8 burner from *The Spirits of Our Ancestors*, he carves a rugged solo through the upper midrange, beginning with some parallel triads and moving into a solo built on repetitions of the dominant and tonic interspersed with quartal lines broken into polyrhythmic motifs, a dissonant interlude in the bass, and a final ascension to the upper range that ends unexpectedly with alternating two-handed clusters, as jarring as an alarm clock. The free structure, parked on a minor I chord, allows Weston to develop his ideas independent of chord changes, a discipline at which he has few equals.

In a similar one-chord solo, during the title cut from *Tanjah*, recorded with a big band in 1973, Weston plays over a propulsive percussion section. He states his theme emphatically, with neat call-and-response subdivisions; he highlights the structure with punchy cadences every two or four bars, often on the tonic. Thumping open fifths—anchored on the fifth above the root—bring this tidy extemporization to an end, and reaffirm the extent to which an ensemble sensibility guides Weston even during his solo spot. This willingness to use improvisation to strengthen the rhythmic foundation of the groove reflects another African aspect of Weston's holistic approach.

61. MAL WALDRON

Born: August 16, 1926, New York, New York

I t is impossible to listen to Mal Waldron without coming eye-to-eye with the spirit of Thelonious Monk. Many pianists have learned from Monk's revolutionary style—its angles and silences, its awkward grace. None have so faithfully replicated his sound as Waldron. So close is his tone, his artful clinkers, and his pacing that, in fact, Waldron can be accused of being one of the most derivative of all the major jazz pianists—or at least the most derivative among those who don't position themselves specifically as guardians of stride, bebop, or some other sanctified style.

It's an especially touchy issue with Monk, who created his sound specifically to avoid sounding like everyone else. He was the living symbol of creative courage, with a dedication to achieving something new that was greater than the doubt kindled by critical derision. The same question vexes blues guitarists today: Can anyone who sounds nearly identical to B. B. King or Stevie Ray Vaughan be taken seriously as an original artist?

In Waldron's case, the answer is yes. As Dick Wellstood had done with the old-guard stride pianists, Waldron developed an original voice on the foundation of Monk. The closer you looked into his music, the more the differences became apparent, in Waldron's loosely swinging phrasing and distinctive bluesy feel. Note repetition became a trademark of sorts, with solos often stalled on a single key that he might hit repeatedly for an entire chorus or two. You could even argue that he succeeded better than his mentor in homogenizing the more jagged elements of his playing; where some of Monk's devices stand out as puzzling eccentricities even today, Waldron boiled them down into a coherent, and often moving, style of his own.

Piano was originally Waldron's second instrument. Though he began classical piano lessons at the age of ten in Queens, he put most of his energy into learning to play alto saxophone. He pursued a music degree at Queens College, where he studied composition with the distinguished teacher Karol Rathaus. Shortly after that, Waldron wandered into a club and had his first live exposure to Charlie Parker. That's all it took to convince him to sell his horn and spend more time at the keyboard.

In 1950 he played his first professional job, with saxophonist Ike Quebec and drummer Kansas Fields at Café Society. Much of his work over the next few years was in borderline R&B bands, with artists like Quebec and "Big Nick" Nicholas; he supplemented his income by playing demo recordings for aspiring songwriters. But he also spent a lot of time listening to other pianists, in particular Bud Powell and Monk. This combination of influences prepared him well for an affiliation with Charles Mingus, which began in 1954. Waldron was a regular participant in the bassist's Jazz Workshop, and played with him two consecutive years, 1955 and '56, at the Newport Jazz Festival. Work picked up quickly: Through a series of sessions he played for artists on the Prestige label, he picked up a gig to remember, as accompanist for Billie Holiday. He played behind her on her last appearances, and came away with as many new insights into phrasing and silences as he had picked up from Mingus and Monk.

He was a fully formed artist by this point, with a very personal improvisational method based largely on repetition and variation. Listen to "Aggression," from the Eric Dolphy album *Live at the Five Spot*, recorded in 1961, on which Waldron takes a call-and-response he had used behind a Dolphy solo, plays it a number of times with slight changes, and then uses the rhythm of the figure to build a right-hand solo driven by more variations on gradually accelerating patterns and a slow movement up the keyboard. A few boppish runs, with modal characteristics, serve only to tie sections of his solo together; far more predominant through the performance is his fixation with turning the minimal figure over and over, inside out, before finally ending on an emphatic dominant note.

Waldron's improvisations have a fragmented quality; one notices the pieces and connections within a line rather than the integrity of the line itself. On *Where?*, Ron Carter's debut album as a leader, Waldron plays somewhat agitated fills behind solos by Carter and Dolphy, with nervous rapid repetitions of chords that nudge against the changes. In his own solo the pianist opens with a syncopated five-note motif, moves it around a narrow range, tentatively stretches it into a longer statement. Then, when he hits the one-chord bridge, Waldron breaks his line down again, shrinking it eventually to edgy repetitions of single notes—a reduction of his earlier accompanimental rhythm concept. His performance does swing, but it speaks from shadows, cryptic and uneasy. Later on the same album, Waldron plays a solo on the Randy Weston tune "Saucer Eyes" that shrinks as it goes along, with note choices narrowing and the line breaking into ever smaller components until one long string of single notes leads to a bass solo.

Within standard song structure, Waldron didn't cling quite so firmly to this device, though it still served as a self-imposed limitation of sorts. His solo on "Like Someone in Love," from the same Dolphy album, has plenty of linear movement, but where the trajectory of a line might lead more mainstream pianists down Bud Powell-like paths through the changes, Waldron interrupts the movement to fall back on one or another stark repetition—an interval of a third played again and again, or an irregular and hesitant descending figure later on. His phrasing acknowledges the rhythm, but rather than play off of it, he creates a self-contained rhythmic structure, filled with unexpected rests and spaces. It's almost an anti-groove—and, on those terms, a beautiful alternative to more predictable formulas for swinging.

Even more minimalist was Waldron's solo on his own tune, "Splidium-Dow," from the 1958 *Trio* album, in which gravity seems to pull him back from a bluesy/boppish first chorus into a minor seventh riff and, finally, to an obsessive reiteration of the tonic note on the third chorus. On subsequent verses he breaks away to hang on the seventh again, and then the flatted fifth, only to find his way back, time after time, to that tonic note. On this performance, and many others, Waldron hammers the root note on the first beat after the final bar to end his solo, as if glad to have put the effort behind him. Listen as well to "Boo," recorded in 1969 for *Free at Last*, the oldest album in the ECM catalog: Though tenacious in his repetition of a single rhythmic motif throughout his solo up to the point where the tempo eases into an extended coda, he moves that figure through a limited series of positions on the keyboard, while concentrating on the placement and attack of his left hand as the true focus of his improvisation. Until a bass note, which he hammers like a blacksmith, grabs your ears, you might not notice just how much development is going on here.

Perhaps this aspect of Waldron's style stems from his relative discomfort with linear improvisation at quick tempos. "Get Happy," on *Trio*, is filled with bracing ideas, but one has the sense that Waldron is running at full speed just to keep up with bassist Addison Farmer and drummer Kenny Dennis. There are places where he falters in the middle of a phrase, out of breath. Only when he slows down into a triplet figure or lapses into note repetition does he get back in sync.

Waldron's abstract temperament dovetailed well with the aggressive character of Mingus's music. His performance on "Pithecanthropus Erectus" in 1956 covers a broad expressive range. In ensemble passages, with saxophonists Jackie McLean and J. R. Montrose whipping the band into a series of frenzied climaxes, Waldron pounds against the relentless bass pulse. In his own solo, however, he returns to his usual approach with a quarter-note repeated motif. Mingus immediately picks up on it, plucking it back and pushing Waldron forward. Throughout this solo the bassist tracks the piano solo; his quick answers and echoes trigger a push and pull of opposite energies, with Waldron laying back and Mingus impatiently prodding him. Even at the minimal volume at which they play, the electricity between them can't be missed.

In 1965 Waldron began a long period of expatriate life, living first in Paris, then moving to Munich after two years. Though a frequent visitor to the States, he continues to keep his distance—and, from the broader view, stand revealed with greater clarity than ever as a true original.

62. MUHAL RICHARD ABRAMS

Born: September 19, 1930, Chicago, Illinois

More than an inventive multi-instrumentalist—piano is only the foremost of his many musical tools—Muhal Richard Abrams is a teacher, through hands-on work and by his own example. With none of the showmanship that made Sun Ra impossible to ignore, and none of the major-label connections that helped make John Coltrane and Ornette Coleman giants in their time, Abrams worked closer to the street. Chicago was his territory in the beginning: His spirit fills not just the streets of his hometown, but the classrooms and clubs, and all the havens of experimental jazz throughout the world.

Abrams—the "Muhal" sobriquet came later, an honorific meaning "teacher"—had no trouble getting into music in Chicago during the forties. The piano attracted him, particularly the East Coast stride of James P. Johnson and the local boogie-woogie beats of Meade "Lux" Lewis, Pete Johnson, and Albert Ammons. Yet he didn't get seriously into playing until he was 17 years old. At that point he began four years worth of indifferent piano study. Before losing interest completely in these drills, Abrams was already writing original material, beginning in 1950 when he created his first arrangements for the King Fleming band.

Working pretty much within the bebop idiom, Abrams spent several years playing gigs and writing for local talent. By 1955, as the once adventurous style began losing its exploratory edge, he began his quest for new methods of improvisation as an important member of MJT+3. For three years this group served as a workshop for Abrams's emerging artistry; when not putting their catalog together and stretching his own playing beyond the borders of convention, he pored over music theory textbooks by Joseph Schillinger and Paul Hindemith and, paradoxically, the old-school exhibitionistic virtuosity of Art Tatum. These ingredients came together as the basis for Abrams's influential activities in the sixties.

With fellow pianist Jodie Christian and saxophonist Eddie Harris, Abrams put together the Experimental Band. More important was the Association for the Advancement of Creative Musicians (AACM), which he co-founded in 1965 as a support group primarily for black musicians who weren't afraid to break barriers. Politics and art played equal parts in this organization, as Abrams explained in an interview with the *Chicago Daily News*: "We had to form the AACM because of the basic nature of the music situation in this country. The people who decide what will be recorded are the business people, not the artists. It was, for us, a question of survival—black cultural survival."

These were revolutionary sentiments, decades ahead of their time. The music produced under the auspices of the AACM was equally far-sighted. But even while performing with and encouraging the Art Ensemble of Chicago, Anthony Braxton, Henry Threadgill, Lester Bowie, and other rising giants of avant-jazz, Abrams defied expectations by performing as well with Eddie "Lockjaw" Davis, Dexter Gordon, and Woody Herman, pillars of the postbop establishment. In 1977 he pulled the ultimate surprise by relocating to New York, where he has become as vital a figure as he had been in the Windy City.

The Abrams catalog is vast and diverse, ranging from duet interpolations with Anthony Braxton on Scott Joplin's "Maple Leaf Rag" to persuasive investigations of electronic synthesis. Solo piano, however, is the truest barometer of his personality as a performer. Abrams's "Young at Heart" (an original improvisation, not the "fairy tales can come true . . ." confection), is a monument in the annals of solo piano. Recorded in 1969 and available on *Young at Heart/Wise in Time*, the piece rejects the large-form free structures of Cecil Taylor and instead follows a modular approach, with short "movements" strung together over a period of nearly half an hour. There are moments in which Abrams approximates Taylor's stiff-fingered, heavily pedaled, jabbing cascades, but these pass quickly and are followed by sections that nod toward stride, Impressionistic pentatonic runs, and other elements—even silences. Throughout this piece Abrams warms his vast sense of organization with a serene inquisitiveness. There are no seams in the fabric of "Young at Heart," only a river-like flow through landscapes as varied as forest followed by field, or mountain by ocean.

A jagged harmonic sense and a very flexible approach to rhythm tie "Young at Heart" together. Abrams makes use of his instrument's limited sound—tinny in the upper range, tubby in the bass—by pedaling sensitively and emphasizing fourths and suspensions, rather than traditional jazz voicings. He also downplays technical display, instead taking time to examine each idea that comes along: A snippet expands into a motif, a simple figure grows brilliant through repetition, like a sparkler in the night sky. For all its ambition, "Young at Heart" is easy to absorb and powerfully communicative.

The flip side of the same album, "Wise in Time," shows a comparable patience and caution in a setting of group improvisation. During much of this 22-minute performance, Abrams either plays simple, semi-repetitive figures, or nothing at all. There's little of the sense one has in a Cecil Taylor ensemble event, in which players sometimes seem to compete with each other—or with Taylor's keyboard eruptions. Abrams imposes himself less obtrusively, which allows for a more subtly interactive energy. Yet the music centers around his piano. Even when he's not playing, a space waits for his entrance, so that when Abrams does come in with a thematic ostinato to kick off his solo, the listener feels a kind of satisfaction with his arrival.

Allow one more comparison with Taylor, as this solo evolves: Rather than overwhelm his colleagues and leave percussionists scampering to keep up, Abrams integrates into the group, with a line that blossoms from a motivic statement into a busy, two-handed abstract flurry that's more like a rippling tide than a volcanic explosion. In fact, Abrams is more the ensemble player than Taylor, less the hair-raising virtuoso. In this contrast we can appreciate the genius that each possesses.

Where appropriate, of course, Abrams was fully capable of setting meter aside and improvising texturally rather than on the basis of note sequence. On the second track from Anthony Braxton's debut album *3 Compositions of New Jazz*—unnamable here, due to Braxton's use of diagrammatic titles—Abrams plays the highly abstract "head" with three horn players, then sustains a kaleidoscopic fury behind each player's frenetic improvisations. Here he embraces Taylor's methodology, in which two or more musicians create a singular improvisation through a kind of sympathetic obliviousness. Instead, his lightly-pedaled splatters and surges go beyond accompaniment to reflect or suggest directions; when violist Leroy Jenkins takes over after Leo Smith's blaring trumpet improvisation, Abrams switches from midrange swirls to thinner sheets of sound higher on the keys. Then when Braxton comes in on alto sax, the piano immediately changes again, this time to thumping polyrhythms in thick, bunched clusters. This is communication masked as incomprehension, filled with risks and rewards for player and listener.

In more conservative settings, Abrams utilizes an accessible, bop-derived melodic sense. On "Seesall," recorded in 1989 for his ambitious orchestral work titled *The Hearing Suite*, he plays a short but intriguing solo over a strong rhythm laid down by drummer Andrew Cyrille and bassist Fred Hopkins. The figure that opens this section seems to clash with the bass line's tonal center, but Abrams uses this dissonance as a device to follow into almost atonal territory. Though he escapes from the gravity of tonality, Abrams pulls a neat trick by doing so through use of familiar-sounding, blues-oriented devices. In just these few seconds, Abrams integrates the traditional and the adventurous, and reminds us of his ability to swing in the most traditional sense of the word.

63. ABDULLAH IBRAHIM

Born: October 9, 1934, Kensington, Cape Town, South Africa

The current of jazz flows through Abdullah Ibrahim's playing, but when channeled into the blood of South Africa a unique sound emerges—a sound that reinvigorates blues and jazz with the traditions from which they were born. For all the great artists who have called South Africa their home, it was Ibrahim and trumpeter Hugh Masakela who first made this connection clear to listeners as well as to their fellow musicians.

This was an invigorating message in the early sixties. For decades up to that point, jazz had been a somewhat insular art form; for all the fantastic variety it had achieved within its brief few decades, the music kept pointing back to African-American roots, with the emphasis on American. Whatever discussion there was about pre-American influences took place either in academic settings or among culturally enlightened blacks. It took this young pianist, with some help from one of the greatest icons in jazz, to set this discussion to a fresh and revealing new music.

Ibrahim was a perfect bearer for this message. His art was eclectic, partially because of his open nature, but largely because of the fact of his upbringing. Francis Davis, in his book *Outcats*, ran down a colorful list of styles that constituted the soundtrack of Ibrahim's youth in Cape Town, especially "the carnival music . . . the traditional 'colored music,' the Malayan strains, and the rural lament." Other elements included "West African ceremonial and popular rhythms, Moslem incantation, British military-band concord, gospel sanctimony and minstrel sanguinity, French Impressionism and modal reverie, Monkian dissonance, and Ellingtonian Cotton Club panache."

Ibrahim was known in those days by his birth name, Adolf Johannes Brand. His lineage was Basuto and Bushman, but daily life was vividly multicultural. He grew up singing in an AME church choir, which his mother accompanied on piano. She gave him his first lessons on the family piano when he was seven years old. It was easy for Brand to discover jazz, which became his touchstone among all the styles that surrounded him. He got his first jazz records from merchant sailors who vended their wares in dockside stalls. Brand was such a frequent customer that he soon picked up a nickname—"Dollar" Brand—that would stick with him for years to come.

Brand was 12 when he began playing gigs with a local dance band. In groups such as the Tuxedo Slickers and the Streamline Brothers, he began toning down his early interest in boogie-woogie and tuning into the subtleties of Duke Ellington's arrangements. In 1959 he and Masakela joined forces in a group called the Jazz Epistles. Unlike his earlier band, the Epistles mixed original compositions into a book that included works by Ellington, Thelonious Monk, and other composers. They quickly built up a following, not just in South Africa but throughout Europe as well, which made it easier for Brand and his wife to settle in Zurich, Switzerland, to begin a three-year engagement at the Café Tropicana in 1962.

It was at that gig that Brand met Duke Ellington. Overwhelmed by his idol's charisma and touched by his attentions, Brand accepted an invitation to record an album with Ellington himself as producer. That disc, fabulously titled *Ellington Presents the Dollar Brand Trio*, opened a number of doors toward greater exposure, through performances at the Antibes Jazz Festival in 1963 and, subsequently, at the Newport Jazz Festival. Within a few years he was well enough situated to cut his ties with South Africa, where the pressures of working under apartheid seemed to grow worse as he found greater success abroad, and move to New York City.

By this time Brand had embraced Islam and taken the name Abdullah Ibrahim. His activities in the States broadened to include a bit of acting, in a modest film shot in Denmark and titled *Portrait of an American Bushman*, as well as writing poetry, scoring for film, working against racism as a member of the African National Congress, and even performing at the piano with Ellington's orchestra. He guested on projects with Max Roach, Elvin Jones, Archie Shepp, and other outstanding jazz artists. Most important, he recorded prolifically as a pianist, leading a series of groups and establishing himself as a performer of enduring distinction.

Ibrahim's approach to rhythm, and specifically to playing within a rhythm section, differs markedly from the idiomatic approaches developed in America. On "Chisa," for example, from the 1989 album *African River*, he parts ways with postbop pianists who interact with the drums and a walking bass; instead, he maintains the central motif of the tune with slight variations throughout the performance. The droning tonic never goes away; the chords never thicken beyond soulful minor sevenths. The horn players are free to blow bluesy solos over this foundation, but Ibrahim keeps his hands deep in African soil.

This marriage of jazz and African elements makes it possible for simple harmonies to convey great emotional potency. In the opening section of "Nisa," from Ibrahim's soundtrack for *No Fear, No*

Die, his accompaniment to a Buster Williams bass solo expands on a I–IV pattern—again, while sustaining a tonic drone—with delicate clusters and relatively unadorned harmonies that shift from a haunting, miniature feel to earthy blues. His ability to underscore someone else's solos is another reflection of Ibrahim's similarity in many ways to Ellington.

The power of this simplicity is more apparent in Ibrahim's solo piano work. His 1992 album *Desert Flowers* offers several examples of its somber beauty. Most of these unaccompanied performances feature original material, so it's especially instructive to look at his approach to standard material. His treatment of "Come Sunday" is a hushed masterpiece, stripped of excess and adornment so that the tune's architecture stands clear. Its opening moments actually evoke Bill Evans, in its brief echo of "Peace Piece." But as Duke Ellington's theme materializes slowly, Ibrahim's vision clarifies. He articulates the chordal movement as if each step were a prayer—which, of course, is appropriate to the piece. But Ibrahim, in this brief recitation of two verses, the bridge, and a final verse, brings us face to face with their solemn majesty; his intention is free of ego, and so the eloquence of Ellington still speaks that much more deeply through him.

64. McCOY TYNER

Born: December 11, 1938, West Philadelphia, Pennsylvania

The evolution of McCoy Tyner has had repercussions far beyond his own experience. The growth that we hear from his earliest recordings through and beyond his work with John Coltrane is actually a process of translation, as the young pianist searched for and found a way to adapt elements of modern jazz to the keyboard. And in learning to rebuild his own improvisatory language under Coltrane's influence, he became an ideal student: Unafraid of new ideas, he achieved something rather like enlightenment.

It is easy to follow Tyner on his mission. He began as a talented but derivative player; like many pianists his age, he emulated Bud Powell, with boppish single lines in his right hand and light comps in the left. His first exposure to Coltrane changed all that. Though they were playing standards and original tunes with fairly traditional structures, the saxophonist kept pushing against convention, letting his lines spill out of meter rather than play off the beat. Listening carefully, Tyner developed a new harmonic sense, based on simple triads juxtaposed in ways that avoided the tendency of more familiar chords to lead through a progression toward resolution on the tonic.

But Coltrane moved further still, toward greater levels of abstraction that would dissolve the whole idea of song structure. Again, Tyner paid attention. As his leader's solos challenged the premise of tonality, the pianist began replacing the triad, which connoted major or minor keys through its articulation of the third, with harmonies based on fourths. He understood that Coltrane needed more intensity and, perhaps paradoxically, more ambiguity from his band. By giving it to him, Tyner became an ideal accompanist, and a better artist as well.

His strength was evident in his quiet demeanor. The oldest of three children, he was a thoughtful child whose interest in spiritual issues led to his conversion to Islam at age 18. His musical gifts were evident much earlier on. Encouraged by his mother, Beatrice, he sang in the Sulzberger Junior High School choir. When he was 13 years old, he began taking piano lessons at the West Philadelphia Music School; for about a year he practiced at any one of three neighbors' homes, until his mother had saved up enough money from her work as a beautician to buy him a spinet piano. Partly because of doubts from his father about pursuing music as a profession, Tyner and his mother set it up at her beauty parlor.

Fate had placed him in a part of town that was teeming with talent. His buddies included pianist Bobby Timmons, saxophonist Archie Shepp, trumpeter Lee Morgan, and bassist Reggie Workman, each one a future jazz headliner. It became their regular routine to hang out at the beauty parlor, talking about music and jamming out ideas. At 15 he formed his first group, a septet with an R&B orientation.

Jazz, however, was Tyner's first love. Along with theory lessons at the Granoff School of Music, he studied the piano styles of Art Tatum, Thelonious Monk, and Bud Powell. When Powell actually moved into his neighborhood, they became acquainted, and young McCoy got to learn from him directly. During summer vacations, he played some of his first professional jobs, with Lee Morgan and saxophonist Paul Jeffries, in Atlantic City.

By this time, the young pianist had already crossed paths with Coltrane. They met when Tyner was 17 as the saxophonist, who was in town to visit his mother, heard him working with a mutual acquaintance, trumpeter Calvin Massey, at a place called the Red Rooster. They spent some time talking, and played two local jobs together. Coltrane was writing "Giant Steps" then, and they spent time polishing it at the home of another friend and future colleague, bassist Jimmy Garrison. Three years later, Coltrane recorded a Tyner composition, "The Believer." But neither was ready to join the other, as Coltrane was in recovery and Tyner was still in high school. He would wait until after graduation in 1959 before committing to music full-time.

At that point he accepted an invitation from saxophonist Benny Golson to join him for a job out at the Jazz Workshop in San Francisco. Things worked out well there, so Golson and trumpeter Art Farmer kept him on board as they formed their Jazztet and cut the soul/bop classic "Killer Joe." Coltrane, meanwhile, was having trouble getting what he wanted from his pianist, Steve Kuhn. Right after letting him go, he asked Tyner to take his place. It was 1960.

Over the next five years, with Elvin Jones on drums and, eventually, Garrison on bass, the Coltrane quartet would turn the practice of jazz inside out. From song form they would move to free improvisation; rhythm itself, the heartbeat of jazz, would change from an articulated swing to a flow of nonmetrical beats, with the saxophone blowing over what sounded to some like three sidemen playing independently—a non-rhythm section.

By the time they were recording albums like *Africa Brass* and *A Love Supreme*, the quartet had moved to a place where Tyner was starting to feel uncomfortable. He had stretched himself into harmonic territory few other pianists had dreamed of exploring, and dug into the mystery of accompanying without reliance on rhythm patterns or even tonal reference. But that was as far as he would go; although transformed by his work with Coltrane, Tyner was ready to cede the piano chair to John's wife Alice Coltrane and get on with his own work.

Many years have passed since his departure from the band and Coltrane's passing from the scene. There were fallow periods, when Tyner had to drive a taxi to make ends meet or take unlikely gigs with performers like Ike and Tina Turner. Generally, though, work has been steady, and Tyner has even tried out a few new tricks with Latin music, big bands, and solo recitals. But little of what he has done on his own reflects the kind of epiphany that he experienced during his apprentice years.

With Coltrane on their historic performance of "My Favorite Things," Tyner showed how a soloist could work with, rather than against, time: A two-chord motif, repeating in his left hand, was his focus. Rather than distract from its hypnotic effect with fiery lines, he put a series of simple patterns together in the upper midrange of the keyboard. Now and then he reduced his right hand to an extension of the chordal pattern, which he repeated against Elvin Jones's backbeat-allergic rhythms.

There was adventure and anticipation in this solo, and in much of what would follow in the quartet's catalog. Unfortunately, one of the lessons of their work was that free improvisation depends greatly on who is in the band. On his version of the Coltrane tune "Naima," recorded for *Echoes of a Friend* after the saxophonist's death, Tyner tries, with only limited success, to transpose the dynamic of the quartet to a solo setting. He runs through a stupendous range of volumes, shows much more hand independence than he allowed himself in his first few years with Coltrane, and strains against the form of the tune, with thunderous fifths prowling through the bass, octave tremolos sparkling high overhead, and one spectacular glissando slashing across the keys into a sudden, delicate open fifth. It is about as strong a performance as Tyner would turn in on his own, yet it is somehow not completely convincing.

True, there are numerous high points in his post-Coltrane catalog; the best of these are usually when Tyner pushes his sound into the sometimes inhospitable contours of a standard tune. His performance of "What Is This Thing Called Love?" offers an example: Recorded with saxophonist Joe Henderson, bassist Ron Carter, and drummer Al Foster for the 1991 album *New York Reunion*, it features a piano solo that begins with two verses played in ear-bending clashes of tonality, with a skipping eighth-note touch and deep tidal chord shifts in the left hand. There's no denying the drama of his playing—but neither can the listener ignore the sense of repetitiveness, especially in the recycling of certain fragments and figures, after several choruses. And on his 1988 solo album *Revelations*, Tyner overwhelms "How Deep is the Ocean" with incendiary tremolos and surging octaves; the irregular rhythms outlined by his left hand are battered by massive booms in the low bass and, at several points, destabilized by diminished fifths pounded out in off-beat octaves. It's unmistakably Tyner, in its technical devices and thrilling intensity, yet it also offers no surprises and few insights into the song itself.

Tyner's accomplishment is gigantic. Very few pianists have contributed as much to the language of modern jazz, and none has developed a style so distinctive; even the untrained ear can identify it after a second or two. Yet this style arrived early, and in the decades that have followed Tyner has almost been its prisoner. Like Tatum, he consistently astonishes within the limits of his own particular virtuosity; unlike Monk, his performances celebrate that virtuosity with little or no concern over what material is being played.

In the final reckoning, as surely as his first performances borrowed from Powell and Monk, Tyner is still chasing after Trane. Those five years with the god of modern saxophone added up to a remarkable journey, which ended far too long ago.

65. DON PULLEN

Born: December 25, 1941, Roanoke, Virginia
Died: April 22, 1995, East Orange, New Jersey

I t was a unique sound, drawn from familiar sources but molded into a harmonious blend of mainstream, modern, and avant-garde, with strong African overtones. Don Pullen's style bore a superficial resemblance to that of McCoy Tyner and his imitators, but at deeper levels the similarities broke down, and Pullen stood alone as a player of under-appreciated power and individuality.

The secret was in his ability to segue from one approach to another in his improvisations, keeping each element pure, compromising nothing, weaving it into a tapestry splashed in clashing colors yet united by the imprint of its creator. Only artists with high standards and imposing will can pull this off; Pullen was one of that breed.

There was nothing surprising in his upbringing. As with so many musicians, Pullen was raised by people who loved music; his grandfather, a preacher, loved to sing, as did several of his uncles. He took piano lessons, played in church, gigged around Roanoke with dance bands. For a while he attended Johnson C. Smith University, then transferred to Jocelyn T. Smith University in North Carolina as a premed student, with some music courses and a steady gig as a restaurant pianist thrown in to keep things interesting. It took just one two-week trip to Chicago, where he met and studied with Muhal Richard Abrams, to pull Pullen out of the classroom and send him on his way to New York.

He got there in 1964 and hooked up with some of the city's more outside improvisers, including Albert Ayler, Sunny Murray, and Giuseppe Logan. But already Pullen was thwarting expectations: When not taking part in ensemble improvisations that earned him premature comparisons to Cecil Taylor, he was backing Big Maybelle and other blues belters as house organist at the Fantasy East in Queens. Even then, Pullen's range was wide; already, he was absorbing from everything he heard and finding ways to make it all fit together.

Pullen had his creative coming of age as the last pianist to work with Charles Mingus. Their affiliation began in 1973 and lasted for two years, during which the pianist formed a long-term creative relationship with saxophonist George Adams and claimed his place among the real innovators on his instrument.

For a taste of his handiwork with the tempestuous bassist, check out *Mingus at Carnegie Hall*, recorded early in 1974. Pullen's backup throughout the long jam on "Perdido" feels always on the verge of exploding. After hanging out in a boppish space, he plunges into atonal whirls, stiff-fingered or fisted out-of-rhythm jabs, and other elemental effects. With soloists like Rahsaan Roland Kirk and Hamiett Bluiett roaring over this turmoil, Pullen has to listen carefully for balance; his switches from more conservative chording to abstract eruptions mirror, echo, and lead the horn players into appropriate directions.

As for his own solo, Pullen takes the first verse cautiously, comps a little restlessly on the bridge while nudging his solo into longer lines a little higher, then follows on the next verse with a few faster licks and some pointed eighth-note lines that push determinedly into very outside territory. By the verse after that Pullen is throwing licks all over the upper range. For relief, going into the fourth verse,

Don Pullen stood alone as a player of underappreciated power and individuality.

he pulls back into the familiar device of two-handed, Peterson-like chords—but only to lead into a finale in which, for the first time, his left hand abandons traditional comps and joins the right in a hailstorm of disconnected, atonal runs. He does remember to bring it home, though, with some more two-handed old-school chords to lead the band into the exit chorus.

When recording his own material in a group setting, Pullen projects that same sense of constricted energy pushing toward release. The labyrinthine structure of his tune "New Beginnings," recorded in 1988 and available on *The Best of Don Pullen: The Blue Note Years*, screws a tight lid on the space that the pianist allows himself for his improvisation. As a result, with bassist Gary Peacock and drummer Tony Williams subtly fanning the flames behind him, Pullen prowls through the chord changes, at first with a jaunty swing as he invents one intriguing line after another on the first couple of choruses. Then, following a ritard written into the tune as a kind of reorientation, he begins pushing against that lid, growing more atonal, dissolving his meticulous sixteenth-note runs into bold smears—making the jump from Pointillism to Pollock, in sound. The final, unaccompanied piano chord—an unadorned triad on the tonic—comments on the simple essence that underlies even the most vexing compositions.

This same restlessness pervaded most of Pullen's solo performances. Recorded in 1977, his trio performances of "Richard's Tune" and "Dialogue Between Malcolm and Betty," from the album *Montreux Concert*, opens with a long unaccompanied passage that's noteworthy for its application of traditional and avant-garde elements in pursuit of a highly focused improvisation. Pullen plays "Richard's Tune" with enormous authority from the start, as he articulates the Muhal Richard Abrams theme with a palpable sense of urgency; even in free time he pushes impatiently against the beat. He constantly shifts his harmonic language, spending most of his time in Tyner territory, with deep tremolos or quartal voicings, or in sudden storms of clusters and atonal scatterings. But he also throws in some mutated stride, and even a few moments of Gershwinesque romanticism. Pullen's fist-pounding barrages exceed Tyner's somewhat more lyrical approach to percussive effect, but while these episodes bring Cecil Taylor to mind, Pullen treats these techniques as one of a number of elements. His focus, as a result, is sectional, as opposed to Taylor's more encompassing perspective.

The solo intro to "Dialogue" is structured differently. From a very simple repeated motif, clearly conceived as a metaphor for conversation, Pullen follows a single line of development through ever more abstract and intense activity to a climactic series of eruptions—those quick, slashing slams, executed without pedal, that function as a trademark of sorts for Pullen. From this point, gently, he brings it down to a soothing chorded ostinato, which cues the somewhat tentative entrance of the percussionists—only to abruptly change direction again and begin an extended interaction with the rhythm instruments that alternates between delicate statements of the theme and staccato keyboard smashes before returning to the ostinato pattern that, this time, brings the rest of the band into the tune.

Pullen has no trouble fitting into a more narrow frame of reference. His solo on "Big Alice," from the 1977 album *Tomorrow's Promises*, cooks in a pot of pure funk. His left-hand comp faithfully emphasizes the Bo Diddley beat as he lays down a long and soulful line with his right hand in stinging straight eighth-notes. Single notes and chords are repeated as percussive sixteenth-note triplets, and sing-song references reflect the festive, playground vibe. Only briefly does Pullen swoop into some of his roller-coaster glisses, which function effectively as a device for contrast. In spirit, and in the precise divisions of his line, "Big Alice" is a bubbling delight.

In the years that ran from Mingus to his own early passing, Pullen performed with heroic energy on countless stages and in studios throughout the world. He and George Adams led their own quartet for ten years; at the same time Pullen began playing solo concerts. In his later years, while teaching at the Yellow Springs Institute in Chester Springs, Ohio, Pullen put together the African Brazilian Connection as a vehicle for cross-cultural exploration. He wrote as if racing to inform audiences on political as well as artistic levels, through ambitious works such as his *Malcolm X Suite*. Driven as much by a respect for the integrity of Third World cultures as by his own musical appetites, Pullen was just beginning to seek connection with Native American music when he succumbed to a two-year battle with lymphoma.

Improvisation as Revelation

KEITH JARRETT

Born May 8, 1945, Allentown, Pennsylvania

Scene One. Inside Louise M. Davies Symphony Hall, in a stark inner sanctum far beneath the airy modern auditorium, guest conductor Charles Wuorinen and a small group assembled from the San Francisco Symphony Orchestra are rehearsing Lou Harrison's *Piano Concerto*. Harrison wrote the piece for Keith Jarrett, who sits at the piano, waiting while the ensemble labors over one passage. Wuorinen stops them, takes them back to the beginning of a thorny phrase, tries it again. Jarrett listens from the bench. His posture is erect and alert. Though he sits motionless—perhaps *because* this unusually animated artist is so still—it's easy to sense that he wants to get on with playing this piece he knows so well. Outwardly he waits; inwardly he fidgets.

After a few minutes, Jarrett turns very slowly, eases off the bench, slips past the page turner, and tiptoes toward the edge of the stage. There, unnoticed by the musicians, he bends over a crumpled paper bag and quietly removes a small hand drum. Crouched now on his haunches, he raises the drum to his ear and taps it gently, once, twice. He pauses, then taps a few times more. Satisfied, he returns the drum to the bag, creeps back to the piano, and takes his place again, looking now like a man refreshed.

Scene Two. The following night, Jarrett, Wuorinen, and the ensemble perform Harrison's *Concerto* before a packed house. Jarrett sticks to the piano; no paper bags litter the glittering expanse of Davies Hall. Earlier, however, he played an original work, *Sacred Ground (For the American Indian)*, in which he led a chamber group from the keyboard and joined them in occasional percussive episodes—isolated taps, shakes, and scrapes on what some people would call primitive ethnic instruments.

Reviews would dismiss *Sacred Ground* as naïve, or simplistic, or just plain dull. The second piece on the program, Wayne Peterson's *Transformations* for chamber orchestra, was more enthusiastically received. *Transformations* prickled with the kinds of dissonances that audiences accept as modern. Critics, professional and armchair, therefore find it easy to applaud, since they are really applauding their own sophistication. Jarrett's work, on the other hand, didn't fit any of the categories listeners associate with contemporary music. The greater the puzzle, the more ambivalent the reaction of those who fail to crack it.

In his program notes, Jarrett anticipated this. "*Sacred Ground* is a musical attempt to reinstate function and context in the innocence available to us before the white man asserted himself in this country," he wrote. "I'm afraid that the people who think it is important to state that this is a piece in many very small sections of different tempos without ritardandos or complete stops, utilizing very simple scales and monotone phrases for the most part, miss the point and probably will also miss the piece."

Fortunately, there were members of the audience whose applause indicated an intuitive connection with *Sacred Ground*. Jarrett would argue that this is the proper level at which to respond to music of quality. As he made his bows before a rack of ancient bangers and clackers that dangled from a rack next to the piano, he seemed to be making a symbolic visual point: that sound, pure sound, resonant in space and magical in its freedom, is the missing cornerstone in our modern musical edifice.

Without it, contemporary music can only crumble into meaningless discord. It is therefore crucial that we learn again to appreciate essential sound.

Scene Three. Some seven years have passed since that night in San Francisco, and Jarrett has only grown more preoccupied on the diminishing importance of tone. In his assessment of this dismal situation, the public has to accept its share of responsibility for letting mystery slip from its music. If there is any hope of restoring it, the first step would be for listeners to begin to *listen*. With growing alarm, he watched as people either mistook his intentions—how could anyone construe his *Köln Concert* as a prototype for new age?—or simply stopped listening. Maybe they were still going to concerts, or buying records by young jazz neo-traditionalists. But they weren't *listening*.

So he spoke out. It was in April 1992, on the night of his solo recital at Avery Fisher Hall in New York's Lincoln Center. After delivering an extended, totally improvised piece, the type of heroic introspection that had become one of his artistic trademarks, Jarrett took a short intermission, then returned to the stage. But rather than sit back at the piano, he went up to the microphone and began what he described as a commentary on "the state of music, as opposed to the state of the union." It began with a disparaging reference to self-styled jazz musicians who "buy their music and their suits at the same store." From a front row, one member of the audience responded with an observation about Jarrett's own attire—"Nice shirt"—which cued Jarrett to begin a more detailed critique of young jazzers who "wear Armani suits and skinny ties." His point, of course, was that the level of experiencing music had sunk so low that listeners were confusing fashion with substance—or, even worse, that the musicians were as well.

Eventually Jarrett returned to the piano and started to play again. But a minute or so into the performance he stopped, returned to the mike, and announced, "There's something else I have to say." What followed was a strenuous and lengthy attack on the world music phenomenon, one that stretched all the way to what would have been the end of the concert.

A *New York Times* writer who was at Avery Fisher that night was moved by this verbal virtuosity to invite the pianist to put his thoughts on paper. Jarrett's polemic, published in the August 16 edition, assaults the icons of modern culture. Its targets include new age music ("Jell-O"), world music ("a hoax"), electronic music ("Waiter, a side order of natural overtones, please"), "opera singers . . . trying to sing black spirituals," and "industry reps dressed as players, players dressed as movie stars."

"The craft of building a resonating instrument has fallen into the hands of toy manufacturers," he wrote. "Music seems to have slipped out of the hands of the true makers and into the hands of the producers and promoters, although the promoters now include the musicians themselves, who seem to love to dress up and watch themselves in the mirror."

Though the article suggested remedies, the litany of abuses overpowered readers. It seemed logical to ask whether *anyone*, in Jarrett's view, was doing anything worthwhile in music. Was Jarrett a visionary, squinting through the smog toward an apprehension of the future? Was he a Cassandra, foreseeing doom and decay? A curmudgeon? Was he simply *jealous* of all those guys in Armani suits?

It was not always so. In the sixties, young jazz artists defied the conventions of their art. Jarrett was one of the brightest of these emerging stars; in his early twenties, he was already a seasoned musician, whose parents had started him on piano lessons when they caught him picking out melodies from the radio on the family upright. Just two years later he made his own broadcast debut, on Paul Whiteman's show. He began composing a year or so after that, as well as performing classical recitals. In a premonition of his marathon solo piano improvisations, Jarrett played a two-hour concert at the age of seven.

Much has been written about the pianist's more adult adventures. He has been a major figure in jazz since the late sixties, when he put in time with Art Blakey's Jazz Messengers, Rahsaan Roland Kirk, and the Charles Lloyd Quartet. In 1969 he organized his own trio, with bassist Charlie Haden and drummer Paul Motian, keeping it together even during his stint with Miles Davis's formidable fusion band in the early seventies, and adding saxophonist Dewey Redman in 1972.

It was the solo piano concerts, beginning in the mid-seventies, that transformed Jarrett into a phenomenon. Entirely extemporized along flowing melodic contours, ballooning at times to more than an hour of uninterrupted ruminations, these performances challenged prevailing ideas about the process of improvising. Even when captured on records, they offer stark insight into the mind of an artist as he tests his own capacity for creativity. Most of the time he was able to meet the challenge, with an unprecedented mixture of lyric inventiveness, legato flow, and ecstatic energy. If Jarrett had retired by 1980, after cutting *Solo Concerts* or the *Köln Concert*, his place in history would have been assured.

But there was much more to follow: a torrent of projects, from Handel on harpsichord to original works for piano and orchestra, from the vexing Shostakovich *Preludes* to jazz standards with bassist Gary Peacock and drummer Jack DeJohnette. Then, in the late nineties, at long last, it seemed that he had reached his limits, as Jarrett withdrew from public view, the victim of a strange ailment that sapped his energy and ambition. Rather than stop him, though, this disability seemed only to focus him more on his journey toward the nucleus, the most universal essence, of all the types of music he had explored.

As he emerged from seclusion late in 1999, Jarrett put forward a gem of an album. *The Melody at Night, With You* presents a selection of familiar tunes, some of them foreign to the jazz catalog, each played with minimal elaboration. These readings of "My Wild Irish Rose," "Be My Love," and other songs in fact come from the same pursuit of purity that fueled *The Köln Concert*, *The Paris Concert*, and perhaps his most revealing recorded improvisation, *The Vienna Concert*. But where those recitals involved emotionally and physically exhausting plunges into the emptiness that precedes invention, *The Melody at Night* is a reverent examination of written material in its barest form. Jarrett turns each chord and melody over with extraordinary delicacy, as a scholar might examine a fragile but priceless relic.

Away from the spotlight, Jarrett is a lover of dialog, often relaxed and quick to laugh; one can imagine him as a student at Berklee, hunched over cups of cold coffee in late-night cafés and relishing the exchange of ideas. Despite his reputation for enigmatic posturing, he places a high priority on communication. Once his inquisitors adapt to his rhythms, they discover a probing, restless individual, whose view of the universe is both coherent and idiosyncratic.

We visited him one cold November day, as the woods of rural New Jersey glistened in mist and a chill rose from a nearby lake into the darkening air. Jarrett led us through his weathered 120-year-old home and out across a sloping hill to his studio, a spare space shared by two harpsichords, an

American Steinway, and a German Steinway. We played the latter, whose glassy resonance seemed the archetype for the ECM sound cultivated by Jarrett's longtime producer Manfred Eicher.

"It is wonderful," agreed Jarrett. "But the thing about the Hamburg Steinway is, you can't play the blues on it."

Only Jarrett—not even Horowitz—would distinguish between two great pianos this way. No other player could negotiate the complexities of Shostakovich, then coax 40-minute exercises in free extemporization from the ether of imagination. The Jarrett we met was, at that moment, an artist of broader vision and deeper ambition than any other pianist we knew. And he wasn't even wearing an Armani suit.

There was a time, when you were recording the album Spirits *back in 1986, that you were reconsidering your relationship with the piano and thinking about getting into more ethnic types of non-keyboard music.*

Well, when you say one thing, you can't say the other side of the coin. If you use words, you cannot help but speak from half of the truth, if not less, because you can't define the whole thing. So if I say something about the piano, I might mean more than that. But what was going through my mind was that even the piano was not a primitive enough instrument that I could consider it essential sound. The more I've been alive and a musician, the more I realize that essential sound, if there's a way of forgetting what I might mean by that for a minute, is the only sound that really touches you despite yourself. Let's say that sophisticated sound is what's on the other side of that coin. That touches you through its own complexities. By the time those complexities have been eliminated, so has half the music. A master flutist, let's say, from a so-called primitive country might be able to touch you right away with his sound, without you even knowing whether he's a good player. Strangely enough, most of the best jazz players have played wind instruments. There are the pianists and the drummers, but in jazz the tendency is for the music to remain more connected to that essential sound. In classical music, it's like getting a sound you want as an ego that's writing a piece; that's different from what I'm talking about.

Essential sound, to you, isn't a tangible component that you can study on an oscilloscope.

That's right. And it involves what I would call the value of the sound itself. If you hear a sound, you automatically are affected by it. If you hear a sound that has value, in the sense that I mean, you are not only affected by it, but you gain from having heard that, even despite yourself. So the more sophisticated the instrument a musician uses, the more he has to be clever about how he gets around having that effect on the audience. And the more clever he is, the more he's playing into the intellectual, technological world that seems to think that all things can be solved by that piling up of things.

Wind players can bring organic nuance to their sound, whereas the piano is fairly locked in. Does that tie into your perception of essential sound?

Yes. Let's say that the locking in is something that's not so good. If you have sound locked in a space, then it can't get out of that space; it's less moving, and less able to touch a human being whose body is constantly changing. So the locked-in thing doesn't have any relationship to the human being. Now, I still love the piano. But my responsibility is as a musician, not as a pianist. If my responsibility takes me away from the piano, that's when I might very likely say something like, "I'm not so interested in the piano at this moment in my life." As a pianist, you really have to phrase impossibly. I think I do that, which is one reason why I still can play the piano and not have to move away from it more often. There are still some magic things the piano can do that are not pianistic. You can still speak through that instrument.

Some of your physical movement as a player reflects a struggle to make the sound of the instrument more organic.

Yes, that's exactly right. I mean, I've never developed a philosophy about my movements. Everybody else does that for me. Most people think they're something that's grafted onto the music. If they could ever see the trio recordings in the studio, with no audience watching, they'd realize that my movements are not grafted on, because that stuff is happening anywhere we play.

Have you ever seen videotapes of yourself playing and been surprised by what they show you?

Not recently, although there's a solo concert that PBS broadcast that was pretty graphic.

Was watching that broadcast something like watching some player other than yourself in the act of creating?

Yeah, I could say that. I'd rather be doing it than watching it [*laughs*].

How did you become aware of the piano's limitations as a source of essential sound?

As long ago as the early sixties, when I was playing with Charles Lloyd, I was talking to people about giving up playing the piano. One note at a time seemed fine. Sometimes I'd be playing just one note, and it seemed so good, I wondered why I'd need the whole piano. This was something I could do without the piano—probably without a key! I could just use anything that was lying around. Okay, let's say that was '64 or '65. Naturally, I was at an age where, if I did that, that would be the end of what I was trying to do. I must have realized that whatever energy I wanted to use had to go somewhere, so since the piano is my instrument, I recommitted myself to the piano. There have been several times since then that I've had the same realization. One of those times was when the solo concerts [temporarily] ended. But each time it's greater; each time it's telling me something. So I ended up having a harpsichord built for me, and a clavichord on which I started doing Baroque music, all the while not realizing that what I was doing was testing the essential possibilities of other instruments. In a way I was testing a theory I had had for 20 years.

What theory was that?

That the piano isn't always the right instrument for what I hear. When I had my first trio, we always fooled around on lots of different percussion things—it was called "fooling around" by most people. But when I made *Spirits* I realized I was actually making the sounds I was hearing, making the piano do something that maybe it shouldn't do. The Shotakovich [recordings] came up as a result of the fact that I'm perfectly comfortable playing the piano. The solo thing is another story.

In what way?

If I want to be analytical about it, it's a context that seems familiar to listeners. Those listeners assume that I'm familiar with it and that it's something that I've been doing. But since a certain point, my doing of it is for a different reason. Now I'm not so much caring about the music in terms of notes. I was curious over the past few years about whether it was possible to take the solo piano thing further, not just for the audience, but in terms of getting onto a recording a document of what I was going through while I was playing. It wasn't so much about coming up with subject matter that I was inspired to do as trying to get the *state* on tape—which is related to *Spirits*. *Spirits* was more of a state than a musical statement. This is also connected to why I'm thinking in words, because I feel that a delicate process is gradually being lost and I don't mind talking about it. It's more delicate than it ever was.

What delicacy are you referring to?

You hear an interesting or clever or intellectually challenging musical idea; that's one thing. But another thing would be to hear the process of coming up with the potential for that idea. Just the other day, someone who had heard the *Vienna Concert* said to me, "I get to these points in listening where I thought I knew what you were going to do, and you didn't do it." And I said, "Well, how did you feel when that happened?" He said, "I became more alert." Now, this is someone I don't know; he had no reason to put words that weren't true out into the air. But that is already justification for me to do what I'm doing. That's what I want to happen. To make someone more alert is the biggest thing that music can do.

But some listeners use your music to facilitate some other process, such as meditation, rather than to induce alertness about the music itself.

You're forgetting the fact that the best way to do that is without music. If somebody is going to get in touch with their environment, it has to be an organic environment. If it's not an organic environment, then there is no relationship. Are you talking about nice music that gets people close to something they've forgotten?

I'm talking about the difference between, on the one hand, sitting in a forest alone and getting a perspective on the relationship to the forest, and on the other hand, letting that process be enhanced by a good flute player who would be able to musically reflect on what's happening.

The better the flute player would be, the less inclined he would be to play the flute in the forest. The whole problem is that we now have a medium that has its own thing to do, to synthetically create maybe the desire to get close to something. And yet, that's a synthetic desire, because either we're doing it or we're not doing it.

If music is such a distraction, why has it been so pervasive in the history of religion and attempts at self-discovery?

Is Keith Jarrett a visionary? A curmudgeon? Is he simply jealous of all those guys in Armani suits?

But, you see, there's a difference. We're living in a society now where we say we have the power of choice. If you belong to a church, you don't have a choice. You go there, and that music is part of the church you go to. That's not the same. What you're saying is that that's parallel with someone deciding that he needs to have something on that can facilitate his spiritual growth, let's say. But that assumes that the person who chooses to do that knows more than he possibly can at that time. How can he know whether he needs music for that? Since he knows that he's not where he wants to be, how can he know what he needs to get there? In the case of churches, you have to assume that somebody decided that hymns are necessary for this church. You can't, as a member of this church, say, "I'm sorry, but I'd like to leave during the hymns." But that's participation! That's not exactly the same thing.

Since each church member would make this choice himself or herself, would you concede that each of us might reach a different but valid conclusion about whether music is appropriate in our own self-examinations?

Okay, but what I'm saying is this: Let's take whoever that person is, and take the music away. I think the person can get quicker to wherever that is without it going through a period of thinking that that's the right thing for him, and then finding out that it wasn't, and *what else is?* See, the question is, what else will it do for you?

You're also saying that if the music is taken away from this person, then he or she will discover that they had a greater dependence on the music in their spiritual process than they should have had.

If he realizes that. We have to assume that he didn't realize that he didn't need it to begin with. So the chances are not that great that he will realize that he didn't need it when he finishes. What he will realize is that he didn't do it, but he won't know what will: "Okay, that didn't work. Or maybe it did. I'm in a haze."

Maybe he should just go out and get another album.

I'm not saying it's bad to be soothed by music. Maybe it can cure; certainly that's not bad. But music cannot make consciousness appear. The biggest thing it can do to consciousness in a listener is to make it even stronger.

Is inducing alertness a conscious goal in your performances?

No, but that's what's so special about the process of improvising. If I am making myself more alert, I can almost guarantee that that's happening out in the hall.

Is there a moment where the process of solo improvisation has changed for you since you began doing it?

I would just say there's a gradual awakening. I've been using the solo concert context ever since I started to learn things about the process of making music from nothing. I've never stopped learning, even though people think, "Oh, he's used to doing this. He could do this with his eyes closed." Well, I could do it with my eyes closed, but I couldn't do it asleep. I need to be more awake each time I do it, because otherwise I'm going to sound like I've always sounded, and why would I want to keep sounding like that? Some people say I have a message in music. I would say that I don't, but the message would be within the process. The alertness that is produced by committing yourself to a process rather than to the subject matter having to be transformed in any particular way demands that you sacrifice what you could do in a certain instant for what the potential of that instant is.

At the beginning of "Vienna, Part 1," you take more than 11 minutes to find a motif and deliberately not embellish it. This must be the kind of document you're talking about: The listener keeps expecting development, and looking for it, but it took forever for you to get it underway.

I think that music is, for the listener, the most experiential thing I've ever done. It's not so much a musical experience as an experience for the listener, and maybe the listener shouldn't even know why. That's why, when I listen to *Vienna*, I can't listen to it again for a while. Experience is like that. Let's say someone is listening to music, and they love what they're hearing. There are people who like sections of the *Köln Concert* and listen to them every day. That's a purely musical thing. What I was aware of after we recorded *Vienna* was that maybe, for the first time, I'd have a chance to detox the *Köln Concert* addicts, because it's absolutely the reverse. The point of reference in *Vienna* isn't the music, it's the ongoing *gestalt* of it, whereas there are sections in the *Köln Concert*; one melody leads to another melody. Whenever you have an existential experience, you don't go right out and get it again. I mean, if you have a fantastic dinner, you don't ask for that same dinner again. But if someone sings you a melody, you'll say, "Hey, I like that. Sing it again."

What do you need in order to play a successful solo improvisation?

First of all, faith. You cannot just have confidence. Confidence is something someone would have if they know how to fix an engine, and they've done it enough times so that they know that whatever goes wrong, they'll be able to fix it. But faith is the ability to deal with a transformed situation. A transformed situation is when you get a different engine than you thought you would get, and you've never learned a thing about it. So I wanted to take the most elemental thing in doing the solo concerts—what one thing, if taken away, would produce nothing valuable, at least to me?—I would say that there's an element of faith, without which the concert would be nothing.

Faith in what?

That's very difficult to articulate. On a more concrete, easy-to-understand level, I do anything that my system asks me to do as we approach the concert time. If I feel like hanging out, I hang out. If I feel like I can't talk to anybody, I don't talk to anybody. Occasionally we'll play dominoes until it's time to start. If my mind wants to focus on the concert, I have to take that focus away.

I assume you would be disinclined to listen to music.

I'd *kill* someone if they brought a radio and turned it on. I'd tell *them* to go out and play the concert [*laughs*]. There have been situations where, for some reason or another, I've been accidentally exposed to a tape of a concert I'd played a couple of nights earlier an hour or two before I'm supposed to play the next one. Someone would put a tape on, and I wouldn't be able to stop it fast enough. Suddenly I'm possessed by this, so when I go out onstage, I have to get rid of it. That's not a concert; that's an enema [*laughs*]. That's not why I'm there. The ideal state to be in, just before I make a sound, would be a state where there is nothing to lose and nothing to gain, no ideas to purge. Because the piano sound itself is instructive. If you take everything else out of your system and all you've got is the sound, you have to reconstruct your system from that sound. That's really what I'm doing in a solo concert; I'm rebuilding myself from a point of awareness.

What do you mean by rebuilding yourself?

It's literally like building a body. You want it to be alive. There are no rules; there are only chemicals at your disposal—the chemicals of the sound—and the audience. If audiences truly understand that, they would never think it's weird if I stop because they're coughing or making noise. I'm a chemist up there, trying to hold the beaker without letting it shake, and then pouring the next ingredient into it.

You put an incredible amount of work into playing even the simplest passages during your solo improvisations. But in your classical recordings there is an enormous technique being applied without, apparently, a comparable effort. It seems as if the processes behind your improvisatory and classical performances are driven by different energies.

That's possible, although I don't think about it unless somebody asks me to. However, essentially—that word again—it isn't true. It's all part of the same flow. To give tiny examples, I asked Lou Harrison if he would be interested in writing a piano concerto. He finally did, and I think the piece is great. One of the problems with it, though, is that it expresses some of the things I'm talking about, and no other musicians who happen to be orchestra players are interested in that. They don't know what that's about. They have a job, and they think whatever they think about this piece. What's really happening is that I'm able to use Lou's piece to say what Lou and I would both like to say about the instrument and some of the assumptions we make about what good and bad music is.

But is it as much physical and emotional labor to play, say, a difficult Shostakovich prelude as it is to do an improvisation from scratch?

Let's put it this way. Shostakovich wrote that music. I can't ask him to keep me awake. I can't say, "Write something that will keep me awake." I can stay awake and play his music. But in the solo concerts I use the music to wake up more. The energy and effort you hear is that. The effort is to stay unpressured by the musical flow. It sounds like it's more effort to do it, but it's really an effort to *resist* the pressure. With Shostakovich I need to have this pressure to play the music, because it's his music and I'm not trying to resist something. I'm not making anything up. You need to have incredible resistance *not* to choose an easy path.

Since the notes are spelled out for you in classical music, the process of playing that material must at some level be more passive than what you go through to dredge up ideas in your improvisations.

Yeah, but when the actual music itself is really happening [in an improvisation], even when it's incredibly intense and fast, it's more passive than someone might think. I'm letting it happen. I once gave a lecture on a classical music cruise that was filled with Mozart people. I decided that no one knew what jazz was, because I kept being asked, "Mr. Jarrett, what is jazz?" So the main subject of the talk was that there's a big difference between jazz and written music. One kind of music, jazz, says, "I have to be able to let it happen." The other kind says, "I have to make it happen." I used the spiritual, "This Little Light of Mine, I'm Gonna Let It Shine," to explain this. Kathleen Battle had sung it the night before, and they were perfect lyrics to describe the difference. That faith is the thing. You can't say "I'm gonna let it shine" if you don't believe there's anything shining. The essence of black spiritual lyrics was a faith that was beyond the function of their lives. That's why it's so important not to confuse it with confidence. Some people would say, "I'm confident. I know how good I am." But they're saying *they* are doing the thing, and the lyric says, "It's your light, but only if you let it shine."

Apparently you feel that many young jazz musicians are latching too firmly onto older models because they're having trouble finding their own lights.

Yes. The only way you can revive a tradition is to be awake at the moment when you're doing what you should be doing. You need to be aware of everything that came before, but to say that you are reviving a tradition, or to school people in the revival of a tradition, which is a tradition of a certain time, takes potential away from these players.

Unless the revived tradition can suggest fresh directions for those players to follow.

Okay, but my next question would be, "How do you really revive a tradition?" How could we ever revive, say, the big band tradition? We couldn't. We could have big bands, but we couldn't revive the tradition of big bands. If we talk about reviving traditions, it starts to scare me in a way that the concept of world music scares me. We don't realize what we're saying when we say "world music" in the sense that we are trying to instruct. The only way to keep a tradition alive is to keep the books open, and not just point to a page.

Look, I frequently play gigs on piano with musicians who play in what you might call a post-bop style . . .

Let me interrupt you. If you play with these guys, are you saying that this is what they do? Or do you notice that they do this? If a player thinks he's revitalizing a tradition, he's already not doing it. If a player says, "Let's play some bebop," he's not going to. There's no such thing as bebop outside of the finding of bebop by playing.

But whether my colleagues on these gigs take that approach or not, I enjoy playing with them. Why is that wrong?

It's not wrong. What's wrong is to think of it at all. Is it the same to revitalize a tradition and to revitalize the awareness of a tradition? I don't think so. What I'm complaining about is the choosing of a position, whereas music is never music unless it's free of choice. If you feel like playing with some players who play bebop, and you have a lot of fun playing with them, I don't see anything wrong with that. But in our world, where media are so strong and messages go too quickly from one place to another, we think we're being educated when we're actually seeing someone restrict themselves to something.

So Charlie Parker wasn't playing bebop because he didn't know what it was yet.

Right. He was *playing*. Luckily, all the most valuable guys in jazz didn't have the faintest idea whether they were bebop players or avant-garde players or whatever. I'm talking about the most crucial players. We should take these players as examples of what it's about. We shouldn't even consider the second string. It's like when you see the top two or three people in tennis playing each other; as soon as you go down to four or five, the game changes. You can't use that game to define the limits of tennis. Gary Peacock and I talk about this all the time, because the trio has been getting more and more to the point of pulse that's nothing *but* bebop. But when we talk about it, Gary might say, "How could we ever have gotten to play this way if we had wanted to?" If we decided to be a bebop trio, we would never have been playing such great stuff. Whether anyone wants to say that we've become a bebop band is behind the point. Somebody will say, "Bebop is the greatest," and somebody else will say, "I can't listen to anything but Dixieland." That's fine for listeners, but it's not cool for someone who wants to be called even a semi-creative musician. Would you say "no" to something that comes into your hands that's not bebop if you're in a bebop band? Would the other players say, "Whoops! What did he do?"

While you begin with a clean slate in your solo concerts, there are actual tunes in your trio sets. Yet you approach these tunes unconfined by the conventions some people associate with those particular songs.

And that's perfectly connected to what we're talking about. Because it doesn't hang on it, because it doesn't have a hook, that makes it possible for us to play these songs. If we said, "Our approach is one of a bebop trio," we'd never get around to sounding like bebop players. We would be bebop *pray*-ers, doing prayers to the bebop church. Meanwhile, the real bebop players would be playing. They wouldn't even be thinking about it. Bebop isn't going to disappear if people are aware. But it will disappear, even with educators, no matter how educated everyone is to know what bebop is, unless there are some actual players who inspire listeners to say, "This is valid. This is happening." And someone says to them, "This is bebop." And they say, "Really? Gee, I didn't know I like bebop."

Jazz listeners, then, must discipline themselves to hear what is actually happening in a performance, without inhibiting their ability to appreciate through the distractions of labels.

What good jazz listeners listen to is closer to what is there than what classical listeners traditionally listen to, or what minimalists are listening to now. They are aware that at any second something might happen that they're not prepared for, so they have to be open. If they're listening to a player from whom something valuable has come out, they listen with a certain openness that differentiates them from other kinds of listeners. Let's say they're willing to sacrifice their preconceptions for the sake of seeing what this person is going to do.

The aware listener, in any kind of music, has to actively interact with the performance.

Yeah. To me, valuable music should not allow you to escape from your own heartbeat, whereas in the Western world over the past several hundred yeas, music means an escape from that, instead of a more vivid seeing of that. I've asked many people about what happened to them during specific parts of my concerts, and no matter where they were sitting in the hall they would tell a similar story if they were listening, or if they knew what I was talking about. First they went through this thing of, "Now what's going to happen? I wonder what's going to happen next?" Then it starts to get boring: "How long is this going to go on?" After they get through this stage, they realize that something is happening anyway. If it stops there, that's minimalism. But if after that experience you could say, "That was that," then something else automatically shows up in the music.

Do your feelings parallel those of the listeners at each point in your concerts?

Yeah. I remember vividly saying to myself, "This should change. Should? Why should it? I don't know. But it should. Well, that's not enough reason." So it stays there. I start hearing different things—let's say harmonics I've never heard before in the three notes I'm playing. It's like going back to a vegetarian diet after a fast, where you realize how strong some of those tastes are that you take for granted. But if you stay on the fast, you don't learn that; you don't have that experience. You get off the thing, and you never get back on, so you have nothing to relate to in terms of what it was about. It may be nice for you physically, but that's not all we are.

The Latin Connection

67. CHUCHO VALDÉS

Born October 9, 1941, Quivican, Cuba

Like his younger compatriot Gonzalo Rubalcaba, Cuban piano legend Chucho Valdés didn't exactly sneak quietly into the U.S. market. His initial recordings and appearances emphasized his titanic technique and the exotic aspects of Cuban-jazz fusion. But there were differences in their strategies for conquest: Rubalcaba had spun heads with his blinding dexterity, and Valdés preferred mowing down his audiences with massive waves of sound. Rubalcaba performances were like blizzards of notes; Valdés brought earthquakes, tidal waves, and other awesome phenomena more to mind.

But there was also a more amiable quality in the music of Valdés. His almost childlike delight in pushing the sonic limits of the piano was hard to resist; where audiences held their breaths until Rubalcaba had finished some high-velocity romp, they often broke into cheers, gasps, and primal hollers in the middle of a particularly eruptive Valdés passage. The older pianist's work was more primal, less intellectual, and more playful; one was much more likely to hear him quote snippets from other songs than the more sober and reflective Rubalcaba.

As was the pianist himself. Valdés makes an imposing physical impression. As tall as he is to begin with, his limbs and hands are still disproportionately huge; at rest on the piano bench, he might let his arms dangle nearly down to the floor in repose. And when he stretches out on the keyboard, his mitts wolf great bunches of notes at a time. An expressive, laugh-lined face and warm personality complete a picture that listeners tended to find impossible to resist.

He was born into a musical aristocracy, the son of Ramon "Bebo" Valdés, who for more than twenty years cut a high profile in Cuba as a pianist and as musical director of the world-renowned Tropicana nightclub. More even than most offspring of musical parents, Chucho was immersed in music throughout his childhood. Before taking his first piano lesson at the age of three, he witnessed sensational jam sessions at his house, with his father and mother taking turns at the piano with the likes of Ernesto Lecuona and Chico O'Farrill.

"I've been playing piano since I have been using reason," Valdés told me during an interview. "They say that I sat down and began to play without anyone having taught me. Yes, nobody taught me how to play the piano. . . . My father was taking a shower, and he sensed that a melody was being played on the piano. He came out without any clothes on to see who was playing." The artist was, of course, his three-year-old son.

Rigorous instruction soon began, followed by lessons in theory and composition that started when Valdés reached the age of five. But never did this regimen undermine the pleasure that music already brought to the young pianist. When not drilling on scales or working on classical repertoire, he was tagging after his father at the Tropicana and listening to such visiting artists as Sarah Vaughan and Nat "King" Cole entertain from the bandstand.

By age 16 Valdés had made his debut at a club called Havana 1900. He was going through a bebop phase, with a style based largely on Wynton Kelly, Horace Silver, and other funk-oriented players. Two years after that he made his recording debut, playing piano with his father's band in 1959. A clear career course seemed open to Valdés, but events beyond his control suddenly changed Cuba's musical landscape. After Fidel Castro's ascension to power, the country's cultural institutions began shutting down jazz clubs and discouraging musicians from playing anything but classical and indigenous music. Chucho's father, like many leading artists, left to live and work abroad; the elder Valdés eventually wound up in Stockholm, Sweden, where he remained vigorous and musically active into the next century.

Chucho, however, stayed behind, a decision he professes never to regret. The restrictions imposed by the state on playing jazz propelled him to pay more attention to native Cuban music. In exploring *los toques de Santos*, or "the sounds of the saints" in the music of Santeria, he began finding ways to apply sophisticated harmonies to its bewitching rhythms. As the Voice of America beamed broadcasts of McCoy Tyner, Herbie Hancock, and other modernists into Cuba, Valdés absorbed their innovations and made them integral to his marriage of Latin and jazz. By the time official pressure on jazz started easing up in the late sixties, he had already created a highly personal sound—one which, he insists, might have eluded him in a more commercial, tolerant climate.

In 1973 Valdés co-founded the seminal Cuban fusion band Irakere, with a group of friends from the Musical Theater of Havana and the Cuban Orchestra of Modern Music. Their daring African-derived clothes, long hair, and electric instrumentation flaunted an indifference to conformity that might have been risky if not for their spectacular level of performance. A long string of recordings captured their energy and breathtaking creativity, though it wasn't until 1978 that U.S. audiences were allowed to see them in person. They made their debut that year in Carnegie Hall, on a bill that included solo piano performances by Mary Lou Williams, Bill Evans, and McCoy Tyner. Many more years would pass before political barriers would finally come down enough to allow Valdés to visit more frequently and be able to perform with a younger generation of American giants, including trumpeters Roy Hargrove and Wynton Marsalis.

The pianist's appeal to great players of all ages is evident on *Live at the Village Vanguard*, a quartet set recorded in 1999. Moderate tempos did little to dampen his attack: Only a few seconds into "Son XXI," with the rhythm section ticking softly in the background, Valdés pounds massive triplet chords that rise into a thunderous tremolo. Though he does switch to rapid but muscular runs later in the piece, he keeps returning to out-of-rhythm, ten-fingered chords punctuated by octaves and low blows in the bass; a long quote from "Summertime," presented as furiously pounded clustered chords, only makes his elemental approach more clear. Like Cecil Taylor, Valdés is intoxicated with sound; unlike Taylor, he finds his power by pouring that sound into forms long established and recognized by two complementary cultures.

Valdés shows the same tendencies when working alone, as documented in his 2001 album *Solo—Live in New York*. Recorded at Lincoln Center, Valdés presents "Somewhere Over the Rainbow" in wild contrasts, beginning with a hushed rendering of the bridge (though he can't resist one thunderous low note before getting to the verse). Within a few bars he is interrupting his relatively restrained reading with heavily pedaled tremolos. The second iteration builds to a galvanic climax, built on a rumbling and roaring pedal tone on the fifth in the bass. By this point the interpretation has become a roller coaster ride, packed with thrills and chills—and, inevitably, an extended quote, this one from *An American in Paris*, played just before yet another massively attacked bridge over, again, a fifth in the bass. The performance ends with another favorite Valdés device—dramatic smears up and down the keys, with two high-range notes added as final punctuation.

Such performances do not lack in drama, but the excitement wears thin after a while, especially when Valdés strays too far from Cuban elements. To his credit, he sustains an extraordinary emotional intensity in all his playing, but even in his most lyrical performances, such as the lilting "A mi madre," from *Solo*, it's instructive to notice how such pianists as Keith Jarrett might achieve similar epiphanies without pushing the instrument to its limits.

It's the old Chopin vs. Liszt equation: What the latter achieved with bravura virtuosity, the former approximated with more minimal gestures. And as Valdés proves, there's nothing wrong with following in the footsteps of Liszt, as well as those of his father.

68. MONTY ALEXANDER

Born: June 6, 1944, Kingston, Jamaica

Born on D-Day, Monty Alexander would launch a one-man Jamaican invasion of America's jazz piano community. His weapons were an ample technique and an ability to use it without letting it dominate his playing. Alexander's spirited style drew occasionally from the music of his homeland, though he tended to keep that side of his work separate from the swing-driven feel that was his stylistic touchstone.

In fact, Alexander is more significant as an inspiration to Latin piano than as head of any jazz vanguard with roots in Jamaica. With reggae and its precursor traditions flowing through the culture, it's more difficult to divert that stream into styles that are less indigenous, than it would be to marry Latin to jazz, with all the harmonic and rhythmic characteristics they share. Perhaps this makes Alexander's accomplishment all that more impressive, in making the leap, like so few of his countrymen, into jazz.

His reasons for moving from a household dominated by calypso toward jazz were actually unusual. "I had a rebellious nature as a kid," Alexander explained to Len Lyons in *Keyboard* magazine. "I rebelled against my teacher because she told me that anything that had a beat to it was almost sinful. . . . Playing jazz was my way of saying, 'Well, I just don't go along with that.'"

That is, of course, only part of the story. Just six years old at the time, and not long into his first piano lessons, Alexander had not yet fallen in love with jazz; that would come in his teens, when he had the opportunity to hear such visiting American giants as Louis Armstrong and Nat "King" Cole at the Carib Theater. In his earlier years he was inspired more by R&B; as a session musician covering American hits by artists such as Bill Doggett and Louis Jordan, he contributed to the evolution of the ska style that would set the stage for reggae. From 1958 through 1960 he scored several Jamaican hits in this style, as leader of Monty and the Cyclones; when they split up, he briefly led another ska-type ensemble, called Doggett.

In 1961 Alexander moved with his mother and brother to Miami, where he almost immediately landed a gig as house pianist at the Bonfire restaurant. Word about the teenage sensation spread quickly, and in 1962 he accepted a gig in Las Vegas with the Art Mooney Orchestra. For the wide-eyed newcomer, who in his own view was still learning the basics of his trade, this engagement brought almost unimaginable exposure—including one fateful night when Frank Sinatra and his friend Jilly Rizzo were in the audience. That's all it took to earn Alexander a ticket to New York to play piano at Rizzo's restaurant, Jilly's.

There was no hotter showbiz hangout than Jilly's in the early sixties. Miles Davis, Erroll Garner, and other jazz luminaries were among the regulars, and Sinatra himself grabbed the mike to sing a few tunes every now and then. This didn't hurt Alexander as he began his own recording career, first with two LPs on the Pacific Jazz label, followed by more on RCA and MGM. In addition to the Jilly's residency, Alexander played at other clubs around town, including the legendary Minton's Playhouse in 1967. There he was heard by bassist Ray Brown and vibes master Milt Jackson, both of whom would perform and record prolifically with Alexander over the next several years.

For more than thirty years now Alexander has kept busy with innumerable guest appearances on sessions by Dizzy Gillespie, Sonny Rollins, and other giants, while also releasing more than fifty albums under his own name. This enormous output has made Alexander's upbeat, sunny style a beacon of sorts for younger, multicultural pianists such as Michel Camilo and Jacky Terrasson to follow. He plays at quick tempos with a fleet, skimming rhythm, with the left hand generally comping in bop style but often switching to quick lines in unison with the right hand. Caribbean or Latin influences are less overt than in the work of other pianists, but their flavor does permeate everything he plays at various degrees of subtlety.

"Accompong," from his 1978 album *Jamento*, offers a good example of Alexander's tendency to separate the straight-ahead and tropical sides of his playing. During the head and the first verse the feel is up-and-down and on the beat, with Larry McDonald's percussion mixing it up behind a straight-four groove from the drums. Yet even there Alexander plays mainly with a swing feel. This creates an

Monty Alexander's upbeat, sunny style is a beacon for younger, multicultural pianists to follow.

agreeable tension between his solo lines (and those of guitarist Ernest Ranglin) and the rhythm bed, so that when everyone switches to a dotted-eighth feel there's a sharp perception of release. Later, when the band returns to the opening feel and anchors on the IV chord, Alexander can kick into a new solo approach, beginning with a few basic funk licks to acknowledge the shift in rhythm, then ripping through a couple of fast passages before returning once more to the head and then tearing past it. There's an excitement in Alexander's projection of complete authority here; when he takes time to quote a boogie-woogie riff, you know he's just amusing himself before digging into a really serious jam.

On the next track, Ray Brown's "Slippery," Alexander again divides his performance between sections of medium-tempo swing and a jazzy interpolation of reggae. His playing emphasizes the complementary nature of the two styles, yet they never come completely together.

Even when approaching a tune from an "island" perspective, Alexander usually does so unambiguously as a jazz pianist. His conception of "Island in the Sun," played solo on *Monty Alexander at Maybeck*, though built on a calypso rhythmic motif, could have been attempted by any jazz pianist of superior imagination, with no regard to cultural background. It's as if Alexander nods toward an aspect of his heritage without immersing himself in it—in this respect his ties to his roots seem less compelling than those of, say, Abdullah Ibrahim.

In recent years Alexander has loosened up a bit and allowed himself to explore his heritage more freely. Two albums serve as milestones in his expansion: *Stir It Up*, a collection of Bob Marley tunes, which he plays with empathy and insight, and *Monty Meets Sly and Robbie*, a fascinating meeting between the pianist and the legendary Jamaican rhythm team of bassist Robbie Shakespeare and drummer Sly Dunbar. Alexander sinks into these steamy drum machine grooves as if they were a seductive hot bath, streaming his improvisation into meticulous, spare lines designed to enhance rather than dominate the track. His only moments of stretching out are over repetitive vamps created to give him space—and even in these episodes, such as the stone reggae arrangement of Joe Zawinul's "Mercy, Mercy, Mercy," Alexander keeps these episodes short and ornamental rather than central to his improvisation.

On ballads Alexander has always been persuasive. Without the up-tempo challenge of having to chase after the highest technical standards, he extemporizes very freely around the melody, building repeatedly to emotional peaks without lapsing into sentimentality. In his performance of "In the Wee Small Hours of the Morning," again with Brown and Ellis, on the 1987 live album *Triple Treat III*, Alexander unfolds an unhurried, legato improvisation, launched from the first three notes of the tune and then shaped masterfully with tiny adjustments to the tempo. Only at one point does he push the intensity with a dramatic left-hand tremolo; in the rest of the solo, Alexander expresses himself purely through the artistry of his melodic invention.

When playing entirely within the jazz mainstream, Alexander is often compared to Oscar Peterson. There are similarities in their approaches to chording; each pianist favors big, ten-fingered voicings, often with sparkling octaves in the right hand and lots of blue notes in the mix. As a soloist, though, Alexander generally kicks into high gear less often. Listen to the tempo switch on "Sweet Georgia Brown," recorded in 1980 with Peterson trio members Ray Brown and Herb Ellis on *Trio*. After some very down-home phrasing in the slow opening choruses—which, like Peterson's, seem more based on visiting the conventions of the style rather than digging deeply into them —Alexander picks up the pace over Brown's pulsating bass. Though his two solo choruses are played with assurance, his lines are shorter than Peterson's, and played with a tad less of the commanding swing that Peterson reveals at these tempos.

There's nothing remotely deficient in these sorts of Alexander performances, but his phrases might taper off just a little more hesitantly, or he might overuse a figure that Peterson would more likely develop and alter—*i.e.*, the turnaround every eight bars during the head and out-chorus of "(Meet the) Flintstones," from the 1982 trio album *Triple Treat*. His quotes—from "When the Red, Red Robin," played with grave deliberation on "Body and Soul," from the same album—can come across as a little heavy-handed. Even when duplicating Peterson's style of block voicings and assertive tremolos, as on the powerfully swinging rendition of "Pure Imagination" from the 1994 album *Steamin'*, when he finishes the opening chorus and begins his single-line improvising, the rising triplet line into the first verse lacks the explosive trajectory that Peterson would have displayed, then stumbles moments later with an awkward figuration that disrupts the momentum that had been so clearly established.

More to the point, there is less distinction when Alexander positions himself under the shadow of players like Peterson than when he's allowing his own voice to emerge. Yet there is always enough of his ebullient personality, projecting an unrestrained joy in playing, that the essence of Alexander is worth whatever slight effort it takes to spot.

MICHEL CAMILO

Born: April 4, 1954, Santo Domingo, Dominican Republic

From the time of its birth in New Orleans, jazz has enjoyed close ties with Latin music. But in the last decades of the twentieth century the pace of their interaction quickened. In the piano realm especially, a crop of gifted young players began staking out a common ground where these styles could blend into a dynamic hybrid sound.

From Jorge Dalto and his smooth backup work with George Benson in the seventies through Hilton Ruiz and Danilo Perez, jazz piano has been enriched by the compatible yet exotic energies of Latin performers. But before the Cuban invasion spearheaded by Gonzalo Rubalcaba and Chucho Valdés, the promise of this movement was embodied in the thrilling performances of Michel Camilo.

There was no shortage of talent in the Camilo family, but it was clear early on that Michel was exceptional. He was only four years old when he discovered an old accordion tucked away amidst other artifacts in his house. It took little time for him to figure out how to work the bellows and start picking out tunes by ear. At the age of nine he was admitted to the National Conservatory, and at 16 he joined the National Symphony as a percussionist.

Camilo's future was secure after he was awarded lifetime tenure with the orchestra, but it was confining as well. To the surprise of no one who had heard him perform around Santo Domingo, Camilo left with his wife to seek his fortune in New York. He was 25 years old when he began taking an exhaustive multidisciplinary program at Juilliard. During off-hours Camilo worked as associate musical director of the Broadway show *Dancin'* and started playing gigs with a group called French Toast, whose members included future longtime collaborators Anthony Jackson on bass and Dave Weckl on drums.

In 1983 Camilo's career took a dramatic turn, as he won an Emmy for the Manhattan Transfer's recording of one of his original tunes, "Why Not?" That same year he began a three-year stint with saxophonist Paquito D'Rivera, while also organizing his own trio with Jackson and Weckl. It was with this lineup that Camilo made his impact on the national jazz scene.

In those early trio performances Camilo made no effort to hide his blazing technique. The opening moments of "Suite Sandrine Part 1," from his self-titled debut album in 1988, feature impossibly precise sixteenth-note octave runs and two-handed chord movement, all at a burning tempo. If nothing else is immediately clear, this performance at least establishes Camilo as a chops monster.

Wisely, he follows this blinding display with a reflective ballad, titled "Nostalgia." With Marc Johnson playing Jaco-like tonalities on electric bass and Dave Weckl inventing free patterns with brushes, Camilo plays a highly melodic improvisation, using space and silence as much as velocity to create expressive surges and aromatic evaporations. A steady on-the-beat comp in his left hand anchors the piece, but the romantic rubato and surging dynamics of his right hand keep the piece from feeling tied down. Compare this with his left hand in "Pra Voce (for Tania Maria)," which keeps a tricky off-beat eighth-note pulse throughout virtually the entire track.

Camilo uses the blues, particularly at faster tempos, as a vehicle for joyful blowing. On "Crossroads," from *Michel Camilo*, the pianist sprints through chorus after chorus of sixteenth-note lines. When his left hand suggests a detour into another tonality, the right follows without dropping a beat, then just as easily wends back to the original key. There's nothing blue in Camilo's blues, and the bright, upbeat feel of his postbop performances suggests a similar disinterest in the moodier shades of jazz. In his boundless exuberance, and in the sunny splatter of his licks and lines, Camilo conveys an agreeable but limited expressive range, for which his technique is called to compensate.

Yet in his later albums a broadening, if not a deepening, is evident. His 1997 album *Thru My Eyes* features trio arrangements of jazz titles that reflect Latin or funk elements. In his rendition of "Watermelon Man," backed by a no-nonsense drum pattern from Cliff Almond and Anthony Jackson's tasteful bass, Camilo stays pretty much in the middle range of the keyboard and keeps his solo on a low boil. He articulates triplets meticulously and never hits a clam over several choruses of improvising, but he also takes his time, building tension through minimal lines that he unfolds with patience and an eye to the long form of the piece. In fact, when he reprises the head at the end, Camilo seems to pass on the idea of building to a big finish; the theme slips back without any fanfare at all.

Later, on "Song for My Father," Camilo presents an invigorating interpretation based first on dazzling melodic concepts, which he follows carefully, even delicately, never letting himself be sidetracked by overplaying. As the solo builds, he begins altering his phrasing to allow a Latin element to surface as a series of triplet figures. Here, too, he applies the effect with taste, treating it as just one seasoning in a rhythm still rooted in Horace Silver's original concept.

On Latin-flavored pieces, Camilo gives even greater exposure to his romanticism and flair for drama. The last track on *Michel Camilo* is an electrifying "Caribe," with an introduction driven by an extraordinarily sensuous habanera, which kicks into a more bracing tempo after a somewhat abbreviated coda. In this idiom, where he can incorporate electrifying montuño passages into his solo, the pianist sounds completely at home.

There's nothing blue in Michel Camilo's blues, and the bright feel of his postbop performances suggests a similar disinterest in moodier shades.

The same is true on "Tropical Jam," from his album *Rendezvous*, a pure bravura exhibition. Despite an opening motif that seems borrowed from hoedown repertoire, Camilo builds most of the piece on an irresistible rumba-like groove laid down by Anthony Jackson and Dave Weckl. But it's the piano playing that brings this piece home, with its soaring and surging dynamics, its race through passages in major thirds and montuño snippets into ecstatic chorded climaxes in the upper range of the keys. In such performances Camilo silences any lingering quibbles over his subtlety. One is too swept up in the festivity of his music to remain a skeptic.

70. ELIANE ELIAS

Born: March 19, 1960, São Paulo, Brazil

Fetchingly attractive, Eliane Elias poses a problem for those who would resist the temptation to stereotype. With tawny long hair and a model's figure, she feels no aversion to glamour shots—it's hard to picture, say, Keith Jarrett in a swimsuit, head tossed back and eyes closed, as Elias is presented on one of her album covers. By the same token, it seems too easy to characterize her playing as feminine, but with her silky legato lines and sensuous tropical rhythms, the description can't be dismissed too quickly.

What can't be denied is her talent as an improvising pianist. A closer scrutiny of her work uncovers a command of mainstream jazz performance; its lessons flow smoothly into the indigenous music that forms the foundations of Elias's style. It's a perfect match which, thanks to her strong technique and canny creativity, establishes Elias as the supreme realization of the Brazilian and jazz traditions.

Almost from birth Elias was raised to play music. Family life was comfortable and secure. Her mother, a classical pianist with an appreciation for jazz, raised Eliane on a diet that mixed Mozart with Monk as equal influences. She began taking formal lessons at age seven, expanding on these five years later with jazz instruction offered by Amilton Godoy under the auspices of a progressive school known as CLAM (in Portuguese, Centro Livre de Aprendizagem). Elias was a dutiful student; meticulous transcriptions of solos by her favorite pianists helped develop her ability to improvise with other musicians. By the age of 15 Elias was rushing through a busy routine that included classes at high school, teaching piano herself at CLAM, and late-night jazz gigs around São Paolo.

She was only 17 when the road beckoned. For three years she toured Brazil with artists such as Vinicius de Moraes and Toquinho. Hungry to expand her horizons, she flew to Paris, where Eddie Gomez, former bassist with Bill Evans, persuaded her to take the leap to New York. Within a few weeks she had found a flat in Manhattan with her mother, rented a piano, and started looking for work. Her first gigs were with Gomez and drummer Bob Moses, followed in 1983 by an extended association with the band Steps Ahead. From this talent-saturated, listenable yet adventurous outfit, Elias found the momentum she needed to establish her own career—as well as a husband, in the form of trumpeter Randy Brecker.

With a fully formed grasp of modern jazz harmonics, Elias matches evocative, intelligent support with tuneful melodic improvisation. On "I Fall in Love Too Easily," from the 2000 album *Everything I Love*, she evokes the eloquent harmonies of Bill Evans, though with a smooth, nuanced touch, even on octaves. Her last chorus, growing from a repeated dominant at the end of the preceding verse, swings into some marvelous extended harmonies on the eighth bar. As she comes to the close of her solo, Elias dissolves into a misty diminuendo, with an unusual combination of rigor and romanticism in her voice movement.

At faster tempos Elias preserves the lyrical quality of her playing. She rarely digs hard into the keys, preferring to build tension by the trajectory of her line. On her free-blowing rendition of Cole Porter's "I Love You," from *Everything I Love*, Elias, bassist Marc Johnson, and drummer Jack De-Johnette shift tonal centers throughout the arrangement, which encourages her to build exhilarating climaxes into her improvised line. The support from her left hand is similarly imaginative, particularly where she locks onto a bitonal chord for the melody to tug against during the last few bars going into the reprise.

In solo context Elias displays even more clearly an unusual fusion of technique and expression. Her 1994 album *Solos and Duets* offers a surging interpretation of "Autumn Leaves," beginning with a thorny motif in the lower register, from which a restless performance emerges. Though IIm-V changes appear at certain cadences, Elias mainly follows a horizontal concept here, with lines rushing and interweaving. Her tempo, though rubato, mirrors the urgency implicit in the tangled voicings of the opening. The Bartókian flavor of this improvisation brings Chick Corea to mind, but Elias's effect here is less intellectual, and somewhat darker.

One notable amplification on Elias's style can be heard on her 1998 album *Eliane Elias Sings Jobim*. With the emphasis on bossa nova, with its spare percussion and sensuous movement, she plays with considerable understatement. On "One Note Samba" her solo follows the melody very strictly, minimally syncopated. And throughout the album her spare accompaniment to her own vocals strips harmonic ideas down to simple, sometimes isolated notes. Though, as the title suggests, the focus is primarily on her voice, Elias demonstrates her command of the idiom and its minimal aesthetic.

It's instructive to compare these performances with Elias's interpretations of bossa material on *Fantasia*, from 1992. Here she approaches "Girl from Ipanema" from a jazz standpoint, with cloudy or clustered chords and strategically placed key changes. Backed by Jack DeJohnette on drums, Eddie Gomez on bass, and Nana Vasconcelos on percussion, she draws from a Keith Jarrett aesthetic, though without his occasional quick bursts and with a more formalized arrangement concept. Elias clearly has the chops, yet she sustains and builds the feel of her solos through rich harmonic movement, motivic variations, and long melodic development. It's a formula that promises to carry her through years of exquisite creativity, regardless of album photos.

71. GONZALO RUBALCABA

Born: May 27, 1963, Havana, Cuba

Gonzalo Rubalcaba hit America like a hurricane in the early nineties, with torrential rhythms and a hailstorm of notes. For a while this storm was mired offshore, stalled by State Department disinterest in allowing Cuban artists into the States. But reports of the pianist's prowess made it through the legal filters, and a series of Blue Note recordings made him impossible to ignore.

He was 28 years old when he made his North American debut—not in the U.S., of course, but at Toronto's El Mocambo. Backed by bassist Charlie Haden and drummer Jack DeJohnette, Rubalcaba delivered a blazing set, fashioned from beginning to end as a single crescendo, from introverted balladry to eruptions of rhythm and velocity. After witnessing this exhibition, I noted in *Keyboard* magazine that his opening numbers were "a kind of Latin take on new age, with long melodic improvisations patiently placed in sixths and unfolded under a hypnotic habanera pattern." By the end of the set, "pedaling sparely, he spins out glitch-free bursts of 32nd-notes [and] unleashes low-register tremolos that rumble like thunder."

It was obvious even then that Rubalcaba was about more than fireworks alone. His romanticism, which endured even at Mach One tempos, pointed the direction in which his style, though still formative, was heading. The fact that he would take such care to make his melodies sing, to shape the details of his rubato even amidst blizzards of rhythm, forecast that the seeds of a mature approach had already taken root. After a decade in the international spotlight—and his relocation from Cuba to the U.S.—Rubalcaba has nurtured this style to the point that it transcends his technique.

Like his compatriot Chucho Valdés , Rubalcaba is a pedigreed virtuoso. His father Guilhermo was a multi-instrumentalist best known for playing saxophone with Enrique Jorrin's popular band. Young Gonzalo tagged along on gigs, where he met Chico Hamilton, Machito, and other giants of Latin jazz. A prodigious talent from the start, he started making waves in his early teens while sitting in with members of Valdés's epochal Irakere ensemble at a club called Jonny Drink. As a piano and percussion major at the Amadeo Roldan Conservatory, and subsequently as a composition student at the Institute of Fine Arts, Rubalcaba chafed against the orthodox curriculum even while mastering its most challenging repertoire. Most of his energy went into catching performances by his favorite local pianists— Frank Emilio, Peruchin, Lily Martinez, Emiliano Salvador, and of course his father—while also studying recordings by Bud Powell, Thelonious Monk, Bill Evans, Keith Jarrett, and Herbie Hancock.

Beginning at age 17, a full decade before his Toronto debut, Rubalcaba was playing outside of Havana. Dizzy Gillespie became a friend and supporter, as did Charlie Haden in 1986. As leader of the fusion-oriented Grupo Royecto, Rubalcaba won critical raves at the Berlin Jazz Festival in 1987. Inevitably, after aggressive lobbying by jazz lovers with government clout, he was finally allowed into the States—on a Dominican Republic passport—in 1993, first to attend Gillespie's funeral, and subsequently to make his high-profile U.S. debut at Lincoln Center. Since then, unencumbered by diplomatic wrong-headedness, Rubalcaba has been able to develop his career through the usual channels, and achieve recognition on the strength of his music, neither helped nor hindered by politics.

Rubalcaba's first U.S. release, *Discovery*, recorded in 1990 at the Montreux Festival, opens with a hair-raising exhibition of polyrhythms and harmonic juxtapositions. The tune, ironically, was Monk's "Well You Needn't," ordinarily played minimally and at moderate tempo; here, Rubalcaba explodes all over the keys with sharp repeated notes and a wild assortment of chords before digging into the theme. But within seconds he's off again; with Haden and drummer Paul Motian essentially keeping time, the pianist builds intensity through an incredible velocity and an almost unprecedented integration of Cuban rhythmic elements and hyperspeed postbop. By the time he's mixing runs in thirds with alternating two-hand jabs and sweeping up from the bass range with a volcanic pedaled smear, he's inviting skeptics to wonder whether there's any fire beneath all this smoke.

Later, on the unaccompanied original tune "Prologo Comienzo," Rubalcaba tears through an improvisation based on a montuño figure. Pedaling lightly, he alternates between variations on the central motif, dazzling runs and layered rhythms, and a few perfunctory spare passages; the five-minute performance batters the listener into a kind of awed submission.

He kept up the same blinding pace on *The Blessing*, his follow-up studio album. As with *Discovery*, Rubalcaba opens at full throttle; "Circuito" has all the flash of "Prologo Comienzo," and in fact falls back on similar devices, from swirling two-handed figures to furious repeated notes and other flashy elements. At least on this track the pianist seems a little more engaged with his sidemen, largely because Jack DeJohnette's drumming seems more responsive and interactive than Motian's.

Later on the same album, Rubalcaba does settle down, to the point of playing "Besame Mucho" at a radically slow tempo. Here he chooses each note with ponderous deliberation, as if to dispel in advance any allegations of showy superficiality. In fact, Rubalcaba does show a supreme ability to animate a melody on this track, through artfully phrasing just behind the beat and using spare intervals, rather than crowded chords, to sustain a languorous mood, as he does on several other performances from the same session. Perhaps recording in the studio rather than before an audience allowed Rubalcaba to explore more reflective possibilities—sometimes to the point of evoking pastoral simplicities, as in the opening moments of his unaccompanied ballad "Mima."

Within a few years Rubalcaba's range broadened noticeably. On *Flying Colors*, a duo project recorded with saxophonist Joe Lovano in 1997, the pianist reveals a more abstract temperament, in which high-velocity bursts play only an abbreviated textural role. His opening rumination on "How Deep Is the Ocean" conveys only subtle Latin elements within a deeper elegiac feeling; with murky low chords and minimal note placements in minor settings, this performance suggests that Rubalcaba is rapidly updating his initial impression as a technical prodigy. Certainly, in their intricate exchanges and deft unison lines throughout the Ornette Coleman tune "Bird Food," Rubalcaba displays a highly tuned sense of interactive improvisation that was absent from his earlier American trio albums.

These characteristics develop even more on *Inner Voyage*, a 1999 trio release. Throughout this album Rubalcaba plays with restraint; his phrasing connects directly with the straightforward grooves laid down by bassist Jeff Chambers and drummer Ignacio Berroa to create a much more unified group feel than he had achieved on previous sessions. On medium swing tunes such as "Promenade" Rubalcaba settles into the rhythm and sustains interest entirely through compelling harmonies and carefully constructed lines. The ballad "Here's That Rainy Day" is even more striking, in its introspective power and employment of extended rests; quarter-notes, played as if in a dream, are far more predominant than even eighth-notes in this performance. Quick flurries still crop up elsewhere on the album, but only where appropriate within the group arrangement. The upshot is that Rubalcaba, in the space of maybe eight years, has achieved a maturity and balance that continues to elude certain other technical dynamos after decades of playing.

The Future Is Now

72. HENRY BUTLER

Born: 1940, New Orleans, Lousiana

Jazz is a music born from diverse elements that had joined together on the common ground of New Orleans. That idea of eclecticism within a specific region is best represented today by Henry Butler, a pianist whose connections to the Crescent City ring clear even when he leaves those connections far behind.

When one speaks of New Orleans piano, Butler is usually not the first artist to come to mind. The relevant lineage begins with Professor Longhair and extends through Tuts Washington, James Booker, and Allen Toussaint—players who play closer to blues than jazz, though with the Latin-influenced syncopations that distinguish the style from more generic permutations. Butler is more than familiar with this style; when he tears into "Tipitina" or some other staple of the repertoire, he's not just visiting that scene—he's speaking from inside of it.

In fact, Butler's background is bigger than blues and jazz alone. Sightless since birth, he spent his earliest years in the city's Calliope housing project, listening primarily to church music and reproducing what he heard on a neighbor's piano. At age six he left for Baton Rouge to study at the Louisiana School for the Blind at Southern University. There, he learned to play drums, valve trombone, and baritone saxophone while channeling his piano performance through classical repertoire. But even though he started playing local gigs in ninth grade, he didn't discover his true enthusiasm for music for another two years, after switching his emphasis from piano to voice.

Of all the pianists featured in this book, Butler is easily the most developed singer, with a masculine baritone formed by an odd collision of gospel music and operatic techniques. His voice is enormous and expressive, disciplined yet resonant with fundamental emotion. Perhaps it was the discovery of this connection that allowed Butler to get past some of the frustration he was feeling in his piano lessons, by channeling that energy from his voice into his work on the keyboard. At the same time, he began exploring jazz and its African antecedents through lessons with clarinetist Alvin Batiste, chairman of the jazz program at Southern University, whom Butler credits for exposing him to the adventurous improvisational techniques practiced by John Coltrane.

After finishing at the School for the Blind, Butler began an exhaustive study regimen. During the academic year he pursued a graduate degree in vocal performance at Michigan State University, working on German lieder, French and Italian art songs, and European composition. Summers were devoted to jazz piano: Before beginning at Michigan he applied an NEA grant to lessons with George Duke, who had just taken Joe Zawinul's place as pianist with Cannonball Adderley. The following summer brought lessons with Harold Mabern, followed a year later by instruction from Sir Roland Hanna, again paid for by the NEA.

As Butler saw it, these disciplines were never separate; Bud Powell, Schubert, and the blues were far closer in spirit than people think. "Bach came closest to what jazz musicians do today," he told me during one interview. "He had to prepare music every week for Sunday services, and it sounds like a lot of the stuff he just improvised. . . . Jazz musicians do that too, you know. They'll take a melody in a live performance, play that head, and then do different improvisations every time they play the tune."

Finally, with his masters degree in hand, it was time for Butler to strike out on his own. He returned to New Orleans in 1974, where he began teaching at the New Orleans Center for the Creative Arts by day and alternating on piano with James Booker at Lu & Charlie's at night. Butler also found

Henry Butler maintains a fondness for powerful attack and, in contrast, quick showers of feathery upper-register notes.

opportunities to reconnect with his local roots through informal lessons with Professor Longhair, and to work with Art Blakey, Gatemouth Brown, and Adderley when they each came to town.

After six years, determined to try his luck in bigger markets, he headed for Los Angeles, where he struggled through an unrewarding life of lounge gigs until one night when Milcho Leviev let him sit in during a trio date with bassist Charlie Haden and drummer Billy Higgins at the Comeback Inn in Venice. Haden, bowled over, immediately arranged for the pianist's recording debut, *Fivin' Around*, released in 1986, with Haden, Higgins, and Freddie Hubbard making up the band. With this album, daring in its eclecticism and emphasis on original material, Butler overnight became a major player in jazz piano.

It was, of course, jazz piano with a strong New Orleans flavor, which would only grow with time. By far the most exciting cut on his 1990 live album *Orleans Inspiration* is the title track, a solo piano performance based on a jangling chorded rhythm and slashed by searing octaves, runs, and soulful figurations. Butler's authority, muscular command of the keys, and incredible rhythm, fully exposed here, would put his brand on more jazz-oriented material as well.

A good example can be heard on his 1996 trio session *For All Seasons*. In his solo on "Blues for All Seasons" Butler demonstrates a punchy, crisp fluency with boppish unison lines, one to each hand, then drops back to funk position for a long, burning blowfest sewn together by smooth segues from blues to more outside languages. When he builds one chorus on two independent lines—a hard-driving, low-register improvisation and a rhythmically and thematically unrelated flurry of notes in the higher range, Butler's authority is impossible to ignore.

For all the bases touched in his solos, Butler maintains a fondness for powerful attack and, in contrast, quick showers of upper-register notes, sometimes in head-spinning octaves but more often as a kind of feathery, out-of-rhythm elaboration behind the melody or someone else's solos. Sometimes all this feels impatient, as if the pianist is trying to push against the tempo; Butler always seems to be in a hurry. It's an intriguing thing to imagine this exciting pianist should he decide to slow down—provided, of course, that it comes at no cost to the intensity that guides his performance today.

73. MULGREW MILLER

Born: August 13, 1955, Greenwood, Mississippi

In the tradition of Hank Jones and Kenny Barron, Mulgrew Miller represents the best of session piano playing. His consistency and intelligence have won him first-call status among his peers and earned him one of the most extensive discographies in jazz. These same qualities distinguish Miller's own albums, though the adaptability that has made him so appealing as a hired gun has also made it harder for him to come across as an artist with his own recognizable style.

As a child in the Mississippi Delta, Miller grew up to the tune of church music. He was six years old when his father brought a piano into the house; the first tune young Mulgrew picked out was from the congregational hymnbook, "Come By Thy Fount of Every Blessing." Without a strong teacher in the area, he essentially taught himself to play on the job as organist for ten years at the local church.

In his early teens Miller started playing gigs with a regional soul band, playing a Farfisa organ on cover versions of hits by Al Green, Aretha Franklin, and James Brown.

Jazz entered the picture when, at age 14, Miller saw Oscar Peterson perform on television. That one experience exposed him to a level of improvisation that he hadn't previously confronted, and inspired him to start some serious woodshedding. Guided by recordings of Art Tatum, Erroll Garner, Ahmad Jamal, and other luminaries, he polished his performance sufficiently to gain admission in 1973 to Memphis State University as a music education major. Along with new friend and fellow pianist James Williams, he attended concerts by visiting artists such as Phineas Newborn, McCoy Tyner, and Chick Corea, while adding some polish to his self-developed technique.

While still a student Miller accepted a call to substitute on a few gigs with the Duke Ellington Orchestra, which was being led at the time by Duke's son Mercer. Two years later, in 1977, Mercer called again, this time to offer him the piano gig full-time. The years he spent with the legendary ensemble helped sharpen Miller's ear for timbre and accompaniment, so that he was able meet the demands of backing Betty Carter when the fiery singer hired him in 1980. From there Miller went on to perform with the Woody Shaw Quintet and saxophonist Johnny Griffin, before accepting an invitation to succeed his schoolmate James Williams as pianist with Art Blakey's Jazz Messengers.

The gigs have come thick and fast since Miller left the Messengers in 1986. His prolific activities leave us a clear and impressive record of performance. Throughout his solo and session projects Miller maintains an understated, thoughtful style, generally unmarred by any sense of urgency. His harmonies bring those of Herbie Hancock to mind, rich with lustrous and romantic clusters. When soloing, he pares down to single lines in the right hand, which typically move easily in and out of relation to the chords. Miller swings in a gentle, unhurried way, neither pushing nor dragging the beat; instead, he keeps pace with it, somewhat like a tourist strolling past and commenting on the sights.

The academic aspects of Miller's performance are apparent on the Wallace Roney recording of "Blue in Green," available as a bonus track on *According to Mr. Roney*. His adaptation to the harmonic aesthetic of Bill Evans is flawless, down to the opening of his swing-oriented solo. However, his rush into double-time toward the end of this brief section does little to encourage the reflective nature of the tune, though it does set the stage for the flurry of notes that kicks off Gary Thomas's tenor solo. Throughout the track Miller's playing displays an uncanny sensitivity, and the extended solo piano coda at the end offers some marvelous extensions of Evans's conceptions, but a sense lingers up to that point that something in the heart of the music eludes him.

Equally typical is Miller's long solo on "Don't Blame Me," from Wallace Roney's *The Standard Bearer*. From the opening verse, he stakes out separate territory for each hand, the long linear work of the right staying in the medium/upper register as the left hand creates a harmonic framework with irregular chords in the lower midrange. Emphasis, in Miller's book, involves occasional coordination of the two hands for rhythmic emphasis, a technique heard on other ballad tracks such as "What a Difference a Day Makes," on his own 1990 trio album *From Day to Day*, but even here his touch is more suggestive than overt. Rather than digging in, his prefers to spread a sheen across the material, often in extended bitonal passages that hardly ripple the surface of his execution, as on "When Your Lover Has Gone." On "Giant Steps" from the same album, and "If I Should Lose You," from his 1995 release

Getting to Know You, Miller shows himself capable of negotiating tougher changes at faster tempos, yet his approach is essentially unchanged, with the same unhurried, almost detached feeling. On more angular material, such as Ron Carter's "Opus One Point Five," from the Roney album *Intuition*, he plays with a measured, almost cautious pointillism, picking out a solo through the tentative starts and stops written into the tune. Its effect is to conform to, rather than challenge, the feel of the material. Elsewhere, however, as on "Ahead" from the same album, Miller explores some vivid harmonic implications with a solo whose restrained execution gives it some extra momentum over the heated interactions between Carter's bass and Cindy Blackman's drums.

Miller, in fact, excels at riding the rhythm, playing along its surface rather than kicking it forward. His comps, and the breezily swinging solo, on "The Way You Look Tonight," from the Lew Soloff album *With a Song in My Heart*, illustrate why he is one of the most popular sidemen in jazz. The dance of his playing never distracts from the leader's personality, in effect completing the package with the right kind of wrapper. On the title track, he delivers a classic postbop solo over several verses, building neatly to a peak on at the end without overplaying or, it seems, working up a sweat at all. And his three choruses on "Bags' Groove," from the Gary Burton album *For Hamp, Red, Bags, and Cal*, show off Miller's command of the blues, as well as his ability, on the second chorus, to take the line just outside enough to make the traditional funk figure work perfectly to close the solo.

But Miller also reflects a McCoy Tyner influence, particularly on material that lends itself to more of a modal improvisational approach. On "La Chambre," an original tune on *From Day to Day* built

Mulgrew Miller can create a strong "outside" impression in solos that in fact adhere to well-established principles.

around a bluesy motif in the chorus, he displays a harder attack, with aggressive spiraling figures, ringing octave tremolos, and overtly funky figurations. The introduction to the title track of *Getting to Know You* seems even more like a Tyner homage, with a 6/8 rhythm feel and muscular quartal chords, before sliding into an approach to the tune that reflects more of a restrained Tyner feel. He's even more aggressive on "Sublimity," from his 1986 trio album *Work!*—here, Miller pounds with an arm-weight attack that's pure Tyner, and swirling figures in his improvisation that draw from that same well. There's little here in common with the salon-like feel Miller cultivates on other sessions, other than a resolute commitment to irregular left-hand comps and long linear solos. At their worst, these moments lack the elegance of his more mainstream work, and often miss its buoyant rhythmic phrasing as well.

Because of his grounding in the postbop model, Miller can create an "outside" impression in solos that in fact adhere to well-established structural and harmonic principles. One excellent example can be heard on "Four," the opening cut from Benny Golson's *I Remember Miles* album, recorded in 1992. The tune opens with a four-bar unaccompanied piano part that suggests a rhythmically free but bop-flavored conception, which Miller delivers immediately after the opening verse. From his unaccompanied pickup he unfurls a long linear improvisation that slips elegantly in and out of the changes. Miller plays throughout his solo with a bracing sense of swing that skims over some vexacious implied harmonies. Notice how, for example, Miller plays through the entire third verse and most of the fourth in several keys that relate only distantly to where the piece is being played, yet when he comes in for a landing back home in the last four bars, everything falls into place, and the pianist's long view turns out to have made brilliant sense.

In a similar performance, Miller offers an exquisite rendering of "Body and Soul" on his 1993 trio album *With Our Own Eyes*. The unaccompanied opening begins at the bridge, with easily recognized chords, which by the second bar have extended into some unorthodox voicings that hit the rest on a diminished fifth. Miller's ruminations through the next verse emphasize both the familiarity of the tune and his willingness to twist it into intriguing angles. His straight eighth-note chords set the ballad pulse for the entrance of bassist Richie Goods and drummer Tony Reedus, then immediately Miller lifts the tune into some quietly iconoclastic chord substitutions and inventive variations on the melody. Now and then he moves from velvety textures into a more pointed passage, but by and large he succeeds at enhancing the mood we've come to associate with the tune with a perspective that's thoroughly modern, even borderline disturbing. It's a wonderful solo by any measure.

74. KENNY KIRKLAND

Born: September 28, 1955, Newport, New York
Died: November 12, 1998, New York, New York

The first in a series of gifted pianists to apprentice in the Wynton Marsalis band, Kirkland was also arguably the most mature at the youngest age. Marcus Roberts, his successor, would more quickly develop a recognizable style, though it could also be criticized as the most affected.

In his theme-oriented albums and extended compositions, Eric Reed would seem the most ambitious. But Kirkland almost immediately exhibited a massive grasp of jazz piano practice, in his understanding of the form and his gift for swing.

Sadly, Kirkland would also be the first of the Marsalis pianists to depart the scene. He was only 43 when he was found dead inside his apartment in Queens, New York; the cause of death was never made clear. In that brief time he was allowed, Kirkland not only realized much of his enormous promise as a straight-ahead improviser in jazz, he also enjoyed his moment in the sun as a media icon with Branford Marsalis's *Tonight Show* band and crossed over to a high-profile career with Sting, who knew the value of surrounding himself with the best players whose services a rock star income could buy.

Kirkland made his impact almost entirely as a sideman, with only one album as a leader to his credit. His ability to fit into a wide range of styles owes to his pursuit of fluency beyond the limits of just one genre. When playing electronic keyboards with Sting, Kirkland showed sensitivity to the nuances that each one offered; like Joe Zawinul with Weather Report, he thought of synthesizers as an arranger rather than as a soloist would. In every setting, whether playing funk, Latin, or R&B, he kept the piano as his primary instrument for improvising.

His education began in Bedford-Stuyvesant, Brooklyn, where he and his three siblings were raised in a Catholic household. His father, sensing Kenny's talent, surprised him by bringing a piano into their apartment—but he also insisted that the six-year-old treat it seriously. It took a while, but when he reached age 13 Kenny suddenly got the message and began to practice diligently. Throughout high school he took weekly lessons in the prep division of the Manhattan School of Music, beginning with piano performance, then moving on into theory and composition. His instruction was classical, though away from the lesson books he sought out R&B/soul stations on the radio.

This extracurricular diet of Sly Stone, James Brown, and Motown led Kirkland eventually to perhaps his greatest influence on the keyboard: Herbie Hancock, whose *Headhunters* project validated and stimulated the young pianist's multi-genre instincts. From there he followed the path back into deeper jazz traditions, beginning with Hancock's funk predecessor Wynton Kelly and, on higher harmonic planes, Bill Evans, Ahmad Jamal, Chick Corea, and other modern pianists with evident ties to tradition.

Still, the young artist wasn't sure that he had what it took to break in as a full-time performer. He was thinking vaguely about pursuing a teaching career when, during his last year at the Manhattan School, a traffic accident forced him to drop out. After he had recuperated, Kirkland went after his first professional gig, as a member of fusion violinist Michal Urbaniak's group, having met Urbaniak through a mutual acquaintance, drummer Buddy Williams of the original *Saturday Night Live* band. In 1977, playing a Rhodes electric piano and a Minimoog synth for the first time, Kirkland hit the road in Europe with Urbaniak and never looked back.

Over the next few years he concentrated on working from his New York home base; his longest engagements were with pop singer Angela Bofill and percussionist Don Alias. When he accepted an offer from Terumasa Hino to tour Japan, Kirkland set himself up for a career-changing encounter there with Wynton Marsalis. Their affiliation led to a series of four albums. On the first of these, titled *Wynton Marsalis* and released in 1982, Kirkland tackled original material that was already more daring than one might reasonably expect from a 19-year-old bandleader. "Father Time" opens with a four-bar rhythm riff on the V chord, which Kirkland pushes with a few well-placed dissonant staccato jolts before the band settles into the opening verse. Though a swing feel kicks things off, the arrangement is filled with changes—to a languid 3⁄4 and, eventually, to a turbulent 6/8 for the solo section. Playing behind other soloists, Kirkland stays out of the way of bassist Clarence Seay and drummer Jeff Watts; his role isn't to paint textures so much as to drop harmonic suggestions, like quick little bombs, when needed in the spaces. On his own solo, Kirkland reins in the chords, with some oddly affecting triads complemented by simple elaborations in the right hand—until Branford Marsalis tears into a rocking solo, which Kirkland quickly answers with sharp tremolos and stabs.

Later, on "Twilight," Kirkland builds his improvisation on interaction with Charles Fambrough. The bassist is hitting the dominant in intense sixteenth-notes as the section begins; when he expands into a walking pattern, Kirkland follows with a burning performance that tears into the upper register, swoops down with powerful chords toward the midrange, then trips through a rising and falling string of contracting and expanding intervals, played first at a leisurely clip, then revved into quicker sequence before dissolving as Fambrough returns to the funky opening riff. In this performance we hear exceptional promise from Kirkland, not only because of the imagination he brings to his improvisation but more specifically because of his ability to pick up ideas from his colleagues.

Kirkland was well on his way to building a name for himself when he appeared as one of the "young lions" featured on the Dizzy Gillespie album *New Faces* in 1984. Throughout this disc he shows the aggressive, somewhat hard-edged approach to rhythm and freewheeling melodic inventiveness that would largely define his improvisational approach. His solo on the Latin burner "Lorraine" builds steadily through two choruses, from a dotted-eighth and repeated-note motif early on to a propulsive line that winds in and out of alternate voicings, returns to a galloping iteration of a single note, then expands into an assertive chorded finale in three-against-two rhythm. What's striking here isn't Kirkland's note selections or technique as much as the urgency in his phrasing. Whether pumping a montuño riff behind the band on the final verse or cooling the proceedings with an ascending, arpeggiated ritard, he devoted himself to feeding, if not defining, the ebb and flow of tension throughout each arrangement.

By 1991, when he cut his only album as a leader, Kirkland had acquired an undeniable authority as a player and was showing signs of great originality as a composer. On the opening track of *Kenny Kirkland*, a blazing quartet performance titled "Mr. J.C.," the pianist blasts from the first chorus into a solo marked by a tremendously aggressive impetus and a daring approach to melody. After paraphrasing from the written motif, he nudges the figure up half an octave, deconstructs it into fragments, then begins an inspired performance marked by an anchor-solid left hand, and a right hand that stutters yet swings through octaves and single lines. He punctuates high-velocity passages with strong polyrhythmic chords, and covers a multi-octave range without trading melodic integrity for gratuitous fireworks. It's the kind of solo one would expect from a master, played in an already distinctive, non-derivative style.

Though Kirkland played ballads with evident feeling, sometimes it seemed as if he was on unsteadier ground than at up tempos. His long solo on "Dienda," from the 1986 Branford Marsalis album *Royal Garden Blues*, shows melodic inventiveness as the pianist extemporizes through the tune's complex changes. But he also restricts his left hand to somewhat wooden comps, often placed squarely on the beat, while keeping to a single line with his right. It's easy to imagine a pianist like Herbie Hancock extending chords much further and varying the texture throughout this kind of material—but then, Kirkland was still in the early stages of his career when he cut this track.

It isn't a stretch to suggest that with his harmonic vocabulary, driving rhythmic phrasing, and temperate use of electronic keyboards Kirkland may have ascended to a position comparable to that of Hancock in the sixties and seventies. As it is, his legacy has a feeling of completeness; rather than leave as an unformed talent, Kirkland had already surpassed his own expectations, whether or not his self-effacing nature would incline him to admit it.

75. FRED HERSCH

Born: October 21, 1955, Cincinnati, Ohio

It's too easy to jump to conclusions about Fred Hersch. His gently dissonant reharmonizations and the almost melancholy contours of his lines encourage listeners to mark him as a disciple of Bill Evans, though the differences between their styles are just as striking.

The irony is that Hersch *is* a follower of Evans, though in terms of spirit more than sound. Both artists committed themselves to serious study and emotional introspection. Each knew that the greater his understanding of the tools available to him as a musician, the more he would be able to discover a unique voice as an improviser.

In Hersch's case, that voice speaks softly. Evans could play just as quietly, but more typically he hit the keys a little harder and pedaled a bit less. His accomplishment was to be able to paint moody pictures with a pointillist technique, as if using a stick instead of brush strokes. For Hersch, the piano is less percussive and more textural. Even on his up-tempo performances there's a silky legato feeling. And when outlining a tune with the playful, connect-the-dots approach that he sometimes enjoys, he keeps his short notes full and soft as well.

In some ways, Thelonious Monk was as important a touchstone for Hersch as was Evans or anyone else. It is the nature of Monk's compositions to encourage younger players to emulate or at least refer to his style, but Hersch found something different in this repertoire. His album *Thelonious: Fred Hersch Plays Monk* probed Monk compositions without a hint of imitation. Other than the occasional whole-tone fragment, *Thelonious* is as much about the pianist's romantic essence as the composer's distinctive, edgy style. By not backing away from either, Hersch honors both Monk's and his own visions, and meets the highest standards of jazz interpretation.

His accomplishments owe much to the parallel experiences of his classical training and extensive apprenticeship as a sideman. After graduating with honors from the New England Conservatory of Music, Hersch settled in New York and started taking gigs with Joe Henderson, Toots Thielemans, Stan Getz, Eddie Daniels, and other headliners. Unlike many of his contemporaries, he also spent a lot of time accompanying singers; with Janis Siegel of the Manhattan Transfer, he established an especially enduring and illuminating relationship.

This experience with singers may account for the sense of breath that infuses much of Hersch's playing. It animates the work he has done with bassist Drew Gress and drummer Tom Rainey, and nudges it closer to the model of Keith Jarrett's performances with Gary Peacock and Jack DeJohnette than to the Evans threesomes. Both pianists build breath-like segments into their lines, which stretch the phrasing away from adherence to a song's formal structure and more toward a more natural, physical energy. In fact, much of the Hersch trio's performance of "For All We Know," from their album *Dancing in the Dark*, could be mistaken for a Jarrett track, except that Hersch holds himself back from playing fast, locks his group into a straight swing rhythm more often—and, thankfully, doesn't squeal and gasp, as is Jarrett's lamentable habit when improvising.

Hersch does share Jarrett's interest in exploring the expressive power of melody, but in a more subdued, less overt manner. In his solo rendition of "If I Should Lose You," also from *Dancing in the Dark*, Hersch structures his improvisation along a kind of textural crescendo and diminuendo, with a very long opening that consists of one line that blossoms gradually into two and then more lines in abstract, spacious counterpoint, builds into some syncopated chords that prod the melody along, and then evaporates down to a delicate final recitation of the theme in the highest range of the keys. In typical Hersch fashion, it's all underplayed and elegant, lacking in flash and fire, yet profound in its quiet way.

Hersch is a languorous player. He encourages the lyric element through a flexible and imaginative use of his left hand. When he does follow the familiar postbop formula for comping, as on his rendition of Dizzy Gillespie's "Con Alma" from *The Fred Hersch Trio Plays . . .*, or from their up-tempo version of "So In Love," from *Dancing in the Dark*, it's with a full but unobtrusive sound just an octave or so below Middle *C* and a fresh sense of placement within the rhythm. These clustered chords sometimes create a muffled timbre, like the tines of an electric piano.

In addition to recording "songbook" albums dedicated to the works of specific performers and composers, Hersch has kept active in his fascination with less mainstream material. His schedule allows for occasional orchestral appearances, as well as an intriguing cross-genre partnership with classical pianist Jeffrey Kahane and more avant-garde appearances at the Knitting Factory and other venues. His compositions include a work for piano and cello, "Tango Bittersweet," which he performed with Erik Friedlander on *Memento Bittersweet*; proceeds from sales of the album are donated to AIDS research.

Since coming out as HIV positive in 1994, Hersch has been a pioneer among jazz musicians in working to combat AIDS. That year saw the release of *Last Night While We Were Young: The Ballad Album*, a collection of performances organized by Hersch to raise money for Classical Action: Performing Arts Against AIDS. He has expressed his reluctance in various interviews over the prospect of being confined in a "poster boy" role, whether as a gay icon or a Bill Evans disciple. It is, he explains, a matter of perspective: His music, not the categories imposed upon him, are what make Hersch one of the most impressive and rewarding pianists of his generation.

76. BILLY CHILDS

Born: March 8, 1957, Los Angeles, California

I t might as well be ordained by law or union regulations that before getting your jazz piano license, you need to collar the nearest music journalist and pay your respect to Art Tatum, Bud Powell, Monk, maybe Bill Evans, and a few other icons of jazz piano. This list of influences is pretty close to universal, and thus at the same time valid and mundane.

Billy Childs, on the other hand, is likely the only major-league tickler to include Keith Emerson among his heroes. Though the rock keyboardist and the rest of Emerson, Lake & Palmer did actually make it onto the cover of *Down Beat*, the leather-clad, shag-coiffed Englishman was about as far from being a jazz cat as a musician could be; when not stabbing his Hammond organ or swilling magnificently from the bottle of brandy perched conspicuously on one of his synthesizers, Emerson was famous for assiduously avoiding dotted-eighths in his solos and crunching Paul Desmond's "Take Five" into a heavy-hoofed, 4/4 lope.

Yet there he is, on Childs's list of inspirations. No echo of this infatuation lingers in his music, unless one squints carefully at his writing—specifically, at the highly structured content of his themes and arrangements. By his own admission a late-bloomer and even then a somewhat half-hearted student, he clearly found in *Tarkus* the conceptual lessons that other pianists may have derived directly from Beethoven and Bartók.

Today Childs is known for his emphatic swing, his assured technique, and a strong instinct for interactive play. His harmonic work has a firm, chiseled quality, which he softens through careful pedaling and lacy ornamental runs. For all his mainstream eloquence, it is difficult to believe that Childs very nearly lost interest in playing until being brought back into action by the prog-rock god.

His first exposure to piano instruction was brief, consisting a few lessons at age six. For the next eight years he did little more than occasionally doodle on the keys. The critical epiphany came in 1971, when as a boarding school student he had his exposure to ELP. On returning to Hamilton High School in L.A., Childs made up for lost time with a spurt of classical instruction and jazz self-education through a diet of recordings by Freddie Hubbard, Chick Corea, McCoy Tyner, Herbie Hancock, and other contemporary giants. At age 17 he was playing pickup jazz dates in L.A. and taking music theory at the University of Southern California. A year later, as a full-time USC student, he was taking Robert Linn's composition course, studying jazz piano privately with Herb Mickman, and sitting in regularly at Onaje's, a club near the campus.

Even before graduating in 1979 with top honors from the composition program, the young pianist had spent time on the road in Japan in trombonist J. J. Johnson's band. Once he nailed his degree, Childs signed up with trumpeter Freddie Hubbard. This was his toughest training: "Things had to be perfect right then and now," he told me in an interview. "Everything had to work. If it didn't, the penalty was that you were fired."

Apparently Childs passed the test, since he spent six years sharing the bandstand with Hubbard. During off-time, he performed with singer Dianne Reeves in the band Night Flight and picked up additional local work with Top 40 acts in L.A. Other gigs came and went during this same period, with Bobby

Hutcherson, Grover Washington, Benny Golson, George Coleman, Dave Holland, Jack DeJohnette, Terence Blanchard, Branford Marsalis, and other headliners.

When he released his debut as a leader, *Take For Example This . . .*, in 1988, Childs was well situated for a solo career. This has included, in addition to a solid sequence of albums, commissions to compose two extended works for the Monterey Jazz Festival, and work with a barrier-breaking group called Prophecy, dedicated to fusing poetry, hip-hop, jazz, and other diverse elements into an integrated experience.

The Childs style was becoming apparent in the title cut from the J. J. Johnson album *Concepts in Blue*, from 1980, on which the pianist follows the rich harmonies of the changes to a finale of right-hand chords sliding over a static voicing in the left. The earlier part of this solo feels a bit forced, especially as Childs pops off some hurried octaves and hits an awkward dead end in a run just before the chorded final section. He obviously brings a real inventiveness to the table, but an organic feel for rhythm hasn't yet asserted itself.

Childs's solo on "'Round Midnight," from the 1981 Freddie Hubbard album *Keystone Bop, Volume 2: Friday and Saturday*, is built on his scampering right hand and daring melodic imagination. We hear some already familiar figures—a triplet motif that alternates an upper note with a descending line in the lower notes, and some descending II-V-I sequences at the beginning of verses. More than on the Johnson album, though, Childs digs in, sometimes with blazing conviction; the heat of his performance fuels some exciting interaction with drummer Steve Houghton and bassist Larry Klein.

On "Birdlike," from Hubbard's *Keystone Bop Sunday Night*, Childs builds his solo on movement between bluesy lines and more florid bitonal explorations, slipping from one to the other on the trajectory of his line. He fleshes out the blues changes with a few chromatic descending chords, which keep the harmonic flavor in constant dynamic flux. Several choruses in he switches to a more pointed attack, with barbed, single-note repetitions for a chorus—a nice lead-in for Hubbard's entry and the following drum solo.

Childs favored prickly, hard-edged sounds on these dates, which allowed him to coherently present his restless chord movement and high-register lines. Though fully capable of locking onto an up-tempo groove, he often slid out to lay triplet or even free-rhythm passages against the beat. On *Take For Example This . . .*, he returns to these practices from a noticeably more mature perspective. His beautiful composition "Quiet Girl" leads to a piano solo distinguished by its thoughtful, well-paced development. Childs's changes are elusive, a challenge for the improviser, but he comes to the fore with a solid first chorus in which the linear implications of the theme break into components and weave together.

At this point Childs doesn't seem to be in as much of a rush as he had been in his days as an apprentice. The fire of his earlier work has cooled, though an appealing balance of feeling and intellect endures. In his ballad playing, Childs shows much more comfort and confidence. On the title cut to *Take For Example This . . .*, he uses spaces between the notes expressively and reverts only occasionally to the stock licks that had formerly clogged his solos; just before drummer Steve Houghton kicks into an emphatic moment, Childs dusts off his alternating triplet figure, but here it serves the purpose of delineating the transition from one section of the tune to the next. He uses it also in a sultry rendition of Ivan

Lins's "The Island," from *Portrait of a Player*, along with his familiar descending three-note figure, once more in order to build an otherwise subdued solo to a peak of sorts.

On later releases Childs still tended to hit notes hard, though he had learned to do so more expressively and less haphazardly. Much of his solo treatment of "Never Let Me Go," on *Portrait of a Player*, is played with an almost shattering impact, as Childs punches out assorted explorations of the theme. Perhaps because of the persistence of this touch, his insights into the tune feel like snapshots of isolated sections, which never quite hang together in a broader picture. The impression is one of virtuosity, even brilliance, but not quite revelation.

It can take time to coax talent to full fruition, and in the case of Childs, whose emergence began so late and from such unlikely antecedents, it is fair to expect that his growth is still underway, with his peak years almost within reach.

77. GERI ALLEN

Born: June 12, 1957, Pontiac, Michigan

You would think that Cass Tech—alma mater to Barry Harris, Donald Byrd, and Frank Rosolino, in the hometown of Hank, Thad, and Elvin Jones—had exhausted the odds of producing more than one jazz giant. Yet common sense was defied as Geri Allen emerged from this historic school with her degree, and a torrent of talent, in her hands. In fact, Allen is one of the strongest candidates of her generation for enduring recognition as a pianist and improviser of the highest order.

The daughter of teachers, Allen began piano lessons at age seven. At Cass she supplemented her studies with jazz instruction from Marcus Belgrave as part of his Jazz Development Workshop. Some of her first important professional contacts were made within this program, including future saxophone star Kenny Garrett and bassist John Hurst, who would eventually work with Wynton and Branford Marsalis. After graduation she enrolled in the Jazz Studies Program at Howard University, where she made another important acquaintance, with fellow student and future trumpet great Wallace Roney, and began private instruction with the city's most respected pianist, John Malachi.

After earning her bachelor's in 1979, Allen briefly pursued graduate studies in musicology at the University of Pittsburgh, where she did some teaching and wrote a thesis on the music of Eric Dolphy. Finally, in 1982, after earning her masters in ethnomusicology, she moved to New York, took advanced lessons from Kenny Barron, and began finding work in a variety of styles, from recording with saxophonist Oliver Lake's band Jump Up to accompanying ex-Supreme Mary Wilson in sets that consisted entirely of Motown hits.

Inevitably the quality and quantity of work began picking up, and over the next few years Allen found herself onstage and in the studio with Steve Coleman and other members of his M-Base collective, in trio gigs with bassist Charlie Haden and drummer Paul Motian, and as head of her own quartet. In the early nineties she worked for several years with singer Betty Carter, and in 1995 became the first pianist in 30 years to perform with avant-garde icon Ornette Coleman.

Allen is a harmonically adventurous player, with a gift for sensitively shaping a phrase at any tempo. Her solo piece "Blue," from the 1989 album *Geri Allen Trio*, shows this talent clearly, along with her eclectic compositional skill. A Satie-like feeling—thoughtful yet brimming with quiet passion—permeates this performance. Allen's moments of improvisation toward the end of the piece, before the coda section, introduce a hint of blues—just enough to impose an earthy fragrance without disrupting the delicate bouquet assembled up to that point.

Equipped with a boundless capacity for harmonic and melodic exploration, Allen shows her gifts especially clearly on "When Kabuya Dances," also from *Geri Allen Trio*, because of the blowing section's foundation on a simple I-chord figure. Beginning with a propulsive line punctuated by note repetitions, she broadens into a passage of lyric thirds, leading into more aggressive out-of-rhythm cyclical figures, and then breaks the barriers with swirls of notes in a passage tempered by an ability to keep even the wildest, most spirited blizzards accessible to those who appreciate when soloists acknowledge the written theme. A brief bass solo by Jaribu Shahid provides a moment for Allen to catch her breath before diving back into another round of exhilarating invention.

In these performances, Allen may bring Lyle Mays to mind; their solo styles both ride on a strong current of linear ideas, with occasional virtuoso displays of hand independence. A similar impression derives from "Ray," Allen's performance with Vernon Reid on acoustic guitar and Mino Cinelu on discreet atmospheric percussion, from *The Gathering*, released in 1998. On this track Reid's performance, and the reverberant production, recall Mays's longtime bandleader Pat Metheny. The differences are in the steely attack and unmistakable Hendrix influence that Reid brings, and in Allen's willingness to balance his emphatic articulation with a more legato approach that derives its power from the liquid flow of her phrasing and the well-formed construction of her lines. On this track, Allen surrenders the emotional spotlight to her colleague, yet makes an eloquent statement of her own by simply opening one of the many other doors within her reach.

At faster tempos, Allen is as formidable. The opening section of "Dark Prince," also from *The Gathering*, is a postbop sprint; with drummer Lenny White and bassist Buster Williams, she hits the first beat at full speed, jamming freely over a crawl of left-hand clusters. Shifting from sixteenth-notes to catch-your-breath triplets and back again, Allen never loses control, and in fact feeds as much back to the band as she draws from them. Then, when Vernon Reid comes in for some guitar atmospherics, she cuts the rhythm feel down to half-time, with well-placed, complex chords that hang in the air over White's continuing rhythm sprint.

Though she plays mainly her own material, Allen has no trouble tackling standards. Her performance of "A Beautiful Friendship," with White again on drums and Palle Danielsson on bass, is a highlight of her album *Some Aspects of Water*. On these sorts of cuts she brings Keith Jarrett to mind—not in how she applies her technique, which doesn't match his in terms of sheer velocity, but in her willingness to expand a tune into configurations that amplify on its original shape. After an opening statement that applies a mixolydian concept to the first thematic variation, she builds quickly from a focus on boppish eighth-notes to counter-rhythmic figurations that break up the line and at the same time push the beat. There's bracing rhythmic interaction between her hands at the peak of this solo—a trademark of sorts for Allen—as well as moments of modal experimentation. On the out chorus, before segueing to the bass solo, she seems to lose a bit of steam—only the slightest blemish on this otherwise solidly conceived performance.

On the following track, her one-chorus solo on "Old Folks," bookended by flugelhornist Johnny Coles's more extended display, offers an almost architectural examination of the tune, as Allen creates a spare but eloquent melody, absent fireworks and with very little left hand. With its beautifully placed peak and diminuendo in the last few bars, this is a miniature masterpiece of improvisation—as impressive, in its hushed presentation, as any of her more emphatic and extended exhibitions. Expressive in miniature settings, and powerful in ambitious large-scale compositions, Allen has only begun to show her strength.

78. RENEE ROSNES

Born: February 24, 1962, Regina, Saskatchewan

A long apprenticeship with distinguished veterans and young innovators equipped Renee Rosnes to perform at the highest level of mainstream modern jazz. To take the next step and emerge as an artist of the first rank is her next and greatest challenge.

Clearly Rosnes was meant to be a musician. She started taking piano lessons at the age of three and continued them through two years at the University of Toronto. During much of this period she also studied violin; one can speculate that her string playing helped guide her toward her smooth, relatively non-percussive style at the keyboard.

After playing in Vancouver for a while, Rosnes moved to New York in 1986 and began to pick up work. The following year she accepted an offer to play piano in saxophonist Joe Henderson's band for a tour throughout the U.S., Japan, and Europe. Another interesting gig followed, with OTB (Out of the Blue), after which Rosnes played successively with saxophonist Wayne Shorter, trombonist J. J. Johnson, and then with trumpeter Jon Faddis in the Carnegie Hall Jazz Band.

Since her debut as a leader in 1989, on an eponymous album that featured guest shots from saxophonist Branford Marsalis and her good friend and fellow pianist Herbie Hancock, Rosnes has come out from the sideman shadows. Support from Marian McPartland, and appearances with artists like Dizzy Gillespie, James Moody, and Wynton Marsalis's Lincoln Center Jazz Orchestra, kept her profile high, but it's her own work that's made Rosnes a headliner.

A strong harmonic vocabulary provides the foundation for her art. This reflects in her compositions: Though often built on a simple motif, such as the droning fifths in the blues variant "Ancestors," they also open into a series of sophisticated changes. This combination of clarity and complexity makes many of her tunes ideal vehicles for solos. Rosnes herself, in playing her own material, often breaks her left hand down to two notes or even one, while suggesting the harmony in the trajectory of her right hand. So it is in her introduction to "Abstraction Blue," from *As We Are Now*, in which she examines a somewhat angular theme through an alteration of vividly voiced chords and stark recitations. Even when she thickens the harmony, she keeps plenty of space around her more pungent dissonances, which she resolves quickly with straight-ahead chords, spare bitonalities, or even bell-like triads, as on the title track to *For the Moment*.

Conceptually, Rosnes follows tradition, with clearly conceived lines that weave over unobtrusive comps. Her articulation is smooth and clean, and her ability to spin out ideas often impresses. She excels particularly with ballads, where the absence of an up-tempo groove poses special challenges to melody-oriented players. Her rendition of "Thinking to Myself," from *For the Moment*, offers a lesson on how to mold a solo line through successive episodes of tension and release.

On the same album, Rosnes performs "Four in One" without succumbing to the imitative temptations that are often part of the practice of playing Monk material. When she finally does one of his whole-tone figurations, her phrasing is watery; rather than jab at the notes, she lets her lines spill over the chord. And when she allows herself a few pointed moments, they reflect her language more than Monk's, with little minor-second trills that adorn the broader melodic line.

These trills are a hallmark in her formula; on any number of extended solos, she lights these sparklers where she feels contrast is necessary to break up the legato flow. She also does variations on this trill, as in her solo on "Nemesis," from *For the Moment*, which begins with a tight triplet figuration. A similar triplet figure occurs several times in her album *Ancestors*, during her first solo statement on "Upo Neguinho," as well as toward the end of her solo on "Chasing Spirits." In both performances she moves the upper note of the figure back and forth to add an internal melodic quality to its decoration of the broader line. She also uses trills as a dynamic effect, as on "Chasing Spirits," also from *Ancestors,* to bring the band's volume down before she begins her solo.

A well-placed trill works well as ornamentation, but when trotted out a little too often it suggests a momentary block. There are times when these trills and sequences seem to mark a brief interruption in the train of ideas. Never a rhythmic player, she can exacerbate this impression of hesitation by not digging into the beat or hitting a syncopation hard to free some fresh stream of ideas.

Despite her gifts, Rosnes has yet to develop a distinctive sound. Perhaps her talent lies more in the compositional realm; if so, she seems destined to claim fame as a writer with more than her share of performance chops.

79. CYRUS CHESTNUT

Born: January 17, 1963, Baltimore, Maryland

I t's not at all unusual for church music to provide early inspiration to jazz pianists. Where Cyrus Chestnut stands out is in the sustaining influence of black religious services, and in his application of this influence into a musicianship forged through extensive formal training. Where gospel elements were prominent in the work of the hard bop and funk pianists of the fifties, Chestnut has built his style on a more discerning adaptation of this tradition into a sophisticated postbop vocabulary.

But there is far more to Chestnut than this. He has a special fondness for applying classical devices in his arrangements; it's often easier to spot a Baroque figuration than a churchy turnaround in a Chestnut solo. While such exercises testify to this pianist's broad range, they also suggest that he has yet to blend his many parts into a fully integrated identity.

Chestnut, an only child, was weaned on church music almost exclusively. His father, McDonald Chestnut, was a postal worker during the week and a gospel pianist on Sundays. When Cyrus began showing interest in the piano at age five, his father started giving him lessons. Within two years the younger Chestnut was performing as well, at the Mount Calvary Star Baptist Church. More advanced study followed at the Peabody Preparatory Institute, where he took instruction in organ, flute, and baritone horn before earning certification in piano and music theory.

By the age of nine Chestnut had also caught the jazz bug, and bits of bop, swing, Art Tatum, and Jelly Roll Morton were suddenly in the house along with the older spirits of Thomas Dorsey, Clara Ward, and J. S. Bach. He took this rich mix with him to Boston's Berklee School in 1981; an eager, energetic student, he was awarded the Eubie Blake Fellowship in 1982, the Oscar Peterson Scholarship in 1983, and the Quincy Jones Scholarship in 1984—while still finding time to play church services every Sunday.

Armed with a degree in composition and arranging, Chestnut went back home to Baltimore in 1985, and started playing casual jobs with a fusion band called Phrase. Soon he accepted an invitation from Phil Wilson, a Berklee faculty acquaintance, to play several cruise gigs, including one with a jazz theme, on which Chestnut was able to perform with Gerry Mulligan, Dizzy Gillespie, and Joe Williams. Word

Cyrus Chestnut is at his best when making use of forms drawn from the music of his formative years.

about the young pianist was already spreading, and in 1986 vocalist Jon Hendricks hired him for a two-year stretch. Subsequently Chestnut performed and recorded with Terence Blanchard and Donald Harrison, made his debut as a leader in 1989 with a gospel album, then played one West Coast tour in 1991 with Wynton Marsalis before leaving for two years as accompanist to Betty Carter.

Since 1993, when his work with Carter came to its end, Chestnut has been on his own, issuing solo albums and working with a variety of artists, from Roy Hargrove to opera diva Kathleen Battle, with whom he recorded *So Many Stars*, a selection of the Baptist hymns on which both were raised.

There's no doubt that Chestnut is well schooled in all aspects of jazz performance. He has a deft and humorous touch with stride, as exhibited on "Nutman's Invention #2," from his 1998 album *Cyrus Chestnut*. There are a few heavy-handed moments, where he'll pound a single chord repeatedly as a turnaround in the music approaches. It's easy as well to notice a tendency to speed up by comparing the tempos at the beginning and end of this track. Still, there's an infectious bounce in Chestnut's quirky stride, which hits sevenths as often as octaves, and his very spare use of the sustain pedal gives every note—including the occasional clam—plenty of exposure. "Nutman" comes across as a combination of Fats Waller and Thelonious Monk—an accomplishment in itself.

Chestnut also has a grip on bop and a talent for infusing it with more modern elements. He launches his solo on "Salt Peanuts," from the 1997 tribute album *Dizzy's 80th Birthday Party*, with a Bud Powell–like extended line on the first chorus, which contrasts with the funk figures and bitonalities that follow. And on the equally sprightly "Bebop," from the same album, he comes up with some rather surprising chords on the second chorus of saxophonist Antonio Hart's solo.

For all his versatility, though, Chestnut still can show rough spots in his articulation, particularly but not exclusively at rapid tempos. Further, he has developed less of an identity than some of his colleagues; where it usually takes just a few bars to identify, say, a Benny Green or Marcus Roberts solo, Chestnut has a more elusive, generic sound. His solo line on "And Then She Stopped," from *Dizzy's 80th Birthday*, is typical: The note choices are solid, the two-handed harmonies toward the end—and, especially, the triplet parallel thirds in the right hand—are appealing. But there's something sluggish in his execution; now and then one note slops slightly into another, and even at this medium clip there are a few nearly imperceptible rhythmic hesitancies. The clunky opening fifth that occurs eight bars into his solo on "Bebop" suggests just this kind of momentary block in the flow of his ideas.

Similarly, following an inspired opening motif that floats gently to the top of the keyboard on "Brother 'K'," also from *Dizzy's 80th Birthday Party*, and a lovely two-bar wait, Chestnut delivers a humdrum solo that's either played rigidly on the beat or scattered slightly out of the pocket. Again, it's a good conception, held back only by tiny imperfections here and there. Even on the *largo* tempo taken with "Great Is the Faithfulness," on *Cyrus Chestnut*, he can't avoid a prominent clinker at one delicate climax toward the end of the performance.

More plentiful examples showcase Chestnut's ability to dig in and play with the groove. On "The Journey," from his eponymous album in 1998, he delivers a fluent improvisation, filled with expressive voicings and a fine swing. Toward the end of this solo Chestnut falls back on one of his favorite devices: eighth-note repetitions of single key intervals, or chords. While this affectation can sound a little forced, it can also build tension when the spirit is with Chestnut, as it is here.

Clearly, Chestnut is at his best when making use of conventions or forms drawn from the music of his formative years. Take his arrangement of Beethoven's "Für Elise," from his interpretations of Vince Guaraldi's *Peanuts* music on *A Charlie Brown Christmas*, whose Latin groove inspires him to burn with untypical intensity. This piano solo is totally self-assured, with emphatic tremolos and sizzling lines. Moments like these are frequent when he tackles or even refers to European repertoire.

But if there's any question whether gospel music remains closest to Chestnut's heart, his 1996 solo album *Blessed Quietness* settles the matter. On such tracks as "Jesus Loves Me," "Silent Night," "The Old Rugged Cross," and "Sometimes I Feel Like a Motherless Child," Chestnut treats the material with delicacy and empathy. His tempos breathe and his phrasing combines an almost surgical precision with a caregiver's tenderness. There isn't a weak moment on this album, precisely because there isn't a moment in which Chestnut loses connection with the material. Chestnut touches greatness on *Blessed Quietness*; it may be his mission to achieve more enduring contact as he explores beyond his roots.

80. BENNY GREEN

Born: April 4, 1963, New York, New York

I
n some respects, Benny Green fit right in with the young jazz musicians of the eighties. He was slim and soft-spoken, disarmingly modest, a dapper dresser from the Marsalis line of fashion. His music, like his look, drew inspiration from the past. At his instrument, he played with assurance and a feathery sense of swing.

But he stood out from this crowd as well. Though most of his contemporaries drew from the blues, Green dug deeper into that mine. Unlike Marcus Roberts, he couldn't be accused of being an academic player; his phrasing was funky rather than abstract, and there was no affectation in his rhythm.

More to the point, Green presented himself as an unambiguous hard bop devotee. Though capable of silky nuance, he enjoyed cutting into the beat with a sharp attack, then dropping down to a whisper in mid-phrase. It was an approach based to a degree on dramatic effect, but more fundamentally it was an honest expression of the Horace Silver aesthetic, with more than a little down-home flavor reminiscent of Mose Allison.

Green was raised on jazz in New York, where his father performed as a tenor saxophonist. He was six years old when his parents brought a piano into the house, and seven when he followed his sister's lead and began taking lessons. He began playing in public at age 12 and found some high-profile work in his teens, which included gigs in a quintet co-led by trumpeter Eddie Henderson and saxophonist Hadley Caliman, and in a larger ensemble fronted by bassist Chuck Israels.

After moving with his family to Berkeley, California, as a high school student, Green continued his piano study with Ed Kelly and Dick Whittington, and in his late teens worked in local club appearances as accompanist to singer Fay Carroll.

Though well on his way to the top of the Bay Area jazz scene with a steady Thursday night spot at Yoshi's in Oakland, Green made the jazz pilgrimage back to New York in the spring of 1982. All of 19 years old, he began scuffling for work and taking lessons from Walter Davis and Walter Bishop. One

Few pianists can drench a song with the juicy flavor that Benny Green brings to the table.

night, while sitting in with Art Blakey's Jazz Messengers, he caught the ear of the brilliant improvising singer Betty Carter, who invited him to audition for the open piano spot in her trio. Green got the gig, and soon he was making his presence known throughout the jazz world.

He worked with Carter until 1987, when a lifelong dream came true and he was invited to join the Jazz Messengers. His two years under Blakey's watchful eye brought a new discipline to Green's performance. Though he would continue to learn during stretches with trumpeter Freddie Hubbard and bass legend Ray Brown, and bring his technique to a new high point through advanced study with Oscar Peterson, Green emerged from his apprenticeship with Blakey a fully formed artist, with a style already well-defined.

On his earliest albums, the hallmarks of Green's style are evident: the crisp two-handed unison lines, steamy harmonies, rumbling Peterson-like tremolos, quick little glissandos, and idiomatic funk figurations. As his career progressed, his sound broadened across the landscape of mainstream jazz; though the swampy feel of funk remained at its heart, Green began to draw from more sophisticated sources as well. On the Billy Eckstine tune "I Want to Talk About You," from his 1994 album *The Place to Be*, he offers an arrangement for six horns that might have been written by Oliver Nelson but was actually drawn up by Green himself and Bob Belden; his playing is close to the chart and light on improvisation, yet impeccably phrased, with the soft pedal adding to the velvety brass timbres.

On subsequent albums the Peterson influence grew more pronounced. "Virgo," the opening track on the 1999 trio album *These Are Soulful Days*, strongly recalls Peterson's work with Ray Brown and

Herb Ellis, from the slick unison statement of the theme by Green and guitarist Russell Malone to the free-ranging lines in Green's solo. The differences are in the nuance: The funky figures that Peterson applies throughout many of his solos feel more natural in the context of Green's playing, though he doesn't quite achieve the overwhelming authority that defines the Peterson style. Where the older pianist grabs the groove and wrestles it into submission, Green tends to coast, a little more behind the beat and with a more organic swing. The strong points of Peterson solos are frequently at their higher dynamics and fastest execution; with Green, it's the slow, sauntering phrases that best define his essence.

These qualities turn "Love You Madly," from Green's 2000 album *Naturally*, into a virtuoso solo piano exercise. Taken at a slow strut, the Ellington standard takes shape through rich chorded passages that practically drip with the sauce of soul. Green walks tenths in his left hand, or plays a bouncy stride against the lagging rubato of his right hand, but his ten-fingered chorded passages, played without rhythmic support, swing hard on their own. A year later, on *Green's Blues*, he delivers a similar performances on several tracks, including "I Wish You Love" and "I've Heard That Song Before," though this time the stride and walking-tenths interludes stay steady as Green adds a few Monk-like melodic twists to a very percussive and expressive right-hand line. There's nothing subtle about these performances, and more than a little slop in some voicings, most of it presumably intentional. Yet few pianists can drench a song with the juicy flavor that Green brings to the table. The joy of his playing, not to mention his knack for writing material that manages to sound both fresh and historic, confirms Green as capable of working within a somewhat dated style to create a sound that's personal as well as relevant to the trends of our time.

81. MARCUS ROBERTS

Born: August 7, 1963, Jacksonville, Florida

At a reception following the announcement that the young pianist Marcus Roberts had been awarded top honors at the first Thelonious Monk International Jazz Piano Competition, a losing contestant peeled me a few sour grapes. "Sure, he can play," he grumbled. "But he won because he obviously studied everything Monk ever played, and that's what he played back for the jury."

There's more to the story than rumors of strategic imitation—though a more prominent pianist told me on another occasion that the Marcus Roberts who won an earlier competition in Jacksonville, Florida, played more like Art Tatum than like Monk, Jelly Roll Morton, or any of the other members of the Stride Memorial Church. Whether premeditated or a natural outgrowth of his own style, Roberts's playing represented something new that night in 1987: the arrival of a different approach to jazz performance. Roberts, like his counterpart Wynton Marsalis, saw redemption in history, and danger in reckless experimentation.

Roberts, though, is no simple nostalgist. Whether performing Scott Joplin's "Maple Leaf Rag" or a nearly somnambulant examination of "Moonlight in Vermont," he never just regurgitates the conventions of years past. Instead, he follows the thread that leads from ragtime through Monk, with an occasional sprinkle of Deco affectation, to come up with a distinctive sound. His stride patterns are looser than those of James P. Johnson, his improvisations built more on bending structure than sticking to it. Yet there is no mistaking that his muse beckons from a bygone time, when pianists and their audiences dressed more formally, and the future of jazz hadn't yet been derailed by any collisions with rock & roll.

Sightless since the age of five, Roberts is an impassive figure onstage. He keeps his posture erect and his expression blank behind dark glasses. He wears the expensive suits that young jazz lions favor, and after each performance he stands stiffly and bows, like a child at his first recital. On his album covers, he affects nonchalance as he stands by the piano in a fantastically lavish columned room, or leans against a tree in a forest with a Steinway positioned nearby amidst leaves and twigs. In these pictures he skirts rather close to pretension. Certainly he follows the Marsalis model of taking himself very seriously, almost to the point of parody.

Though drenched in blues, his music also bears the weight of formality. It isn't so much academic reverence; though capable of whipping listeners into frenzies through intricate polyrhythms, he never loses that look of reserve, and though the spirits in his music strain against the traditions that hold them, they never quite break free. This is the source of the tension in his art, as well as of the impression it creates of never quite fulfilling its promise.

The singing of his mother in a church choir led Roberts into music. She bought him a piano when he was eight years old, and after a period of teaching himself and playing at her church, he took lessons

Marcus Roberts, like his counterpart Wynton Marsalis, saw redemption in history and danger in reckless experimentation.

from ages 12 through 21. He got a solid grounding in classical performance through study at the University of Tallahassee with Leonidas Lipovetsky, a protégé of Juilliard master pedagogue Rosina Lhevinne.

Like many jazz musicians his age, Roberts launched his career more through channels provided by schools than through the dwindling resources of the club circuit. His prize-winning performance at the National Association of Jazz Educators convention in 1982 won notice from Wynton Marsalis, who soon introduced himself and became his friend and mentor. When Kenny Kirkland left the Marsalis band, Roberts was recruited to fill the piano chair for six productive years.

The two were an interesting match. Each has a cool temperament, though Marsalis is capable of building his solos to technically polished peaks of emotion. Roberts, in contrast, prefers keeping things at a constant simmer rather than heating up to a boil. Over two or three or more choruses, he will work through motifs, as if trying to solve a puzzle. His ability to find infinite variations within a limited range remains a hallmark of his style.

Clear examples of this approach are evident on his 1991 solo piano release, *Alone with Three Giants*, conceived as a tribute to Jelly Roll Morton, Duke Ellington, and Thelonious Monk. His patient, methodical style works well on one-chord solos, as on his version of Morton's "Jungle Blues." Without a chord progression to rely on in building tension, he lets the spell of the blues unfold through fragmented figures and, eventually, a submission to the three-chord temptations of the form. On the following track, "Mood Indigo," Roberts seems to have all the time in the world. He plays at a very free rubato, with simple harmonies and the use of some staccato pedaled figurations as a motivic device. The performance ends, significantly for the theme of the album, with an alternation of Monkish bitonalities and elementary triads.

It's instructive to compare Roberts's versions of Monk with those of another devotee of the pianist, Chick Corea. Where Corea uses the material as a reference for freewheeling explorations into the harmonic implications of the tune, Roberts strips away extraneous elements to get close to the blues skeleton. "Trinkle Tinkle" typifies his isolation of the core of Monk, down to an evocative and somewhat imprecise stride; for Roberts, unlike true stride pianists, the left-hand pattern is an expressive device rather than a musical form to which one must show fidelity. By smearing through stride and blues, Roberts alludes to the mystique of African-American essence rather than strive to master the technical intricacies conquered by Waller, Johnson, and their colleagues.

The same approach applies in group performances. His solo on "Nebuchadnezzar," from *Deep in the Shed*, maintains a thoughtful, meditative focus at subdued volume. There are no hills and valleys; instead, the music flows along, more hypnotic than cathartic. The listener, like the piano playing itself, floats over the groove, never quite locking in but never losing the connection either.

At times this approach pushes us toward incredulity. On "What Is This Thing Called Love," from the 1993 solo album *If I Could Be With You*, his left hand devolves into a series of thumping fifths. Their primitive effect demands a decision on the part of the listener: Is Roberts expecting us to accept a simple affectation as an even deeper descent into the basics of the blues? Similarly, the bass line on the unaccompanied version of "Cherokee," from *As Serenity Approaches*, rejects references to acoustic walking lines in order to pound out each sixteenth-note with an almost angry attack. Frankly, it is too stylized to swing.

Roberts is one of the most easily recognized pianists of our time. Some perspective is needed, though, before we can determine whether that individuality will take him to a higher level of accomplishment as an improviser, or leave him settled in a niche defined more by its manipulations of styles rooted in the past.

82. JACKY TERRASSON

Born: November 27, 1965, Berlin, Germany

There's no more amiable improviser among jazz pianists than Jacky Terrasson. With little apparent feeling for blues or pure bop, the French pianist builds his identity on a breezy, easy-going approach. On ballads as well as up-tempo pieces, he sounds as if he's having a blast. It's not the most profound or ambitious aesthetic, but even at a superficial level Terrasson is undeniably fun to listen to. Though obviously equipped with a roaring technique, Terrasson has learned not to unleash it too carelessly. Particularly on his earlier material, he slipped into high gear either to push his rhythm section a little harder or—unique among his peers—to inject some humor into the sometimes serious business of improvisation.

Like jazz itself in modern times, Terrasson is a product of multicultural influences. Born in Germany to a French father and an African-American mother from North Carolina, he was brought up in Paris on a diet of classical instruction and, after discovering his mother's collection of albums, jazz. He came to the States at the age of 19 to study at the Berklee School in Boston, quit after a while to perform trio gigs in Chicago, then returned to Paris to perform with bass legend Ray Brown, singer Dee Dee Bridgewater, and other headliners.

In 1990 Terrasson moved to New York, where he worked with trumpeter Wallace Roney, spent two years with drummer Arthur Taylor's Wailers, recorded with tenor saxophonist Javon Jackson, and then accompanied Betty Carter for eight months. Though the jazz community was fully aware of this incendiary young pianist, it took a victory at the Thelonious Monk Piano Competition in 1993 for him to win wider attention. From that point, through increasing exposure with his own trio, a high-profile collaboration with singer Cassandra Wilson in 1997, and continued appearances with other major artists, Terrasson shows every sign of maintaining his front-rank status.

Terrasson spent several years on sideman duty before putting out his own album in 1994. On one such session, with Wallace Roney on the trumpeter's 1991 release *Seth Air*, he makes a powerful impression on "Melchizedek." Through the head and the long solos that follow by Roney and his saxophonist brother Antoine, only bassist Peter Washington and drummer Eric Allen are at work. This makes Terrasson's entrance that much more explosive; after a unison passage by the Roneys, he hits one barbed dissonance, melts it down through a descending whole-tone line as the rhythm section cools, then proceeds to blow through a solo that bristles with what will soon be recognized as some of his favorite devices—tight cycling rhythms and very active left hand that frequently locks onto harmonies or unisons with a right-hand line. When he brings his solo down to a deliberately anticlimactic two-handed call-and-response sequence of chords, one can almost see him grin and shrug, as if to say, "You ain't heard nothin' yet."

On his eponymous debut album, recorded with bassist Ugonna Okegwo and drummer Leon Parker, Terrasson comes across as a kind of high-powered piano imp. His arrangements reveal a sense of ironic humor: On "I Love Paris" the trio trips through wildly contrasting sections of the song, with slippery key changes, unexpected dynamic shifts, and long silences that function almost as false endings. Later on the same album, he opens "For Once in My Life" with a turgid 6/8 left-hand ostinato, over which he plays the theme in a contrasting 4/4 meter. There seems to be no reason for this beginning, except to end it abruptly and switch to a lighter feel entirely in four, and then quickly double that tempo and jam over it with delicate, nimble lines that dart around the higher octaves. Then, of course, comes the recapitulation, which ends with the snarling opening figure and a final emphatic crash.

Elsewhere on *Jacky Terrasson*, "Bye Bye Blackbird" begins as a blowing session, on which Terrasson swings mightily at a medium-up tempo, with aggressive lines and occasional low-register rumbles that in no way refer to the theme of the piece. After a couple of choruses, the group suddenly gooses the tempo to a feverish accelerando, and Terrasson continues to tear it up with deft lines that splinter now and then into ascending spirals or other effects. A few moments later, they speed it up even more; Terrasson stays on top of the tempo, with punchy clustered jabs and sizzling licks that trade fours with Parker. Only at the very end of the piece, when everyone suddenly hits the brakes and the tune eases down to a slow-motion final verse, does the pianist refer to the written melody for the first time.

The same trio performs on *Reach*, also recorded in 1994. Here, Terrasson opens "Just One of Those Things" with a thoughtful free-tempo exploration of the theme, which includes an unexpected simple triad just before the bridge. As Okegwo jumps in with a steady bass pulse, followed by Parker a verse later, Terrasson plays with the groove, at one point stretching out past a full verse and bridge with a trill in his right hand above an edgy left-hand improvisation. Once they get out of that, the group characteristically slams into double time for a while; Terrasson rides this current, building momentum with fleet repeated figures and wrapping it up with a jarring dissonant lick in the first half of the bridge. All of this seems to skim the surface, creating pleasant effects rather than probing the material or, on the other hand, obscuring it with fireworks for their own sake.

Five years later, on the album *What It Is*, Terrasson shows less inclination toward gimmickry, perhaps because the material here is his own. On "Toot-Toot's Tune," a medium-tempo vehicle, he builds his solo conscientiously, moving from textbook funk chords, right-hand octaves, and a blues lick toward slightly more dissonant voicings and counter-rhythmic figurations. As if to signal that this is a Terrasson performance, a trill sparkles toward the end over some crackling left-hand chord movement; the mood is as buoyant as ever for this pianist, without the encumbrance of slapstick devices. (Significantly, the most affected performances on *What It Is* are on the only two non-original titles: a steamy paraphrase of the Ravel *Bolero*, which includes an extended 7/8 section, and a "*cinema vérité*" interpretation of Pink Floyd's "Money.")

His collaboration with Cassandra Wilson, *Rendezvous*, represents a watershed in Terrasson's catalog. As with many speed-demon pianists, accompaniment exerts a tempering effect here. Even when not backing the vocalist, Terrasson reflects the lessons learned from holding back and letting the spirit of the tune speak. His performance of "Chan's Song," written by Herbie Hancock and delivered here on both acoustic and Rhodes electric piano, establishes from the outset a respect for the space around the theme and the chord changes. Terrasson takes plenty of time to outline the melody, playing almost inaudibly at times. His chords draw from Hancock's style, though his improvised line, particularly in a meticulous ascension of broken sixths, a skipping descent of dotted-eighth triplets, and a few rapid but brief figurations, reflects Terrasson's more playful temperament. The important point is that the pianist has learned to project his artistic personality more economically and with none of his old shtick.

By the time of *A Paris . . .*, released in 2000, Terrasson's style has become familiar. Throughout this record he plows through devlish left-hand ostinato figures and terraced tempo changes ("Jeux interdits"), reduces "La vie en rose" to a samba over a vexatious rhythm riff in the left hand, and turns "La Marseillaise" into a meditative waltz. He even comes up with another whimsical arrangement of "I Love Paris," this time over a strutting funk backbeat, which collapses into a wispy dissection of the theme before sinking slowly to a whispery final note.

With this subdued eloquence, Terrasson parallels the recent process of maturity achieved by another keyboard dynamo, Gonzalo Rubalcaba. Each has learned to say more with fewer notes, a development that promises to make their influence that much more remedial for tomorrow's young prisoners of technique.

83. BILL CHARLAP

Born: October 15, 1966, New York, New York

Of all the younger jazz pianists, Bill Charlap is the most refined—a technically assured player, with a cool, sometimes wry approach that recalls André Previn. Yet their reputations differ somewhat. Some jazz purists as far back as the fifties dismissed Previn as a dilettante—an enormously gifted one, but nonetheless a dabbler for whom jazz might have been a hobby more than a conviction.

Not so with Charlap. Though cerebral by his musical nature, and apparently born with a classicist's temperament, he is above all else a jazz interpreter. Previn has spoken of standard tunes as fundamentally springboards into improvisation, certainly incomparable to the great classical repertory. Charlap, in contrast, treats the material with a delicate respect, lingering over the contours of each song and, rather than lose the melody, following it as a beacon throughout his solos.

This attitude came naturally to Charlap, who was raised in a climate of reverence for popular songs. He was born smack in the middle of the Theater District in Manhattan, the son of Sandy Stewart, a singer who had toured with Benny Goodman, and Moose Charlap, a highly regarded Broadway composer whose credits include most of the music for the stage production of *Peter Pan*. Piano training in that household was as inevitable as learning to walk, and Bill showed evidence of prodigious talent. Like some gifted kids, though, he managed to bluff his way through his early lessons; already Gershwin, Cole Porter, and Irving Berlin meant more to him than Czerny and Chopin.

Still, Charlap polished his performance through private instruction with Jack Reilly and Eleanor Hancock, and four years at the High School for the Performing Arts, after which he was admitted to SUNY-Purchase as a piano major. It was already too late, though, and after enduring the classical curriculum for only a little more than a year Charlap happily dropped out to hit the road in the late eighties as successor to his friend Bill Mays in baritone saxophonist Gerry Mulligan's quartet.

These past ten-plus years have seen Charlap expand his activities through accompanimental work with Carol Sloane and Sheila Jordan, advanced study with Dick Hyman, a music director assignment with *Midnight in the Garden of Good & Evil: A Celebration of Johnny Mercer* for the JVC Jazz Festival, and a spell with the Phil Woods Quintet, beginning in 1995. He has also recorded under his own name, in the process spreading his reputation as the most elegant of retro-oriented contemporary jazz pianists, a master of velvety texture and the cantabile line. His style is based on caressing rather than pushing against the material, and swinging only up to the point that the rhythm threatens to disrupt the interpretive reverie. Tradition is essential to this kind of approach, and Charlap has obviously done his homework: As Whitney Balliett observed in *The New Yorker*, "Charlap has absorbed every pianist worth listening to in the past 50 years. . . . His ballads are meditations on songs, homages to their composers and lyricists."

This is true even when he's tackling material that was conceived not for tony theater audiences but for bebop carving sessions. Charlap's intro to "Donna Lee," on his album *Along with Me*, is hushed and tender—as unexpected a setup as this Charlie Parker burner has ever received. When Charlap does dig into the tune, with bassist Andy Eulau and drummer Ron Vincent, his solo coasts over the changes, in pearly timbres, with no sense of urgency. After a couple of brief choruses, the pianist brings it all to a surprising close—no bass solo, no drum break, no trading fours. As Charlap sees it, "Donna Lee" is as much an *objet d'art* as something by Sondheim.

In live settings he is equally unruffled. His approach to "In a Sentimental Mood," on the 1998 album *Gene Bertoncini with Bill Charlap and Sean Smith*, emits an exotic perfume, with clouds of whole-tones and intoxicating clustered chords that float over a droning dominant pedal in the bridge. At times Charlap seems nearly to be playing in his sleep, so heavy is his rubato; yet his dreams of bewitching harmonic color glow seductively in this stillness.

At faster tempos Charlap maintains composure and executes rapid passages with no apparent effort. On his arrangement of "In the Still of the Night," from the 2000 album *Written in the Stars*, he lets bassist Peter Washington and drummer Kenny Washington lay down a blazing backup as he improvises a long, light-speed single line. Although played much faster than typical for Charlap, this solo's intimate dynamic detachment make it still feel like a ballad.

No matter where jazz piano is headed, performers like Charlap will always have their place. Though he will never epitomize anyone's idea of innovation, it's just as sure that there will always be audiences that identify with his serene and high-class aesthetic.

84. HARRY CONNICK, JR.

Born: September 11, 1967, New Orleans, Louisiana

Perhaps it's ironic that the contemporary pianist who would most absorb and adapt the influence of Thelonious Monk would be a media-savvy, rakishly handsome white kid from the Deep South. More than ironic—for some who revered the memory and example of Monk, it would prove difficult to accept. Yet the music spoke for itself, and from a very early age Connick proved to be an original, an artist whose disparate parts assembled into a unique musical package.

The package's point of origin was New Orleans, where Harry Connick, Sr. was one of the more controversial attorneys in a city known for its vivid characters on both sides of the law. His support for Jim Garrison's attacks on the Warren Report endeared him to enough voters to elect him district attorney. As if that weren't enough gravitas for one household, the D.A.'s wife was also a lawyer, and a judge to boot.

Given the inbred histories of crime and jazz in New Orleans, it's hard to imagine a background less likely to produce a finger-snapping, swaggering performer with deft chops and a way with a camera. That, however, is exactly what happened in the case of Harry Connick, Jr.

The signs were there early—as early as 1973, when the five-year-old prodigy played "The Star-Spangled Banner" at his father's swearing-in ceremonies as D.A. He took his first piano lessons from his cousin Georgia, showing so much promise that he soon was studying with two members of the city's musical aristocracy, Ellis Marsalis and, more intermittently, James Booker. A fraction of the age of Eubie Blake, he shared the spotlight with the ancient ragtimer one memorable night. At the age of nine he made his recording debut; four years later he played his first nightclub gig, at the Famous Door.

Already seasoned at age 18 by years of work up and down Bourbon Street, Connick hit the well-worn jazz path to New York. After a few years of working private parties and at relatively modest establishments, such as the boho Empire Diner in Chelsea, he released an eponymous instrumental album in 1987. On his sophomore effort, *20*, he began singing as well, in a smart croon that made comparisons with the young Frank Sinatra inescapable. Bookings started coming from out of town. Executives at his label, Columbia, picked him as their next hot commodity after he wowed them at the company convention in Boca Raton. With reports of his progress filtering back to New York he got himself a booking at the city's top cabaret, the Oak Room at the Algonquin Hotel, in January 1989. Here, finally, is where the Connick phenomenon broke, and suddenly the young entertainer became the hottest ticket in town.

Later that year, when director Rob Reiner recruited him to sing a set of standards for the soundtrack to *When Harry Met Sally*, Connick crossed that river that separates the lean and hungry jazz world from the airier territory where celebrities glisten and gleam. Though he kept making music—and not just romantic ballads amidst billowy orchestrations—he had grown too big for his old world. With starring roles in big-time movies and glitzy big-band tours filling his calendar, the piano receded to a small part of the picture—a prop, almost, for a cameo in *Cheers* or a hyperventilating boogie-woogie break in his stage show.

Even so, Connick hasn't forgotten the importance of the instrument in his music. In a 1990 interview with *Down Beat* he carefully outlined his evolution from a Chick and Herbie wannabe to a genuine student of old-school masters. "I hated Monk," he insisted. "I hated Duke. I hated Erroll Garner. I said, 'Why can't I do this? Why can't I play like Monk? It sounds so easy!'" That became his motivation for excavating every gem he could find in those deep reserves of tradition: "Jazz is becoming popular again! Wynton started it, and Branford, and I'm continuing it." As if to remind himself of his roots, Connick has made it a point to go back to that well every five years and cut an instrumental, piano-centered album, with his own age at the time serving as the title.

The album that won him attention, though, was the non-numeric *Harry Connick, Jr.*, released in 1987. Playing unaccompanied or as a duo with bassist Ron Carter, the 20-year-old pianist displays an easy-going familiarity with stride piano, at least when taken at a moderate tempo and seasoned with a bit of Crescent City spice. On tracks such as "Love Is Here to Stay" and "Sunny Side of the Street" Connick projects a slouching, shambling hipness in his elastic tempos and, especially on the latter, swooping, showbiz smears. That untied stride feel owes a lot to Monk, yet in his treatment of a Monk tune, "I Mean You," he doesn't even try to follow the idolators who affect the composer's jagged phrasing; his solo statement of the theme, in fact, grabs attention through its pure presentation, without even a single fudged note, deliberate or otherwise. Then, with Carter delivering a brisk walking bottom, Connick digs into several choruses distinguished by their powerful swing and conceptually solid construction. It's a confident, even cocky performance, though the decision to play the one Monk tune on the album in a non-Monk fashion suggests both a superficial irony and plenty of room for interpretive growth.

By the time we get to the trio album *Lofty's Roach Souffle* in 1990, Connick has achieved a real synthesis of Monk and New Orleans on a set of original material. Even so, in their mismatched components, stinging minor ninths, and resolution to the major third, "Hudson Bommer" and "Harryonymous" are unabashedly derivative. Connick punches out each note with a deliberation that borders on gimmickry, especially on "Hudson Bommer"; clearly it doesn't take much effort to assemble the line he eventually constructs, unless one is trying more to sound like Monk than to draw something fresh from his example.

On *25*, from 1992, aside from a few tracks with guest artists, Connick performs solo. It's a gutsy act to update the unaccompanied tracks on his *20* album, when dubious listeners might make allowances for his youth. Still, Connick doesn't disappoint. The staggered syncopations, clustered bass accents, and barbed dissonances of "Music, Maestro, Please" reflect his Monk lineage; while the performance feels more facile than insightful, Connick does bring an original voice to the mix in his loping stride, easy rhythmic sense, and playful quotes from "Laura" and other tunes. On the New Orleans chestnut "After You've Gone" Connick manipulates the tempo of his stride with unusually sensitivity, and structures his articulation of the theme and subsequent improvisation on an Erroll Garner model of octaves, tremolos, and splashy, tinkling chords. In a far more adventurous tune, John Coltrane's "Moment's Notice," his left hand displays extraordinary rhythmic expressiveness beneath a long single line; however, Connick can't resist cramming a couple of graceless quotes into the song and stumbling into an ill-advised quick stride just before the finish. On this sort of material, there's a sense that he's stretching, sometimes very obviously beyond the limits of his comfort.

Connick's future as a force in jazz piano is conjectural. It is difficult to maintain real excellence when the distractions and obligations of fame begin to intrude—just as it was for Nat "King" Cole. But because of his own respect for the instrument and its traditions, Connick will surely remain capable of delivering at any time a surprising chorus, or maybe even an entire album, that will catch the skeptics by surprise and remind listeners of what he may yet achieve.

85. STEPHEN SCOTT

Born: March 13, 1969, Queens, New York

If jazz at the beginning of the new century is about learning from the past, Stephen Scott has the advantage of paying dues directly to the people who were there. But his idea of the past differs from those held by Marcus Roberts and his mentor Wynton Marsalis. Few traces of pure bebop color his playing, and fewer still of stride. Instead, Scott summons the spirits of early Herbie Hancock, McCoy Tyner, and Ahmad Jamal, with maybe a taste of Duke Ellington added for his sleek distillations of the blues.

Yet there's nothing shallow in Scott's music. And it's refreshingly free of museum dust. Antique references that shape the work of others from his generation would distract from what he wants to say. All that defines his music stems from the fifties and the pre-fusion sixties.

He was only 18 when Betty Carter hired him. Playing in her band was like learning to swim by being thrown into whitewater, but Scott was up to the task. Soon he was guesting on albums with Sonny Rollins and Joe Henderson, as well as leading his own dates. But he made his first widespread impact as a member of the Harper Brothers band in the early nineties.

In their straight-ahead sound he grew as a harmonic player whose specialty was tight chords placed mainly in the middle of the keyboard. When playing within the rhythm section, he left most of the responsibility for the groove to the bass and drums and concentrated on painting a pointillistic picture with quick, off-beat jabs. It wasn't his style to coast over a walking bass line; instead, he planted chords like signs on the highway, guiding the soloist toward his destination without getting in his way.

In this respect, Scott recalls Dave Brubeck, another pianist known for his harmonic profundity and sometimes non-swinging placement. Scott's composition "Keynote Doctrine," from the Harper Brothers album *Remembrance*, follows this model. Throughout the song, as the soloists blow, Scott plays nothing but block chords, without a single line or figure to vary their impact. The approach doesn't change much when the tempos are slower, as on Roy Hargrove's rendition of "End of a Love Affair," on *Public Eye*. With a strong soloist, though, Scott can trigger fresh ideas; a diminished fifth toward the end of a Wynton Marsalis improvisation on "Johnny Come Lately," from the Joe Henderson album *Lush Life*, bumps the trumpet line into a harmonically adventurous final phrase.

As heavy as his chording could be, Scott's solos typically slim down to light, right-hand lines that swim through entire verses before coming up for breath. Particularly on his earlier recordings, Scott plays with an energy untempered by reflection. But when freed from his self-imposed formula of sticking to solid chords, Scott can allow his left hand to map out some exciting possibilities for his own

Stephen Scott—who has expressed a growing disinterest in being a sideman—may be strongest of all when working solo.

solos. On "They Say It's Wonderful," from the Sonny Rollins album *+3,* for example, he departs three or four times from fairly predictable patterns into more outside territory, mainly as amplification on the dense voicings of his chords. It's almost as if he's surprising himself, as much as he might some other soloist.

On Ron Carter's *Orfeu,* called upon to play in a bossa-nova setting, Scott floats with the breezy feel but doesn't abandon his thick chording style; throughout many of the comping sections, he maintains his habit of moving chords around chromatically to build tension against the root. His solo on the medium-tempo "Obrigado" has a singing quality, with a strong melodic integrity; his line is eminently musical and idiomatic, his flow of ideas unforced and unblemished by technical display.

Scott delivers an especially magnificent solo on his Monk tribute "Always Know," from *Remembrance.* It's a brilliant exhibition, thoughtful yet swinging, reverential without being derivative. He absorbs elements of the Monk style—notably, the dissonant minor seconds—but takes off from them through an extended performance that leaves and then returns to this starting point, with a nod or two toward Monkish whole-tone arpeggios. He hits the same high standard on "Public Eye," essentially a minor blues, from the Roy Hargrove album of the same name: When he shifts from accompaniment to a few solo choruses, the transformation is striking. His lines roam into bitonal territory but are flavored with enough bluesy phrases to remain listenable.

When leading his own session, Scott allows himself even more latitude. His treatment of "Solitude," on his trio album *Renaissance*, inverts the solemn treatment that the tune usually receives. Here, Scott plays casually, whacking left-hand accents and tossing off licks as if they were incidental afterthoughts. In the same free-thinking spirit, he follows with a performance of "Tenderly" that shimmers like a mirage over Clarence Penn's soft mallet patterns on the drums; the hallucinogenic impression deepens in the chorus, which he stretches into slow motion as dreamy chords sink in a whole-tone descent. These performances, like his sprint through Herbie Hancock's "Maiden Voyage" and the metrical trickery added to the theme to "Just Friends," aren't irreverent; rather, Scott wants to show that the great tunes can tolerate limitless interpretation.

Perhaps Scott is strongest of all when working solo. His long unaccompanied spot on "Lotus Blossom," from *Lush Life*, takes the listener from a simple triadic starting point through affecting passages of introspective harmony, less knotty than his usual style, and into a balletic stride that falls in and out of rhythm, as if from playfulness to tragedy. Precisely because he uses the stride device so seldom, this passage speaks very emotionally.

The key, then, to Scott's artistry is freedom. He has said in interviews that his interest in being a sideman is in rapid decline, and it's easy to hear why in his music. The more room he has, the clearer his emergence as an artist. His apprenticeship is over; his future rests in his hands now.

86. ERIC REED

Born: June 21, 1970, Philadelphia, Pennsylvania

E ach player to have occupied the piano bench in the Wynton Marsalis band has developed a unique voice; there's no mistaking Marcus Roberts for Kenny Kirkland. And Eric Reed, the third in this distinguished line, is just as distinctive. Reed's sound is the most elegant of the three, and perhaps the least affected.

He was also likely the youngest to show signs of talent. The son of a Baptist preacher, Reed began playing on the family piano when he was just two years old. By the age of five he was playing before his father's congregation as well with the Bay State Singers, the elder Reed's gospel vocal group. Like his Baltimore compatriot Cyrus Chestnut, Eric grew up in a rich milieu of African-American church music, especially as performed by his favorite group at the time, the Edwin Hawkins Singers.

Reed began taking formal lessons when he was seven years old, at the Settlement Music School in Philadelphia. Unlike Chestnut, he was an unenthusiastic student, with only a passing interest in the classical regimen. When his family moved to Los Angeles in 1981 Reed was subjected to another series of lessons, this time at the R. D. Colburn School of the Arts. After a while it became apparent to his family and teachers alike that most of what he would learn at the piano would be through self-instruction, in response primarily to the soulful jazz of Art Blakey, Horace Silver, and Ramsey Lewis, as well as recordings by Dave Brubeck, Oscar Peterson, Erroll Garner, and his favorite pianist, Ahmad Jamal, whose music he discovered through a percussionist at his father's church. The neighborhood library, which was well stocked with vinyl, was his academy of higher jazz learning during those years.

The young pianist was 14 years old when he briefly met his future mentor Wynton Marsalis; by that time he was well on his way to a performing career. While still in high school he gigged frequently throughout L.A. and learned how to fit into a big-band setting through work with Gerald Wilson. As a freshman at Cal State Northridge, Reed took time off to play his first gigs with Marsalis, during a short trek to Chicago. One year after that he left academia to become a member of the trumpeter's band, with one short interruption, from 1990 through '95—that interruption was spent working with Freddie Hubbard and Joe Henderson, under whose direction Reed claims to have learned to play better through more perceptive listening.

Reed's first album, *Soldier's Hymn*, was recorded when he was 19 years old, with Dwayne Burno on bass and Greg Hutchinson on drums. From the late nineties onward he continued to release albums under his own name, some of them built along ambitious conceptual themes, as were two Marsalis projects, *Citi Movement* and *In This House, On This Morning*, in which he had participated. On each of these Reed showed a willingness to serve the theme of the album rather than just stretch out on chorus after chorus.

This approach shows itself in the bracing originality he brings to arranging some familiar titles on *Manhattan Melodies*, a 1998 release offered as a tribute to New York. The opening cut is a fresh, full-bodied take on "59th Street Bridge Song." In place of thin-chested warbles of "feelin' groovy" Reed offers an introspective reworking of the theme, with a complete rearrangement of the monotonous written chord sequence. By the time he hits his solo he's pouring on the funk over the changes, with Hutchinson sizzling on brushes and Reginald Veal laying down a stuttering bass line. Reed makes every cliché sound vital and leaves us with an unexpected appreciation for the sentiment, if not the craft, behind the Paul Simon composition. This sort of interpretation can best be compared to an artist rendering a new take on something old and familiar—a street scene in this case, tranquil at dawn and bustling as the day begins.

The blues quality in Reed's playing throughout *Manhattan Melodies* animates his work even within more restrictive arrangements. On the Wynton Marsalis ballad collection *The Midnight Blues: Standard Time Vol. 5*, it's Reed's job to scatter some soul behind the trumpeter's romantic melodies and amidst the plush orchestrated strings. He does this with thoughtful solos, as on "After You've Gone," starting here with an echo of Marsalis's closing figure that develops into a decidedly blue commentary over hushed bass and drums. Throughout this oddly positioned improvisation, which begins three bars into one verse and ends on the fifth bar of the next, Reed's playing is grit and velvet, perfectly balanced for the arrangement.

Outside of this orchestrated context Reed can struggle with keeping a ballad conception together. His trio version of Monk's "Ask Me Now," from the Joe Henderson tribute album *Thank You, Joe!*, lacks the kind of originality that's necessary to sustain interest at tempos this slow. His solo, over predictable voicings, seldom strays beyond the limits of the written chords; rather than let the spaces speak for themselves, as Monk could do, Reed seems to let too much air into this performance, robbing it of any emotional density. Quotes from "Never Let Me Go" and "Too Close for Comfort" add little as well.

On some up-tempo cuts a similar, vaguely unsatisfying impression has characterized Reed's performance. His arrangement of "42nd Street," from the album *Pure Imagination*, is all about jamming over a rocking groove concocted by Hutchinson and bassist Reginald Veal. Almost everything he plays is based on sixteenth-notes fired over clustered comps. While he certainly swings here, he doesn't sustain interest over the long haul; after several verses, the lack of variety becomes evident. Where a McCoy Tyner would have pushed the harmonic envelope and altered his textures more, Reed doesn't quite dig in or spread out enough.

On the medium-up "Black, as in Buhaina," from his 1996 album *Musicale*, the results are more impressive. Backed this time by Ron Carter on bass and Karriem Riggins on drums, Reed follows a solid opening chorus, which shifts from 6/8 to swing time, with a long, meticulously crafted solo. He takes his time building momentum, moving from deliberate note choices in the opening verse through two different segments based on punchy eighth-note triplets, which Reed uses at one point to push the line upward and, briefly, mirror it with a descending figure in his left hand—it's a small touch, but unorthodox and refreshing. In the end, his combination of disparate elements—percussive attack applied to a stream-like current of melodic ideas—makes this solo work.

The same is true in his unaccompanied rendering of "You'll Never Walk Alone," from *Pure Imagination*. The approach is unadulterated gospel, in a stately 6/8 that begins with a statement of the theme and builds through call-and-answer chords, aggressive octave work, and a restless octave bass line to the kind of climax that normally accompanies congregational shouts and choral frenzies. Unfortunately, Reed's performance is a little too self-consciously derivative, as if his intention is to pay respects toward an entire style—a lesson learned, perhaps, under Wynton's tutelage—rather than express something more personal and spontaneous. It sounds, in the end, distressingly like a student recital.

However, when Reed allows elements of his gospel background to filter into a jazzier context, the results can be more satisfying. The mellow ballad "Felix the Cat," from his album *The Swing and I*, combines familiar jazz harmonies with some bass line movement and occasional triadic chords, whose power stems from their placement within the chord sequence and from Reed's sensitive articulation. The rubato ending, played unaccompanied, evokes the gospel element more clearly, in the I to VI minor vamp.

On most of his work Reed reveals himself as a more than competent player, capable of thoughtful ballad interpretations (as on "Old Flame," with bassist Rodney Whitaker and drummer Gregory Hutchinson, from *The Swing and I*). He has yet to show either the intensity or originality to mark him as an essential force, but with his abundant good taste and adaptability, Reed could well become a mainstay pianist in the Hank Jones mold.

87. BRAD MEHLDAU

Born August 23, 1970, Jacksonville, Florida

There's something so breezy, so offhand, about the first track on the 1995 release *Introducing Brad Mehldau*. In the pianist's arrangement of "It Might as Well Be Spring," the 7/4 meter blows past, as simple as the arrival of the new season. You marvel as well at the arrival of a new talent, even as you sense that Mehldau is having a little fun with your incredulity.

There's a lot of intellect involved in Brad Mehldau's method, and he makes sure his audience knows it.

A similar impression emerges right after the solo piano verse that kicks off "It's Alright With Me," from *Live at the Village Vanguard*. Everything Mehldau plays seems to set the stage for bassist Larry Grenadier and drummer Jorge Rossy to blast in with a conventional swing feel; he begins with the bridge and plays the tune in tempo, but when the rest of the trio joins him, instead of an emphatic cymbal crash and an explosion of rhythm, we get disconnected taps and shards of bass. Mehldau jumps immediately into the non-groove and begins breaking the tune into fragments. Rather than mirror our expectations of jamming through the changes, he breaks the mirror and reassembles the pieces to reflect an almost Cubist interpretation.

It's an unfashionable approach, and maybe a little cocky. Other pianists affect a reverent posture in their treatment of familiar tunes. In fact, Mehldau respects the standard repertoire, though his approach is based on a powerful confidence in his ability to transfigure it into something wholly new. There's a lot of intellect involved in his method, and he makes sure his audience knows it: In case anyone misses his references to Brahms and Teutonic philosophy in interviews, he reproduces excerpts of poetry from Rilke in the package for *The Art of the Trio, Volume One*, and simultaneously pontificates and satirizes himself in a 12-page discourse that accompanies his *Live at the Village Vanguard*.

Lots of pianists have gone through the kind of classical training that Mehldau underwent without being transformed into Gothic apostles. Maybe his outlook has something to do with the cultured atmosphere in which he was raised, as the son of a doctor in West Hartford, Connecticut, as well as his flight from the comforts of his youth into a dalliance with heroin. In any event, it is possible to overplay the German thing. Even after making several pilgrimages to the Fatherland, Mehldau doesn't exactly drench his music with the scent of Schumann or Schubert. The jazz imprimatur remains much clearer than any Romantic pallor.

It takes patience to squint through his ruminations on Beethoven, Socrates, Brecht, and "erotic onanism." A similar commitment is helpful in listening to some of his explorations on piano, but it's more worth the effort: The displacement of the theme in the opening of "The Way You Look Tonight" seems contrived at first, especially when contrasted with a conventional reading of the bridge. But these eccentricities emerge as new motifs, distinct from the written ones, in Mehldau's improvisation. With Grenadier and Rossy churning rhythms but avoiding an articulated swing, the piano has structure to refer to and freedom to ignore it. In lesser hands, a train wreck would be likely; with Mehldau at the keys, we're rushed through fascinating scenery and delivered intact at the end.

His work on the Lee Konitz album *Another Shade of Blue* is even more intriguing. The saxophonist's drum-free threesome takes an elastic approach to rhythm: Tempos stay steady, but implications of the pulse are filtered through extraordinarily fluid interactions between the pianist and bassist Charlie Haden on a number of standards. And on "Everything Happens to Me" Haden sits out, leaving his colleagues to probe into the tune. The most impressive moments on this track occur in Mehldau's accompaniment: As Konitz outlines the theme and begins an economical improvisation, the piano part floats along, functioning not so much as a rhythm section as a kind of light shining overhead, changing color and shape but always illuminating a route through the tune. Played almost entirely in the middle range of the keyboard, Meldau's inquisitively dissonant chords and brief linking passages form a perfect complement to Konitz's cerebral inventiveness—a darker echo of some of the classic Brubeck/Desmond performances.

Though clearly occupied with his own convictions, Mehldau is supremely capable of adjusting himself to fit into the vision of other artists. With his friend Joshua Redman, he abandons the analytical approach taken with Konitz and leans more toward a hard bop mentality. His licks on "Rejoice," from *MoodSwing*, draw from the Bobby Timmons well, with churchy minor sevenths and turnarounds. When the quartet breaks from the simple rhythm riff into a swing groove, Mehldau beefs up his voicings, but by keeping the gospel feel intact he creates continuity and builds tension throughout Redman's solo.

His strong grounding in jazz, through study with modernists such as Fred Hersch and Kenny Werner and bluesmeister Junior Mance, creates the framework for Mehldau's art; his interest in Germania nudges him toward perspectives that are certainly unusual within that context. Wherever all this takes him in the decades to come, he has already been lauded by mainstream media as the most important pianist of his generation. Nothing he has done suggests otherwise.

88. GEOFF KEEZER

Born: November 20, 1970, Eau Claire, Wisconsin

His roots are musical—a father who plays drums, a mother who plays French horn. Intelligence runs in the family too—Dad and Mom both teach, at the University of Wisconsin and at a local junior high school, respectively. Yet even this lineage can't explain the phenomenal gifts of Geoff Keezer, who is quite likely to claim his place on the pedestal of jazz piano immortals.

What it comes down to is this: Keezer shows no weak spots. From his first note, he shows who's boss; in the brawn of his tone and his unshakable confidence, he is fully the equal of Oscar Peterson. His harmonic knowledge is vast and intuitive, yet he is learning to find a new level of expressiveness through a more simplified language. (Of course, Keezer's idea of simplification exceeds the grasp of many players of comparable ambition.) His rhythm doesn't just swing; it roars and blazes, scattering the slowpokes who stand in his way. To say that he has been guilty of overplaying, particularly at slower tempos, is to grasp for the feeblest of straws.

Keezer in fact represents a synthesis of historic and modern aesthetics. He knows every corner of the standard repertoire, and he plays it all with reference to performance precedent. But his relationship with tradition is stormy; one senses love, but also impatience, as he distends and twists his chord structures. His fleet lines strain impatiently against conventions of tempo. The last challenge may be to find the balance between performer and material that, ironically, can come easier to pianists of more typical capabilities.

He was three years old when the piano lessons began. The regimen was classical from day one, though the revelations brought by exposure to jazz pretty much defined Keezer's ambitions in his teens. The International Association of Jazz Educators saw what was coming and gave Geoff their Young Talent Award when he was just 17 years old. After a year of studying at the Berklee College of Music, he was referred by his teacher James Williams to Art Blakey, who happened to be looking for a pianist at the time. Keezer was 18 when he hit the road with the legendary drummer, as the last of the line of great pianists to play with the Jazz Messengers.

Through work with Art Farmer, T. S. Monk, and the Mingus Dynasty band, Keezer built a reputation as a pianist of boundless potential. By 1992 he was leading his own group, a quartet of future all-stars, with Joshua Redman on sax, Christian McBride on bass, and Leon Parker on drums. Perhaps his most rewarding affiliation was with bassist Ray Brown, in whose trio he sharpened his playing in a more focused mainstream setting.

On "Close Your Eyes," from the Brown album *Some of My Best Friends are . . . the Piano Players*, even Keezer's statement of the theme in the opening verse projects restless ornamentation: the triplet treatment of the restated three-note motif, the slight lag behind the beat in his phrasing, the funk figure at the end of the sixteenth bar, and much more. By the time he begins his solo, over an arranged rhythmic figure, Keezer is ready to break out of the changes with a daring examination of the melody's implications. The second chorus features the pianist roaming way outside of the tune, easily moving bluesy figures in unexpected directions, yet always swinging. Even his locked-hands treatment on the third chorus undergoes significant alternations as it moves along; while playing thick harmonies at an up tempo, Keezer has no trouble working with the inner voicings in compelling ways. And dig his mutation of the three-note motif as he begins the out chorus. The man never stands still, yet never leaves the music behind.

With an imposing technique and a superb sense of line, Keezer routinely hits the highest levels of sophisticated swing in his improvisations. He opens his solo on "Our Delight," from the Brown album *Some of My Best Friends Are . . . the Trumpet Players*, with an inspired figure in triplets, based on descending modified sixths. He ends his phrases emphatically, takes his solo into bitonal territory where the effect best builds momentum, smoothly moves from the upper midrange to the low bass and back, and ends with emphatic chords that lead to trading fours with trumpeter Roy Hargrove. Another example of his extraordinary fluency can be heard in his opening chorus to "Close Your Eyes," from *Some of My Best Friends are . . . the Piano Players*; from a simple statement of the three-note motif in unisons, Keezer uses Monkish intervals as a suggestion for some extremely pleasing harmonic extensions. They rush past rather quickly, but leave a satisfying taste in their wake.

Like Dave Brubeck, Keezer has been known to trot out crowd-pleasing devices, including rumbling tremolos and funk/jazz clichés. But Keezer presents these without the any sense of playing to the gallery, as one can sometimes sense from Brubeck. On a strutting, soulful arrangement of "When I Fall in Love," from the Ray Brown Trio's *Live at Starbucks*, Keezer erupts from a tremoloed crescendo after a Blakey-like drum roll into a gospel figure that recalls Les McCann. From that point he digs into a steamy solo that whips through funky eighth-notes in snappy unison lines that split and spiral in opposite directions. In the final two bars Keezer breaks into a breathtaking spurt that picks up velocity even as it melts out of the way for a Brown bass chorus.

He shares another trait with Brubeck: a sly humor that manifests itself in song quotes. "Bali Ha'i" provides the opening motif for Keezer's solo on "Blue Walk," from the Benny Golson album *One Day, Forever*. In fact he sticks with this joke halfway through the first verse, playing the theme in a widely spaced unison. The playfulness continues with the second verse, in a paraphrase from "Blues in the Night," but after a few seconds Keezer gets down to business and, in the remaining bars, hammers home some resonant, percussive chords, and a rapid exit run, again in unisons, that brings the band down for a Dwayne Burno bass solo.

Another album in the Ray Brown "friends" series offers an especially revealing insight in Keezer's artistry. Not every pianist—and especially not every pianist with a truckload of chops—can ease back into a supportive role behind singers. But on *Some of My Best Friends Are . . . the Singers*, Keezer dispels whatever doubts there may have been about his skills as an accompanist. What impresses most here is his ability to rip through dazzling solos that in no way clash against the singer's style. When playing behind a vocal on a medium or up tune, he often restricts himself completely to full-blooded block chords, positioned to draw maximum energy from the bass and drums. The single lines don't jump in until his solo breaks, and there they generally build to roaring climaxes before dropping back down for the vocalist's return.

Take "I Thought About You," on which Diana Krall delivers a sultry but very literal reading. Keezer starts his solo by circling around the tune for a while, then he detours into some more outside lines during the second half of the bridge; with the groove and the changes well established, he allows himself some speedy indulgences and eyebrow-raising twists before coming back home with funky unison lines that drop straight back into the pocket for Krall's return. The nearly inaudible "yeah" uttered by the singer just before her entrance says just about all that needs to be said about this impeccably structured performance. On the following track, "Poor Butterfly," Etta Jones strays more than Krall from the tune, but Keezer repeats his formula of rock-solid chords behind the vocal, then turns up the heat in his solo choruses. This time he begins with a big harmonic statement of the theme, answers it with a swinging four-bar response, reprises the theme with more meaty chords, and finally takes off from there into an improvisation that includes one head-spinning lick—off-beat quarter-notes from the left hand, illuminated by flittering triplets around each ascending note—yet deferentially cools down as Jones, inspired, hits the lyric hard for the final verses.

On ballads, Keezer's adherence to the same formula can create more of a disruption: When doing "More Than You Know" with Dee Dee Bridgewater, his inability to resist popping off a few sixteenth-note sparklers toward the end of his solo may not have offered quite as seamless a segue back to the vocal as something more ruminative and less edgy.

In fact, ballads aren't this pianist's forte; his quick imagination makes him sound a little confined at sleepwalking tempos. And his curiosity about the melodic possibilities of even the most straightforward tunes makes his every fast-clip solo a potential thrill ride. There's an almost terrifying intensity his treatment of the old swing standard "Stompin' at the Savoy," from his 1997 album *Turn Up the Quiet*. It's a drum-free date, with Christian McBride on bass and Joshua Redman on tenor sax, and Keezer seems eager to prove that no percussive help is necessary. Over Redman's opening solo, the pianist hurls chords up and down the keys for two verses, in a driving off-beat pattern; when they reach the bridge, he shifts to a series of rocking chords, hitting on the beat with his right hand and in-between with his left, and from there he treats the third verse to an angular whole-tone stalk down the keyboard, harmonized in ninths. Even while backing up another soloist, Keezer is bouncing in the back seat, eager to grab the wheel.

In unaccompanied settings, Keezer displays abundant ambition—which he generally tempers with taste. From the *Starbucks* album, his medley of "This House Is Empty Now" and "I Should Care" takes its time to develop, slipping in and out of tempo before the rest of the trio jumps in. Keezer's ability to glide from one style to the next, from a Eastern modal run to rapid improvised counterpoint, is without equal in contemporary jazz. No pianist since Tatum has been able to execute independent and simultaneous improvised melodies as dazzlingly as Keezer.

And on *Turn Up the Quiet*, he grabs the challenge of playing "Lush Life" with a spirit far more free than most pianists dare to bring to this piece. Traditionally it's treated almost as an art song; certainly it's not the kind of standard that one can sketch out in chord symbols and jam on. That doesn't stop Keezer, who only six bars into the piece breaks the sedate texture with an alarm-like repeated note, which points the way to a moment of aromatic modal exotica. In a few seconds he reaches the bridge, which is distinguished by a shift in meter, a delicate brief ostinato, and a moment of exploratory chord movement that ends with a simple unison figure and a return to the verse. For three minutes new angles on "Lush Life" fly by in an audacious, colorful blur. His performance is like a whirling dance around a delicate vase, which at the end remains intact and, under an entirely new light now, undiminished in its beauty.

Since the *Quiet* album, Keezer has shown a willingness to streamline a bit—not by extinguishing all the flash and fire, but by exploring the possibilities of leaving space in his material. *Zero One*, a solo piano collection released in 2001, contains a few ill-advised special production effects. More intriguing is the new group of original works by Keezer, in which he lets his stupendous chops unfold in material that shows a romantic, even new age inclination. The opening cut, "These Three Words," conveys a rustic feel, with straightforward chords that make it possible to derive expression from well-crafted inversions. The bridge on this tune swirls with guitar-like textures that recall Michael Hedges; this leads to an improvisation that, like everything Keezer plays, trumpets his total technical control—yet does so in consonant lines, including a series of descending sixths, broken and articulated as smooth, slippery triplets.

Keezer is nearing a milestone on *Zero One*—a synthesis of velocity, authority, imagination, and, at least now and then, economy. When all these elements lock up, the bar will raise, and jazz piano will be transformed yet again.

Photo Credits

Photo by Frank Driggs: 1, 7
Photo by Charles Peterson, Courtesy of Don Peterson: 14, 18, 21, 25, 64, 57,
Photo by William P. Gottlieb: 31, 111, 224,
Photo by Michael Spector: 41
Photo by Veryl Oakland: 46, 95, 109, 151, 167, 191, 241, 261,
Photo by Duncan Schiedt: 51
Photo by Ray Avery's Jazz Archives: 55, 81, 116
Photo by Kathy Sloane: 73, 247
Photo by Herman Leonard Photography, L.L.C.: 86, 186, 286, 319
Photo by Tom Copi: 99, 130, 141, 143, 200, 221, 259, 289
Photo by Harriet Hoffman: 107
Photo by Raymond Ross: 123, 176
Photo by Jon Sievert: 277
Photo by James Lee Suffer: 132
Photo by Nova: 163
Courtesy CBS Records: 172
Courtesy Concord Jazz Records: 183
Courtesy Columbia Records: 213
Courtesy Blue Note Records: 216
Photo by Justin Freed: 231
Photograph © Carol Friedman: 233
Michael Ochs Archives.com: 267
© 2001 Enid Farber: 301
Photo by Clayton Call: 306
Photograph © 1998 Jack Vartoogian/FrontRowPhotos, NYC: 315

Index

A

Aaron, Andy, 203
Abercrombie, John, 207
Abrams, Muhal Richard, 219, 251–253, 260
Abrams, Ray, 125
Adams, George, 258, 260
Adams, Pepper, 103
Adderley, Cannonball, 149, 210, 287
Ailey, Alvin, 45
Akiyoshi, Toshiko, 190–193
Alexander, Monty, 104, 275–278
Alias, Don, 291
Allen, Eric, 308
Allen, Gene, 119
Allen, Geri, 204, 297–299
Allen, Steve, 67–68
Allen, Woody, 179
Almond, Cliff, 280
Alvis, Hayes, 90
Ambrose, Bert, 158
Ammons, Albert, 251
Amos, Ernest, 24
Amsterdam, Morey, 178
Anderson, Gene, 8
Arlen, Harold, 183
Armstrong, Louis, 22, 54, 66
    Hines and, 32, 34, 36
    Morton and, 2, 7, 9
    Peterson and, 77
    Valdés and, 276
Arnold, Horacee, 89
Ashby, Irving, 77
Avakian, George, 70, 169
Ayler, Albert, 258

B

Babbitt, Milton, 149, 210

Bacon, Paul, 113
Bailey, Dave, 173
Bailey, Mildred, 49
Baker, Chet, 134, 149, 207, 227
Baker, Harold "Shorty," 44
Balchard, Terence, 204
Ballard, Butch, 26
Balliett, Whitney, 6, 54, 87, 104, 192, 201
Bampton, Claude, 158
Baraka, Amiri, *See* Jones, LeRoi
Barker, Danny, 9
Barksdale, Everett, 66, 67
Barron, Kenny, 203–206, 287
Baryshnikov, Mikhail, 236
Basie, Count, 39–42, 92
    Akiyoshi and, 193
    Billy Taylor and, 187
    Byard and, 97
    Dameron and, 91
    Ellington and, 26
    Jamal and, 72
    Johnson and, 15
    Lewis and, 167
    Monk and, 117
    Peterson and, 77
    Ra and, 222 223
    Tatum and, 62, 68
    Waller and, 20
    Weston and, 245
Bates, Bob, 170
Bates, Norman, 170
Battle, Kathleen, 270, 302
Bauer, Billy, 224, 225
Beal, Eddie, 68
Bechet, Sidney, 11, 161, 181, 182
Beiderbecke, Bix, 2, 48, 144, 161
Beirach, Richie, 206–208

Belden, Bob, 304
Benford, Tommy, 8
Benjamin, Joe, 174
Bennett, Tony, 103, 154, 162
Benson, George, 279
Berlin, Irving, 65, 311
Bert, Eddie, 119
Bertoncini, Gene, 174
Best, Denzil, 158
Bethune, Lebert, 88
Bigard, Barney, 36
Bishop, Walter, Jr., 90, 303
Blake, Alex, 247
Blake, Eubie, 17, 30, 32, 52, 312
Blake, Ran, 229–232
Blakey, Art, 71, 98, 122, 128, 135
    Billy Taylor and, 187
    Bley and, 228
    Brackeen and, 202
    Butler and, 287
    Green and, 304
    Jarrett and, 264
    Miller and, 288
    Reed and, 316
    Walton and, 193
Blanchard, Terence, 296, 302
Blanton, Jimmy, 26, 71
Bley, Carla, 228
Bley, Paul, 23, 137, 202, 227–229
Blocker, Bill, 101
Blount, Herman. *See* Sun Ra
Bluiett, Hamiett, 258
Bobo, Willie, 199
Bofill, Angela, 291
Bonnemere, Eddie, 90
Booker, James, 285, 286, 312
Bowie, Lester, 252
Boyd, Nelson, 92, 167
Boyette, Lippy, 17, 63
Boykins, Ronnie, 221
Brackeen, Charles, 202
Brackeen, JoAnne, 201, 201–203
Bradford, Perry, 9
Braff, Ruby, 179
Brand, Adolf Johannes, 254
Braxton, Anthony, 232, 252, 253

Brecker, Randy, 122, 281
Brice, Percy, 189
Bridgewater, Dee Dee, 323
Britt, Stan, 28
Broadbent, Alan, 154
Brookmeyer, Bob, 142, 149, 173, 216
Brooks, Roy, 107
Brooks, Russell, 20
Brown, Clifford, 83, 89, 92
Brown, Ed, 68
Brown, Gatemouth, 287
Brown, Grace Johnson, 97
Brown, James, 288, 291
Brown, Lawrence, 236
Brown, Louis, 24
Brown, Ray, 74, 86, 177, 185
    Green and, 304
    Valdés and, 276, 277
Brubeck, Dave, 69–70, 92, 145, 168–172
    Cecil Taylor and, 236
    Kuhn and, 196
    Ra and, 220
    Reed and, 316
    Shearing and, 160
Bryant, Ray, 127–129
Buckley, William F., 180
Buckner, Milt, 157
Budwig, Monty, 176
Burno, Dwayne, 317, 322
Burns, Ken, 229
Burrell, Kenny, 104, 135, 139, 174
Burton, Gary, 161, 200, 289
Butler, Henry, 285–287
Byard, Jaki, 97–100, 104
Byas, Don, 85
Byrd, Donald, 125, 194

C
Cage, John, 210
Calhoun, Eddie, 70, 72
Calloway, Cab, 22, 34, 91
Camilo, Michel, 276, 279–281
Capone, Al, 8, 20, 34, 49
Carle, Frankie, 201
Carr, Ian, 149, 151
Carr, Mancy, 33

Carroll, Fay, 303
Carter, Benny, 50, 68, 177
Carter, Betty, 297, 304, 314
Carter, Francis, 63
Carter, Ron, 100, 109, 138, 315
 Barron and, 204
 Hancock and, 139, 140
 Kuhn and, 197
 Waldron and, 250
 Walton and, 195
Cary, Dick, 36
Case, Brian, 28
Casey, Al, 66
Cassarino, Ray, 230
Catlett, Sid, 36, 66, 85
Chaloff, Margaret, 197
Chaloff, Serge, 197
Chambers, Jeff, 284
Chambers, Joe, 199
Chambers, Paul, 80, 101, 105, 127
Charlap, Bill, 310–311
Charles, Ray, 121
Charles, Ennis, 236
Cherry, Don, 202, 228, 231
Chestnut, Cyrus, 300–303, 316
Chestnut, McDonald, 301
Childs, Billy, 295–297
Christian, Charlie, 84, 114
Christian, Jodie, 251
Clark, Dick, 36
Clarke, Kenny, 79, 84–88, 92, 98, 105, 165–168, 215, 227
Clarke, Stanley, 199
Clayton, Buck, 40
Cleaver, Eldridge, 231
Cobb, Jimmy, 107, 127, 149, 151
Cole, Cozy, 68
Cole, June, 62
Cole, Nat "King," 52–54, 94
 Flanagan and, 103
 Jamal and, 72
 Peterson and, 77
 Valdés and, 276
Coleman, George, 138, 207, 296
Coleman, Ornette, 79, 251

Allen and, 297
Bley and, 228
Brackeen and, 202
McPartland and, 162
Rubalcaba and, 284
Coleman, Steve, 297
Collins, John, 71
Colomby, Harry, 117
Coltrane, Alice, 256
Coltrane, John, 93, 95–96, 202
 Abrams and, 251
 Beirach and, 207
 Butler and, 286
 Cecil Taylor and, 241
 Connick and, 313
 Ellington and, 26
 Evans and, 145, 149
 Garland and, 101, 102
 Kuhn and, 196, 197
 Monk and, 117–118
 Tyner and, 255–257
 Walton and, 194
 Zawinul and, 211
Condon, Eddie, 184
Confrey, Zez, 30
Connick, Harry, Jr., 312–314
Cook, Junior, 122, 194
Copeland, Ray, 245
Corea, Chick, 138, 145, 198–201
 Barron and, 204
 Childs and, 295
 Elias and, 282
 Kirkland and, 291
 Makowicz and, 214
 Miller and, 288
 Roberts and, 307
 Zawinul and, 210
Costa, Eddie, 149
Crawford, Ray, 72
Crosby, Bing, 66
Crosby, Israel, 73
Crouch, Stanley, 144–145
Crowley, John, 45
Crowser, Henry, 8
Cyrille, Andrew, 253

D

Dailey, Albert, 202
Dalto, Jorge, 279
Dameron, Radd, 44
Dance, Stanley, 62
Daniels, Eddie, 293
Danielsson, Palle, 298
Dapogny, James, 8
Darensbourg, Joe, 10
Davern, Kenny, 179
Davis, Eddie "Lockjaw," 252
Davis, Francis, 253
Davis, Frank, 231
Davis, Miles, 92, 199
    Beirach and, 207
    Billy Taylor and, 187
    Bryant and, 128
    Cecil Taylor and, 235, 242
    Corea and, 199
    Evans and, 144, 149, 150–151
    Flanagan and, 104
    Garland and, 101, 102
    Hancock and, 137, 138, 141
    Harris and, 106
    Hyman and, 178
    Jamal and, 71
    Kelly and, 125, 126
    Kuhn and, 197, 198
    Lewis and, 164, 167
    Peterson and, 76
    Ra and, 219
    Valdés and, 276
    Zawinul and, 209, 211
Davis, Sammy, Jr., 97
Davis, Walter, 104, 303
Davison, Wild Bill, 178, 181
Dawson, Alan, 213
Dawson, Mary Caldwell, 72
Debray, Regis, 231
DeFrancesco, Joey, 106
DeFranco, Buddy, 158
DeJohnette, Jack, 153, 194
    Barron and, 204
    Beirach and, 207
    Childs and, 296
    Elias and, 282
    Hersch and, 294
    Jarrett and, 264
    Rubalcaba and, 283, 284
Dennis, Kenny, 152, 250
Deppe, Lois, 28
Desmond, Paul, 169, 171, 295
Dexter, Dave, 66
Dickenson, Vic, 48
Dickerson, Carroll, 32, 33
Dillard, Gladys, 103
Dixson, Arti, 75
Dodds, Baby, 181
Dodge, Joe, 170
Doggett, Bill, 276
Dolphy, Eric, 99, 100, 140, 249, 250, 297
Donaldson, Lou, 194
Donegan, Dorothy, 84
Dorham, Kenny, 86, 122–123, 194
Douglass, Bill, 68
Dowdy, Bill, 185
Drew, Kenny, 134
Duke, George, 286
Duke, Vernon, 192
Dukes, Amboy, 102
Dunbar, Sly, 278
Dunlop, Frankie, 119
Duvivier, George, 95, 107

E

Eager, Allen, 85
Eckstine, Billy, 35, 92, 96, 304
Edison, Harry "Sweets," 53
Eicher, Manfred, 227
Eldridge, Roy, 48, 66, 77, 104
    Billy Taylor and, 187
    Harris and, 106
Elias, Elaine, 281–282
Ellington, Duke, 14, 16, 23–27
    Akiyoshi and, 192, 193
    Billy Taylor and, 187
    Cecil Taylor and, 235, 239, 242
    Dameron and, 91, 93
    Green and, 305
    Hines and, 34, 36

Hyman and, 179
Ibrahim and, 254, 255
Jamal and, 72
Lewis and, 164
McPartland and, 161, 163
Miller and, 288
Morton and, 2–3, 9
Peterson and, 77
Petrucciani and, 216
Powell and, 84
Ra and, 222, 223
Rowles and, 175
Scott and, 314
Tatum and, 58, 62–63, 65
Walton and, 193, 194, 245
Williams and, 44
Ellington, Mercer, 288
Ellis, Herb, 277, 305
Emerson, Keith, 295
Emilio, Frank, 283
Eubanks, Kevin, 127, 203
Eubanks, Robin, 127, 203
Eubanks, Vera Bryant, 203
Eulau, Andy, 311
Evans, Bill, 38, 47, 92, 144–155
Barron and, 206
Beirach and, 207
Billy Taylor and, 189
Childs and, 295
Elias and, 281
Garland and, 101
Hersch and, 293, 294
Hyman and, 177
Ibrahim and, 255
Kelly and, 125, 126
Kirkland and, 291
Lewis and, 166
Miller and, 288
Petrucciani and, 214
Rubalcaba and, 283
Shearing and, 160
Valdés and, 274
Evans, Elaine, 153, 154
Evans, Gil, 244

F

Faddis, Jon, 299
Fambrough, Charles, 292
Farmer, Addison, 250
Farmer, Art, 149, 256
Keezer and, 321
Kuhn and, 197
Walton and, 194
Farrell, Joe, 199
Feather, Leonard, 70, 78, 142, 158
Fellman, Jim, 31
Feldman, Victor, 137
Ferguson, Maynard, 76, 98, 134, 210
Fields, Herbie, 147
Finck, David, 197
Fischer, Clare, 137
Fitzgerald, Ella, 77, 78, 96
Flanagan and, 103, 104
Lewis and, 165, 166
Flanagan, Tommy, 97, 102–106, 108
Fitzgerald and, 103, 104
Rowles and, 175
Walton and, 194
Forman, James, 134
Fortune, Sonny, 203
Fournier, Vernel, 73
Fox, Ed, 34
Fox, Harold, 61
Franklin, Arethra, 288
Friedlander, Erik, 294

G

Gammage, Gene, 77
Gant, Willie, 181
Garland, Red, 72, 100–102, 246
Garner, Erroll, 68, 69–71, 76, 133, 178, 185
Connick and, 313
Miller and, 288
Reed and, 316
Ra and, 221, 222
Valdés and, 276
Garrett, Kenny, 297
Garrison, Jimmy, 152, 256

Gaye, Marvin, 131
Gaylor, Hal, 228
George, Russell, 173
Gershwin, George, 53, 59
    Charlap and, 311
    McKenna and, 183
    Pullen and, 260
    Ra and, 221–222
    Tatum and, 65
Getz, Stan, 122, 142
    Barron and, 204
    Beirach and, 207
    Evans and, 148
    Hersch and, 293
    Kuhn and, 197
    Rowles and, 176
Giannini, Bruto, 13
Gillespie, Dizzy, 44, 45, 68, 77, 85, 87, 94
    Barron and, 204
    Billy Taylor and, 187
    Bryant and, 127
    Chestnut and, 301
    Corea and, 199
    Dameron and, 91
    Hersch and, 294
    Jamal and, 72
    Kelly and, 125, 127
    Kirkland and, 292
    Lewis and, 165
    Monk and, 116
    Powell and, 85
    Valdés and, 276
    Walton and, 194
    Zawinul and, 210
Gilmore, John, 90
Gitler, Ira, 87, 91
Giuffre, Jimmy, 149, 228
Glaser, Joe, 32, 153
Glaser, Martha, 71
Gleason, Ralph, 78
Golson, Benny, 135, 194, 256, 290, 296, 322
Gomez, Eddie, 154, 197, 202, 281
Goodman, Benny, 40, 49–50, 94, 109, 152
    Charlap and, 310

    Harris and, 185
    Hyman and, 178
    Makowicz and, 212
    McPartland and, 161, 162
    Rowles and, 175
    Williams and, 44
Goods, Richie, 290
Goodstein, Oscar, 87
Gordon, Dexter, 86, 87
    Abrams and, 252
    Brackeen and, 202
    Harris and, 107
    Timmons and, 136
Goss, Carol, 228
Gould, Glenn, 154
Grant, Henry, 24
Granz, Norman, 59, 67, 77, 192
Grappelli, Stephane, 176, 215
Grauer, Bill, 246
Gray, Glen, 62
Gray, Nettie, 130
Green, Al, 288
Green, Benny, 90, 302–305
Green, Freddie, 42
Green, Lil, 220
Greer, Sony, 235
Grenadier, Larry, 319, 320
Gress, Drew, 294
Griffin, Johnny, 288
Grimes, Henry, 189
Grimes, Tiny, 66, 127
Gryce, Gigi, 119, 194
Guaraldi, Vince, 98, 135, 168, 205
Guevara, Che, 231
Gulda, Friedrich, 210

H
Hackett, Bobby, 184
Haden, Charlie, 202, 228
    Barron and, 204, 205
    Butler and, 287
    Jarrett and, 264
    Rubalcaba and, 283
Hadlock, Richard, 33

Haig, Al, 227
Hakin, Omar, 210
Hall, Al, 50, 66, 70
Hall, Jim, 154, 166, 215
Hall, Specs, 70
Hamilton, Chico, 283
Hammond, John, 15, 40, 49, 178
    Jamal and, 72
    Makowicz and, 212
Hampton, Lionel, 55, 79
Hancock, Eleanor, 311
Hancock, Herbie, 130, 134, 137–142
    Billy Taylor and, 189
    Childs and, 295
    Corea and, 199
    Kirkland and, 291, 292
    Rubalcaba and, 283
    Scott and, 314
    Terrasson and, 310
    Valdés and, 274
    Zawinul and, 209
Handy, W. C., 5, 8, 9, 10, 20
Hanna, Sir Roland, 103, 104, 108–110, 286
Hargrove, Roy, 274, 302, 322
Harris, Barry, 90, 103–104, 106–109
Harris, Eddie, 133, 195, 251
Harris, Gene, 184–186
Harris, Reuben, 63
Harris, Wynonie, 220, 221
Harrison, Donald, 302
Harrison, Lou, 262
Hart, Clyde, 84
Hawkins, Coleman, 42, 44, 62, 66, 94, 101
    Hancock and, 137
    Harris and, 106
    Lewis and, 165
    Monk and, 116
    Morton and, 9
    Ra and, 220
    Shearing and, 158
    Silver and, 122
    Weston and, 246
Hayes, Edgar, 68
Hayes, Jois, 195
Haynes, Roy, 87, 105, 199, 204
Heard, J. C., 50, 158

Heath, Albert, 166
Heath, Jimmy, 203
Heath, Percy, 166, 168
Heath, Ted, 92
Hedges, Michael, 324
Henderson, Eddie, 138
Henderson, Fletcher, 62, 63, 164, 220
Henderson, Joe, 103, 127, 141–142, 202, 207, 215, 220
    Hersch and, 293
    Monk and, 317
    Tyner and, 257
    Ra and, 223
    Walton and, 194
Hendrix, Jimi, 298
Henry, Ernie, 92
Hentoff, Nat, 69, 115
Herman, Woody, 175, 184, 210, 230
Hersch, Fred, 293–294, 320
Higgins, Billy, 90, 202, 195, 228, 247
Hill, Teddy, 114
Hindemith, Paul, 251
Hines, Earl, 23, 27–38
    Bryant and, 128
    Byard and, 97
    Donegan and, 55, 56
    Evans and, 144
    Hank Jones and, 94
    Lewis and, 164
    Peterson and, 76
    Rowles and, 175
    Shearing and, 158
    Tatum and, 65
    Williams and, 43, 45
    Wilson and, 48
Hino, Teumasa, 291
Hinton, Milt, 182
Hodeir, Andre, 116
Hodges, Johnny, 194, 236, 240
Hoffman, Joseph, 13
Holiday, Billie, 49, 103
    Monk and, 117
    Rowles and, 175
    Tristano and, 223
Holland, Dave, 207, 228, 296
Holley, Major, 109

Holmes, Groove, 133
Holzman, Adam, 215
Hope, Elmo, 246
Hopkins, Claude, 90
Hopkins, Fred, 253
Horne, Lena, 22, 244
Horne, Onzie, 79
Houghton, Steve, 296
Howard, Darnell, 36
Hubbard, Freddie, 100, 207, 287, 295, 296
Hucko, Peanuts, 158
Hudson, George, 72
Humes, Helen, 15
Hurst, John, 297
Hutcherson, Bobby, 202, 295–296
Hutchinson, Greg, 317
Hyams, Marge, 158
Hyman, Dick, 22, 76, 177–182, 311

I
Ibrahim, Abdullah, 254–255, 277
Irwin, Dennis, 192
Israels, Chuck, 150, 153
Ives, Charles, 247

J
Jackson, Anthony, 279, 280, 281
Jackson, Bull Moose, 92, 246
Jackson, Chubby, 224
Jackson, Michael, 239
Jackson, Mike, 65
Jackson, Milt, 92, 95, 103, 119
    Lewis and, 164, 165, 166
    Valdés and, 276
Jackson, Oliver, 36
Jackson, Reggie, 105
Jackson, Tony, 5
Jacquet, Illinois, 165, 167
Jamal, Ahmad, 71–75, 288
    Kirkland and, 291
    Reed and, 316
    Scott and, 314
Jarrett, Keith, 140, 145, 214, 262–272
    Allen and, 298
    Elias and, 281, 282
    Hersch and, 294

Rubalcaba and, 283
    Valdés and, 275
Jeffries, Paul, 256
Jenkins, Leroy, 253
Johnson, Alphonso, 210
Johnson, Brooks, 219–220
Johnson, Bud, 35
Johnson, James P., 9, 13–15, 230
    Basie and, 39
    Ellington and, 24
    Hines and, 30
    Hyman and, 177
    Tatum and, 61, 63
    Makowicz and, 212
    Monk and, 114
    Roberts and, 306
    Waller and, 19, 20, 22
    Wellstood and, 181
    Willie Smith and, 17, 18
Johnson, J. J., 86, 104, 296, 299
Johnson, Marc, 154, 279, 282
Johnson, Pete, 251
Jones, Clarence, 77
Jones, Elvin, 103, 104, 106
    Barron and, 204
    Brackeen and, 202
    Ibrahim and, 254
    Tyner and, 256, 257
Jones, Eta, 323
Jones, Hank, 93–97, 100, 103, 108
    Barron and, 203
    Hanna and, 109
    Miller and, 287
Jones, Jo, 50
Jones, LeRoi, 219
Jones, "Philly" Joe, 80, 93, 127, 149, 152–153
Jones, Sam, 107, 150, 195
Jones, Thad, 103, 105, 106, 109, 119, 162
Jones, Willie, 90
Joplin, Lottie, 8
Joplin, Scott, 8, 46
    Abrams and, 252
    Brubeck and, 168
    Roberts and, 305
    Waller and, 20
Jordan, Clifford, 128

Jordan, Duke, 245
Jordan, Louis, 276
Jordan, Sheila, 311
Jorrin, Enrique, 283

K
Kahane, Jeffrey, 294
Kaminsky, Max, 18, 178
Kay, Connie, 164, 166, 246
Keane, Helen, 153
Keepnews, Orrin, 15, 60, 102, 147
Keezer, Geoff, 321–324
Kellaway, Roger, 172–174
Kelly, Ed, 303
Kelly, Wynton, 125–127, 137, 150, 274
        Beirach and, 207
        Kirkland and, 291
Kennedy, Rick, 8
Kerouac, Jack, 157
Kerr, Brooks, 19
Kessel, Barney, 77
Khan, Eddie, 140
King, B. B., 249
Kirby, John, 84, 85
Kirk, Andy, 44, 46–47
Kirk, Rahsaan Roland, 104
Kirkeby, Ed, 22
Kirkland, Kenny, 290–293, 316
Klein, Larry, 296
Konitz, Lee, 149, 225, 227
        Beirach and, 207
        Billy Taylor and, 187
        Evans and, 149–150
        Mehldau and, 320
        Petrucciani and, 214
        Rowles and, 176
        Tristano and, 226
Kotick, Teddy, 95
Krall, Diana, 322
Krupa, Gene, 49, 49–50, 184
Kuhn, Steve, 196–198, 256
Kyle, Billy, 84, 85

L
LaBarbera, Joe, 153, 154
Lacy, Steve, 227, 236

LaFaro, Scott, 149, 152
Lake, Oliver, 297
Lambert, Donald, 84, 181
Land, Harold, 202
Lange, Art, 230
Larkins, Ellis, 104
LaRoca, Pete, 197
Lateef, Yusef, 90, 106, 203, 204
LaVerne, Andy, 217
Lecuona, Ernesto, 274
Lee, George E., 36
Lee, Jeanne, 230–231
Lee, Peggy, 162, 175
Lees, Gene, 125, 153, 155
Leonard, Harlan, 91
Leonard, Jack E., 173
Leth, Jorgen, 88
Leviev, Milcho, 287
Levy, John, 158
Lewis, John, 101, 107, 164–168
Lewis, Meade "Lux," 65, 222, 251
Lewis, Mel, 109, 162
Lewis, Ramsey, 129–132
Liebman, Dave, 207
Lincoln, James, 3
Lindsey, John, 7
Linn, Robert, 295
Lins, Ivan, 296–297
Lipovetsky, Leonidas, 306
Lipski, Mike, 181
Lloyd, Charles, 202, 215, 266
Logan, Giuseppe, 258
Lomax, Alan, 4, 5–6
Lovano, Joe, 215, 284
Lowe, Mundell, 147
Lunceford, Jimmie, 62, 77, 92, 122, 164, 187
Lyons, Jimmy, 236
Lyons, Len, 228, 229–230, 276

M
Mabern, Harold, 286
McBride, Christian, 201, 204, 321, 323
McBrowne, Lennie, 228
McCann, Butch, 129
McCann, Les, 131–134, 203, 322
McCoy, Freddy, 202

McCurdy, Roy, 211
McDaniel, Thomas, 89
McDonald, Larry, 276
McFerrin, Bobby, 215
McIntyre, Dianne, 236
McKenna, Dave, 182–184, 198, 202
McLean, Jackie, 194, 195, 227, 250
McPartland, Jimmy, 161–162, 163, 173
McPartland, Marian, 43, 104, 134, 161–163, 299
McRae, Carmen, 128
McShann, Jay, 65
Makowicz, Adam, 79, 212–214
Malachi, John, 297
Malcolm X, 231, 260
Malik, Ahmed Abdul, 36
Malone, Russell, 204, 305
Mance, Junior, 320
Mann, Herbie, 104
Manne, Shelly, 225
Marable, Fate, 8
Mariano, Charlie, 98, 192
Marley, Bob, 277
Marmarosa, Dodo, 71
Marsalis, Branford, 292, 296, 297
Marsalis, Ellis, 94, 193, 312
Marsalis, Wynton, 142, 199
    Allen and, 297
    Billy Taylor and, 187
    Chestnut and, 302
    Evans and, 144–145
    Kirkland and, 290, 291
    Reed and, 316–318
    Roberts and, 305, 207
    Scott and, 314
    Valdés and, 274
Marshall, Eddie, 192
Marshall, Wendell, 26
Marterie, Ralph, 173
Martin, Kelly, 70
Martinez, Lily, 283
Mason, Fats, 61
Massey, Calvin, 256
Matthay, Tobias, 188
Maupin, Bennie, 122, 138
May, Earl, 187, 189
Mayhew, Virginia, 206

Mays, Lyle, 298
Mehegan, John, 155
Mehldau, Brad, 208, 214, 318–320
Metheny, Pat, 298
Mezzrow, Mezz, 15
Michelot, Pierre, 88
Mick, Sticky, 24
Mickman, Herb, 295
Militello, Bobby, 171
Miller, Glenn, 158
Miller, James, 72
Miller, Mitch, 71
Miller, Mulgrew, 287–290
Millinder, Lucky, 116
Mingus, Charles, 79, 87, 98, 99
    Akiyoshi and, 192
    Billy Taylor and, 187
    Bley and, 228
    Evans and, 149
    Hanna and, 109–110
    Keezer and, 321
    Pullen and, 258
    Rowles and, 176
    Waldron and, 251
Minton, Harry, 114
Mitchell, Billy, 104
Mitchell, Blue, 122, 199
Mitchell, Red, 147, 184
Mobley, Hank, 122, 123
Monette, Louise, 4
Monk, Thelonious, 3, 44, 47, 112–120
    Akiyoshi and, 193
    Barron and, 204
    Basie and, 41
    Beirach and, 207
    Blake and, 230, 232
    Bley and, 227
    Brackeen and, 202
    Cecil Taylor and, 236, 239
    Childs and, 295
    Connick and, 313
    Corea and, 200
    Dameron and, 93
    Evans and, 144, 154
    Garland and, 101
    Hank Jones and, 94

Hanna and, 109, 110
Hersch and, 293
Ibrahim and, 254
Johnson and, 15
Jones and, 93
Lewis and, 165
Makowicz and, 214
Peterson and, 76
Powell and, 82, 84, 87, 90
Ra and, 220–222
Reed and, 317
Roberts and, 305, 207
Rowles and, 175, 176, 177
Rubalcaba and, 283
Scott and, 315
Timmons and, 135
Tristano and, 226
Tyner and, 256, 257
Waldron and, 248–249
Weston and, 247–248
Zawinul and, 209
Montrose, J. R., 250
Moog, Bob, 228
Moore, Bill, 61
Moore, Don, 90, 203
Moore, Michael, 174
Morello, Joe, 170
Morgan, Frank, 105
Morgan, Lee, 90, 108, 128, 194, 256
Morrell, Marty, 153
Morris, Marlowe, 84, 181
Morton, "Jelly Roll," 2–11, 16, 17
Chestnut and, 301
Evans and, 144, 145
Hines and, 29, 32
Hyman and, 178
Roberts and, 305, 207
Williams and, 43, 44, 45
Morton, Mabel, 11
Mosca, Ray, 189
Moses, Bob, 197, 281
Moses, J. C., 140
Motian, Paul, 148, 152, 153
Allen and, 297
Bley and, 228
Jarrett and, 264

Rubalcaba and, 283
Mraz, George, 109, 208, 213
Mulligan, Gerry, 187, 301, 311
Murray, Sunny, 236, 258
Musso, Vido, 91
Mussulli, Boots, 184

N
Nance, Ray, 26
Navarro, Fats, 86, 92, 101
Neidlinger, Buell, 181, 236, 238
Nelson, Oliver, 137
Nero, Peter, 173
Newborn, Phineas, 78–80, 125, 288
Newhall, Scott, 28
Newman, David "Fathead," 193
Nicholas, Albert, 3, 11
Nichols, Herbie, 246
Noone, Jimmie, 33, 34
Norvo, Red, 66, 178
Nugent, Ted, 102

O
O'Farrill, Chico, 274
Ogerman, Claus, 154
Okegwo, Ugonna, 309
Oliver, King Joe, 6, 7, 33

P
Paderewski, Ignace, 20
Page, Oran "Hot Lips," 101, 240
Palmieri, James, 207
Parker, Charlie, 44, 94
Bley and, 227
Bryant and, 127
Corea and, 199
Evans and, 148
Flanagan and, 103, 104
Garland and, 101
Hank Jones and, 95
Harris and, 107
Hyman and, 178
Lewis and, 164, 165, 167
Marian McPartland and, 162
Monk and, 115
Powell and, 84, 85, 88

Tatum and, 67
Waldron and, 249
Walton and, 194
Wellstood and, 181
Parker, Leo, 321
Parker, Leon, 309
Pass, Joe, 77, 161
Pastorius, Jaco, 210
Patitucci, John, 199
Patton, George S., 169
Paudras, Francis, 88, 89
Peacock, Annette, 228
Peacock, Gary, 228, 294
Jarrett and, 264, 271
Pullen and, 259
Pechet, Mimi, 5
Peiffer, Bernard, 78
Penn, Clarence, 316
Pepper, Art, 127
Perez, Danilo, 279
Perlo, Don, 228, 229–230
Perry, Doc, 24
Peterson, Oscar, 42, 66, 68, 75–79
Akiyoshi and, 192
Blake and, 230
Cecil Taylor and, 234
Evans and, 155
Hancock and, 137
Makowicz and, 213, 214
Miller and, 288
Monk and, 116
Reed and, 316
Valdés and, 277
Petrucciani, Michel, 214–217
Pettiford, Oscar, 66, 79, 86–88, 158, 227
Phillips, Bill, 29
Phillips, Flip, 182
Pierce, Kyle, 6
Pomeroy, Herb, 98
Porter, Cole, 192, 212, 311, 246
Potter, Tommy, 105
Powell, Bud, 44, 67, 82–90, 93, 95, 103–106, 115–116
Akiyoshi and, 192
Beirach and, 207
Brackeen and, 202

Bryant and, 128
Butler and, 286
Cecil Taylor and, 236
Childs and, 295
Corea and, 199
Evans and, 148
Hancock and, 137, 138, 139
Hank Jones and, 94
Hyman and, 178
Kuhn and, 197
Lewis and, 130, 164
Monk and, 117
Rubalcaba and, 283
Shearing and, 160
Silver and, 121
Timmons and, 134
Tyner and, 256, 257
Waldron and, 250
Walton and, 194
Powell, Mel, 158
Priester, Julian, 138
Pullen, Don, 258–260

R
Ra, Sun, 219–223, 228, 251
Raglin, Junior, 26
Rainey, Overton G., 61
Rainey, Tom, 294
Ramirez, Ram, 84
Randolph, Willa, 220
Ranglin, Ernest, 277
Rathaus, Karol, 249
Rawls, Lou, 133
Redman, Dewey, 264
Redman, Joshua, 201, 320, 321, 323
Reed, Eric, 291, 316–318
Reed, Lucy, 147
Reedus, Tony, 290
Reese, Lloyd, 66
Reeves, Dianne, 295
Reid, Vernon, 298
Reilly, Jack, 311
Rich, Buddy, 204
Richard, Little, 220
Riley, Ben, 95, 109, 204
Rivers, Sam, 228, 236

Rizzo, Jilly, 276
Roach, Max, 85–86, 90, 95, 101
  Cecil Taylor and, 236
  Harris and, 106
  Ibrahim and, 254
  Lewis and, 167
  Weston and, 245
Roberts, Charles "Luckey," 13, 17, 30
Roberts, Marcus, 76, 106, 193, 290, 302–303, 305–308
  Makowicz and, 214
  Reed and, 316
Roberts, Ozzie, 77
Roberts, Ralph, 68
Robinson, Bill "Bojangles," 22, 34
Robinson, Red, 33
Rodgers, Richard, 65
Rodney, Red, 106–107
Rodriguez, Wallie, 174
Roker, Mickey, 96
Rollins, Sonny, 86, 101, 104–105, 137, 141, 227
  Bley and, 227
  Bryant and, 127, 128, 129
  Kellaway and, 174
  Scott and, 314
  Valdés and, 276
Roney, Wallace, 288, 297, 308
Rosnes, Renee, 299–300
Ross, Diana, 223
Rossy, Jorge, 319, 320
Rouse, Charlie, 92, 112, 118–119, 204
Rovinsky, Anton, 178
Rowles, Jimmy, 175–177
Rubalcaba, Gonzalo, 214, 273, 279, 282–284, 310
Ruedy, Phil, 173
Ruiz, Hilton, 279
Rushing, Jommy, 39
Russell, Curly, 85
Russell, George, 149
Russell, Ross, 34
Ryder, Mitch, 102

S
Sakamoto, Ryuichi, 190
Salvador, Emiliano, 283
Sanchez, David, 204

Santamaria, Mongo, 199
Sargent, Gray, 184
Sawson, Alan, 98
Schickele, Peter, 199
Schillinger, Joseph, 251
Schuller, Gunther, 53, 100, 115, 149, 230
  Blake and, 231
  Tristano and, 223
Schwartz, Arthur, 183
Scott, Stephen, 314–316
Scott, Tony, 90, 147
Scruggs, Mary Elfreida, 43
Seay, Clarence, 292
Senior, Milt, 62
Shakespeare, Robbie, 278
Shapiro, Harold, 149
Shapiro, Nat, 69
Shaughnessy, Ed, 184
Shaw, Artie, 16, 187
Shaw, Arvell, 36
Shaw, Woody, 122, 199
Shearing, George, 137, 144, 146, 157–161, 173
Shepp, Archie, 227, 254, 256
Shorter, Wayne, 136, 141, 210, 215, 299
Siegel, Janis, 293
Silver, Horace, 121–125, 199
  Blake and, 232
  Bryant and, 128
  Cecil Taylor and, 236
  Evans and, 148
  Green and, 303
  Hancock and, 137
  Reed and, 316
  Valdés and, 274
Sims, Zoot, 175

Sinatra, Frank, 276
Singleton, Zutty, 11, 32, 33
Sissle, Noble, 52
Slay, Emmett, 106
Sloane, Carol, 311
Smith, Bessie, 212, 220, 223
Smith, Bill, 170
Smith, Charlie, 187
Smith, Jimmy, 126, 133
Smith, Lester, 61

Smith, Leo, 253
Smith, Stephen, 10
Smith, Willie "The Lion," 16–19, 177, 178
    Ellington and, 25
    Monk and, 114
    Tatum and, 63
    Waller and, 20
    Wellstood and, 181
Soloff, Lew, 289
Spanier, Muggsy, 36
Spellman, A. B., 238
Springsteen, Bruce, 212
Stearns, Marshall, 15, 246
Stewart, Rex, 62, 63
Stewart, Sandy, 310
Stewart, Slam, 66, 67, 71
Stitt, Sonny, 85, 86, 92
Stollman, Bernard, 90
Strayhorn, Billy, 23, 71, 92
Strong, Jimmy, 33
Subotnick, Morton, 210
Sutton, Ralph, 181, 182
Swallow, Steve, 197, 199
Swartz, Harvie, 197

T
Tabackin, Lew, 192
Tate, Grady, 109, 139, 174
Tatum, Art, 24, 45, 49, 58–68, 79, 127
    Billy Taylor and, 187
    Brackeen and, 202
    Brubeck and, 171
    Chestnut and, 301
    Childs and, 295
    Cole and, 52
    Donegan and, 54, 55
    Evans and, 144
    Flanagan and, 103
    Garland and, 101
    Garner and, 70
    Hank Jones and, 97
    Hanna and, 108, 110
    Jamal and, 72
    Keezer and, 323
    Lewis and, 165
    Makowicz and, 212, 214

    Miller and, 288
    Newborn and, 79
    Peterson and, 75, 77
    Powell and, 82, 84
    Roberts and, 305
    Rowles and, 175
    Shearing and, 158
    Timmons and, 134
    Tyner and, 256
    Walton and, 194
    Wellstood and, 181
    Weston and, 246
Taylor, Art, 226
Taylor, Billy, 58, 68, 90, 187–190
Taylor, Cecil, 45, 55, 97, 234–244
    Abrams and, 252, 253
    Evans and, 144, 145
    Hyman and, 178
    Pullen and, 258, 260
    Ra and, 219
    Valdés and, 275
Taylor, Creed, 153
Taylor, Gene, 124
Teachout, Terry, 152
Teagarden, Jack, 62, 66
Terrasson, Jacky, 276, 308–310
Terry, Clark, 137, 173
Tesser, Neil, 72
Threadgill, Henry, 252
Thielemans, Toots, 154, 293
Thigpen, Ed, 77
Thomas, Gary, 288
Thompson, Lucky, 103
Thornton, Argonne, 85
Timmons, Bobby, 134–136, 187, 203, 320
Tjader, Cal, 161, 170
Tolliver, Charlies, 122
Torff, Brian, 160
Toussaint, Allen, 285
Towner, Ralph, 231
Travis, Dempsey, J., 32
Travis, Nick, 119
Tristano, Lennie, 207, 223–226
Tucker, George, 109
Turner, Ike, 257
Turner, Joe, 63, 65

Turner, Margaret Marian, 161
Turner, Tina, 257
Turrentine, Stanley, 122, 133, 185
    Barron and, 204
    Billy Taylor and, 189
Tyner, McCoy, 55, 72, 194
    Beatrice, 256
    Childs and, 295
    Kuhn and, 197
    McCoy, 255–257
    Miller and, 288, 289–290
    Pullen and, 258, 260
    Reed and, 318
    Scott and, 314
    Valdés and, 274
    Zawinul and, 211

U

Ulanov, Barry, 59, 225
Ullman, Michael, 230
Urbaniak, Michael, 291

V

Vadim, Roger, 166
Valdés, Chucho, 273–275, 279, 283
Vast, Jimmy, 203
Vaughan, Sarah, 35–36, 77, 92
    Corea and, 199
    Hanna and, 109
Vaughan, Stevie Ray, 249
Veal, Reginald, 317
Ventura, Charlie, 184
Vincent, Ron, 311
Vitous, Miroslav, 199, 210

W

Wald, Jerry, 147, 148
Waldron, Mal, 117, 230, 248–251
Waller, Fats, 19–22, 94
    Basie and, 39
    Billy Taylor and, 187
    Byard and, 97
    Cecil Taylor and, 239
    Ellington and, 24
    Flanagan and, 103
    Johnson and, 13, 14, 15

    Lewis and, 165
    McPartland and, 161
    Monk and, 114
    Morton and, 9
    Rowles and, 175, 177
    Shearing and, 158
    Tatum and, 63, 64
    Wellstood and, 181, 182
    Williams and, 43, 44
    Willie Smith and, 16, 18
Waller, Maurice, 63, 64
Walton, Cedar, 193–196, 203
Ware, Wilbur, 117, 220
Warren, Butch, 119
Warren, Earle, 62
Washington, Dinah, 125
Washington, Grover, 296
Washington, Kenny, 311
Washington, Peter, 308, 311
Washington, Tuts, 285
Waters, Ethel, 34, 220
Watters, Johnny, 31
Watts, Jeff, 292
Webb, Speed, 48
Webster, Ben, 94, 106, 133, 187, 211
Webster, Freddie, 91
Weckl, Dave, 199, 279, 281
Wellstood, Dick, 15, 180–182, 236, 249
Werner, Kenny, 320
Wess, Frank, 109
Wessell, DaVid, 242
Weston, Fitz, 61
Weston, Randy, 90, 245–248, 250
White, Josh, 44
White, Lenny, 298
Whiteman, Paul, 62, 63, 264
Whyte, Zack, 91
Wilber, Bob, 179, 180, 184
Williams, Buddy, 291
Williams, Buster, 204, 255, 298
Williams, James, 288
Williams, Joe, 301
Williams, Mary Lou, 42–48, 55
    Blake and, 230
    Cecil Taylor and, 234
    Cootie, 84, 115

Hyman and, 178
Martin, 197
Monk and, 113, 114, 119
Valdés and, 274
Williams, Tony, 138, 140, 142
Wilson, E. E., 14
Wilson, Gerald, 317
Wilson, Phil, 301
Wilson, Shadow, 92, 117
Wilson, Teddy, 47–51, 72, 97, 103, 104, 175
Akiyoshi and, 191
Hyman and, 178
Lewis and, 168
McKenna and, 184
Shearing and, 158
Wilson, Cassandra, 308, 309–310
Winding, Kai, 227
Winston, George, 205
Winter, Paul, 231
Wittington, Dick, 303
Wolfolk, Ephraim, 75
Wonder, Stevie, 163

Woods, Anthony, 45
Woods, Phil, 119, 137
Workman, Reggie, 256
Wright, Eugene, 170
Wright, Gene, 220
Wuorinen, Charles, 262

Y
Yancey, Jimmy, 170
Youmans, Vincent, 63
Young, Emma D., 30
Young, Lester, 40, 51, 94, 101, 106, 117, 165, 166
Bryant and, 127
Corea and, 199
Rowles and, 175

Z
Zawinul, Joe, 36, 209–211, 278, 286, 291
Zigmund, Eliot, 153
Zschorney, Valery, 210
Zurke, Bob, 158